Principles and Practices of Teaching Reading

EIGHTH EDITION

Principles and Practices of Teaching Reading

Arthur W. Heilman
The Pennsylvania State University
Professor Emeritus

Timothy R. Blair
University of Central Florida

William H. Rupley
Texas A&M University

Merrill, an imprint of
Macmillan College Publishing Company
New York

Maxwell Macmillan Canada
Toronto

Maxwell Macmillan International
New York   Oxford   Singapore   Sydney

Cover photo: Unicorn Stock Photos ©
Martha McBride
Editor: Linda James Scharp
Developmental Editor: Carol S. Sykes
Production Editor: Linda Hillis Bayma
Art Coordinator: Lorraine Woost
Photo Editor: Anne Vega
Text Designer: Anne Flanagan
Cover Designer: Robert Vega
Production Buyer: Patricia A. Tonneman

This book was set in Meridien by The Clarinda
Company and was printed and bound by R. R.
Donnelley & Sons Company. The cover was
printed by Lehigh Press, Inc.

Macmillan College Publishing Company
866 Third Avenue
New York, NY 10022

Macmillan College Publishing Company is part of
the Maxwell Communication Group of
Companies.

Maxwell Macmillan Canada, Inc.
1200 Eglinton Avenue East, Suite 200
Don Mills, Ontario M3C 3N1

Library of Congress Cataloging-in-Publication Data

Heilman, Arthur W.
  Principles and practices of teaching reading /
Arthur W. Heilman,
  Timothy R. Blair, William H. Rupley.—8th ed.
     p. cm.
  Includes bibliographical references and index.
  ISBN 0-02-353001-4
  1. Reading (Elementary)   I. Blair, Timothy R.
II. Rupley, William H.   III. Title.
LB1573.H325   1994
372.4—dc20   93-17672
                                              CIP

Printing: 1 2 3 4 5 6 7 8 9
Year: 4 5 6 7 8

Photo credits: All photos copyrighted by
companies or individuals listed. Rich Bucurel,
p. 259; Jean Greenwald/Macmillan, p. 13; KS
Studios, pp. 16, 283, 390, 470; Barbara
Schwartz/Macmillan, pp. iii, 3, 17, 27, 33, 51, 81,
85, 135, 162, 167, 208, 223, 228, 232, 247, 267,
277, 303, 310, 339, 344, 381, 386, 417, 425, 457;
Anne Vega, pp. 39, 42, 56, 60, 69, 84, 96, 140,
154, 176, 273, 317, 341, 350, 428, 431, 435, 441,
451, 466; Tom Watson/Macmillan, p. 474.

To our wonderful wives,
Jeanné and Agnes,
for their patience,
continued understanding,
and love

Flashback Credits

Preface

*T*he eighth edition of *Principles and Practices of Teaching Reading* is based on the premise that effective teachers of literacy need to be knowledgeable, skillful, exciting, motivated, and caring people. It has become almost a cliché to say that the classroom teacher has a profound influence on how successful students will be in learning to read and write and how much students learn. Coupled with the universal beliefs that schools today must require students to reach higher levels of cognitive functioning and must foster the practice of lifelong learning, the importance of the classroom teacher remains paramount.

The field of literacy has progressed in the past 15 years, building a substantive knowledge base both in teaching and in understanding the reading process. The new edition of our text reflects this growing knowledge base by clearly presenting new topics and expanding other significant literacy topics for teachers-in-training. One of the trademarks of this text continues to be presentation of multiple perspectives representing a balanced viewpoint in teaching children to become literate.

Major changes for the eighth edition of *Principles and Practices of Teaching Reading* include:

- Complete discussion of reading as an interactive process.
- Expanded coverage of emergent literacy.
- Increased emphasis on the reading-writing connection in the language arts and content areas.
- A revised chapter on literature-based reading by Donna Norton, author of the classic textbook on children's literature, *Through the Eyes of a Child.*
- An updated chapter on teacher effectiveness.
- Increased emphasis on comprehension strategies.
- Focus on alternative assessment strategies.
- An updated chapter on teaching in a multicultural society.
- A new appendix providing suggested games and activities for all reading skills and strategies.
- A new Instructor's Manual that includes test questions, discussion questions, and blackline masters that can be made into transparencies.

As in previous editions, this text includes a variety of instructional activities. Throughout, the text presents practical examples, lesson plans, and classroom activities to provide concrete ideas for instruction. In addition, instructors can make use of a set of audiotapes containing 20- to 30-minute lecture-discussions on hot topics in literacy development: emergent literacy, literature-based reading, comprehension, word recognition, diverse learners, and motivation and reading.

The flashback features have been retained and updated. Students and professors using the book say the flashbacks serve as learning tools that provide a valuable historical perspective to the process of teaching literacy.

We wish to express our appreciation to the following professors for their insightful reviews of the text: Reta D. Hicks, Western Kentucky University; Donna Kerstetter, University of Tennessee at Chattanooga; Peter Quinn, St. John's University; Mary S. Rogers, University of Alabama; Leo Schell, Kansas State University; and Lawrence L. Smith, Ball State University.

In addition, we would like to thank Angie Feliciano for her patience and her careful typing. Finally, sincere appreciation is extended to the Macmillan staff, especially Jeff Johnston, Linda Scharp, Carol Sykes, and Linda Bayma, and to free-lance editor Megan Rowe, for their support, guidance, and continued good humor.

Contents

II Teaching Students to Become Strategic Readers

4

Word Identification

III   *Developing Literacy and Teaching Reading*

7

13

Principles and Practices of Teaching Reading

I

Foundations of Literacy Instruction

OVERVIEW

Children's literacy growth and development depend on a knowledgeable, caring, and thoughtful teacher. Helping students learn to read and write is an exciting, rewarding, and honorable responsibility. The first part of this text covers the overwhelming importance of the teacher in a successful literacy program, as well as the nature of the reading process, guiding principles of a sound literacy program, specific characteristics of successful teachers, and language—the core from which effective literacy instruction follows.

INTEGRATING PRINCIPLES OF TEACHING READING

Individual principles of reading instruction, which will be presented in Chapter 1, will serve as guiding fundamental ideas throughout the text. The first three chapters will reinforce the following principles:

- Reading and writing are language processes.

- Reading and writing are interrelated and interactive processes, and literacy instruction should capitalize on this relationship.

- Instruction should lead children to understand that reading is a meaningful, active, and strategic process.

- The key to successful literacy instruction is the teacher.

1

Principles of Reading Instruction

For the Reader

As you are preparing to become an effective teacher of reading, it is important that you understand your enormous influence on whether students will learn, the features of quality reading instruction, and the process of reading. Reading is a basic communication skill and a primary means of learning in our society. You most likely are a competent reader, one who gives little thought about how you read and how you get meaning from what you read.

Reading is a complex process. It depends on a variety of factors, such as experimental and conceptual backgrounds, word recognition strategies, reasoning abilities, purposes for reading, environment, motivation, and text complexity. These features of reading influence our attempts to construct meaning from what we read. This chapter presents some basic aspects of the reading process and sets forth principles to help guide you at all grade levels of reading instruction.

Key Ideas

- Reading is interaction with language that has been coded into print.
- The result of reading is construction of meaning.
- Reading is a language process.
- Learning to read is a developmental process.
- Many methods can be used to teach reading effectively.
- Instruction must be tailored to the needs of each student.

Key Terms

reading an active process of constructing meaning from written text in relation to the experiences and knowledge of the reader.

literacy ability to read and write proficiently.

decoding identifying the pronunciation and meaning of a word.

schema the background knowledge structure for an idea, object, or word meaning.

interactive theory of reading theory that readers use the information from the text, their experiential and conceptual backgrounds, and the context in which reading occurs to arrive at meaning.

experiential and conceptual backgrounds readers' experiences that are both concrete and abstract (knowledge) as well as their reasoning abilities in using this knowledge. This is also known as background knowledge.

automaticity ability to decode words with minimal effort.

assessment procedures used by teachers to identify students' literacy strengths and weaknesses in planning and executing instruction to meet the students' needs.

exceptional children culturally and linguistically diverse, disabled, and gifted learners.

This book is based on the premise that you will have a profound influence on how well students learn to read. Teaching is a major challenge and a complex process. As you will learn throughout this text (and especially in Chapter 2), research has made tremendous advances in determining how effective reading teachers teach. As a teacher-in-training, you should be aware that how you promote *literacy* in the classroom will have a profound effect on students' lives. The ability to read—that uniquely human process that results from a multitude of factors—is truly a magical phenomenon. It can open the minds of children to new worlds, emotions, insights, and imaginative ideas; information of all types; and exciting, new creative pursuits. It can also help them further their education and career opportunities and increase the quality of their lives through personal enjoyment. This is exactly why being a teacher of literacy is such a challenging, exciting, and rewarding experience.

Unfortunately, not all children experience the rewards and joys of literacy, and you will need to customize your instruction to suit students' varying strengths and weaknesses and to suit an intended instructional goal. If all reading instruction were the same for all students in each grade, teaching it would be easy. One thing that makes teaching so rewarding and challenging, however, is the fact that children are different. They differ in a multitude of ways—in intelligence, background knowledge, language background, social awareness, thinking abilities, creativity, and interests, to name a few. Learning to read is a complex process, affected by a host of factors (many of which are under your control and some that are not). Your knowledge and expertise can help you make a difference in children's lives. You will have much to say about guiding children in developing their language abilities to the fullest; your involvement is both indispensable and a privilege. Historian Henry Adams articulated it best: "Teachers affect eternity; they never know where their influence will end."

THE READING PROCESS

Do you sometimes read without thinking of or understanding some of the writer's message? We all have experiences where we read material but are thinking of other things. You may still be able to read aloud from your high school French, Latin, or Spanish textbook, but can you understand or comprehend all of what you read? The reading process is a dynamic one, requiring active, meaningful communication between the author and the reader. This text defines *reading* as the process of constructing meaning from written text in relation to the experiences and knowledge of the reader.

The major goal of reading instruction is to foster in students the ability to interact with and to understand printed language. Reading is an internal, mental process that cannot be observed or studied directly. Many investigators relate reading to thinking and argue that the two are inseparable in understanding printed language. In a much-quoted study of reading comprehension, Thorndike (1917) defined reading as thinking:

> The reading of a paragraph involves the same sort of organization and analysis as does thinking. It includes learning, reflection, judgment, analysis, synthesis, problem-solving behavior, selection, inference, organization, comparison of data, determination of relationships, and critical evaluation of what is read. It also includes attention, association, abstraction, generalization, comprehension, concentration and deduction.

Reading once was thought to be a passive process: It consisted of a hierarchical list of word identification and comprehension skills which, once mastered, would enable one to comprehend what one was reading. Instruction emphasized *decoding* skills, since they were more easily taught. If teachers accept the idea that a major aspect of reading is comprehension, then they must put into proper perspective the two facets of reading instruction: (1) decoding words rapidly and accurately and (2) combining information from the text with existing knowledge to construct meaning. The following examples deal with these two important aspects and illustrate the basic features of reading. Anyone who reads English will have no trouble with decoding or intonation:

Some squares do not have four sides.

Thomas Jefferson was a friend of tyranny.

Reading these sentences, like all written material, demands reader interaction. The reader must relate existing knowledge to the ideas that the text represents and use this knowledge to make sense of that text.

A person reading "Some squares do not have four sides" might react in any number of ways: "This is a misprint—it should say, 'All squares have four sides.' No, maybe that's not the kind of square it means; Reginald Philbut is a square, and he doesn't have four sides. No, that's not what it means. What is the author talking about? Well, no matter. I don't see how he can say that some squares do not have four sides. Maybe this is a trick statement. I had better read more to see if I can figure out what this statement means."

The last example illustrates how we use existing knowledge to make sense of what we read. The reader is using knowledge both about squares as geometric figures and knowledge about squares in a figurative sense (representing an individual). In addition, the reader employs a strategic approach by using this knowledge about text to realize that this may be a trick statement or that further reading may help explain the sentence. This reader is thus exercising the thinking abilities Thorndike described.

In the second sentence, a reader who knows little of Thomas Jefferson might reason, "Well, it's good to be apprised of this man's character. I'll be suspicious of everything he says or writes, particularly about government and people's rights." However, anyone who knows much about Jefferson might react by saying, "How ridiculous! Who is writing this stuff? Where was this book published? I had better read more; this might be a misprint. Didn't Jefferson say, 'I have sworn eternal hostility to every form of tyranny over the mind of man'?"

FLASHBACK

One characteristic of Americn education is the commitment to the concept of universal education. Evidence of this commitment is seen in our compulsory school attendance laws. Massachusetts was the first state to enact a compulsory school attendance law in 1852. In the 1800s only a small percentage of students completed high school.

/ / /
/ / /
/ / /
/ / /
/ / /
/ / /
/ / /
■

UPDATE

Today 70 to 90 percent of students complete the twelfth grade. Additionally, the school's population is becoming increasingly culturally diverse in nature. According to a recent report from the National Assessment of Educational Progress (NAEP), students are doing well in acquiring basic knowledge, but few students are learning to use this knowledge effectively in thinking and reasoning. Thus, teachers of reading today are being encouraged to promote comprehension of ideas requiring higher cognitive thinking. The authors of *Becoming a Nation of Readers* (Anderson et al., 1985) stated, "Discussions before reading and discussions and questioning after reading should motivate children's higher level thinking, with an emphasis on making connections with their prior knowledge of the topic" (p. 58).

The last examples put the two essentials of reading—automatic decoding and comprehension—in proper perspective. Fluent reading demands rapid and accurate decoding of printed words, but mere decoding of words is not reading until it evokes the meaning or meanings that those words represent.

NEW PERSPECTIVES

Just as the field of teacher effectiveness has seen advances, so our understanding of how children learn to read has improved in the last two decades. This greater understanding of the reading process has emerged primarily from the field of cognitive psychology (Samuels & Kamil, 1984). While word identification is crucial, today's concept of the reading process stresses the process of meaning construction.

Two theoretical models, supported by an abundance of research, have helped shape our understanding of the reading process: *schema* and *interactive theories of reading*. Schema theory recognizes that reading involves many levels of analysis at the same time but at different levels. Levels include both text features (e.g., letters, word order, and word meaning) and the reader's background knowledge (e.g., content and hypotheses about meaning). A central component of this theory relates to the interrelated and interdependent relationship between text comprehension and the reader's background knowledge. Each student has schemata (plural of schema), which are background knowledge structures for various ideas, objects, or word meanings (see Chapter 6 for an illustrated discussion of schema theory). As students read, they use past experiences (schemata are activated) to interact with new information presented in the text. The integration of old information with new information results in an improved or elaborated schemata (Tierney & Pearson, 1985). Thus, as readers process printed words, they construct meaning from them based both on the words and on background knowledge. For example, in reading about how to grow vegetables, readers integrate knowledge about gardening and related experiences with new information. They process the text to formulate hypotheses that make sense in light of existing background knowledge.

Directly related to schema theory is the interactive theory of reading, which holds that reading is an active process in which, to comprehend, students interact with a multitude of factors related to themselves, the text being read, and the context in which reading occurs. Figure 1.1 depicts the interactive nature of reading by grouping significant factors under the headings of reader, text, and context. Central to the interactive theory (Rumelhart, 1985) is the reader's use of prior knowledge and various strategies to interact with text. In this sense, the reader is an "active" participant interacting with the text by applying specific strategies to construct meaning. The term *strategic reader* reflects the view that readers consciously apply strategies to enhance the understanding of ideas. Chapters 2 and 6 will discuss schemata and interactive theories as well as specific comprehension strategies students can use to make sense out of what they are reading. Dole, Duffy, Roehler, and Pearson (1991) provide a concise summary of the latest thinking on the reading process:

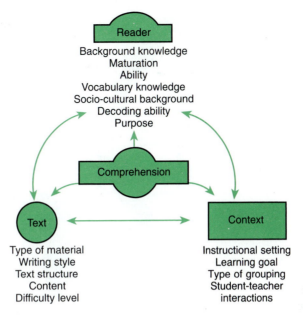

FIGURE 1.1
Interactive reading factors

The cognitive views of reading present a different view of the reader. The traditional view assumes a passive reader who has mastered a large number of subskills and automatically and routinely applies them to all texts. The cognitive view assumes an active reader who constructs meaning through the integration of existing and new knowledge and the flexible use of strategies to foster, monitor, regulate, and maintain comprehension. The only thing that becomes automated in the newer view is the disposition to adopt strategies to the particular constraints in the act of comprehending a particular text. (p. 242)

OVERVIEW OF THE READING CURRICULUM

Before moving on to stages of reading development, principles of teaching reading, and then specific reading approaches and strategies, it is helpful to have an overall view of the major strands of an elementary school reading curriculum and major areas of a complete reading program. Most literacy programs cover the following strands: word recognition, word meaning, comprehension, reading study skills, independent or recreational reading, and literature. Each strand is fostered through instruction and an abundance of practice in meaningful text. The strands are analogous to braiding hair or weaving a basket, with each strand (i.e., section of hair or piece of twig) woven together in a continuum. The strands must be woven correctly to achieve the desired result. In most reading programs today, such skills, strategies, and understanding are developed increasingly through the reading of quality literature. (See Figure 1.2.)

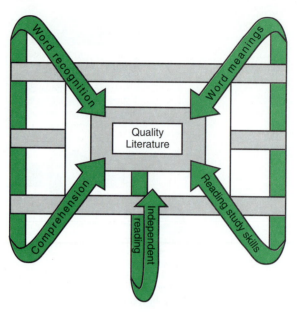

FIGURE 1.2
Major strands of an elementary school reading curriculum

It is also helpful to understand the major areas of a complete reading program. Regardless of grade level, the reading curriculum includes experience in each of the following five areas: developmental reading, application-transfer, independent or recreational reading, content reading, and functional reading.

Developmental reading involves sequential development of reading skills and strategies. Students need interesting, varied practice on new material (application-transfer) if they are to master reading. In the recreational component, students apply their reading skills and strategies to a variety of literary forms to expand their interests and develop lifelong reading habits. The content reading component includes systematic instruction in reading study skills and comprehension strategies so that students are able to understand content material. Finally, the functional reading component includes experiences in which students apply their reading strategies in practical situations: Students receive instruction and practice in filling out job and loan applications, using telephone books, and reading magazines and newspapers.

Figure 1.3 provides a view of the major areas of the reading curriculum along with the purposes of each and materials used to implement their instructional goals.

PRINCIPLES OF READING INSTRUCTION

Sound instructional principles tend to be learner-oriented. They can be applied consistently to children who have noticeably different learning capacities, interests, and experiences. While learning to read is a complicated process, you al-

Components	Purposes	Materials
Developmental reading	Systematic learning of word identification, word meanings, comprehension, content skills, and strategies. Development of proficient, strategic readers who comprehend written language.	Literature-based, basal reader, language experience, and content-area programs.
Application-transfer	Reading experiences designed to help students master skills and strategies taught in the main program component and to enhance the transfer of reading skills to other reading situations.	Various types of literature, high-interest/low-vocabulary readers, supplemental basal reader programs, games, audiovisual aids, workbooks, teacher-made materials, newspapers, magazines, content texts.
Recreational reading	Literary experiences to which students apply their reading abilities to expand their knowledge of a variety of subjects and become lifelong readers.	Various types of literature, paperback books, book clubs.
Content reading	Specific learning of skills and strategies to use in content areas.	Various types of literature, encyclopedias, card catalogs, almanacs, atlases, maps, charts, graphs, tables, diagrams, content texts.
Functional reading	Instruction in how to use reading to gain basic, practical information needed in everyday activities.	Telephone books, newspapers, catalogs, driver's manuals, job and loan applications, magazines.

FIGURE 1.3
Components of a complete reading program

ready know many effective learning principles from your study of educational psychology. You must integrate these principles with specific knowledge in developing reading abilities.

Learning to read depends on the same learning principles as other cognitive skills, such as past experiential and conceptual backgrounds, purposes for learning, learner motivation, task difficulty, and instructional quality.

The principles discussed in this section can serve as guidelines for teacher behavior. Principles of teaching reading should evolve from the best knowledge available in general psychology, educational psychology, curriculum planning, studies in child growth and development, reading research, and child guidance and psychological clinics. In formulating principles, it is necessary to consider all facets of human growth and development, including intellectual, physiological, psychological, and emotional. Some of you may believe that some of the following principles are not absolutely valid. Such questioning is healthy, especially if it stimulates the formulation of rational alternatives.

1. Reading and writing are language processes.

Teachers must understand the relationships between reading and writing and children's oral language. Children's oral language reflects their experiences with objects, ideas, relationships, and their interaction with their world. Much has been written about what children bring to school and the role of the school in building on each child's abilities. Teachers should help children transfer the language background children bring to school directly to their reading and writing (Norton, 1993).

Recent studies have shown that experiences that promote success in reading occur long before a child begins formal schooling (Weiss & Hagen, 1988). For example, before starting school, many children can recognize letters of the alphabet, write their names, identify brand names, use books properly, and retell all or parts of favorite stories (Kontos, 1988). Many children also exhibit knowledge of written language and its purpose to communicate. They may scribble (write) letters and stories and read their compositions to others, make up spellings, and create letter-like forms (Martinez & Teale, 1987). In addition, children often demonstrate an understanding of stories and use stories to bring meaning to their play (Roskos, 1988). These behaviors indicate an understanding of language that can form the foundation for effective literacy instruction. Anderson, Heibert, Scott, and Wilkinson (1985) highlight the importance of oral language facility to the reading process:

> Reading instruction builds especially on oral language. If this foundation is weak, progress in reading will be slow and uncertain. Children must have at least a basic vocabulary, a reasonable range of knowledge about the world around them and the ability to talk about their knowledge. These abilities form the basis for comprehending text. (p. 30)

Unfortunately, teachers ignore many of the early signs of understanding language, and children's early experiences in literacy mask the fact that they are engaged in a language process. Beginning reading and writing programs often ask children to focus on isolated parts of the literacy process.

Children's learning background directly determines where and when to begin reading instruction (see Chapter 7). Children who come from homes full of rich literary experiences bring a wealth of language abilities and understandings with them (Lipson, 1988; Neuman & Roskos, 1993). They may already be reading with understanding and have strategies to help identify words. For such children, reading instruction should begin beyond basic decoding instruction. Children who have had limited language and literacy experiences before entering school, however, should focus on the concepts that language serves a communicative function and that print and oral language convey meaning (see Chapter 13).

The relationship of oral language development is crucial to reading, as are the other language processes. The language arts—listening, speaking, reading, and

The meanings acquired from reading are closely related to our experiential and conceptual backgrounds.

writing—are the tools of communication. All of the language arts are interrelated; growth in one reinforces and facilitates growth in the others. While it may be convenient to discuss the language arts separately, they are inextricably intertwined. A primary method to promote all the language processes is through their integration in reading quality literary selections (see Principle 5).

Listening, the first language process to be developed, is the basis for oral language growth. Listening skills also are important in learning to read—especially in acquiring word-pronunciation or decoding skills and strategies. Likewise the processes of reading and writing are interrelated and interdependent. The development of one enhances the other. While reading involves interacting with and making sense of written symbols, writing involves creating text that will communicate ideas to others. This relationship has been highlighted recently and given much emphasis in today's reading programs. To reflect its increased importance, our next principle stresses this unique relationship.

2. Literacy is a developmental process.

If teachers accept that reading and writing are constructing meaning (comprehension), then there is no such thing as mastery of literacy ability; rather, it is a constantly evolving process. Individuals' experiential and conceptual backgrounds continue to grow. As one's background knowledge grows, so does one's ability to interact with text and acquire new information; therefore, literacy capabilities are constantly expanding. Reflecting the belief that reading is a developmental process whereby children move through various stages in an orderly and predictable manner, many authors have proposed that each child moves through various stages of reading development. While the stages are not entirely separate, they do provide teachers with an overall view of development and how their students' growth and their instruction fit into the big picture. Chall (1983) views reading development as a sequence of stages (see Figure 1.5). Stage 0 focuses on learning to recognize and identify letters; Stage 1 (grade 1) emphasizes decoding or word-pronunciation abilities and comprehension of simple stories; Stage 2 (grades 2–4) centers on making decoding abilities automatic and increasing comprehension; Stage 3 (grades 4–8) encourages comprehension in a variety of different texts, including content-area books and complex fiction.

3. Reading and writing are interrelated and interactive processes, and literacy instruction should capitalize on this relationship.

Recent research (Teale, 1989) has highlighted the close relationship between reading and writing. Both are communicative processes that involve the interaction and understanding of ideas. Writing abilities improve with the development of various reading abilities, such as knowledge of how stories are constructed, the ability to use prior knowledge to create new meanings, decoding skills, and word meanings. Likewise, children's reading abilities benefit from those same skills used in the writing process, such as the abilities to revise one's thinking to delete or add important information, to predict and plan written ideas, and to summarize information.

4. Instruction should lead children to understand that reading is a meaningful, active, and strategic process.

Reading is more than a mechanical process. Beginning reading should deal with more than mechanics, with meaning inserted later in the learning continuum. The product of interacting with printed language should be comprehension. Reading involves *automaticity* (ability to decode words with minimal effort) and a host of other text, reader, and contextual factors. Readers must be "active"; that is, they must use all available resources to construct meaning and make sense of the text. Reading involves the interaction of several factors, including textual factors, background knowledge, and the social setting in which reading occurs. In addition, the effective reader applies various reading strategies at the right time and in the right doses for understanding: The student becomes a "strategic" or flexible reader. Flexible readers choose from a variety of strategies to fulfill their purposes in comprehending text.

5. Early in the learning process, the student must acquire ways of recognizing words independently.

Developing independence in reading requires acquiring methods of identifying words, interacting with the text, and constructing meaning. Whether using clues about analyzing spelling to help with pronunciation, looking at the structural parts of a word, or considering the context in which the word appears, one must develop facility in identifying (i.e., decoding) printed word forms. These clues are best taught and practiced in conjunction with sentences and/or whole texts, not in isolation. Thus, students learn to decode in the context of real reading or the whole reading process. This principle is not in conflict with previous statements that the student must see reading as an active, meaning-making process. Research has supported the close relationships between decoding facility and total reading performance (Anderson et al., 1985). Once students can decode words at an automatic level, they can spend more time and energy on comprehension.

6. The use of quality literature should be an integral part of literacy instruction throughout the entire school curriculum.

The time has passed when literature was thought to be an add-on or a separate entity reserved only for the recreational or independent reading program. Quality literature of all types should be an integral part of the daily reading language arts program and should be fused into content subjects (Cullinan, 1992). Entire works of quality literature or authentic texts can be the main vehicle for learning the language processes and achieving various instructional goals: learning basic vocabulary and decoding knowledge, comprehension strategies, content reading skills and strategies, inferential and critical thinking abilities; and promoting a joy of reading.

7. Literacy instruction needs to be an integral component in all content areas.

Successful learning in content areas depends on students' application of reading study skills, comprehension strategies, and writing ability. A literacy program is not complete without adequate attention to content areas. Success in the regular literacy program does not automatically guarantee success in the content areas. Many students experience difficulties in these areas that are further compounded when they are not becoming independent learners. If we truly believe in the educational platitude of independent learning, we must devote more time to teaching the skills and strategies needed in the content areas. For students to be independent learners, we must teach them how to pursue the ever-increasing amount of knowledge in nearly all fields. In other words, they must learn how to learn.

8. Teachers need to foster students' abilities to reason and critically evaluate written ideas.

Learning decoding and basic comprehension are important but not sufficient in today's world. Children must understand how to interact with ideas above a basic level. Successful readers and writers can collate or synthesize, analyze, and critically evaluate ideas to increase their knowledge. Teachers can use quality literature in a variety of ways and effective instructional strategies (e.g., using cooperative groups) to help children apply literacy skills to fulfill their own goals.

9. Proper literacy instruction depends on the ongoing *assessment* of each student's reading strengths and weaknesses.

The teacher's ability to assess students' needs lies at the heart of effective instruction. Effective reading teachers make instructional decisions based on assess-

The effective literacy program integrates the entire curriculum across all content areas around reading, writing, listening, and speaking activities.

ment information. A key to correctly assessing students' progress in reading is to obtain information from multiple sources, both formal and informal. Teachers should ensure that the assessment process permeates all aspects of instruction, from making initial placement decisions to adjusting daily instruction based upon yesterday's lesson.

10. Any given technique is likely to work better with some students than with others.

Many methods can be used to teach reading and writing effectively. Using only one method to the exclusion of others makes it difficult to adjust instruction to meet students' individual needs. Student differences must be a primary consideration in literacy instruction. Effective literacy instruction addresses the needs of each student.

11. Motivation contributes to the development of literacy.

Motivation is an important feature of both acquiring literacy and associating value with literacy. Students who are motivated to read and write for school and enjoyment become better readers and writers, because the more students read and write, the better readers and writers they become. Teachers who use strategies that promote high levels of student engagement and provide a wide range of meaningful literacy activities encourage the development of positive attitudes toward literacy.

12. The key to successful literacy instruction is the teacher.

Results of research do not recommend any particular literacy method or material as best for all children. The teacher is one of the major variables determining the effectiveness of reading instruction (Rupley & Blair, 1989; Rupley, Wise, & Logan, 1986). Numerous investigations have identified instructional practices of effective reading teachers: ongoing assessment of students' literacy development, structure and direction of students' learning, provision of opportunities to

The key to successful literacy instruction is the teacher.

practice and apply skills in meaningful context, and maintenance of a high level of student involvement in learning (Rupley & Blair, 1988).

13. Teachers must provide for the needs of *exceptional children* in regular classroom literacy instruction.

Exceptional children often need different literacy instruction than what is typically found in most classrooms. Literacy instruction is generally more effective when teachers accept and accommodate the differences of exceptional children rather than forcing them to adjust to the demands of instruction (Banks, 1991).

14. Teachers must be able to create, manage, and maintain an environment conducive to learning.

Teaching children what they need to know and advancing their literacy abilities are a tall order. With a small group of students, classroom management, however, is less important. As you already know, you will be responsible for a class of 20 to 30 students. In addition, many school systems are organizing the early grades into primary blocks, which group students from different age and grade

---

1. Reading and writing are language processes.
2. Literacy learning is a developmental process.
3. Reading and writing are interrelated and interactive processes, and literacy instruction should capitalize on this relationship.
4. Instruction should lead children to understand that reading is a meaningful, active, and strategic process.
5. Early in the learning process, the student must acquire ways of recognizing words independently.
6. The use of quality literature should be an integral part of literacy instruction throughout the entire school curriculum.
7. Literacy instruction needs to be an integral component in all content areas.
8. Teachers need to foster students' abilities to reason and critically evaluate written ideas.
9. Proper literacy instruction depends on the ongoing assessment of each student's reading strengths and weaknesses.
10. Any given technique is likely to work better with some students than with others.
11. Motivation contributes to the development of literacy.
12. The key to successful literacy instruction is the teacher.
13. Teachers must provide for the needs of exceptional children in regular classroom literacy instruction.
14. Teachers must be able to create, manage, and maintain an environment conducive to learning.
15. Teachers of literacy must forge partnerships with the home and community to promote reading growth.

FIGURE 1.4
Principles of reading instruction

levels. Studies on teaching reading have clearly shown that effective teachers are proficient in classroom organization and management (Emmer & Evertson, 1980). Proper planning, managing of group instruction, and monitoring of student progress can help the teacher deal with a broad range of student abilities.

15. Teachers of literacy must forge partnerships with the home and community to promote reading growth.

Without a doubt, teachers alone cannot do a complete job of educating students. Teachers must have a cooperative relationship with parents and the community as a whole to have a successful literacy program. Parents—a child's first teachers—are in a unique position to provide meaningful literacy experiences for their children (Edwards, 1991; Handel, 1992). In *Becoming a Nation of Readers* (Anderson et al., 1985), the Commission on Reading recommended two ways parents can help their children:

■ Parents should read to preschool children and informally teach them about reading and writing. Reading to children, discussing stories and experiences with them, and—with a light touch—helping them learn letters and words are practices that are consistently associated with eventual success in reading.

■ Parents should support school-aged children's continued growth as readers. Parents of children who become successful readers monitor their children's progress in school, become involved in school programs, support homework, buy their children books or take them to libraries, encourage reading as a free time activity, and place reasonable limits on such activities as TV viewing. (p. 117)

Parents can contribute a great deal to every stage of reading development. Teachers need to communicate with parents what we know about reading development, how we teach reading, and specifically how parents can help (Silvern & Silvern, 1990). Figure 1.4 summarizes the 15 principles of reading instruction.

THE ELEMENTARY SCHOOL READING PROGRAM

Reading programs are said never to rise above the quality of instruction found in them. Teachers must understand students as learners and must view learning to read as a developmental process. Several reading authorities have offered considerable support for the developmental view of reading. Important reading behaviors identified by Clay (1979), Stanovich (1986), and Chall (1983) focus on well-developed decoding strategies and understandings of meaning.

Jeanne Chall developed a comprehensive illustration of the reading development stages for kindergarten through grade 9. Her proposed reading stages (Figure 1.5) illustrate the major qualitative reading characteristics for grade ranges, the ways students acquire reading abilities, and the relationship of reading to listening comprehension.

It is important to understand that stages may overlap and are not fixed. That is, a first grader could be in stage 3 and a sixth grader could be in stage 1. The

1 Stage Designation	2 Grade Range (Age)	3 Major Qualitative Characteristics and Masteries by End of Stage	4 How Acquired	5 Relationship of Reading to Listening
Stage 0: Prereading, "pseudo-reading"	Preschool (ages 6 months–6 years)	Child "pretends" to read, retells story when looking at pages of book previously read to him/her; names letters of alphabet; recognizes some signs; prints own name; plays with books, pencils, and paper.	Being read to by an adult (or older child) who responds to and warmly appreciates the child's interest in books and reading; being provided with books, paper, pencils, blocks, and letters.	Most can understand the children's picture books and stories read to them. They understand thousands of words they hear by age 6 but can read few if any of them.
Stage 1: Initial reading and decoding	Grade 1 & beginning grade 2 (ages 6 & 7)	Child learns relation between letters and sounds and between printed and spoken words; child is able to read simple text containing high frequency words and phonically regular words; uses skill and insight to "sound out" new one-syllable words.	Direct instruction in letter-sound relations (phonics) and practice in their use. Reading of simple stories using words with phonic elements taught and words of high frequency. Being read to on a level above what child can read independently to develop more advanced language patterns, knowledge of new words, and ideas.	The level of difficulty of language read by the child is much below the language understood when heard. At the end of stage 1, most children can understand up to 4,000 or more words when heard but can read only about 600.

FIGURE 1.5
Stages of reading development for primary, intermediate, and junior high reading instruction
(From Jeanne S. Chall, *Stages of Reading Development* [New York: McGraw-Hill Book Co., 1983], 85–86. Reprinted by permission.)

1 Stage Designation	2 Grade Range (Age)	3 Major Qualitative Characteristics and Masteries by End of Stage	4 How Acquired	5 Relationship of Reading to Listening
Stage 2: Confirmation and fluency	Grades 2 & 3 (ages 7 & 8)	Child reads simple, familiar stories and selections with increasing fluency. This is done by consolidating the basic decoding elements, sight vocabulary, and meaning context in the reading of familiar stories and selections.	Direct instruction in advanced decoding skills; wide reading (with instruction and independently) of familiar, interesting materials which help promote fluent reading. Being read to at levels above their own independent reading level to develop language, vocabulary, and concepts.	At the end of stage 2, about 3,000 words can be read and understood and about 9,000 are known when heard. Listening is still more effective than reading.
Stage 3: Reading for learning the new Phase A Phase B	Grades 4–8 (ages 9–13) Intermediate, 4–6 Junior high school, 7–9	Reading is used to learn new ideas, to gain new knowledge, to experience new feelings, to learn new attitudes; generally from one viewpoint.	Reading and study of textbooks, reference works, trade books, newspapers, and magazines that contain new ideas and values, unfamiliar vocabulary and syntax; systematic study of words and reacting to the text through discussion, answering questions, writing, etc. Reading of increasingly more complex fiction, biography, nonfiction, and the like.	At beginning of stage 3, listening comprehension of the same material is still more effective than reading comprehension. By the end of stage 3, reading and listening are about equal; for those who read very well, reading may be more efficient.

characteristics associated with each stage should be viewed as representative. They should serve as guidelines for planning quality reading instruction and understanding the curriculum.

SUMMARY /

The ability to read is a uniquely human process that can open worlds to children. Teaching students to read is an exciting, rewarding, and honorable responsibility. Effective teachers of reading are knowledgeable, skillful, exciting, and caring. This first chapter discussed the reading process, an overview of the reading curriculum, principles of teaching reading, and stages of reading development.

Reading is defined as a process of constructing meaning from written text in relation to the reader's experiences and knowledge. Reading is a complex process; our knowledge of it has been reshaped recently primarily from research on schema theory and from viewing reading as an interactive process. Reading is an active, dynamic, and strategic process whereby readers use cues from themselves, the text, and the context in which the reading occurs to construct meaning.

An overview of the reading curriculum was presented. The major strands of the elementary school curriculum—word recognition, word meaning, comprehension, reading study skills, independent or recreational reading, and literature—were covered for each grade level. A complete reading program includes developmental reading, application-transfer, independent or recreational reading, content reading, and functional reading.

To synthesize major understandings and provide a foundation for the rest of the text, principles for teaching reading were presented with brief explanations of each. Key elements of the principles were the importance of the teacher and the integration of reading development with the other language arts in quality literature. Finally, Chall's stages of reading development were presented with the qualitative characteristics for the primary, intermediate, and junior high grades.

YOUR POINT OF VIEW /

Discussion Questions

1. In your opinion, which of the principles of teaching reading are the most important for improving the quality of reading instruction? Provide a rationale for your choices.
2. Refer to Chall's stages of reading development (Figure 1.5) and reread the category "How Acquired" for each stage. What features would a reading instructional program need in order to develop the reading abilities associated with each stage?
3. Assume that you are assigned to improve the teaching of reading in a school and you want teachers to realize that reading instruction should lead to improved comprehension. How would you illustrate this for teachers? What examples would you use to show them that reading is a process influenced by

the reader's decoding abilities, experiential and conceptual backgrounds, purposes for reading, motivation, and setting?

Take a Stand For or Against

1. A teacher's definition or concept of reading will, in the final analysis, have little impact on practices used in teaching students to read.
2. A child's problems in learning to read can usually be attributed to one factor.
3. A regular classroom reading program can effectively address the reading needs of exceptional children.

BIBLIOGRAPHY /

Anderson, P. C., Hiebert, E. H., Scott, J. A., & Wilkinson, I. A. G. (1985). *Becoming a nation of readers: The report of the commission on reading.* Washington, DC: The National Institute of Education.

Anderson, R. C., & Pearson, D. P. (1984). A schema-theoretic view of basic process in reading comprehension. In P. D. Pearson (Ed.), *Handbook of reading research.* New York: Longman.

Banks, J. A. (1991). *Teaching strategies for ethnic studies* (5th ed.). Boston: Allyn and Bacon.

Chall, J. S. (1983). *Stages of reading development.* New York: McGraw-Hill Book Co.

Clay, M. M. (1979). *The patterning of complex behavior.* Auckland, New Zealand: Heinemann Educational Books.

Cullinan, B. E. (Ed.). (1992). *Invitation to read: More children's literature in the reading program.* Newark, DE: International Reading Association.

Dole, J. A., Duffy, G. G., Roehler, L. R., & Pearson, P. D. (1991). Moving from the old to the new: Research on reading comprehension instruction. *Review of Educational Research, 61*(2), 239–264.

Edwards, P. A. (1991). Fostering early literacy through parent coaching. In E. H. Hiebert (Ed.), *Literacy for a diverse society* (pp. 199–214). New York: Teachers College Press.

Emmer, E. T., & Evertson, C. M. (1980). Synthesis of research on classroom management. *Educational Leadership, 38,* 342–347.

Handel, R. D. (1992). The partnership for family reading: Benefits for families and schools. *The Reading Teacher, 46,* 116–126.

Kontos, S. (1988). Development and interrelationships of reading knowledge and skills during kindergarten and first grade. *Reading Research and Instruction, 2,* 14–28.

Lipson, E. R. (1988). *The New York Times parent's guide to the best books for children.* New York: Times Books.

Martinez, M., & Teale, W. H. (1987). The ins and outs of kindergarten writing programs. *The Reading Teacher, 4,* 444–451.

Neuman, S. B., & Roskos, K. (1993). *Language and literacy learning in the early years: An integrated approach.* Orlando: Harcourt Brace Jovanovich.

Norton, D. E. (1993). *The effective teaching of language arts* (4th ed.). New York: Merrill/Macmillan Publishing Co.

Roskos, K. (1988). Literacy at work in play. *The Reading Teacher, 6,* 562–567.

Rumelhart, D. E. (1985). Toward an interactive model of reading. In R. Ruddell & H. Singer (Eds.), *Theoretical models and processes of reading*. Newark, DE: International Reading Association.

Rupley, W. H., & Blair, T. R. (1988). *Teaching reading: Diagnosis, direct instruction, and practice* (2nd ed.). New York: Merrill/Macmillan Publishing Co.

Rupley, W. H., & Blair, T. R. (1989). *Reading diagnosis and remediation: Classroom and clinic* (3rd ed.). New York: Merrill/Macmillan Publishing Co.

Rupley, W. H., Wise, B. S., & Logan, J. W. (1986). Research in effective teaching: An overview of its development. In J. V. Hoffman (Ed.), *Effective teaching of reading: Research and practice*. Newark, DE: International Reading Association.

Samuels, S. J., & Kamil, M. L. (1984). Models of the reading process. In P. D. Pearson (Ed.), *Handbook of reading research*. New York: Longman.

Silvern, S. B., & Silvern, L. R. (1990). *Beginning literacy and your child*. Newark, DE: International Reading Association.

Stanovich, K. E. (1986). Matthew effects in reading: Some consequences of individual differences in the acquisition of literacy. *Reading Research Quarterly, 21*, 360–406.

Teale, W. (1989). Emergent literacy: New perspectives. In D. S. Strickland & L. M. Morrow (Eds.), *Emerging literacy: Young children learn to read*. Newark, DE: International Reading Association.

Thorndike, E. L. (1917). Reading as reasoning: A study of mistakes in paragraph reading. *Journal of Educational Research, 8*, 323–332.

Tierney, R., & Pearson, P. P. (1985). Learning to learn from text: A framework for improving classroom practice. In H. Ruddell & H. Singer (Eds.), *Theoretical models and processes of reading*. Newark, DE: International Reading Association.

Weiss, M. J., & Hagen, R. (1988). A key to literacy: Kindergartners' awareness of the functions of print. *The Reading Teacher, 6*, 574–579.

2

Teacher Effectiveness in the Literacy Program

For the Reader

Teachers' tremendous influence upon learning has been documented and emphasized for years. Specific instructional behaviors that have the greatest impact on learning have not been at issue until relatively recently, however. General qualities, such as mental health and enthusiasm, are certainly important, but what specifically sets apart more effective teachers of literacy from those who are less effective?

If you have had experience teaching, you realize the tremendous responsibilities that teachers have in the classroom. If you are preparing to become a teacher, the realities and complexities of working with 25 to 35 students in a teaching situation may (justifiably) seem overwhelming. Every day, teachers are responsible for covering certain material, ensuring learning, minimizing discipline problems, and maintaining a pleasant atmosphere for learning. You may ask, "What exactly does an effective teacher of literacy do?" "Where should I place my efforts so that the classroom experience is rewarding and profitable for both me and my students?"

The overall objective of this text is to provide you with the essential knowledge, concepts, and skills of an effective teacher of literacy. This chapter synthesizes teacher characteristics that make a difference in teaching.

Key Ideas

- Studies of teacher effectiveness have pointed out a number of characteristics related to student learning of basic reading skills.

- The six areas of importance to competent reading instruction are (1) assessment, (2) interactive instruction, (3) opportunity to learn, (4) student attention to learning tasks, (5) teacher expectations, and (6) classroom management.

- A pattern of teaching practices is more likely to promote learning than is a single practice.

- The most pervasive conclusion of school and teacher effectiveness studies in the 1970s and 1980s was that teachers profoundly influence how much students learn.

- Guidelines for effective literacy instruction must be applied differently in each classroom, depending upon a host of variables including students' needs, material content, grade level, and learning objectives.

- Teaching is a decision-making process, and the judgments teachers make are the keys to the success or failure of literacy programs.

- Effective teachers of literacy continually reshape teaching decisions, depending on each student's progress.

Key Terms

interactive instruction   imparting new information to students through meaningful teacher-student interactions and guiding student learning.

skills   learning that is specific in nature and amenable to behavioral objectives.

strategies   learning that is less specific and represents higher-level cognitive thinking to be used in interacting with text information.

direct/explicit instruction   systematic teaching in which the teacher models and demonstrates learning and gradually turns the responsibility for learning over to the student. This teaching method emphasizes students' understanding the "when" and "why" of utilizing various capabilities and strategies.

mediated instruction   intervention or guidance that another person (such as a peer, parent, or teacher) provides in the teaching-learning process.

scaffolds   "forms of support provided by the teacher (or another student) to help students bridge the gap between current abilities and the intended goal" (Rosenshine & Meister, 1992).

opportunity to learn   allotment of time and exposure to instruction.

academic engaged time (time on task)   classroom time in which students are actually attending to the valued learning.

academic learning time (ALT)   classroom time in which students are actually attending to the work at hand with a high success rate (80 percent or more).

STUDIES OF TEACHER EFFECTIVENESS

It is generally accepted that the teacher plays a major role in determining the effectiveness of a literacy program. Recognition of this significant role is not new. Over the past 50 years, a number of major studies have demonstrated the importance of the teacher. Gates (1937) found that although mental age is correlated with beginning reading success, the type of teaching and the teacher's expertise and effectiveness are equally important. In her 3-year study, Jeanne Chall (1967) concluded that even more than the instruction materials, the teacher generally determines students' attitudes toward learning to read.

The importance of the teacher was apparent in a major investigation that compared different reading instruction methods at the first-grade level (Dykstra, 1967). The study noted wide differences in reading achievement among classes and school systems that were using similar instructional methods. The differences underscore the importance of the teacher's role in reading instruction.

Early studies on effective teaching yielded little specific information on what a teacher does in the classroom that is effective, however. Being a good, decent individual who is interested in students is clearly insufficient. As Pescosolido stated in a personal communication in 1980, "Just being a 'nice' person doesn't a teacher of reading make, but a nice person doing some important things in terms of the reading process results in good teaching and good learning."

RECENT RESEARCH

In early studies of teacher effectiveness, researchers looked at what went on inside classrooms. Researchers identified several factors that explained why students in some classrooms seemed to learn more than did students of similar ability in other classrooms. This early research in reading teacher effectiveness did not specify exact instructional guidelines. Yet, the studies generally associated the same characteristics with student learning of basic skills.

To avoid simplistic explanations of teacher effectiveness, it must be acknowledged that the majority of recent studies have been nonexperimental, thus prohibiting the conclusion that specific teacher behaviors actually cause student achievement. Until recently, the research has focused predominantly on word-identification skills and literal-comprehension skills as measured by standardized tests. Critical and creative reading skills, essential goals of education, have not received much attention. Thus, it is entirely possible that teacher behaviors that appear to promote basic reading skills also deter the development of other skills such as the ability to evaluate and to synthesize information. The following discussion therefore should be regarded as providing tentative guidelines.

We believe that it is reasonable to expect a teacher to benefit from knowing about practices of competent teachers. Before proceeding, however, another cautionary note is needed. Keep in mind that no teaching strategy or method works best for all students all of the time. Student factors, such as socioeconomic status, experiential background, language capabilities, grade level, and learning style, are also important to consider.

Arthur I. Gates was one of the most influential scholars in reading. His research and writing in areas of vocabulary control, reading interests, spelling, diagnosis, remediation, reading readiness, and disabled children have influenced reading instruction and materials since the 1920s. Arthur I. Gates was truly a "man ahead of his time." He pointed out in the 1930s that a key factor in determining pupils' success in beginning reading was the teacher. Professor Gates' contribution to reading was recognized by the International Reading Association in 1961 when he received the Citation of Merit and again in 1968 with the International Award.

UPDATE

Teachers can expend their time and effort in a variety of ways in teaching reading. Research on teaching and on reading development in the past 25 years has helped us discern which efforts are helpful. Research on teacher effectiveness in the 1970s and 1980s looked at how classrooms of effective teachers operated. These efforts yielded principles of teaching that, when applied appropriately, enhance student learning and growth.

A more recent view of effectiveness builds on this research and emerges directly from new understandings of the reading process and how teachers can promote student understanding of text. Much of the newer understandings of effectiveness came from researchers at the *Center for the Study of Reading* at the University of Illinois and the *Institute for Research on Teaching* at Michigan State University. This new view stresses teachers' ability to tap students' prior knowledge on a subject, to interact with students in a variety of ways regarding the comprehension of ideas and when and how to use strategies to enhance understanding, and to practice new skills and strategies using more authentic reading situations rather than isolated exercises.

CHARACTERISTICS OF EFFECTIVE LITERACY INSTRUCTION

The areas that appear to be of primary importance in competent literacy instruction include the following:

- Assessing students' literacy strengths and weaknesses.
- Structuring literacy activities around an interactive instructional format.
- Providing students with opportunities to learn and apply skills and strategies in real-life literacy tasks.
- Ensuring that students attend to the learning tasks.
- Believing in one's teaching abilities and expecting students to be successful.
- Maintaining effective classroom control. (Blair, 1984)

Assessing Students' Reading

The ability to teach students what they need to know relies on the premise that teachers of literacy continually use a blend of formal and informal measures to identify students' strengths and weaknesses in interacting with text. Without a pervasive concern for knowing and responding to students' needs, literacy instruction can be irrelevant and mindless drudgery for all concerned. This pervasive concern for assessment can be related to Chall's stages of reading development (see Chapter 1). Teachers should provide instruction that reflects the student's level of reading development.

Teachers' use of reading assessment and its effects on reading achievement have been part of many research investigations that span more than 30 years. Pescosolido (1962) appraised the effects of a variety of teacher factors on achievement. A major factor associated with level of reading achievement was the teacher's ability to judge accurately students' attitudes toward reading.

Blair (1975) found that teachers who secured and used supplementary materials, provided differentiated instruction, kept records of student progress, and arranged conferences dealing with student progress were effective in improving student reading skills. Results indicated significant differences in class-achievement scores for teachers who exerted more effort on the job.

Finally, Rupley (1977) found that effective teachers of reading used more ongoing assessment than did less-effective teachers.

More recently, assessment has received increased emphasis. External assessment of procedures, such as standardized tests, typically focus on students' basic skills in reading and writing and provide little information for instructional decision making (Calfee & Hiebert, 1991). Today's teachers of literacy realize that testing is only one small part of assessment and that literacy is the ability to use reading and writing as tools for learning, thinking, and problem solving (Brandt, 1989). In a recent survey regarding the National Assessment of Educational Progress (NAEP) in reading, this view of literacy was reflected by teachers, researchers, and administrators associated with literacy instruction (Commeyras, Osborn, & Bruce, 1992). The respondents indicated that assessment should focus on the reading and writing processes, reading to inform, and reading to perform a task. Defining literacy as much more than basic skills has direct implications for effective instruction.

Effective teachers of literacy rely on a variety of assessment tools, including interviews, observations, samples of students' work, portfolios, and students' judgments of performance (Henk & Melnick, 1992). Such assessment procedures give teachers information about their students and help them make informed instructional decisions to maximize their teaching effectiveness.

Using assessment as an integral part of effective instruction requires several provisions. First, effective literacy teachers employ informal, ongoing assessment procedures rather than infrequent administration of standardized tests. Second, their procedures aim to determine appropriate instructional practice rather than simply students' grade level placement. Third, ongoing assessment allows effective teachers to evaluate student outcomes more regularly in relation to actual classroom instruction. Effective teachers of literacy use a variety of assessment techniques to adjust instruction frequently to increase students' chances of success in instructional tasks.

The fact that effective teachers assess students' literacy more frequently using a variety of procedures (see Chapter 11) than do less effective teachers should be carefully analyzed. By itself, assessment has no beneficial effects. Therefore, you cannot expect students' literacy achievement to improve simply by increasing the frequency of assessment. Effective teachers of reading and writing expend considerable effort in developing and using ongoing assessment. How they incorporate this information into their instruction probably determines students' reading achievement.

Another plausible explanation is that effective teachers select instructional strategies appropriate to the desired student outcomes in relation to the students' existing literacy capabilities. Instructional tasks that are too difficult for students limit their chances of successful learning. Teachers who pace their instruction by progress in small, closely related steps to maximize students' success in literacy activities increase students' chances of success. Ongoing assessment that focuses on pupils' literacy strengths and weaknesses enables teachers to identify instructional procedures that increase success. A balance of high- and medium-success tasks, with greater emphasis given to high-success tasks, results in students who achieve more at the end of the school year, retain more over the summer, and have a positive attitude toward school (Schneider, 1979).

In summary, effective teachers of literacy employ a variety of ongoing, informal assessment to:

Adjust instruction in terms of its impact on students' learning.

Identify instructional activities and tasks that maximize student success.

Select instructional strategies appropriate to desired literacy outcomes in relation to students' existing reading capabilities.

Pace reading instruction by progressing in small, related steps to maximize students' success rates.

Interactive Instruction

Effective teachers of reading teach students what they need to know. Although it seems simplistic and obvious, teachers of literacy "teach"; that is, students do not become independent learners through maturation alone. *Interactive instruction* means imparting new information to students through meaningful teacher-student interactions and guiding student learning. The key to interactive instruction is the active communication and interaction between teacher and student. An interactive style of teaching can be very direct or indirect, well structured or less structured in nature. The type of learning distinguishes the degree of directness or structure. A majority of learning objectives in teaching literacy can be classified as being either "skill" or "strategy" learnings. Both types of learning are important for success in literacy; however, they require different lesson-presentation methods. *Skills* require lower-level cognitive processing, are specific in nature, and "are more or less automatic routines" (Dole et al., 1991). Examples of literacy skills include learning the various decoding abilities of phonics, structural analysis, and context; specific comprehension skills such as sequential development, fact versus opinion, and stated main idea; reading-study skills such as use of an index and interpreting a bar graph; and writing skills such as capitalization, punctuation, and spelling. *Strategies* require higher-level cognitive

The key to interactive instruction is the active communication and interaction between teacher and student.

processing, are less specific and "emphasize intentional and deliberate plans under the control of the reader" (Dole et al., 1991). Examples of cognitive strategies applied to literacy include summarizing a story, reacting critically to what is read, and editing a piece of writing. Both types of learnings require different degrees of directness and control by the teacher (see Figure 2.1). As shown, skills require more control and direction by the teacher than strategies, which require less teacher directness and are more under the control of students. However, teaching is neither direct nor indirect—on a continuum, a given teaching lesson is more or less direct than another. Both types of interactive teaching—for skills and for strategies—are important, and both types of lessons should be included in a teacher's repertoire.

Skill Learning. Skill learning is particularly suitable to the ***direct/explicit instruction*** approach. Summarizing the literature on the teaching procedures for direct instruction, Rosenshine and Stevens (1986) delineated six instructional functions (see Figure 2.2). Teachers who use these procedures consistently see higher-than-average achievement among their students.

At the heart of the direct/explicit instruction method are explicit explanation, modeling and guided practice. Explicit explanation can include defining a reading skill, modeling or demonstrating its use in an actual reading situation, and thinking aloud with students about what the skill is and how it is used (i.e., showing how to apply it in context) (Blair & Rupley, 1988). Effective teachers provide varied, meaningful practice to ensure mastery and transfer of a skill to other meaningful reading situations (Rupley & Blair, 1988). Directly controlled by the teacher, this practice is characterized by varying degrees of teacher-student interaction. In this process, the teacher acts as a mediator. Based on Vygotsky's theoretical work (1962), ***mediated instruction*** involves providing guidance to a student in learning a particular skill. During practice, the amount of guidance is great at the beginning; it declines to little or none. Walker (1992) emphasizes both the teacher guidance and continuous assessment of instruction in mediating instruction.

Guiding student learning is certainly not new; it has been an effective teaching strategy for years. The renewed interest today is the result of new research on the teaching-learning process and the social environment of the classroom.

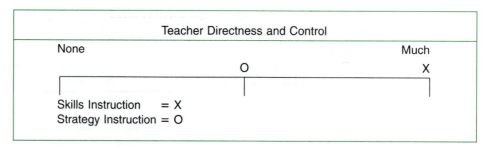

FIGURE 2.1
Skill versus strategy learning: Teacher directness and control

Figure 2.3 depicts this gradual shift of responsibility for the application of a reading skill.

Strategy Learning. Teaching students strategies or strategic reading behaviors to interact with and comprehend text requires a different style of interactive teaching. Most strategies require higher-level thinking as opposed to skills, which are more factual or literal and amenable to specific learning objectives. Strategies are behaviors a reader applies before, during, and after reading to construct and understand the author's message. Examples of strategies include the ability to preview a selection, ask questions to understand and clarify ideas while reading, summarize a passage, and react critically to what was read. Referring back to Figure 2.3, it is important to note that teaching students strategies requires a different style of direct/explicit instruction. The emphasis is on helping students understand the when and why of utilizing various strategies. Teaching a strategy still requires teachers to explain, inform, model, or demonstrate what they want students to know, but it is not a strict step-by-step procedure under complete control of the teacher (as it is for skill instruction). Teaching cognitive strategies also follows the gradual shift of control and responsibility for the learning and application of a reading strategy (Figure 2.3). Rosenshine and Meister (1992) described the teaching of cognitive strategies as including the following steps:

1. Present the new cognitive strategy.
2. Regulate difficulty during guided practice.
3. Provide varying contexts for student practice.
4. Provide feedback.
5. Increase student responsibility.
6. Provide independent practice. (p. 27)

Central to teaching strategies is the use of instructional procedures called ***scaffolds*** to aid students while they learn the strategy (see Chapter 6). Rosenshine and Meister defined the term:

> Scaffolds are forms of support provided by the teacher (or another student) to help students bridge the gap between their current abilities and the intended goal . . . . Instead of providing explicit steps, one supports, or scaffolds, the students as they learn the skill. (p. 26)

Scaffolds can be general aids such as modeling or demonstrating a strategy or specific aids used to teach a strategy. For example, in learning the strategy of generating questions, teachers may use the scaffold of teaching students the meaning of reporters' questions (who, what, where, when, why, and how) in questioning what they read. In teaching any cognitive strategy, the teacher acts more as a facilitator than a director in helping students learn to interact critically with text.

The importance of giving analytical consideration to classroom structure and direct teaching as a means for improving literacy teaching effectiveness seems clear. The literacy program should not be regimented and inflexible. Structure and direct instruction depend on the desired reading outcomes and the grade

1. Daily Review and Checking Homework
   Checking homework (routines for students to check each other's papers).
   Reteaching when necessary.
   Reviewing relevant past learning (may include questioning).
   Review prerequisite skills (if applicable).

2. Presentation
   Provide short statement of objectives.
   Provide overview and structuring.
   Proceed in small steps but at a rapid pace.
   Intersperse questions within the demonstration to check for understanding.
   Highlight main points.
   Provide sufficient illustrations and concrete examples.
   Provide demonstrations and models.
   When necessary, give detailed and redundant instructions and examples.

3. Guided Practice
   Initial student practice takes place with teacher guidance.
   High frequency of questions and overt student practice (from teacher and/or materials).
   Questions are directly relevant to the new content or skill.
   Teacher checks for understanding (CFU) by evaluating student responses.
   During CFU teacher gives additional explanation, process feedback, or repeats explanation—where necessary.
   All students have a chance to respond and receive feedback; teacher insures that all students participate.
   Prompts are provided during guided practice (where appropriate).
   Initial student practice is sufficient so that students can work independently.
   Guided practice continues until students are firm.
   Guided practice is continued (usually) until a success rate of 80% is achieved.

FIGURE 2.2
Instructional functions
(From "Teaching Functions." In M.C. Wittrock [Ed.], *Handbook of Research on Teaching* [New York: Macmillan Co., 1986], p. 379. Copyright 1986 by the American Educational Research Association. Reprinted by permission.)

level. Analyzing how these variables influence students' reading and making changes when necessary enhance teacher effectiveness.

In summary, effective teachers of literacy utilize an interactive style of teaching to:

■ Maximize pupil involvement in tasks or academic activities related specifically to lesson content and desired outcomes.

■ Control pupil behavior using task-related comments rather than criticizing or scolding.

■ Monitor and guide the direction of learning.

■ Vary the degree of structure in relation to desired behavioral objectives: less structure and less-direct instruction are employed for strategy or creative outcomes and more structure and control for skill outcomes.

4. Correctives and Feedback

Quick, firm, and correct responses can be followed by another question or short acknowledgement of correctness (i.e., "That's right").

Hesitant correct answers might be followed by process feedback (i.e., "Yes, Linda, that's right because...").

Student errors indicate a need for more practice.

Monitor students for systematic errors.

Try to obtain a substantive response to each question.

Corrections can include sustaining feedback (i.e., simplifying the question, giving clues), explaining or reviewing steps, giving process feedback, or reteaching the last steps.

Try to elicit an improved response when the first one is incorrect.

Guided practice and corrections continue until the teacher feels that the group can meet the objectives of the lesson.

Praise should be used in moderation, and specific praise is more effective than general praise.

5. Independent Practice (Seatwork)

Sufficient practice.

Practice is directly relevant to skills/content taught.

Practice to overlearning.

Practice until responses are firm, quick, and automatic.

Ninety-five percent correct rate during independent practice.

Students alerted that seatwork will be checked.

Student held accountable for seatwork.

Actively supervise students, when possible.

6. Weekly and Monthly Reviews

Systematic review of previously learned material.

Include review in homework.

Frequent tests.

Reteaching of material missed in tests.

Note: With older, more mature learners, or learners with more knowledge of the subject, the following adjustments can be made: (1) the size of the step in presentation can be larger (more material is presented at one time), (2) there is less time spent on teacher-guided practice and (3) the amount of overt practice can be decreased, replacing it with covert rehearsal, restating and reviewing.

FIGURE 2.2
Continued

- Utilize a pattern of instruction at the primary level that allows pupils to contact the teacher, work in small groups, and use a variety of materials.
- Utilize a pattern of instruction at the intermediate level that allows larger instructional groups, more discussion at higher cognitive levels, less teacher direction, and greater pupil-initiated learning.

Opportunity to Learn

Opportunity to learn refers to whether students have been taught the skills relevant to the areas for which they are assessed. Teachers who specify literacy behaviors prior to teaching and who teach content relevant to these outcomes of-

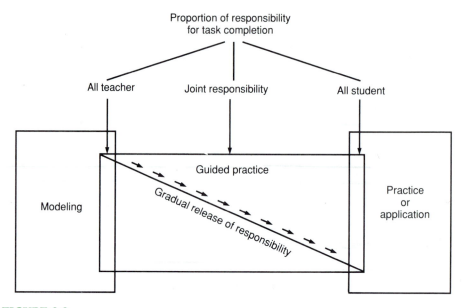

FIGURE 2.3

The gradual-release-of-responsibility model of instruction
(After Campione, 1981. Reprinted with permission from P. D. Pearson and M. C.
Gallagher, *The Instruction of Reading Comprehension* [Urbana, IL: University of Illinois,
Center for the Study of Reading, October 1983], p. 732.)

ten have pupils who achieve at a higher reading level than do teachers who do
not (Rupley, Wise, & Logan, 1986).

Opportunity to learn is a variable associated with direct instruction. Teachers
could employ structure and direct instruction, but if the instruction does not relate to an assessed learning task or a valued outcome, then students have not
had an opportunity to learn the product. For example, students who do well in
learning isolated reading skills as a result of intensive instruction but who do
poorly in actual reading may lack the opportunity to learn how to apply such
skills in actual reading tasks.

A study of 1,828 Philadelphia fourth graders (Vicino, 1979) indicated the importance of providing students with opportunities to apply their reading skills in
actual reading tasks. In addition to daily whole-class or small-group reading instruction groups, the students spent a large portion of their class time reading
silently. The result was more advanced reading skills.

The importance of providing opportunities for students to apply their reading skills in real-life tasks is apparent in a reading program developed by the Irwin School in Charlotte, North Carolina (Cohen & Irons, 1979). In addition to
increasing the amount of students' engaged time, using ongoing assessment to
plan instruction, and maintaining appropriate levels of structure and direct instruction, teachers focused on applying reading skills to comprehension tasks and
literature appreciation activities. Preliminary results indicate that the third,

Students should gradually assume more control and responsibility for their own learning.

fourth, and fifth graders involved in the program were progressing at a rate of 3 months' growth for every 2 months of instruction.

Providing pupils with opportunities to apply their reading and writing skills in meaningful content areas appears to be extremely important; however, teachers must use materials that students can handle. The more time students spend on actual reading with which they can be highly successful, the more they will probably learn. The more they are involved in actual reading tasks that limit success, the less likely they are to enhance their learning.

Practice activities in reading are of the utmost importance. Such activities are best designed around three areas: (1) planning for practice, (2) delivering effective practice, and (3) evaluating the effectiveness of practice assignments.

When planning for practice, teachers should ask:

- Is the intended practice related to the students' needs?
- Is the level of the materials appropriate and interesting?
- Is the content of the practice within the students' experiential background?
- Are different ways of practice provided to meet students' needs and maintain their interest?
- Is the amount of practice appropriate for the instructional period?

- Are directions and examples provided to students to ensure understanding (i.e., are they clear)?
- Is it necessary to vary the type of practice in one class period (having students work on two or three different types of materials relating to one aspect of reading), or will one practice activity be sufficient?

When delivering practice, teachers should ask:

- Are several exercises completed with the students before they work on their own?
- How will the students' progress during practice sessions be monitored?
- Do individual students know how to get help if the teacher is working with another student?
- What should students do if they finish an activity early?
- Do the students understand how the practice activity relates to reading in meaningful text?

When evaluating the effectiveness of practice assignments, teachers should ask:

- Did the practice accomplish its goal?
- What are the students' patterns of correct and incorrect responses?
- How will the results of this practice session modify the next practice activity? (Rupley & Blair, 1987)

Opportunity to learn is not equal to coverage of materials and topics. Opportunity to learn, ongoing assessment, structure, and direct instruction are related. The reading instruction that is offered must relate to assessment data, desired outcomes, instructional format, and application in actual reading tasks. Opportunity to learn should reflect the desired learning outcomes, not simply cover the content.

In summary, effective teachers of reading attend to students' opportunity to learn and apply skills in actual reading situations to:

- Ensure that instruction focuses on desired and valued reading outcomes.
- Guard against isolated reading skills and strategies becoming an end in themselves rather than a means to effective reading comprehension.
- Provide for application of reading skills and strategies in silent reading tasks that ensure maximum student success.
- Ensure that students understand how to apply their reading skills and strategies for reading enjoyment.

Attention to Learning Tasks

Students' attention to learning tasks and engagement in pertinent learning materials logically fall under the direct supervision of the teacher. The historic Beginning Teacher Evaluation Study, Phase II (McDonald, 1976) provided clear support for the importance of maintaining a reasonably high level of student involvement. Appropriate reading materials alone are not sufficient to maximize achievement. Effective teachers use not only appropriate materials but also attend to actively engaging students in learning from the materials. Simply requiring that all students complete similar learning tasks does not ensure maximum attention. Students approach various learning tasks with varying interest, capabilities, and understanding. Effective literacy teachers take these factors into account as they attempt to engage students in meaningful reading instruction.

Academic engaged time, or *time on task,* refers to the classroom time when students are actually attending to the work at hand. Classrooms in which students are actively engaged in learning for a large proportion of the time demonstrate higher achievement in reading and writing. Engagement is the key; merely completing reading and writing activities does not mean learning.

Researchers have extended time on task to include students' success rate while working productively. Fisher et al. (1979) label this concept *academic learning time (ALT).* They define the term as "the amount of time a student spends engaged in an academic task he/she performs with high success" (p. 52). A high success rate is considered to be above 80%. Allocated time, student engagement, and student success rate define academic learning time. Collectively, academic learning time occurs when a student has the time or opportunity to learn, is actively engaged with the task at hand, and is succeeding at the task.

Attention to learning and engagement in materials are important for learning in both directed and individual instruction. The key is *active engagement* in reading and writing instruction, not necessarily the total *time* allocated. Students may be passive or indifferent to instruction, even though a teacher devotes a large amount of instructional time to reading and writing. Alone, the number of minutes allocated for instruction does not affect level of reading achievement. However, with all other things equal, the greater the time spent on instruction, the higher the achievement will be (Schneider, 1979).

In summary, effective teachers of literacy help maximize students' focus on learning tasks by:

- Allocating more time to reading instruction.
- Keeping students actively engaged in learning during the instructional period.
- Providing academic feedback to students about their work to increase attention to tasks and amount of engaged time.
- Setting purposes for learning.
- Presenting an overview of what is to be learned.
- Using examples and illustrations to relate new learning to what has been presented previously and to help students understand how to apply what they are learning.
- Monitoring students' involvement to ensure a high success rate.

Effective teachers monitor students' involvement to ensure a high success rate.

Teacher Expectations

The most pervasive conclusion of school and teacher effectiveness studies in the 1970s and 1980s was that a teacher of reading profoundly influences how much students learn. This influence stems from both classroom actions and belief systems. Effective literacy programs have teachers who believe in themselves and expect their students to succeed in learning. Simply put, students learn more if you hold high academic expectations for them. Thus, expectations for students may bias teachers' actions: If students perform according to what is expected of them, expectations can become self-fulfilling prophecies.

Having different expectations for different students is natural as long as the expectations reflect diagnostic data (such as achievement scores, specific strengths and weaknesses in comprehension, and motivational concerns) rather than socioeconomic status, gender, race, or ethnic background. Good and Brophy (1987) showed that students for whom teachers have low expectations may:

- Receive less instruction.
- Be expected to do less work.
- Receive less-frequent praise.
- Be called on less often.

- Receive less time to respond to questions.
- Be asked predominantly factual questions.
- Be seated farther from their teachers.
- Receive less eye contact.
- Be smiled at less often.
- Be criticized more frequently for incorrect responses.
- Receive less help.

Luckily, some students are not as affected by low teacher expectations as others. However, it is important to realize the potential impact that expectations can have on students.

In addition to holding high, realistic expectations for students and communicating them, effective teachers have a strong sense of efficacy, or the expectation that their efforts will result in valued outcomes (Fuller et al., 1982). In effect, teachers with a high sense of efficacy say, "I know I can teach these students!" These teachers believe in themselves and believe that investing substantial effort into their work will raise student achievement.

Being aware of the power of expectations and translating this awareness into sound instruction takes effort. That effort involves:

- Ensuring that reading instruction is based on diagnostic data.
- Communicating goals and expectations to students.
- Ensuring that all students participate in the reading lesson.

Classroom Management

Directly related to student achievement in reading is the teacher's classroom management ability. Without the ability to manage complex interactions, a teacher's best intentions and instructional techniques are ineffective. Researchers have shown that teachers of high-achieving students in reading are good classroom managers (Emmer, 1987). Effective classroom management creates and maintains an atmosphere conducive for learning. Managerial skills include planning for instruction, developing routines to manage group interactions, devising monitoring procedures, and responding to off-task behavior (Blair, 1988). Chapter 12 covers classroom management in detail. That chapter discusses specific techniques and strategies for the teacher of reading and writing.

In summary, effective teachers of reading manage the classroom to:

- Ensure conditions that are conducive to student learning.
- Plan meaningful reading activities.
- Manage group instruction.
- Monitor student progress throughout the reading period.
- Respond appropriately to student misbehavior.

DECISION MAKING IN READING INSTRUCTION

While the literature on effective teaching has yielded specific guidelines for teaching reading, the guidelines apply differently to each classroom depending upon a host of variables, including student needs, material content, grade level, and learning objectives. This realization underscores the notion of effective teachers of reading as decision makers: Teaching is a decision-making process, and teachers' judgments are the keys to the success or failure of reading programs.

To teach students what they need to know, teachers must base their decisions about planning and instruction on assessment information (as opposed to race, gender, socioeconomic status, ethnic background, or personal characteristics). Studies of teacher planning have reported that many focus on instructional activities when making decisions (Stern & Shavelson, 1983). This contradicts the traditional thinking that teachers should focus on specific objectives in making

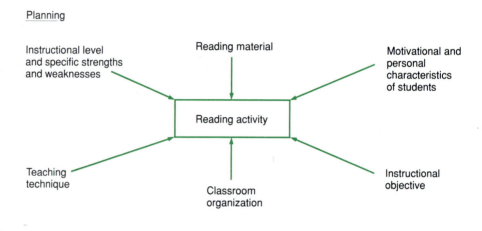

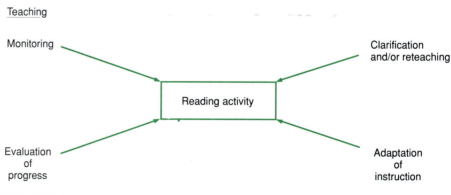

FIGURE 2.4
Interactive decision making

Diagnosis

Focus: Pupils' reading strengths and weaknesses

Features: Ongoing—combining both informal and standardized measures of reading outcomes related directly to instructional goals. Data are used to plan appropriate classroom structure and instruction.

Guiding questions:
- Are the students placed on their instructional level of reading materials (that is, not too difficult and not too easy)?
- Are you continually using informal observational techniques and diagnostic tests to detect strengths and weaknesses in word identification and comprehension?
- Is the instruction based on a diagnosis of student needs?
- Are you adjusting your instruction according to the students' progress?

Direct Instruction

Focus: Instructional organization and process.

Features: Stated purposes for learning in terms of academic skills. Direct instruction emphasizes the importance of the teacher in learning. It provides a focus on the product for identifying and conceptualizing instruction. Such instruction is differentiated by grade level and type of task.

Guiding questions:
- Do you vary the amount of structure in your class depending on student characteristics, grade level, and objectives?
- Do you allow for less structure when teaching more complex tasks (for example, do you solicit emotional responses to a story or judgment of the desirability or acceptability of a character's behaviors)?
- Do you devise more structured lessons when teaching basic reading skills (such as word identification and comprehension)?
- Do you give your students appropriate feedback?

Opportunity to Learn

Focus: Instruction aimed at measurable and desired reading outcomes. Application of skills in actual reading tasks.

Features: Matching the instruction to desired outcomes and teaching content relevant to these. Opportunity to learn maximizes pupils' understanding of the purposes for learning skills and of applying these skills to actual reading situations.

Guiding questions:
- Do you allow sufficient instructional time to teach what your students need to know?
- Do you allow time for your students to practice their reading skills in actual reading situations?
- Do you plan ways to monitor student practice of targeted reading skills?
- Are your students practicing their reading skills in materials that will ensure a high degree of success?

Classroom Management

Focus: Creating, managing, and maintaining a classroom environment conducive to learning.

Features: Preparation of materials and activities prior to actual teaching to prevent management difficulties. During instruction, successful managers grasp the total classroom situation, monitor students' work, and respond appropriately to student misbehavior.

Guiding questions:
- Do you prepare materials in advance and distribute them at appropriate times?
- Do you select and apply appropriate group management techniques to manage student misbehavior?
- Do you monitor student progress by responding quickly and appropriately to student responses to material?

Teacher Expectations

Focus: Believing one's students can learn and communicating this expectation to them.

Features: Ensuring that instruction is based on diagnostic information. Teachers convince students that they will be successful in the classroom.

Guiding questions:
- Are your instructional decisions based on diagnostic data?
- Are all students involved in the reading class?
- Do you communicate to your students that they will be successful in your reading class?
- Are you exhibiting a positive attitude toward teaching and continually striving to learn and to grow?

Attention to Learning Tasks

Focus: Maintaining a high level of pupil involvement in learning.

Features: Maximizing pupils' involvement and attention to learning. Attention to the learning tasks looks at pupils' needs, based on diagnostic data. It involves pupils in instruction at a moderate level of difficulty, monitors their engagement in the instruction, and maximizes attention to learning by focusing on tasks related directly to desired outcomes.

Guiding questions:
- Do you clearly communicate the specific purposes of each lesson to your students?
- Do you plan your instruction to ensure a high percentage of academic engaged time?
- Do you design seatwork assignments to ensure student involvement?
- Do you use a reward system with students to reinforce specific positive behaviors?

FIGURE 2.5
Summary of effective teacher practices

decisions. A focus on activities should not be interpreted to exclude objectives in the planning process, however. Student characteristics should help shape reading and writing activities into meaningful experiences.

Figure 2.4 outlines the decision-making process for planning and actual teaching (interactive decision making). As shown, instructional implementation depends on decisions made both before and during teaching. Planning decisions center on the ability to modify and adapt the major reading activity to meet learning needs. Students' instructional levels, strengths, weaknesses, and personal qualities will factor into decisions. The teacher's learning objectives (e.g., basic word identification or critical thinking), teaching techniques (e.g., directed reading activity, language experience approach, direct instruction, or reciprocal teaching), and grouping or classroom organization will also influence decisions.

Planning instruction, however, does not mean the end of decision making. Effective teachers modify their instruction based on student responses (either mastery of material, which requires no modification, or difficulty, which requires further explanation or reteaching). The goal should be to progress at a speed that maintains student involvement and achieves instructional goals.

Figure 2.5 summarizes six areas that characterize quality instruction. Attention to these areas should enable teachers to better determine and improve the effectiveness of their reading instruction.

SUMMARY /

Time and time again, research has demonstrated the importance of the teacher in effective literacy instruction. Admittedly, we have much to learn about what makes an effective teacher. However, a great deal of the available information warrants careful consideration. We know, for example, that teachers who include provisions for ongoing assessment, interactive instruction, opportunity to learn, attention to learning tasks, accurate expectations, and efficient classroom management are more effective than teachers who do not include provisions for these practices.

All teachers of literacy can benefit from knowing about the practices of competent teachers. Teacher-effectiveness research identifies some characteristics associated with effective teaching of literacy. Teachers of literacy should sort out and analyze these characteristics in terms of their own capabilities and classrooms.

YOUR POINT OF VIEW /

Discussion Questions

1. What reasons account for the different characteristics of effective primary-grade teachers versus effective intermediate-grade teachers?
2. What are the implications of direct instruction for teaching of critical thinking skills?

Take a Stand For or Against

1. Good teachers are born, not made.
2. Opportunity to learn is the most powerful variable in education.
3. Small-group direct instruction is more beneficial than large-group direct instruction.

BIBLIOGRAPHY /

Blair, T. R. (1975). *Relationship of teacher effort and student achievement in reading.* Unpublished doctoral dissertation, University of Illinois, Urbana.

Blair, T. R. (1984). What makes an effective reading program effective? In R. Thompson (Ed.), *Reading research review.* Afton, MN: Burgess Publishing Co.

Blair, T. R. (1988). *Emerging patterns of teaching: From methods to field experiences.* New York: Merrill/Macmillan Publishing Co.

Blair, T. R., & Rupley, W. H. (1988). Practice and application in the teaching of reading. *The Reading Teacher, 41,* 536–539.

Brandt, R. (1989). Strategies for teaching and learning strategies. *Educational Leadership, 46,* 2.

Calfee, R. & Hiebert, E. (1991). Classroom assessment of reading. In R. Barr, M. Kamil, P. Mosenthal, & P. D. Pearson (Eds.), *Handbook of reading research* (Vol. II) (pp. 281–309). New York: Longman.

Chall, J. S. (1967). *Learning to read: The great debate.* New York: McGraw-Hill Book Co.

Cohen, R. G., & Irons, B. R. (November 1979). Doubling up in reading. *The Allyn and Bacon Reading Newsletter, 7,* 4.

Commeyras, M., Osborn, J., & Bruce, B. (1992). The reactions of educators to the framework for the 1992 NAEP for reading. In C. K. Kinzer & D. Leu (Eds.), *Literacy research, theory, and practice: Views from many perspectives* (pp. 137–152). Chicago: National Reading Conference.

Cruickshank, D.R. (1990). *Research that informs teachers and teacher educators.* Bloomington, IN: Phi Delta Kappa.

Dole, J. A., Duffy, G. G., Roehler, L. R. & Pearson, P. D. (1991). Moving from the old to the new: Research on reading comprehension instruction. *Review of Educational Research, 61,* 239–264.

Dykstra, R. (1967). *Continuation of the coordination center for first-grade reading instruction programs (*Final Report). Washington, DC: U.S. Department of Health, Education, and Welfare, Office of Education, Bureau of Research.

Emmer, E. T. (1987). Classroom management and discipline. In V. Richardson-Koehler (Ed.), *Educators' handbook: A research perspective* (pp. 233–258). New York: Longman.

Fisher, C., Marliave, R., & Filby, N. (1979). Improving teaching by increasing academic learning time. *Educational Leadership, 39,* 52–54.

Fuller, B., Wood, K., Rapoport, T., & Dornbusch, S. (1982). The organizational content of individual efficacy. *Review of Educational Research, 52,* 7–30.

Gates, A. I. (1937). The necessary age for beginning reading. *Elementary School Journal, 37,* 497–508.

Good, T. L., & Brophy, J. E. (1987). *Looking in classrooms* (4th ed.). New York: Harper & Row.

Henk, W., & Melnick, S. (1992). The initial development of a scale to measure "perception of self as reader." In C. K. Kinzer & D. Leu (Eds.), *Literacy research, theory, and practice: Views from many perspectives* (pp. 111–118). Chicago: National Reading Conference.

McDonald, F. J. (1976). *Summary report: Beginning teacher evaluation study: Phase II, 1973–74.* (Final report: Vol. 1). Princeton, NJ: Educational Testing Service.

Pescosolido, J. D. (1962). *The identification and appraisal of certain major factors in the teaching of reading.* Unpublished doctoral dissertation, University of Connecticut, Storrs.

Rosenshine, B. V., & Meister, C. (1992). The use of scaffolds for teaching higher-level cognitive strategies. *Educational Leadership, 49,* 26–33.

Rosenshine, B. V., and Stevens, R. (1986). Teaching functions. In M. C. Wittrock (Ed.), *Handbook of research on teaching* (3rd ed.) (pp. 376–391). New York: Macmillan.

Rupley, W. H. (1977). Stability of teacher effect on pupils' reading achievement gain over a two-year period and its relation to instructional emphases. In P. D. Pearson (Ed.), *Reading: Theory, research and practice* (pp. 69–72). Clemson, SC: National Reading Conference.

Rupley, W. H., & Blair, T. R. (1987). Assignment and supervision of reading seatwork: Looking in on 12 primary grade teachers. *The Reading Teacher, 40,* 391–393.

Rupley, W. H., & Blair, T. R. (1988). *Teaching reading: Diagnosis, direct instruction, and practice* (2nd ed.). New York: Merrill/Macmillan Publishing Co.

Rupley, W. H., Wise, B. S., & Logan, J. W. (1986). Research in effective teaching: An overview of its development. In J. V. Hoffman, *Effective teaching of reading: Research and practice.* Newark, DE: International Reading Association.

Schneider, E. J. (Fall 1979). Researchers discover formula of success in student learning. *Educational R&D Report, 2,* 1–6.

Stern, P., and Shavelson, R. J. (1983). Reading teachers' judgments, plans, and decision making. *The Reading Teacher, 37,* 280–286.

Vicino, F. L. (Ed.). (1979). Philadelphia study pinpoints factors in improving reading achievement. *Pre Post Press, 5,* 1.

Vygotsky, L. (1962). *Thought and language.* Cambridge, MA: M.I.T. Press.

Walker, B. J. (1992). *Diagnostic teaching of reading: Techniques for instruction and assessment* (2nd ed.). New York: Merrill/Macmillan Publishing Co.

3

Language: The Key to Literacy

For the Reader

Language continually shapes our views of the world and ourselves. Whether it is a child saying "cookie," a scientist explaining a new theory, an author writing a book, or a student reading a textbook, the central purpose of language is communication of meaning. Reading is based on language, as are listening, speaking, and writing. Language cuts across every goal and function of the school. Everything that is taught in the school passes through a communication process before students learn it. Schools must take advantage of the listening, speaking, and writing abilities of their students if they are to nurture and develop understanding of written language. Educators can best do this by integrating language activities and building on students' language.

Key Ideas

- Reading and writing are related to all language functions found in the elementary school curriculum.

- Learning to read and write is related to, and built upon, past language experiences.

- Literacy instruction should be a natural outgrowth of students' past language experiences.

- Literacy learning is a developmental process related to continued language development.

- Different methods of teaching literacy may be justified, but a method should build logically and systematically on students' language capabilities.

Key Terms

oral language   the language abilities of listening and speaking.

literacy   the language abilities of reading and writing.

decontextualized language use   the basis for literacy, requiring developing language awareness.

grapheme-phoneme relationships   the relationships between written letters and letter combinations and the sounds they typically represent.

semantics   the meaning features of a language.

syntax   the word order or grammar of a language.

culturally and linguistically diverse learners students whose culture and language or dialect differ from that of the school.

dialects   the ways people speak in different parts of the country or specific cultures.

whole language   a style of reading instruction based on the idea that students learn best when literacy is naturally connected to their oral language.

shared reading   students see the text as it is read aloud to them—usually from big books—and are invited to read along.

paired reading   one student reads aloud as another follows along in the text.

response journals   written letters or dialogues that students share with each other and their teacher on a regular basis.

THE INTERACTIVE FEATURES OF READING

Reading is a language process requiring the understanding of written language. Language provides a bridge that enables ideas, information, and data to pass between parent and child, teacher and student, and student and peers. Reading has a unique relationship with language. Since we acquire or refine most of our concepts and reasoning capabilities through the use of language, reading enables us to go beyond what we can see or manipulate. In a broad sense, reading frees both language and thinking from immediate experiences (Wells, 1981).

Reading involves the learner in solving two codes. One is accessing the text or print by understanding the relationship between the orthography (the writing system) and the phonemes (speech units represented by the writing system). This understanding permits the reader to recognize, decode, or approximate the pronunciation of words not recognized as whole words. Reading research has documented the importance of children understanding the relationship between letters and letter combinations and the sounds they represent (Perfetti, 1991); however, an ongoing debate concerns how best to facilitate this development in reading instruction. Children who are emerging readers and writers need to know the relationship between their own speech sounds and how these are represented in print. Some children find this difficult because they are not aware of how words and sounds are marked in their speech and that they are perceived as distinct units (Dickinson, Wolf, & Stotsky, 1993).

Constructing meaning is the second important code. Readers interact with writers so that there is communication between both. Writers of books, notes, lists, directions, and so forth are using language to communicate with a reader. Interaction between the text and reader depends on the reader's experiential and conceptual backgrounds, purposes for reading, and setting, as well as the text content (see Chapter 1). This interaction involves a strategic approach that requires knowledge of language structures, comprehension monitoring, and getting meaning. Such interaction is language-related, but it goes beyond the reader's oral language background, because much of this interaction involves reading and writing experiences that support and extend all language capabilities.

Oral Language and Reading

The *oral language* capabilities of listening and speaking are related to the language processing capabilities of reading and writing *(literacy)*. Three important relationships between oral language and literacy are (1) oral language capabilities develop to a fairly high level of proficiency before written language development, (2) oral and written language share the same vocabulary and grammar, and (3) knowledge of oral language is used extensively by students in learning to read and write (Sticht & James, 1984). Literacy builds a bridge of understanding between oral language capabilities and reading and writing.

One view of the relationship between oral and written language is that in the beginning stages of reading development, children depend on their oral language abilities to comprehend. That is, emerging readers' comprehension of print is linked closely to their spoken language capabilities and experiences with environmental print. At this early stage of learning about words, called the logo-graphic stage (Frith, 1985), children learn words as wholes; these words are often embedded in a logo, such as McDonald's golden arches (see Chapter 7 for an elaborated discussion of emergent literacy). As children's reading becomes more automatic and proficient, their dependence on spoken language abilities in comprehending print generally disappears, and print is comprehended in terms of its structural and meaning features. This capability is reflected in Stage 2 of Chall's (1983) reading stages (presented in Chapter 1), where children begin to become more proficient in using letter-sound relationships in their reading. Samuels (1988) has attributed this to word recognition becoming more automatic; that is, requiring less attention for sounding out words, and more attention for comprehension. Research findings have shown that children experience difficulty reading text containing features and structures they have not yet acquired in their oral language. They also have problems with text containing structures that they are in the process of acquiring.

Research supports the idea that students undergo developmental shifts in the importance of oral language in comprehending text. Young children often depend more on their oral language. Older students, who are more proficient in reading, depend more on their experience with reading and writing. Emergent readers who are learning about orthographic features and acquiring word-recognition skills are also developing an understanding of how print functions, the nature of stories, and other important components of literacy that will enhance their comprehension. As they build experience with print, emergent readers rely less upon the speech code representation and focus more on meaning.

This phenomenon suggests a reciprocal relationship between literacy and oral-language development. Students' language awareness depends heavily on their literacy experiences, which help them to understand language features, such as syntax and semantics, and to develop and expand their vocabularies. Direct experiences with reading and writing enhance and facilitate development of language awareness, which enhances and facilitates reading and writing development (Stahl, 1992). Language awareness, which includes knowledge about phonemes, words, sentences, story structure, and communication of meaning evolves primarily through direct experiences with print in both reading and writing situations.

Reading Instruction That Builds on Oral Language

Reading for meaning is in many ways closer to children's previous experiences with language than is associating visual symbols with the sounds they typically represent. Prior to reading instruction, children have spent several years listening to and speaking meaningful language. Most children begin school with a speaking vocabulary of approximately 8,000 words and are capable of using language to express themselves. However, they use this language within familiar contextual settings and focus on communication with others. The process and the demands of literacy are based on *decontextualized language use,* which requires developing language awareness. Decontextualized language has three characteristics that are more closely associated with written language than oral language:

1. *Information* must be conveyed that is new to the hearer.
2. *Background knowledge* necessary for the hearer to interpret the message needs to be provided.
3. The information must be communicated through words and *syntax,* not by relying on intonation and extra-linguistic resources such as gestures. (Dickinson, Wolf, & Stotsky, 1993, p. 372)

Experiences with language in their environment begin to enhance children's development of decontextualized language skills. As children learn to recognize words by associating logos (Coke, Crest, McDonald's, K-Mart, etc.) with them, engage in pretend writing in their play, distinguish print from pictures, understand the features of books, and so forth, they begin developing decontextualized language capabilities.

Because children learning to read and write rely heavily on their language backgrounds and their early experiences with literacy, they can experience difficulties if asked to do something that does not build on their existing capabilities. Failure to build on children's existing language capabilities may result in their failure to see that they are really involved in a language process. The materials and methods used for reading instruction often divorce the act of reading from language involvement by emphasizing letter-sound relationships and failing to stress the language-meaning features of print.

Lack of balanced reading instruction may or may not be deliberate. Our concern is how the learner perceives what is going on. Phonics, for example, can provide motivation only for a limited time—it is not a self-sustaining activity. Only direct involvement in actual reading and writing will help children develop literacy capabilities that complement and extend their language development.

Teachers who are teaching and facilitating reading must be aware of children's experiences and growth before they enter school. Many children will have had pleasant language experiences that form a solid foundation for their experiences with reading. Children whose parents read to them often will begin to make connections between print and oral language, recognize some words as whole words, know the features of a book, relate pictures to text, and understand many other points about the relationships between oral and written language. Children who have not had opportunities to engage in informal reading activities may not.

As noted earlier, children's oral language will influence their ability to benefit from literacy activities. They are not likely to be able to read language that is too different from their speaking and listening capabilities. They are not likely to be able to write better than they can talk, for example. Oral-language capabilities set the limits for literacy at the beginning stages and at each stage that follows. Teachers of reading should view children's experiences both in and out of school as bound together with language and communication: all involve developing and extending concepts. Children build comprehension skills in reading and expression skills in writing on these concepts (Lundsteen, 1989).

Experiences with print that build on children's existing language capabilities ensure their involvement in meaningful literacy activities.

STRUCTURE OF LANGUAGE

Language instruction has its own distinct terminology. Teachers of literacy will frequently encounter these terms in their readings about literacy instruction, as well as in many of the instructional materials and reading programs used to teach literacy.

Terms Associated with *Phonology*

Phoneme: the smallest unit of sound within a language. When the word *man* is pronounced, three phonemes are utilized: /m/, /ae/, /n/.

Grapheme: a written symbol (letter and letter combination) used to represent a sound in a language. The word *man* has three graphemes representing three phonemes. The word *chop* has three graphemes representing three phonemes (*ch* is a consonant digraph representing one sound).

Grapheme-phoneme relationship: the sound(s) represented by a letter or letter combinations. Also referred to as letter-sound correspondence.

Phonics: different approaches and strategies designed to teach the orthographic code (written code) of language and relationships between spelling patterns and speech sounds represented by the spelling patterns.

Terms Associated with Meaning Features of Language

Semantics: describes the meaning relationship among words. Semantic acquisition refers to how children acquire vocabulary and how they begin to acquire semantic systems that are based on simple vocabulary acquisition.

Morpheme: the smallest unit of meaningful language. They can be one of two types—free and bound. A free morpheme functions independently in larger language units. For example, *son* is a free morpheme composed of three phonemes. A bound morpheme must be used with another morpheme. This class includes affixes and inflectional endings. If *s* is added to *son* to form a plural, the *s* in *sons* is a bound morpheme, therefore the word *sons* contains two morphemes.

Terms Associated with Structural Features of Language

Syntax: the term used to describe the patterns found within language (the grammar of the language). Syntax includes the various patterns in which words can be strung together. It also includes the ways in which words may function in different language patterns.

Light the fire. (verb)

She saw the *light.* (noun)

He danced *lightly* across the ring and threw a *light* punch. (adverb, adjective)

Research (Adams, 1990; Stahl, 1992) has supported the idea that children need to learn about the relationships between word spellings and pronunciations to become successful readers. Many of the language-development characteristics and features presented earlier must be taken into consideration. However, reading instruction can overemphasize words as individual units. Overemphasizing words inhibits development of abilities in using syntax and semantic features to arrive at meaning. Furthermore, it does not reflect the purpose of phonics, which is to develop automatic word recognition so children can devote their attention to comprehension. Understanding the importance of language in teaching literacy is essential to developing a quality instructional program.

LANGUAGE VARIATIONS

Children acquire the language to which they are exposed—generally that of their parents, which reflects the parents' geographic region (Goldfield & Snow, 1993). Although most languages share some common features (syntactic, semantic, and phonetic features were discussed in the Language Structure section), variations occur among speakers of a language. Dialects, for example, differ from region to region. Another important variation that influences children's literacy acquisition is when they are learning to read and write in English but have a first language (Spanish, Vietnamese, Navajo, etc.) different from English.

Culturally and Linguistically Diverse Learners

Culturally and linguistically diverse learners (see Chapter 13 for further information on diverse learners) refer to children whose culture and language or dialect differ from that of the school. The term refers to speakers from diverse ethnic and racial backgrounds. Difficulty in learning to read has been a major educational problem for some students from these groups (Weber, 1991).

Dialects, broadly conceived, are the ways people speak in different parts of the country or in specific cultures. The components of dialect are pronunciation, grammar, and vocabulary. Generally speaking, phonological divergences are differences in speech sounds within words; a grapheme (written letter symbol) may represent different phonemes (speech sounds) in different dialects. Grammatical and syntactical divergences are differences in inflectional changes, verb forms, verb auxiliaries, and the structures of phrases and sentences.

Since many culturally diverse children speak a dialect, a question raised by linguists and pondered by teachers of reading is: Do dialect divergences cause difficulties in literacy acquisition in standard English? Martin and Castaneda (1980) hold that children who enter school speaking a dialect other than standard American English encounter noticeable difficulty in learning to read and have a higher failure rate than do children who speak standard American English. But do the children fail in reading because of their dialect or because of their lack of experiences that relate to reading, the quality of instruction they receive, teachers' expectations, or other factors?

Linguistically diverse (bilingual and non-English-speaking) students who lack competency in the language of the classroom do not enter the school setting from a linguistic void. These students have mastered a language and its systems of significant speech sounds, grammatical structures, and meaningful vocabulary. Linguistically diverse children often face the expectation that they will read and comprehend English with competency as part of their school curriculum. Many factors, however, inhibit rapid acquisition of English as a second language, while others facilitate linguistically diverse students in becoming bilingual in their native language and English. For example, linguistic components such as phonology, syntax, and semantics make learning English difficult. *Phonology* refers to the inventory of meaningful speech sounds used to form grammatical structures in a particular language system. Vietnamese children who are learning English as a second language, for example, have never heard in their native language the sounds /s/, /es/, /t/, and /d/ at the end of a word. Languages other than English can follow a different syntax. Spanish, for example, contains no possessive forms of nouns (That is my dad's car), so children who are native Spanish speakers can experience difficulties with such language structures in English. The semantics of other languages are also different. A Navajo speaker learning English would perceive the concept of the word *rough* as a series of many attributes, each having different labels depending on the texture of the object.

Reading development is linked to students' strengths and weaknesses in their oral language capabilities (listening and speaking). Many linguistically diverse students cannot distinguish among some of the speech sounds of English, so they experience extreme difficulty in using phonics as an aid to reading. Several important strategies and considerations for teaching reading and writing to linguistically and culturally diverse learners are presented later in this chapter and discussed throughout this book.

For culturally and linguistically diverse learners, a lack of experience in curricular topics or themes also inhibits reading development. Therefore, language expansion and concept development contribute to such students' literacy development. A word, even if pronounced correctly, is nonsense to a student who attaches no meaning to that word. Providing opportunities for students to broaden and enrich both their language and informational backgrounds promotes their success in reading.

Instructional Guidelines for Working with Culturally and Linguistically Diverse Students

Classroom reading and writing instruction can benefit from the teacher's understanding of the differences between the student's language or dialect and the language of instruction. Literacy instruction that provides meaning in rich contexts is likely to be most effective in increasing literacy of diverse learners. By making reading and writing activities central to students' life experiences, teachers can emphasize the communicative intent of literacy.

The following guidelines for working with culturally and linguistically diverse students should form the foundation for effective classroom instruction—and they are equally crucial for all students.

- Learning must be continuous, built from the known to the unknown, and consistently reinforced.

- Because learning must occur in meaningful contexts, the student's language must be accepted and used as a foundation for learning literacy skills. A wide variety of authentic texts reflecting many cultures can be selected to build on the existing background knowledge of culturally and linguistically diverse students.

- The teacher must maintain and enhance students' sense of self-worth by establishing an effective climate. Teachers need to respond in an accepting manner toward culturally and linguistically diverse students if the students are to feel good about themselves in the classroom. Such acceptance benefits their learning of the language and culture of the school.

- Different students respond differently to various approaches and techniques. What works well with some students may be ineffective with others. Students' literacy progress should be periodically assessed to monitor the effectiveness of reading and writing instruction.

- Instruction in standard English should be based on the interrelated nature of the language arts. Reading, writing, speaking, and listening should be used together to promote students' use and understanding of language.

Linguistically diverse students' success in a literacy program depends greatly upon what abilities the students develop concurrently in listening, speaking, and writing. Reading is constructing meaning, and instructors should guard against

Literacy instruction that provides meaning in rich and concrete context is likely to be most effective.

teaching skills in isolation. Linguistically diverse students, as all students learning to read, must be assisted in understanding that reading is a tool for communication.

THE READING AND WRITING CONNECTION

The connection between reading and writing should be apparent, although each is often treated separately. As with listening, speaking, and reading, the purpose of writing is to communicate meaning. Students who understand that others can read their writing and that they can read the writing of others better realize the communicative concept of reading and are more likely to understand that reading is constructing meaning, not just sounding out words.

Researchers have found reading and writing to be interactive processes that share similar components (McCarthy & Raphael, 1992). Tierney and Pearson (1983) consider both reading and writing acts of composing. Writers compose meaning as they record their thoughts on paper; readers compose meaning as they process text. Reading and writing don't merely share the composition of meaning, however. Other researchers (Beck, 1985; Raphael & Englert, 1989) indicate that both readers and writers operate at several levels—using word-recognition strategies, using and understanding language structure, organizing ideas, applying background knowledge, and monitoring the composition of meaning process. These shared features emphasize the importance of language in children's literacy development.

As discussed earlier in this chapter and in Chapter 1, many factors within students influence their reading, such as knowledge of letter-sound relationships, knowledge of language functions and structure, and background knowledge of the text they are reading. Also, as students progress through school their reading capabilities increase as they learn more about language through literacy activities and expand their experiential and conceptual knowledge. Writing development seems to follow a similar pattern. Students with excellent language capabilities are often better able to organize their writing and produce text that is more coherent and longer. An important relationship seems to exist between students' reading ability and writing ability (Spivey & King, 1989).

Some of the key strategies that successful readers and writers use were summarized by Larry Lewin (1992). He points out that good readers and writers routinely and knowingly use the following strategies:

1. Prepare by:

   - Tapping their existing knowledge background for a topic before they read and write.
   - Determining their purpose(s) for reading and writing.
   - Predicting how what they are reading or what they are to write will turn out.
   - Self-selecting topics they want to read about or write about.

2. First draft by:

   - Monitoring their own understanding of their text and the text of others.
   - Monitoring their own reactions to text.
   - Relating new information in their reading and writing to what they already know.
   - Expanding their vocabulary both during and after a first draft of reading or writing.
   - Knowing where to get help and assistance when either the reading or writing "breaks down."
   - Distinguishing in their reading and writing the important from the less important ideas.

3. Repair by:

- Reconsidering the first draft meaning that they construct in their reading and writing.
- Repairing their text to improve its meaning by rereading or rewriting.
- Appreciating an author's craft and working to expand and enhance their own writing craft.

4. Share by:

- Sharing their reactions with others to their own and others' writing.
- Applying their newly acquired information to future reading and writing tasks.

Students' experiential and conceptual backgrounds for both reading and writing are important in both comprehending text when reading and composing comprehendible text when writing. Students can write best about things in which they have background knowledge. Likewise, they can read with comprehension about things that are in their experiential and conceptual backgrounds. A most important feature of reading and writing is that they both enhance children's language resources, particularly their oral language capabilities.

Interactive Features of Reading and Writing in Constructing Meaning

The connections between reading and writing suggest that teachers should integrate reading and writing throughout instructional programs. The key strategies noted earlier are those that teachers can develop, nurture, and polish by combining reading and writing in the classroom to better develop children's literacy. Shanahan (1988) developed seven instructional principles based on the reading-writing relationship. Each principle illustrates how to combine reading and writing in the classroom.

Teach Both Reading and Writing.   Although many individuals argue that reading and writing are similar in terms of the skills, strategies, and cognitive processes they involve, Shanahan does not consider them so similar. This suggests that children need opportunities to be taught both. Students do not become writers only through reading instruction, nor do they become readers only through writing instruction. Students need both reading and writing opportunities for each skill to enhance the development of the other.

Introduce Reading and Writing From the Earliest Grades.   Although Shanahan recommends early introduction, it is best to make reading and writing a pervasive part of the curriculum. Teachers who create a literate environment in their classroom don't treat literacy as something with a scheduled period. Language is an integral part of the learning environment, and reading and writing opportunities should abound throughout each day.

Reading typically is introduced early in children's formal education, but writing is often delayed until later. Sulzby and Barnhart (1992) argue that reading and writing should be taught in the first year of formal education because children begin school with much literacy learning. Building on and nurturing this early literacy learning is what enables young children to develop conventional literacy. These early reading and writing behaviors, called emergent literacy, are discussed in Chapter 7.

Reflect the Developmental Nature of the Reading and Writing Relationship in Instruction. (This relationship is also found in Chapters 5, 6, and 7.) Tierney (1992) suggests that reading and writing are developmental processes and that different abilities are dominant at different points in development. Shanahan notes that at the beginning stages of reading, spelling and word recognition are dominant. These findings coincide with Chall's (1983) research on stages of reading development and Adams' (1990) analysis of beginning reading development. With more-capable readers, the connection between reading and writing focuses on comprehension, vocabulary, and organization. What students learn at differing points in their reading and writing development can have important implications for instruction.

Reading and writing can be integrated at developmental stages by using writing activities appropriate to students' level of reading and oral-language development. Teachers can use multiple types of text in teaching students to read, write about, synthesize, evaluate, or analyze. Writing activities that encourage children to use new words can reinforce vocabulary development. Such writing activities focus on real-life experiences to ensure that the language structure and text reflect students' background knowledge. Writing activities can also replace or supplement many of the independent practice and application activities recommended in reading instructional materials.

Make the Reading and Writing Connection Explicit. Teaching a particular reading or writing skill does not guarantee that it will transfer to actual applications. Students need direct instruction in reading and writing and close supervision by the teacher to promote learning. They also need to understand when to use a skill or strategy. Lessons in reading and writing should therefore complement each other. In other words, when appropriate, what students learn in reading should be transferred for use in writing, and vice versa. Reading and writing instruction can be simultaneous, showing students the specific purpose of and the relationships between the two subjects. Students learn much about the nature and structure of writing through instruction in story grammar (see Chapter 6), process writing, expository writing patterns (see Chapter 9), and other reading instruction that focuses on text processing. Learning these aspects of reading enables students to better use them in writing and, thus, develop more mature writing styles. Younger students often pattern their writing after books they have read or listened to. Schell (1993) points out a classic example, *Brown Bear* by Bill Martin, where children model the story language in their writing (Brown dog, brown dog, what do you see? I see a fat cat looking at me). Literary aspects (see Chapter 9), such as characterization, irony, foreshadowing, dialogue, and sarcasm that teachers focus on in their reading programs also are modeled for students in their writing.

Emphasize Product and Process Knowledge in Instruction. Shanahan urges teachers to be aware of the differences between product knowledge and process knowledge. Product knowledge is substantive (vocabulary and word knowledge), while process knowledge is related to reasoning ability. The latter is concerned with strategies and procedures of solving problems and carrying out complex activities. Readers and writers both must monitor themselves to make sure that text makes sense and must use strategies to aid comprehension.

Reading and writing instruction that focuses on vocabulary knowledge and relates text to students' background knowledge can expand product knowledge. Most teachers do a good job of teaching in this area. The process aspect of reading and writing, however, requires a focus on the *how and why.* In process instruction, students discuss how they preview text, how they predict outcomes and events, how they come up with ideas about text they have read or stories they have written, how and why they choose to revise their thinking about text, and why they edited or would edit text. As noted earlier, reading and writing share many processes. Awareness of these processes benefits both reading and writing acquisition and development.

Emphasize Communication.   Reading and writing are communication processes; readers and writers are concerned with meaning. This text emphasizes that language is communication of meaning and that reading must be recognized as a language process. Highlighting the communication function of language capitalizes upon the essentials of language growth—(1) *people to talk to, read about, and write to and* (2) *things to read and write about*—that are meaningful to students.

Teach Reading and Writing in Meaningful Context.   The functional features of language (see Figure 3.1) are valuable for teaching reading and writing in meaningful context. Teachers can explore and develop these features by integrating reading and writing.

Teachers can have students write explanations of text, rewrite text, prepare lists, write directions, write and evaluate advertising aimed at encouraging consumer use, write and edit a class newspaper, write books and stories for other classes and students, keep minutes of group meetings, plan schedules, and so forth. The central point for teachers to consider is that students have opportunities to integrate reading and writing in a variety of literacy experiences.

CONSIDERATIONS FOR A LANGUAGE-RICH CLASSROOM ENVIRONMENT

Many of the teachers we have visited do an excellent job of creating a language- and literacy-rich classroom environment. What varies, however, is how they integrate this environment into their literacy program. Much of the variation reflects teachers' different philosophies about the best way to teach literacy.

Some teachers think students learn best when reading and writing are naturally connected to their oral language. This perspective or orientation is referred to as **whole language.** Whole language is not a method or program of reading instruction, it is an orientation toward development of literacy. Whole-language advocates believe that language acquisition (including reading and writing) is an essential part of an individual functioning within the environment. Whole language assumes that (1) the function of language is making meaning; (2) writing is a language activity, so what is true for oral language is also true for written language; (3) cue systems of language (structural features) are present and interact in all instances of language; (4) language use occurs in real-life situations; and (5) real-life situations are crucial to the meaning aspect of language.

A teacher who has a true whole-language orientation would not use materials or activities (such as published reading materials) intended for teaching specific literacy skills and abilities (such as phonemic awareness, vocabulary, and story grammar). Early concepts of whole language viewed subskill-practice activities as work substitutes that did not accurately reflect the acquisition and use of language (Goodman & Goodman, 1983). Today, a broader view of whole language would include the basic components (big books, shared reading, guided reading, and writing activities) used to practice needed skills independently in a meaningful context.

In talking with many teachers who believe they have a whole-language orientation toward literacy development, we have found that the term means many things to different teachers. Vacca and Rasinski (1992) noted similar variations in teachers' working definitions of whole language:

> In practice, teachers will vary in their working definitions [whole language], usually placing emphasis on certain dimensions of their concepts of whole language. If, for example, you were to ask a room full of teachers to associate one or two words that come to mind quickly when thinking about whole language in their classrooms, their responses undoubtedly would vary. Some might use words that associate whole language with child-responsive environments for learning; others, with literature-based instruction; still others, with curriculum integration. (p. 6)

Even though how teachers perceive whole language varies, their classroom environments exhibit many similar features. A whole language–oriented teacher's classroom would be rich in print. The teacher would make little, if any, use of materials developed specifically to teach reading. The teacher would instead use literature, big books, shared reading, creative writing, and print (such as real recipes for making cake, butter, and ice cream) (Edelsky, Altwerger, & Flores, 1991). In addition, in such classrooms the teacher would read aloud, vary organizational schemes, and interact with the students. The pervasive characteristic of such a classroom is that it develops literacy from a real-life perspective. Students engage in communication of meaning for reading and writing and apply their skills in meaningful context.

As we noted earlier, whole language means various things to different teachers. We have talked with teachers who say they do some whole-language activities, but focus more on text-processing skills. We have spoken with other teachers who use a literature-based reading program and believe that they are teaching reading from a whole-language perspective, even though they follow the recommendations in the teacher's guide for teaching reading.

We believe that there is not one best way to teach reading. Instead of devel-

Instrumental Language—The teacher can:

1. Be accessible and responsive to children's requests, but teach independence by having children state their requests effectively.

2. Encourage the use of instrumental language with other children, helping them to expand their own language through providing help and direction to peers.

3. Analyze advertising, propaganda, etc., to help children become aware of how language can be used by people to get what they want.

Regulatory Language—The teacher can:

1. Create situations that let children be "in charge" of small and large groups.

2. Find instances in which regulatory language is used inappropriately to teach appropriate regulatory language or the alternative, instrumental language.

3. Attempt to use less regulatory language as a teacher.

Interactional Language—The teacher can:

1. Create situations that require children to share work areas or materials and talk about how they are to do it.

2. Find ways of having small group (especially pairs or trios) discussions in a variety of subject areas. Through these discussions, students not only learn the subject matter more thoroughly, they practice communication.

3. Let students work together to plan field trips, social events, and classroom and school projects.

4. Whenever possible, mix children of different ages, sexes, races in work groups or discussion groups.

5. Have informal social times and, as a teacher, engage in some talk that is not "all business."

Personal Language—The teacher can:

1. Use personal language to give permission to children to share personal thoughts and opinions.

2. Be willing to listen and talk personally during transition times; for example, when children are coming in in the morning. Converse with children while on cafeteria or playground duty.

3. Provide some comfortable, attractive areas in the classroom where students can talk quietly.

4. Encourage parents and family members to visit and participate in classrooms.

5. Read stories or books that prompt a very personal response from students.

FIGURE 3.1

Instructional strategies to promote language functions
(From G. S. Pinnell, "Ways to Look at the Functions of Children's Language." In A. Jaggar and M. T. Smith-Burke [Eds.], *Observing the Language Learner* [Newark, DE: International Reading Association, 1985], pp. 68–69. Reprinted with permission of Gay Su Pinnell and the International Reading Association.)

Imaginative Language—The teacher can:

1. Create situations that naturally elicit spontaneous dramatic play; for example, house corner, dress up, blocks for younger children, and drama and roleplaying for older children.

2. Read stories and books which feed the imagination and which are a stimulus for art, drama, and discussion.

3. Provide time for children to talk in groups and/or with partners before they begin their writing or imaginative topics.

4. Encourage "play" with language—the sounds of words and the images they convey.

Heuristic Language—The teacher can:

1. Structure classroom experiences so that interest and curiosity are aroused.

2. Create real problems for children to solve.

3. Put children in pairs or work groups for problem-solving activities.

4. Use heuristic language to stimulate such language in children. Saying "I wonder why" often promotes children to do the same. (This should, however, not be contrived; it should be an honest problem.)

5. Try projects which require study on the part of the entire class, including the teacher. Find some questions that no one knows the answer to.

Informative Language—The teacher can:

1. Plan activities which require children to observe carefully and objectively and then to summarize and draw conclusions from their observations (field trips are a good opportunity).

2. Require children to keep records of events over periods of time and then to look back at their records and draw conclusions; for example, keeping records on classroom pets.

3. Use questioning techniques to elicit more complex forms of information giving.

4. Instead of having tedious classroom reports, have children give their reports to small groups and encourage feedback and discussion of those reports.

FIGURE 3.1
Continued

oping an orientation that is rigid, teachers need first to look at each student and ask themselves, "What does this child bring to the reading and writing situation?" "How can I capitalize upon the student's capabilities to maximize his or her reading and writing growth and development?" The whole-language concept has helped spur a re-evaluation of how reading is taught: We now know that quality literacy instruction teaches skills for reading and writing and applies them in meaningful context.

Providing students opportunities to interact with print in a language-rich environment is essential, regardless of the teacher's beliefs about how best to teach reading. Several important considerations for such a language-rich environment are presented next, along with recommendations for their implementation in literacy instruction.

Features of a Language-Rich Environment

When considering how to create a language-rich environment in the classroom, a teacher should ensure two important qualities. One is creating a classroom environment to encourage and support literacy development. The second is incorporating language-rich environmental features and activities into reading and writing instruction.

Sulzby and Barnhart (1992) describe what a literacy-rich environment generally would look like:

> Materials are at children's reach and there is sufficient time during the day for children to interact with those materials. Reading and writing tend to become less visible as separate activities and become more deeply embedded in other aspects of classroom life. (p. 125)

Language-rich classroom environments have features that promote and encourage students to interact with language; that is, they have things to talk about, read about, and write about.

Classroom Centers

Centers to promote literacy development can be set up in the classroom. Such centers can focus on reading, writing, and oral language. A writing center could provide children with access to such things as a typewriter, a computer, pencils, pens, markers, lined and unlined paper, notepads, staplers, scissors, and other materials that encourage students to write and share their writing with others. To stimulate students' imagination and motivation to write, many teachers have also included in their writing centers old magazines, pictures, stamp pads, and other objects they have collected.

A reading center is more that just a library with a collection of books. It is an area in the classroom that invites children to read. A large collection of reading materials would include books on a variety of topics and reading levels—including big books, read along books, audio-taped books, rebus books, and picture books—along with catalogs, magazines, stories written by children in the class, newspapers, and travel brochures. A variety of reading materials for all grade levels is recommended (our undergraduate students still get excited when reading children's books, as do many fifth- and sixth-grade students). Furniture for the reading center can range from comfortable chairs to old bathtubs, but it should be comfortable and inviting for students.

Centers to promote oral language (speaking and listening) are not as well defined as writing and reading centers; however, any classroom arrangement that brings students together to talk and listen to one another can promote oral-language development. Many of the suggestions presented in Figure 3.1 can be the focus of a permanent or temporary center in the classroom. For example, a drama center stocked with old clothes, hats, shoes, puppets, and other materials can be used to stimulate role playing and dramatic play resulting in spontaneous interaction.

A garden or plant center where students gather to watch and care for the plants will create interest and stimulate their curiousity. Projects such as this can help students begin to better understand heuristic language as the teacher encourages them to interact with each other by asking questions that begin with "I wonder why."

How teachers use their activity centers to promote literacy depends on what function the centers serve and how much direct instruction the teachers do. The instructional strategies to promote language functions (Figure 3.1) can serve as guidelines to help determine the function and purpose of the centers and plan appropriate learning activities.

In addition to using centers to promote reading and writing development, teachers can display examples of students' writing; encourage them to write stories to take home; label objects in the classroom (this is the door, here is our light switch); write dictated lists and schedules; place notepads, paper, and writing tools in activity centers; establish pen pals for the students; set up a classroom post office; write class newspapers; and encourage diary and journal writing.

Any classroom arrangement that brings students together to talk and listen to one another can promote language development.

Reading Activities and Instructional Opportunities in a Language-Rich Environment

Incorporating a classroom's language-rich features into reading and writing instruction capitalizes on the benefits of such an environment. Suggestions for integrating and promoting language development in literacy instruction appear throughout this book; expanded discussions are found in chapters dealing with emergent literacy, comprehension, meaning vocabulary, and instructional materials and programs.

Reading aloud to students of all ages has several benefits and has been frequently cited (Adams, 1990; Teal, 1984) as a major factor contributing to reading and writing development. First, it can help students understand that the purpose of reading is to communicate meaning. Students often cry, laugh, or express other emotions when listening to stories read to them. Such reactions indicate that they comprehend what they hear.

Second, reading aloud to students can foster a desire to read and can help students associate value with reading. Most students look forward to the teacher's reading aloud to them daily. Later, the children may read many of the books and magazines from which the teacher reads.

Third, reading aloud to students can enable the teacher to take advantage of "teaching moments." Teaching moments are situations that arise during a school day when the teacher can reinforce, reintroduce, or illustrate something taught previously. For example, if a lesson about different meanings of words preceded reading aloud to children, and what is being read aloud has some multiple-meaning words, the teacher can point this out and illustrate it with examples from the selection being read.

Students in the lower grades often will benefit from hearing the same books read aloud to them several times. If these books are then made available for students to read independently, often these become the books they enjoy reading the most. In addition to reading books, students enjoy hearing poetry, limericks, and song lyrics. Students at all grade levels enjoy being read to, and teachers at all grade levels should be encouraged to make reading aloud part of their daily instruction.

Reading aloud to students gives them the opportunity to see the relationships between reading, writing, speaking, and listening. It is one way to enable them to connect, through the use of language, old learning with new learning. Encouraging students to discuss and ask questions about what is read aloud to them engages them in the reading and language relationship. Questions broaden their experiences and reinforce the concept that reading is a communication process. Therefore, questions that encourage children to express their feelings about their favorite parts of a story, the author's language, and the characters—and questions about possible upcoming events in the story—are more beneficial than questions about literal information. Reading written materials aloud to students helps them acquire and develop language skills and creates an enjoyable experience for both teacher and students.

Shared reading is similar to reading aloud except the students see the text as the teacher reads aloud to them. Students are invited to read along and the fo-

FLASHBACK

Reading teachers have long recognized reading aloud to children as a means to promote students' interest in reading. In years past, elementary school teachers, predominantly in the early grades, recognized that their students benefited greatly from listening to good literature.

Some of the direct benefits of reading aloud to students that these teachers realized were gaining an appreciation of life's possibilities, helping to satisfy basic needs vicariously, nurturing young minds, motivating wide interests, and providing an escape into the worlds of fantasy and imagination.

UPDATE

Today, teachers view the practice of reading aloud to children with even more importance both in the early and the upper grades. Reading aloud is viewed not just as a worthwhile activity that is added on to the curriculum, but rather as an integral component in the literacy program. By reading aloud to students, the teacher is helping them develop important concepts about literacy, concepts such as print communicates meaning and stories follow a structure.

cus is still on enjoyment of the story. Big books, which are large books with enlarged print and pictures that students in group settings can easily see, are frequently used in the early grades for shared reading. The language of most big books is repetitive and predictable, which helps the students to read along easily. Big books are discussed further in Chapter 7.

Although shared reading is typically associated with kindergarten and first grade, it can be used successfully at all levels. One benefit of shared reading is that it is a way to immerse students in language-rich activities regardless of their grade level or reading capabilities. An additional benefit is that shared reading can allow students to apply their reading skills in a meaningful reading situation. For example, the teacher can point out beginning letters and letter combinations and encourage students to respond to the sounds represented, direct students' attention to common phonograms *(tion, at, et)* found in words within the context of the story, ask students to predict what the next word might be within the syntax of the story, and ask students to predict what events might happen next in the story.

Paired reading is a modification of shared reading. In this version, one student reads aloud as another follows along. Students can take turns reading and following along as they read text. Paired reading is often used with a less-capable reader, who follows along as a more-capable reader reads the story aloud. This technique enables the students to support each other in their reading of text and provides valuable practice time for both students. The less-capable reader should also be given opportunities to read as the more-capable reader follows along. Paired reading is an enjoyable activity for older students, who can help younger students with their reading. For example, a fifth grader might do paired reading with a second grader.

Independent reading is the cornerstone of successful reading instruction, since students need opportunities to practice and apply their reading skills in meaningful text. Independent reading is similar to individualized reading instruction, presented in Chapter 12. In independent reading, the teacher acts as facilitator and role model—providing students with a wide range of readily available reading material, encouraging them to read, and initiating informal discussion with them about their reading. Time should be set aside daily for students at all grade levels to read independently. Teachers should also read during this time to provide students with a model that demonstrates the value and enjoyment of reading. The practice and application of their reading capabilities make students better readers, expand their meaning vocabularies, enhance their reasoning capabilities, and associate value with reading.

Writing Activities and Instructional Opportunities in a Language-Rich Environment

A language-rich classroom environment gives students the opportunity to participate in a variety of writing activities. Examples of such activities include displays throughout the classroom of writing by both teacher and students, notecards and notepads placed in activity areas (e.g., library, block center, drama center, science center, and other center areas), story starters (beginnings that students devise based on their experiences and that the teacher uses to illustrate how stories are written), and discussions with students about what their attempts at writing (scribbles, invented spellings, letter strings, text for artwork, first drafts, and final drafts) mean to them.

Establishing a classroom to promote literacy development will encourage students to engage in writing activities throughout the day. Implementing Atwell's (1987) beliefs about writing could serve teachers well in creating a language-rich environment for encouraging children to write:

- Writers need regular chunks of time.
- Writers need their own topics.
- Writers need response.
- Writers learn mechanics in context.
- Children need to know adults who write.
- Writers need to read.
- Writing teachers need to take responsibility for the knowledge and teaching. (pp. 17–18)

Teachers can integrate reading and writing at developmental stages by using writing activities appropriate to students' level of reading and oral-language development. Teachers can use multiple text to read, write about, synthesize, evaluate, or analyze. Vocabulary can be reinforced through activities that encourage students to use the words in their writing. Such writing activities would focus on real-life experiences to ensure that the language structure and text reflect the students' background knowledge. In addition, writing activities can replace or supplement many of the independent practice and application activities recommended in reading instructional materials.

Kenneth and Yetta Goodman (1983) listed several reading and writing activities that focus on the practical functions of both. Activities such as making lists (birthdays, attendance, library books) can help students understand organizing, categorizing, and alphabetizing. Most students are aware of list making because they see their parents and teachers doing it. Similar to making lists is writing labels for items in the room, writing instructions for the care of plants and animals, and writing out job responsibilities. The intent of these activities is similar to the use of informative language presented in Figure 3.1.

Although students enjoy writing lists, such activities do not focus on the communicative features of printed language to the extent that diary and journal writing do. Diary writing is personal writing that students can easily read because it is based on their own experiences and concepts. Students can record classroom and personal events in their diaries. A classroom diary can be kept for the whole class, where all members participate by dictating to the teacher experiences with birthday parties, field trips, special occasions, and so forth.

Journal writing encourages students to share their feelings, noting important events in their lives. Such writing is intended for the teacher to read, and therefore students must communicate with a reader. In *response journals* (see Chapter 11), the teacher reads and responds to the students' journals. The teacher's written response provides students with a model of writing and reinforces the connection between reading and writing.

Note and letter writing connects a writer with one or more readers. Classroom pen pals, teachers, parents, brothers, sisters, and other familiar individuals can be the audience to whom students write notes and letters. Since the writer and reader share many common experiences, the writer need not communicate as completely for the reader to construct meaning.

Writing notes and letters to less-familiar people offers an opportunity to communicate with new audiences. Students can write notes and letters to their favorite authors, to national and community leaders, or to pen pals. The responses that their letters generate provide students with further opportunities to understand the communicative features of literacy.

One of the important features of promoting numerous and varied opportunities for classroom writing is that the teacher demonstrates models of the writing process. Routman (1991) identified several ways that teachers can model writing. Many of these are presented and further discussed throughout this book; however, those listed here illustrate how teachers can model the writing process for their students. A key feature of these modeling activities is that the teacher writes in front of the students and talks about the process involved in writing the message, story, outline, or whatever he or she is writing.

- Many teachers in schools that we visit write their daily schedule and classroom events on the chalkboard to help students know what will be occurring during the day. Rather than writing this information before students arrive, however, teachers can capitalize upon an opportunity to model writing by doing so in front of the students and talking with the students about the process. For example, "Today is Bryan's birthday. He is seven years old today." could announce the birthday of a classmate to the students. The teacher could discuss with the class why certain words are capitalized, why certain punctuation is used, and so forth. It is best to write the information in paragraph form rather than just listing events. The teacher can ask questions that encourage students to figure out the structure of the writing as well as its convention.

- Brainstorming writing topics as a class enables the teacher to focus on students' interest and to model features of the writing process. Students can generate topics—which the teacher lists—and the teacher can demonstrate how to elaborate upon the topics and write a first draft. Students participate in both topic elaboration and writing and revising the first draft. The teacher can use this first draft again to model for the students how to revise and polish their writing.

- Whole-class and small-group rewriting and revising can help further model the writing process. Teachers can select examples of writing that students have generated together or can use examples of their own writing for modeling. The teacher can direct students to focus on word choice, descriptions, topic choice and other features by questions such as, "Is there another word that would work better here? I like that this describes. . . . How could you expand this section so the reader knows exactly what you mean?"

Modeling for the students what is involved in the writing process, ranging from capitalization to communication of ideas, helps them better understand how writing functions. Many of the language functions presented in Figure 3.1 can form the basis for writing activities and help direct teachers' focus on what to model for the students.

SUMMARY /

Reading is a language process related to all language functions found in the elementary school curriculum. Students' language awareness depends on literacy experiences, which help them to understand language features such as syntax and semantics, develop and expand their vocabularies, and refine and extend their knowledge of text. Literacy builds a bridge of understanding between oral language and reading and writing.

Oral-language capabilities contribute to students' literacy development. In the beginning stages of learning to read and write, their comprehension of print is linked closely to their spoken language. This important linkage should be reflected in instruction, which should be based on oral-language development. Culturally and linguistically diverse learners also need instruction that broadens and enriches both their language and informational background to encourage their success in literacy.

It is generally accepted that reading and writing are interrelated. Both reading and writing compose meaning, which involves interaction between an individual's experiential and conceptual backgrounds and the text. Although both are similar in many respects, each must be taught, and students need many varied opportunities to engage in reading and writing activities.

Literacy instruction must include a sense of involvement with language. A language-rich classroom environment is essential to promoting literacy growth. Such an environment does not treat reading and writing as separate subjects, but rather emphasizes them in all aspects of classroom life. A language-rich environment in the classroom should have two important components. First, it should encourage and support literacy development. Second, it should incorporate language-rich features and activities into reading and writing instruction.

YOUR POINT OF VIEW /

Discussion Questions

1. How does students' development in speaking, listening, and writing affect their reading development?
2. Why is it important for teachers to plan language activities that are meaningful to students and related to their existing language capabilities?
3. Why should teachers integrate reading and writing instruction in the literacy program?
4. Why is it important for teachers to understand the language and literacy needs of culturally and linguistically diverse learners?

Take a Stand For or Against

1. The processes of learning to speak and learning to read are basically the same.
2. Reading and writing are so similar in their development that reading can be taught by teaching writing only.
3. Formal language instruction is not necessary in today's school.
4. A language-rich classroom environment allows the teacher simply to guide students' literacy acquisition and little or no instruction is necessary.

BIBLIOGRAPHY /

Adams, M. J. (1990). *Beginning to read: Thinking and learning about print.* Cambridge, MA: M.I.T. Press.

Atwell, N. (1987). *In the middle: Writing, reading, and learning with adolescents.* Portsmouth, NH: Heinemann.

Beck, I. L. (1985). Five problems with children's comprehension in the primary grades. In J. Osborn, P. T. Wilson, & R. C. Anderson (Eds.), *Reading education: Foundations for a literate America* (pp. 239–253). Lexington, MA: Lexington Books.

Chall, J. S. (1983). *Stages of reading development.* New York: McGraw-Hill Book Co.

Dickinson, D., Wolf, M., & Stotsky, S. (1993). Words move: The interwoven development of oral and written language. In J. Berko Gleason (Ed.), *The development of language* (3rd ed.) (pp. 369–420). New York: Merrill/Macmillan Publishing Co.

Edelsky, C., Altwerger, B., & Flores, B. (1991). *Whole language: What's the difference.* Portsmouth, NH: Heinemann Educational Books.

Frith, U. (1985). Beneath the surface of developmental dyslexia. In K. E. Patterson, K. C. Marshall, & M. Coltheart (Eds.), *Surface dyslexia: Neuropsychological and cognitive studies of phonological reading.* Hillsdale, NJ: Lawrence Erlbaum Associates.

Goldfield, B. A., & Snow, C. E. (1993). Individual differences in language acquisition. In J. Berko Gleason (Ed.), *The development of language* (3rd ed.) (pp. 299–324). New York: Merrill/Macmillan Publishing Co.

Goodman, K. S., & Goodman, Y. (1983). Reading and writing relationships: Pragmatic functions. *Language Arts, 60,* 590–599.

Lewin, L. (1992). Integrating reading and writing strategies using an alternating teacher-led/student-selected instructional pattern. *The Reading Teacher, 45,* 586–591.

Lundsteen, S. W. (1989). *Language arts: A problem solving approach.* New York: Harper & Row.

McCarthy, S. J., & Raphael, T. E. (1992). Alternative research perspectives. In J. W. Irwin & M. A. Doyle (Eds.), *Reading/Writing connections: Learning from research* (pp. 2-30). Newark, DE: International Reading Association.

Perfetti, C. A. (1991). On the value of simple ideas in reading. In S. A. Brady & D. P. Shankweiler (Eds.), *Phonological processes in literacy* (pp. 211–218). Hillsdale, NJ: Lawrence Erlbaum Associates.

Raphael, T. E., & Englert, C. S. (1989). Integrating reading and writing instruction. In P. Winograd, K. K. Wixson, & M. Y. Lipson (Eds.), *Improving basal reader instruction* (pp. 231–255). New York, NY: Teachers College Press.

Routman, R. (1991). *Invitations: Changing as teachers and learners K-12.* Portsmouth, NH: Heinemann.

Samuels, S. J. (1988). Decoding and automaticity: Helping poor readers become automatic at word recognition. *The Reading Teacher, 41,* 636–647.

Schell, L. (1993). Personal communication.

Shanahan, T. (1988). The reading-writing relationship: Seven instructional principles. *The Reading Teacher, 45,* 636–647.

Spivey, N. N., & King, J. R. (1989). Readers as writers composing from sources. *Reading Research Quarterly, 24,* 7–26.

Stahl, S. A. (1992). Saying the "p" word: Nine guidelines for exemplary phonics instruction. *The Reading Teacher, 45,* 618–625.

Sticht, L. G., & James, J. H. (1984). Listening and reading. In P. D. Pearson (Ed.), *Handbook of reading research* (pp. 293–318). New York: Longman.

Sulzby, E., & Barnhart, J. (1992). The development of academic competence: All our children emerge as writers and readers. In J. W. Irwin & M. A. Doyle (Eds.), *Reading/writing connections: Learning from research* (pp. 120–144). Newark, DE: International Reading Association.

Teal, W. H. (1984). Reading to young children: Its significance for literacy development. In H. Goelman, A. Oberg, & F. Smith (Eds.), *Awakening to literacy* (pp. 110–121). Portsmouth, NH: Heinemann.

Tierney, R. J. (1992). Ongoing research and new directions. In J. W. Irwin & M. A. Doyle (Eds.), *Reading/writing connections: Learning from research* (pp 246–259). Newark, DE: International Reading Association.

Tierney, R., & Pearson, P. D. (1983). Toward a composing model of reading. *Language Arts, 60,* 568–580.

Vacca, R. T., & Rasinski, T. V. (1992). *Case studies in whole language.* New York: Harcourt Brace Jovanovich.

Weber, R. (1991). Linguistic diversity and reading in American society. In R. Barr, M. L. Kamil, P. B. Mosenthal, and P. D. Pearson (Eds.), *Handbook of reading research* (Vol. II) (pp. 97-119). New York: Longman.

Wells, G. (1981). Writing and the teaching of reading. *Language Arts, 60,* 600–606.

II

Teaching Students to Become Strategic Readers

OVERVIEW

Just as a fine orchestra studies and practices interrelated parts of a performance with the ultimate goal of putting the parts together in splendid fashion, the teaching of literacy involves a host of interrelated understandings that must be studied and practiced and ultimately combined in an efficient and effective "performance." An effective literacy program stresses the instruction and application of the essential strategies, skills, and abilities that produce strategic readers and writers. The ability to interact successfully with text demands the simultaneous use of several tools in our language. Chapters in this part will focus on the role of word pronunciation and vocabulary growth and the development of strategies to comprehend written ideas.

INTEGRATING PRINCIPLES OF TEACHING READING

The following principles, presented in Chapter 1, will be reinforced in this part:

- Early in the learning process, the student must acquire ways of recognizing words independently.

- Any given technique is likely to work better with some students than with others.

- Instruction should lead children to understand that reading is a meaningful, active, and strategic process.

- Teachers need to foster students' abilities to reason and critically evaluate written ideas.

- Literacy learning is a developmental process.

4

Word Identification

For the Reader

The core of an effective literacy program is the instruction and application of skills and strategies that produce good readers. This assertion applies equally at all grade levels, with specific instruction dependent upon student learning needs. Regardless of the instructional materials utilized, research suggests that good literacy programs include emphasis on word identification, comprehension, writing, and reading study skills and strategies. Because learning to read is a long-term, developmental process, building a solid foundation in the essential reading abilities should be a goal of every education program. This chapter focuses on developing the various word-identification skills and strategies that skilled readers need.

Key Ideas

- Students need a variety of word-identification skills and strategies to arrive at the meaning of what they read.
- Basic sight vocabulary, phonics, structural analysis, and contextual analysis are word-identification skills and strategies that children should learn so that they can comprehend written language.
- Students must have opportunities to apply word-identification skills and strategies in meaningful authentic reading situations.
- Students need to develop flexibility in identifying words so that they can use all available cue systems to arrive at meaning.
- Each student needs to develop and continually expand a basic sight vocabulary.
- The major purpose of teaching word-identification skills and strategies is to provide tools for deriving meaning from reading.
- Word-identification skills and strategies are best taught through direct/explicit instruction.

Key Terms

word identification   the process of arriving at the pronunciation of a word, given the printed letter representations (also known as decoding).

sight vocabulary   words that a reader recognizes and comprehends instantly.

whole-word approach   a word-identification strategy that focuses on learning words as wholes rather than by any form of analysis.

phonics   a word-identification strategy that uses letter-sound relationships to arrive at the pronunciations of unknown words.

structural analysis   a word-identification strategy that focuses on visual or structural patterns and meanings that change as a result of adding inflectional endings, prefixes, and suffixes and combining root words.

contextual analysis   a word-identification strategy that helps students figure out the meanings of words by how they are used in the context of sentences or passages.

analytic phonics   a phonic approach using letter-sound relationships by referring to words already known to identify a new phonic element.

syllabication   the division of a word into its basic units of pronunciation.

syntactic clues   a contextual-analysis strategy using the knowledge of word order in our language to identify an unknown word.

semantic clues   a contextual-analysis strategy using the meanings of known words in a sentence or passage to identify an unknown word.

WORD-IDENTIFICATION STRATEGIES

Learning to read involves the interrelationship of two broad areas: (1) word identification and (2) comprehension. **Word identification** is the process of decoding written symbols. Comprehension involves understanding and interacting with the ideas expressed in text (or decoded text). Obviously, the ability to identify words is necessary for comprehension. To become proficient in identifying words, readers must employ a variety of strategies. Beginning readers must continually expand their sight vocabularies. A **sight vocabulary** is made up of words that are recognized instantly. Many of these words are not spelled the way they sound (e.g., *to, know,* and *they*); these irregular words are taught using the **whole-word approach. Phonics** instruction consists of teaching letter-sound relationships to provide an approximate pronunciation, whereby the sound elicits a meaningful association of the word meaning in the text. Instruction in **structural analysis** looks at visual patterns and meanings that change as a result of adding inflectional endings (e.g., *-s, -ed, -ing,* and *-ly*), prefixes (e.g., *ex-* and *pre-*), and suffixes (e.g., *-ment* and *-ous*) and combining root words to form compounds (e.g., *sidewalk* and *playground*). Instruction in **contextual analysis** helps students figure out meanings of words by how they are used in the context of text.

Knowing words on sight, applying letter-sound relationships, recognizing word parts, and using context clues are important parts of decoding; that is, arriving at the pronunciation of a word, given the printed letter representations (Anderson, Heibert, Scott, & Wilkinson, 1985). Equally important is an understanding of how to use all available word-identification cues simultaneously to comprehend written information. A number of studies support the idea that proficiency in using these cues for word identification is developmental (Fowler, 1992; Juel, 1991). Students who are learning to read rely predominantly on letter-sound relationships to identify words. More skilled and mature readers use larger units (e.g., word parts and whole words) and attend primarily to meaning because their word-identification strategies are automatic (Samuels, 1988).

Children develop several language-cue systems simply through learning to communicate with oral language. The communicative function of spoken and written language is one cue system related to success in learning to read and write (Downing, 1979). Reading and writing also involve the student's awareness that words are strung together in meaningful units governed by structure and syntax. These features of language apply both to spoken and written text. The learner can transfer this knowledge of spoken language to master the reading process.

When teaching word-identification skills, remember the following:

- Word-identification instruction is not reading; it is providing tools to help understand the meaning of written language. Instruction must provide opportunities for students to apply their word-identification skills in meaningful reading situations.

- Students must develop flexibility in identifying words so that they can use all available cue systems to determine meaning. They need to develop independent and fluent mastery in the areas of whole-word recognition, phonics, structural analysis, and contextual analysis (Stahl, 1992) to focus on the *meaning* of

Students must develop flexibility in identifying words so that they can use all available cue systems to determine meaning.

what they read rather than just word pronunciation. The ability to decode a word with minimal effort is called automaticity of word identification.

Integration in Authentic Reading Situations

With automatic decoding of printed symbols a goal of reading instruction and a prerequisite for students to be able to devote a large percentage of their attention to processing meaning, an important consideration is how word-identification or decoding skills (i.e., whole-word recognition, phonics, structural analysis, and context) are taught and practiced in our schools. Chapters 2 and 6 discuss the direct/explicit instruction approach and its effectiveness in teaching reading skills. The actual teaching and guided practice of a particular skill precedes independent practice of it. Meaningful practice should be provided to ensure transfer of a new skill to a variety of situations. This stage—independent practice—signals a change in instructional practice. With our new understandings of the reading process, particularly its interactive nature, the emphasis for independent practice has switched from a reliance on isolated worksheets to integrating independent practice in more authentic reading situations; that is, through a variety of experiences in quality literature. Workbooks and other types of practice materials (including games) are still used, but their use is supported through story content to ensure that students can apply the skill in recreational or independent reading.

Students must have opportunities to apply word-identification skills and strategies in meaningful, authentic reading situations.

FOUR MAJOR INSTRUCTIONAL TASKS

In mastering the reading process, four instructional tasks represent the major thrust of beginning reading instruction. These instructional tasks help students to:

1. Understand that reading is a language process.
2. Develop and expand sight vocabulary.
3. Learn to associate visual symbols with speech sounds.
4. Realize that reading is always a meaning-making process and that printed word symbols represent language.

Some instructional materials and activities overlook or give undue emphasis to one or two tasks. Students can learn much of what is taught through such an instructional approach, but in doing so they run the risk of developing attitudes and habits harmful to the concept of reading. Beginning reading instruction that overemphasizes the mechanics and ignores comprehension is not meaningful.

Too much emphasis on word-identification skills can be detrimental. Students may develop a set of behaviors that neglects one or more aspects of the reading process. This may result in habits that handicap the reader in later development. For instance, a student may develop a set to sound out every word she encounters in reading. This means she will be sounding out the same word the 10th, 20th or even the 50th time she sees it in reading. She has learned that reading is sounding out words, and this becomes her goal in all reading situations.

On the other hand, overemphasis on learning whole words rather than other word-identification techniques forces the student to make fine visual discriminations when minimal sounding techniques would have made the task much easier. Knowledge of whole words combined with context and minimal sounding clues are more efficient than using one technique alone.

The premise underlying this discussion is that major instructional tasks are inseparable parts of one total instructional process. Students should learn to use all of the cue systems in written language—whole-word recognition, phonics, structure, and context—in learning to read. Thus, the major task of reading instruction is to blend these instructional components properly.

What makes reading instruction complicated is that no blueprint spells out precisely where and how much instructional time and effort teachers should devote to each cue system. Second, no blueprint tells us which instructional techniques work the best with individual learners. Understanding individual differences among learners offers the answer to these questions.

SIGHT VOCABULARY

Students increase their sight vocabulary directly through instructional procedures, independent reading, and activities and indirectly through television, road signs, bulletin boards, carton labels, and the like. Obviously, the most important source of learning is meaningful reading situations, such as those provided by charts, teacher-written stories, predictable books, big books, and easy-to-read trade books. A skill of such significance to the total reading process should be taught effectively. Following are a number of justifications for learning words as wholes:

- A child who knows a number of words as whole words can better understand, see, and hear similarities between these known words and new words. Having a large sight vocabulary is invaluable in helping identify other words.
- When words are recognized instantly, analysis is minimal. The reader can focus on reading for meaning.
- Numerous high-frequency words (e.g., was, the, those, etc.) should be learned as units simply because students see them over and over in any reading situation and they contribute significantly to using syntax as a means of getting meaning from reading.

There is a difference between learning certain frequently used words and learning to rely extensively on one word-identification strategy in beginning reading, whether that strategy is whole words, phonic analysis, or context. The normal pattern of learning dictates that the student develop a sight vocabulary or learn some words as wholes through the whole-word approach.

The normal student's experience with reading results in a constantly growing stock of words recognized as wholes. The student establishes automatic stimulus-response patterns for dozens of frequently used words, such as *that, with, be, are, and, was, it, the, in, to, than, you, they, said, when,* and *can.* A number of these structure words and other frequently used words must be learned to the point where recognizing them is automatic (Samuels, 1979).

The most popular list of high-frequency sight words is the 220-service-word Dolch list. Developed by Edward Dolch (1948) more than 40 years ago, this list includes a high percentage of irregularly spelled words found in beginning reading materials. Palmer (1986) recently tested whether the Dolch list applies to today's reading materials. Her findings agree with previous studies, which concluded that the Dolch list remains relevant. The Dolch words constituted 60 percent of the vocabulary in four of five basal series passages analyzed. Other common words in a student's sight vocabulary include words of personal interest, words in content areas, and words in reading and language arts books from preschool.

The whole-word approach focuses on learning words as wholes rather than through any form of analysis. Irregular words (i.e., those not spelled the way they sound) are best taught through this approach in meaningful context. However, regular words (i.e., those spelled the way they sound) can also be learned through this approach. This is especially true when teaching new words as a way of building background knowledge before reading. As will be discussed later in the chapter, teaching new words as whole words in conjunction with teaching a story is a main avenue for word learning. The following is a step-by-step procedure detailing the teaching of a word through the whole-word approach:

- Present the word visually (e.g., on a posterboard or chalkboard) and pronounce the word.

- Pronounce the word for the student again, making sure the student is looking at the word at the time the teacher says the word.

- Use the word in written context familiar to the student. Ask the student to make up a sentence containing the word and write the sentence on the board. Ask the student to discuss the meaning of the sentence.

- Present the word again visually and ask the student to pronounce it.

- Provide an abundance of meaningful practice in authentic reading situations (e.g., experience stories, big books, and writing).

A major avenue for teaching whole words is the Directed Reading Activity (DRA) for a story. A main component in a DRA is building vocabulary. Most vocabulary words are taught through the whole-word approach. The practice component of the whole-word approach is built into this instructional method through the ensuing story to be read and the variety of practice activities associated with most reading programs. The activities systematically present, integrate, and repeat new vocabulary words in a variety of authentic reading situations. If the teacher is using trade books for instruction without an accompanying teacher's guide, the teacher must select the key vocabulary to be taught and design appropriate independent practice. Words selected for emphasis should be those that contribute to understanding the story to enable students to recognize, understand, and use the words.

Teachers can include the teaching of whole words in the literacy program in innumerable ways. A few of the ways include:

- In conjunction with literature (narrative and expository).
- Language-experience stories.
- Reading aloud using big books and predictable books.
- Written activities including using the typewriter and computer, writing diaries and journals, and writing creative stories and poems.
- Oral-language activities and games.
- Development of scrapbooks.
- Various games and puzzles.
- Reading of newspapers and magazines.
- Reading aloud to students.
- Independent reading.

Regardless of the means used to develop sight vocabulary, the application must be meaning-based, relating new vocabulary to prior knowledge and experience.

Names

One of the first printed words a child learns is his or her name. The practice of learning names in printed form provides the basis for teaching letter-sound relationships. Children also can begin to recognize names of common objects in the classroom that are labeled.

INSTRUCTIONAL ACTIVITIES

- **Reading Children's Names.** Tape each child's first name on the front of his or her desk. Use other words with it so that each name is within a meaningful context. Doing this will more likely result in processing print as it is related to comprehension.

Mary sits here.	Mike sits here.
Sarah sits here.	Sandy sits here.

Children learn the names of other children in meaningful context just as they learn the words in the sentence. Children also learn very quickly to recognize a number of names in printed form. Use chalkboard announcements involving students' names.

Hand out books
John and Helen

Water the plants
Jean and Billy

■ ***Labeling Objects.*** Print naming words in short phrases on separate oaktag cards to make naming labels and attach to objects in the room.

a door

a book

a plant

the chalkboard

the big table

Collect a number of pictures that depict objects or animals within the range of the children's experiential and conceptual backgrounds (photographs of the school and community are appropriate). Paste the pictures on cardboard and print the naming words in short phrases beneath them. Use these to generate language-experience stories.

a cat

a cow

a horse

a house

To add the kinesthetic mode to the words, duplicate a page of drawings and leave space for children to copy the names from models displayed on the chalktray. In the first experience, outline the printed words with dots. Have each child mark over the dots and "write" the words.

a bear

a house

a car

Later exercises may omit the dotted outlines. Have each child copy from the printed models on the chalktray, chalkboard, or bulletin board.

■ **Writing Short Stories.** As children begin to recognize many words, provide many opportunities for them to apply this skill in context. Write short, meaningful sentences that relate directly to the names of the children and objects in the classroom. Children are more likely to succeed because the concepts represented are meaningful to them. Combine the sentences to construct a story.

<u>Our Class</u>

John and Helen hand out books.
Jean and Billy water the plants.
Mary, Mike, and Sarah sit at the big table.
A plant, a book, and a door are in the room.

Develop similar application activities for objects and animal names. Read a short phrase and direct students to select from a list the words that make sense in the sentence. Write the words in the spaces and call on pupils to read each sentence. If several choices make sense, ask about the meaning of each word selected.

On his farm there is ___ ___.
In the woods lives ___ ___.
Sandy went to the farm in ___ ___.
At the farm she saw ___ ___.

a cat   a cow   a bear   a horse   a car

Language-experience stories enhance sight vocabulary in meaningful context (Heilman, 1992). Stimulate students to dictate group-experience stories by posing questions that encourage them to use words introduced in teacher-directed instruction. For example, ask "What do we do at school? What is in our classroom? What do we know about a cat, a cow, and a horse?" to stimulate students to compose stories that make meaningful application of sight-word instruction.

See the Appendix for more practice activities and games.

A picture dictionary is excellent for developing word meanings as well as a multitude of other skills, such as letter sounds and letter names.

INSTRUCTIONAL ACTIVITIES

■ **Making a Picture Dictionary.** Secure a number of small pictures from workbooks, magazines, and the like. Have one page devoted to each letter of the alphabet. Let the students paste pictures of animals whose names begin with each letter on the appropriate pages. Then print a picture-naming word beneath each picture. (Note the use of *a* or *some* with the words to focus attention on them.) A partial *M-m* page follows.

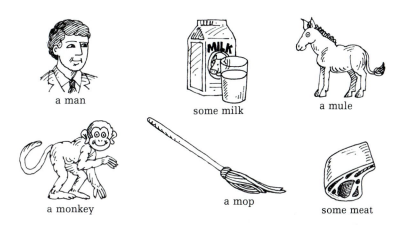

a man

some milk

a mule

a monkey

a mop

some meat

■ **Using a Picture Dictionary.** Use the picture dictionary in determining other words that make sense in the sentences and stories. For example, ask students to find two words in their picture dictionaries that have the long *a* sound. Use examples and illustrations to model for students how to use the dictionary to identify and select words for their writing activities.

Reporter Questions

Instruction on and practice with reporter questions (How? What? Where? When? Why?) help children learn some important terms used in reading instructions and in following directions. Each experience with these important words helps students learn them as sight words.

INSTRUCTIONAL ACTIVITY

■ **Using Reporter Questions.** Write the words *how, what, where, when,* and *why* on the chalkboard. Say the words (making sure each student is thinking about the word as it is pronounced), and point to each word as you say it. Use the chalkboard, an overhead projector, or duplicated materials to present materials similar to the following:

Direct students' attention to the written context for each of the materials. Encourage discussion and write their responses next to each question.

Circle A

How many dots?   There are four dots.
How did you learn this?   We counted them.
When did you count them?   Just now!
What color are the dots?   They are black.
Where is the circle?   Around the dots!
Why is the circle around   So we could ask how,
the dots?   what, when, where, and
                                  why questions.

Circle B

Where are the letters?
How many letters are there?
What are the letters?
What is around the letters?
Why is it around the letters?

Position Words

The importance of teaching the meanings of certain crucial terms used in reading helps avoid unnecessary instructional problems. Students must understand the position words *in, on, above, below, over, under,* and the like.

INSTRUCTIONAL ACTIVITY

■ *Using Position Words.* Use a format similar to the following circle-square-table. Prepare cards on oaktag and put them on the chalktray or tape them on the chalkboard so all can see. Provide each participating student with three or four word cards. Each card should have the same position word printed on both sides. As children hold up the requested card, check for accuracy.

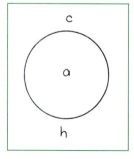 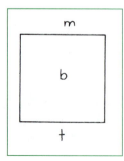 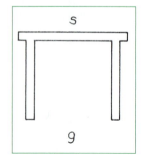

Read the following directions:

Hold up the word *in* (pause) What letter is in the circle?

Hold up the word *over.* . . What letter is over the square?

Hold up the word *on.* . . What letter is on the table?

Continue using all of the word cards issued to the children. Each can be used more than once if desired—for example—*in* the circle, *in* the square, *under* the circle, square, table.

Words Often Confused

Students need varied and interesting practice on confusing words commonly found in their reading materials. This practice should help them recognize the words at sight.

INSTRUCTIONAL ACTIVITIES

■ *Presenting Individual Words.* Use the chalkboard, an overhead projector, or duplicated materials consisting of words frequently confused in early reading. Present these words in pairs and direct students' attention to the differences in letter combinations. Following are several examples.

their	every	when	four	which
there	very	where	for	with

■ *Presenting Words in Sentences.* Present words in meaningful context, underlining the frequently used words. Paying heed to the underlined words, read the sentences in unison with the class or a group. Focus discussion on the meaning features of the words.

<u>Their</u> house is over <u>there</u>.
<u>Every</u>one said it was <u>very</u> cold.
<u>When</u> <u>were</u> they taken there?
These sell <u>four</u> <u>for</u> a dollar.
<u>Which</u> boy will go <u>with</u> you?

■ *Using Words in Meaningful Context.* Prepare a short text that contains blank spaces. Write the two words that will complete the sense of the context. Ask students to write the correct word in each blank space. You may have to read the sentences aloud for many of the students. Discuss both the meaning features and graphic features of their word choices.

(to, two)	**1.** The _____ boys were going _____ the store.
(for, four)	**2.** These boxes sell _____ _____ a dollar.
(think, thank)	**3.** I _____ you should _____ him for it.
(very, every)	**4.** _____ teacher was _____ busy.
(you, your)	**5.** Have _____ had _____ dinner?

Scrambled Sentences

Practice in assembling scrambled sentences helps students acquire a basic sight vocabulary and a knowledge of terms used in reading instruction (such as period and question mark). Understanding basic sentence structure also aids in comprehension.

INSTRUCTIONAL ACTIVITY

■ *Arranging Words into Sentences.*   On separate cards, print individual words from sentences used previously on the chalkboard. Present them in scrambled order, then ask students to arrange the words in proper order. Follow each sentence with a card bearing the proper punctuation. This is one of many ways to repeat frequently used words.

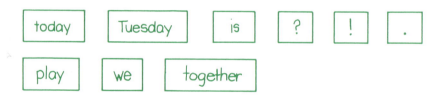

Classification

Classifying words is a good way to introduce and practice sight vocabulary. It is also a beginning step toward successful comprehension. Classifying interesting and concrete terms can motivate students to succeed.

INSTRUCTIONAL ACTIVITIES

■ *Classifying Words.*   Write classification words on the board and underline them. Point to each word and read it. Ask students to repeat each word after you pronounce it. On oaktag or cardboard, print each of the other words to be used in the exercise. Hold up one card at a time and call on a student to pronounce the word and to tell under which heading the word belongs.

animals	clothing	food	school
a dog	a hat	my milk	a book
a cat	the shoes	my cookies	a desk
a cow	a dress	my pie	the paper

As a variation, place a number of appropriate words in a box at the bottom of the page. Ask students to copy the words under the correct heading. They can work individually or in small groups. Focus discussion on why words were grouped together.

■ **Using Classifications in Context.** Develop further categories. Have students complete short sentences by selecting the words that make sense in context. See the following for an example.

animals	*animal sounds*	*animal homes*
a dog	it moos	the farm
a cow	it barks	the house
a cat	it oinks	the woods
a bear	it meows	

_____ _____ barks.

_____ _____ is the home of a cow.

A dog _____.

On _____ a cow moos.

A cat meows in _____ _____.

PHONICS

Purposes of Phonic Instruction

Phonic instruction consists of teaching letter-sound relationships so that the learner can identify new words in print. Since English is alphabetic in that written words represent a collection of speech sounds, phonic instruction is crucial in helping beginning readers understand how our language works (Adams, 1990; Juel, 1991). Beginning readers inevitably encounter many words they do not recognize. By applying knowledge of letter-sound relationships in combination with available context clues and understanding that printed language must make sense, students can better comprehend what they read. Most likely, a written word that puzzles a student is one he or she has spoken or heard many times, so applying letter-sound relationships determines the pronunciation or yields an approximate pronunciation.

A purpose of phonic instruction is to teach the beginning reader that printed letters and letter combinations represent speech sounds heard in words. The sounds heard in words are quite different from sounds heard in isolation. In the sentence "The cat ran after the mice," the written word cat blends three phonemes just as they are in the oral word. But readers should not produce three syllables: *kuh-ah-tuh* (cat). Phonic instruction should teach the learner to blend the sounds that the printed letters represent when encountering a new word (Eeds-Kneip, 1979; Stahl, 1992). Blending permits a child to determine whether or not the word is in his or her speaking or listening vocabulary and whether it makes sense in context.

Phonic instruction should teach the learner to use all available cue systems in combination with letter-sound relationships to identify words and comprehend written text, giving primary attention to word meanings and comprehension. Too much emphasis on using letter-sound relationships to identify isolated words will cause the learner to think these relationships constitute reading. Initial instruction should stress that reading is a meaning-making process.

Phonics instruction improves children's ability to identify words.

Tasks in Phonics

Phonics involves a series of tasks taken together. Phonics teaching materials include a number of techniques common to all approaches. They may differ in the sequence in which skills are introduced, the emphasis on learning rules, the number of steps taught, and the degree of phonic instruction included in beginning reading. The major phonics tasks include:

- Discriminating speech sounds in words.
- Using written letters to represent the speech sounds.
- Using the sound represented by a letter or letters in a known word to unlock the pronunciation of unknown words in which these particular letters occur.
- Identifying sounds of consonants in initial and final positions.
- Blending consonants.
- Identifying special consonant digraphs (such as *th, ch, sh,* and *wh*).
- Discerning short and long vowel sounds.
- Distinguishing double vowels, vowel digraphs, and diphthongs.
- Identifying vowels followed by *r*.
- Identifying the effect of a final *e*.
- Discerning the sounds of *y*.

All of the preceding tasks are not equally important in learning to read, and each should not receive the same amount of instructional time. They are simply the framework, since some include many specific elements.

The actual learning of phonics as it relates to reading usually begins early in the preschool years (see Chapter 7). The child learns the sound of a word like *mommy* and can easily differentiate it from similar-sounding words. He may have a pet kitty and a playmate Kathy. He can differentiate if asked "Where is Kathy?" even though the kitty is also present.

Phonic instruction begins when an adult talks with an infant, thus providing the child with a model. A child who associates sounds with objects and does not confuse words that are very similar—such as *mommy, money, monkey,* and *maybe*—is mastering auditory discrimination, which is important for phonic analysis in the reading process. The later tasks in learning phonics depend on mastery of this basic language function. Beginning reading instruction in the school should build on the child's previous language experiences. In reading, students must discriminate among written word symbols and learn that these symbols represent the speech sounds of words they speak and understand.

Phonic Instruction

While a variety of specific techniques can help students learn the relationships between letters and speech sounds, the main approach is the analytic (or implicit) approach. Regardless of the approach, however, teachers should remember that (1) an important goal of phonic instruction is the approximate, not exact, pronunciation of words, (2) letter-sound correspondences are best communicated through direct/explicit instruction, and (3) phonic instruction should include an abundance of practice in contextual reading situations.

The last two points highlight the importance of mastering automatic word-identification skills. Without direct instruction and meaningful practice to the point of overlearning and automaticity, students are less likely to understand and interact with the ideas in the text.

Analytic Phonics. **Analytic phonics** teaches letter-sound relationships by referring to words already known to identify a particular phonic element. Walker (1992) describes this analytic approach as "decoding by analogy." Decoding by analogy is another way of describing the inductive technique in teaching. Inductive instruction occurs when a teacher begins by giving examples and guides the students to a conclusion.

As an example of the inductive technique for teaching the initial consonant *b,* assume that the students know the words *ball, bat,* and *bundle* or that the words are taught through the whole-word approach. The teacher asks students what is similar about the words, and they discover that the words contain the letter *b,* which represents the *b* sound. The teacher solicits other words with the sound of *b.* Then the teacher presents the *b* words in context. Finally, the teacher gives practice exercises using the words in context (Rupley & Blair, 1989).

Direct/Explicit Teaching of Phonics

The most beneficial teaching method to implement the analytic approach is direct/explicit instruction. As stated in Chapter 2, skills are best taught and learned through the direct/explicit instruction approach. A teaching sequence that emphasizes direct/explicit instruction will ensure student mastery of phonic, structural, and contextual analysis skills and strategies. In direct/explicit instruction, the teacher gives direct, step-by-step explanations of a particular skill or strategy. Viewing this approach from an interactive viewpoint in the reading process, it also emphasizes the "when" and "why" of using various skills and strategies. Closely related to Rosenshine and Stevens' description in Chapter 2, another view of the process of direct/explicit instruction includes the following steps:

Stage One: Planning

1. Area of needed reading instruction
2. Intended learning outcome
3. Past learning

Stage Two: Teaching

4. Building background
5. Teacher-directed instruction
6. Independent student practice
7. Ongoing diagnosis
8. Modifying instruction (Rupley & Blair, 1988)

In the planning stage, the teacher (1) selects the desired area of reading instruction appropriate to students' needs, (2) identifies specific learning outcomes and appropriate instructional features reflecting assessment information, and (3) determines areas of related past learning from assessment information. The first phase in teaching a skill or strategy is to review past learnings with students and to motivate them to participate in the lesson. The second phase is to explain formally, model, and/or demonstrate the goal of the lesson for students. Easy, concrete examples based on students' experiential background are most suitable for the actual instructional activities. This phase also includes teacher-directed or supervised practice of the particular skill or strategy. At this point, the teacher "walks" the students through an individual or group activity to make sure they all understand the skill or strategy and when and why they are to use it. In the next phase, independent practice, students are expected to complete an activity on their own to apply the skill and strategy in a real reading or authentic situation. Next, ongoing diagnosis focuses on assessing students' progress to ensure mastery of the intended goal. Last, in the modifying instruction phase, the teacher responds to his or her own monitoring of instruction and ongoing assessment procedures. Figure 4.1 provides an example of a direct/explicit instruction lesson on a word-identification skill.

Phonics in Proper Perspective

Throughout the history of reading instruction, phonics has occupied a variety of roles. While no one approach—whole-word or phonics—is used exclusively in learning to read, the pendulum swings back and forth between an emphasis on learning words as wholes or through sound-symbol relationships.

From the colonial days to 1840, letters and sounds were taught haphazardly. The year 1840 marked the publication of Josiah Bumstead's *My Little Primer*, a beginning reader based on the whole-word approach. Due in large part to Horace Mann's influence, the following years ushered in several other readers emphasizing the whole-word approach.

Rebecca Pollard's Synthetic Method, introduced about 1890 (Pollard, 1889), advocated reducing reading to a number of mechanical procedures, each of which focused on a unit smaller than a word. Reading became mechanistic and, when mastered, often produced individuals who were adept at working through a given word. The result among both teachers and students was that reading became equated with facility in calling words. Beginning around 1920 and continuing until 1950, phonics went out of favor again.

Rudolph Flesch's *Why Johnny Can't Read* was an influential book published in 1955. It advocated a return to intensive phonics. Since the mid-1950s, phonics has assumed a more dominant place in early literacy instruction.

Equally noteworthy was the publication of Jeanne Chall's 1967 classic, *Learning to Read: The Great Debate*. In this text, Chall underscored the importance of decoding in beginning reading. Since the publication of Chall's book, commercial programs in reading have emphasized decoding.

No other aspect of the literacy curriculum has received as much critical attention as phonic instruction. Each generation of reading teachers faces both old and new controversies about phonic instruction. Even today, unfortunately, many people believe that phonics is an enemy of reading for meaning. Individuals who oppose phonics argue that teaching students to read by focusing on letter-sound relationships interferes with comprehension. We, too, oppose phon-

- **Area of Needed Reading Instruction**

Understanding of the vowel diphthongs *oi* and *oy*.

- **Intended Learning Outcome**

Given a series of words containing the vowel combinations *oi* and *oy*, students will be able to pronounce the words correctly.

- **Past Learning**

Students know the vowel sounds (long and short).
Students know vowel principles.

- **Building Background**

Review with students the vowel principle that helps them pronounce the words *heat* and *boat*. Remind students that when you discussed this principle, you reminded them that it did not hold true all of the time. Tell them that today they will learn two vowel combinations that do not follow the double vowel principle.

- **Teacher-Directed Instruction**

On the board write two lists of known words that contain the *oi* and *oy* vowel combination. For example:

oil	toy
soil	boy
boil	joy

Ask students to pronounce the words. Next ask: How many vowels are there in each word? What usually happens when there are two vowels together in a word? Do you hear the sound of the first vowel in *oil* and *toy*? Tell students that *oi* and *oy* are special vowel combinations that usually stand for the sound heard at the beginning of *oil*. Isolate the sound of *oi* for students. Solicit other words that have this sound. Lead students to the conclusion that *oi* and *oy* represent the vowel sound found in the word *oil*. Present a new list of real and nonsense words containing the vowel combinations *oi* and *oy*. Make sure they can pronounce the words correctly.

- **Independent Student Practice**

Write the following words on the chalkboard and ask students to fill in the sentence blanks with the correct words. After they finish, read the sentences aloud to check mastery of *oi* and *oy* combinations.

FIGURE 4.1

Direct/explicit instruction lesson

(Reprinted with the permission of Macmillan Publishing Company from *Teaching Reading: Diagnosis, Direct Instruction, and Practice,* Second Edition by William H. Rupley and Timothy R. Blair. Copyright ©1988 by Macmillan Publishing Company.)

soil	enjoy
boy	moisture
coin	toy
noise	poison

The plastic airplane was his favorite _____.

The _____ is dry and needs to be watered.

The insects were killed with _____.

That 1923 dime is a rare _____.

I hope you will _____ the picnic.

The _____ in the air caused rain.

The _____ in the yellow shirt threw the ball.

The neighbors next door make a lot of _____.

▪ Ongoing Diagnosis

Read with each student individually during the silent reading section of a directed reading activity. Note the student's application of the vowel combination of *oy* and *oi* and decide if further direct instruction and/or practice is necessary.

▪ Modifying Instruction

The independent student practice can be simplified by using pictures representing the words that students are to select to complete the sentences. Write the naming words beneath each picture to emphasize the written text that represents the pictures. Another modification is to write a choice of words beneath the blank and have students select the one that makes sense to complete the sentence. For example:

The plastic airplane was his favorite _____.

                        toy   enjoy   soil

This can be made easier by giving the students only two words from which to select.

The difficulty level can be increased by providing several choices that make sense in each sentence; have students identify all words that would meaningfully complete the sentences.

FIGURE 4.1
Continued

ics if it requires a student to sound out every word with the correct pronunciation of words becoming the primary goal of reading instruction.

The first objective in sounding out unknown words is to establish their identity, but this is not the end of the process. Words are identified to utilize their contribution to the meaning of the sentence. A student who sounds out a word without pursuing the meaning of the sentence is a casualty of either poor instruction or inadequate instruction. The objective in using letter-sound relationships is to identify unknown words to read for meaning, not to identify words simply because they are there (Taylor & Nosbush, 1983).

As mentioned, several studies have found that students' word identification skills progress developmentally. In the early stages, learners depend primarily on

FLASHBACK

Horace Mann was responsible for the first educational reform related to reading in the nineteenth century. Mann was the secretary of the Massachusetts Board of Education in the mid 1830s. He was extremely critical of the prevailing ABC method of teaching reading. In a report to the board, Mann argued that using the alphabetic method to teach reading was presenting information to children that was totally unfamiliar to them. Mann's criticism had a major impact on the reading instruction practices used nationwide in this time. By the 1880s the alphabetic method had been abandoned in most of the progressive schools and replaced with the word method for teaching reading.

UPDATE

Today, a main goal of reading programs is automatic word identification. This goal is primarily achieved through teaching phonics and its content. Other strategies to promote automatic word identification include sight vocabulary learning through the whole-word approach, structural analysis, and contextual analysis. The importance of phonics was highlighted in the landmark book, *Becoming a Nation of Readers: The Report of the Commission on Reading* (1985). The authors of this important work summarized recent research on the reading process and the teaching of reading.

Though most children today are taught phonics, often this instruction is poorly conceived. Phonics is more likely to be useful when children hear the sounds associated with most letters both in isolation and in words, and when they are taught to blend the sounds of letters to identify words. Phonics instruction should be kept simple and it should be completed by the end of the second grade for most children.

knowledge of letter-sound relationships to identify words. Children who come to school knowing how to read usually possess basic phonic skills. Donald D. Durrell and Helen A. Murphy (1978), who have devoted more than 50 years of work to beginning reading instruction, state:

> The [letter names, writing letters, letter name sounds, and syntax matching] appear to be early stages of reading which all children acquire before they become successful readers. Children who learn to read before coming to school invariably have these phonic skills; occasionally a child cannot write the letters, but the other abilities are always present. (p. 389)

Phonic instruction today is central to most reading programs. After reviewing classroom research on beginning reading and the effectiveness of phonics, the authors of the influential book *Becoming a Nation of Readers: The Report of the Commission on Reading* (1985) recommend phonics as an essential ingredient of beginning reading programs. The authors state, "Thus the issue is no longer, as it was several decades ago, whether children should be taught phonics. The issues now are specific ones of just how it should be done" (p. 37). The authors' conclusions on the role of phonics are:

> Phonics instruction improves children's ability to identify words. Useful phonics strategies include teaching children the sounds of letters in isolation and in words, and teaching them to blend the sounds of letters together to produce approximate pronunciations of words. Another strategy that may be useful is encouraging children to identify words by thinking of other words with similar spellings. Phonics instruction should go hand in hand with opportunities to identify words in meaningful sentences and stories. Phonics should be taught early and kept simple. (p. 57)

Stahl (1992) presented a balanced view of phonics instruction, emphasizing the necessity of all types of reading programs to include attention to the generalizations about the connections that exist between the spelling and pronunciation of a word. Noting the often-heard opposite extreme views on the use of phonics, he stated, "With these strong feelings, though, extreme views have been allowed to predominate, seemingly forcing out any middle position that allows for the importance of systematic attention to decoding in the context of a program stressing comprehension and interpretation of quality literature and expository text" (p. 618). He then discussed the following components of "exemplary phonics instruction," stating that "These components could be found in classrooms based on the shared reading of literature, as in a whole language philosophy, or in classrooms in which the basal reader is used as the core text" (p. 620).

Stahl says that exemplary phonics instruction:

1. Builds on a child's rich concepts about how print functions.
2. Builds on a foundation of phonemic awareness (awareness of sounds in spoken words).
3. Is clear and direct.
4. Is integrated into a total reading program.

5. Focuses on reading words, not learning rules.
6. May include onset and rime. (An *onset* is the part of the syllable before the vowel and a *rime* is the part from the vowel onward.)
7. May include invented spelling practice.
8. Develops independent word recognition strategies, focusing attention on the internal structure of words. (pp. 620–623)

Rather than taking extreme positions for or against phonic instruction, teachers must analyze how they will teach literacy. The optimum amount of phonic instruction for each student who is learning to read is not simply a matter of hours of instruction—it is the amount needed to make them independent readers. As in the case of all instruction, teachers hold the key to students' success in reading. Keep in mind that letter-sound analysis is most effective when used in combination with other skills.

The following instructional activities can be used to supplement a literacy program based on students' interaction with meaningful language. Reading and writing activities based on real-life experiences are invaluable.

Consonant Sounds. Some instructional materials used in beginning literacy advocate that the teaching of the letter sounds start with consonants because one of the most important clues to the sounds of vowels comes from consonants that follow vowels. A consonant-vowel-consonant pattern usually results in a short vowel sound—such as *cat, den,* and *can.* The same is true if the vowel is followed by two consonants (e.g., *cattle, dentist,* and *canvas*). Starting from the premise that children have learned to recognize a few words at sight—which for illustrative purposes we will assume includes the words *be, back,* and *ball*—they are ready to associate the sound of *b* in these words with the written symbol *b.*

INSTRUCTIONAL ACTIVITIES

Bb
be
back
ball
bear
boat
big
Bobby

■ ***Introducing Initial Consonants.*** Print an uppercase *B* on the chalkboard and say, "Today we will learn all about the letter *B*. Next to the uppercase *B*, I will print a lowercase *b*. This uppercase *B* is also called a capital *B*. Now I am going to write some words that begin with lowercase *b*."

Write *be, back,* and *ball* on the chalkboard. Point to each word and pronounce it. Stress the initial sound of *b* without distorting it. Direct pupils to look at each word as it is pronounced. Ask, "Who can give us another word that begins with the sound heard in the words?" Answer, "Yes, *bear, boat,* and *big.* We write *Bobby* with a capital *B* because it is somebody's name."

When a number of examples have been given, ask, "What sound do we hear at the beginning of each of these words?" Continue, "That's right, they all begin with the sound of *b—be, back, ball, bear, boat, big,* and *Bobby.*" (Point to each word as it is pronounced.) Note that in no instance were the children asked to sound the letter *b* in isolation.

■ *Applying Initial Consonants.* To provide for immediate meaningful application of the sound represented by the letter *b* and ways that initial consonants combined with context can provide clues for word identification, write sentences such as the following on the board:

B_____ put the b_____ in the water.
We will b_____ coming b_____ to class after lunch.

Announce, "You all have done well telling me words that begin with the *b* sound. Look carefully at each word on the board as I say it. Each word begins with the letter *b* and the sound of *b*. I am going to read a sentence for you two times that has two words missing. The missing words begin with the letter *b* and the *b* sound. (Point to blanks and letter *b*.) Listen and watch carefully as I read this sentence one time. (Point to first sentence and move your hand left to right under the words as you read each sentence to the children.) Now, I want each of you to listen and watch carefully as I read the sentence again. Tell me which of the words from our list makes sense in the context." Point to the list and read aloud each word as you point. Read each sentence, asking a student for a word from the list that makes sense in each blank. Write each response in the appropriate blank.

Engage all students in instruction by asking them if the word choices sound like something they would say. Ask if they could draw a picture of what is happening. Tell them why their choices are either correct (make sense) or incorrect.

Both of the preceding activities for teaching letter-sound association possess features of effective reading instruction. Specifically, these features include:

■ Relating new learnings (letter-sound association) to past learnings (sight words).

■ Asking literal-level questions such as, "Who can give other words beginning with the sound represented by *b*?" and "Does the sentence make sense?"

■ Using direct instruction.

■ Moving in small, related instructional steps.

■ Providing for immediate application of skills in meaningful reading situations.

■ Rewarding students' efforts and thinking and not just the correctness of responses.

In addition to the group work just described, you can begin to make the transition to student use and application by giving each child an opportunity to practice and apply the concept. Applications can be done in the group setting by using meaningful text that is similar to the earlier examples. Read the text several times as students follow along. Have them select and discuss their word choices for each blank. Monitor their performance closely to ensure that they are successful.

Most of these kinds of activities provide no opportunity to apply auditory discrimination skills in meaningful context and are intended to be supplementary. Application is extremely important, and the teacher must provide for it.

INSTRUCTIONAL ACTIVITIES

■ *Identifying Objects.* In a row of pictures such as the following, ask each student to mark the objects whose names begin with the same sound as the name of the object in the picture on the extreme left.

■ *Matching Pictures and Words.* Show the picture of an object and follow it by four words, none of which names the picture but one or more of which begin with the same sound as the name of the pictured object. Ask students to draw a circle around the boxes or words that begin with the same sound. For example:

 house | baby | cup | bath

Show a picture of a familiar object along with the word represented by the object in the picture. The example shown here is a bell. Let the children see the letter *b* and hear the sound *b* represents. Then ask them to mark all the other words in a supplied list that begin with the same sound.

bell

be   play
lake   boat
book

■ **Identifying Sounds in Words.** Show a series of boxes, each containing three words. Pronounce one of the words and direct students to underline the word pronounced. They need not know all of the words as sight words, provided they are familiar with the initial sound of each. In the following example, you could pronounce the italicized words.

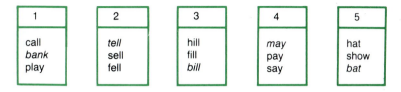

1	2	3	4	5
call *bank* play	*tell* sell fell	hill fill *bill*	*may* pay say	hat show *bat*

■ **Matching Words.** In columns, present words, some of which begin with the same sound and the same letter. Ask students to draw a line from the word in column A to the word in column B that begins with the same sound. For example:

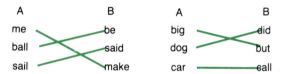

A	B		A	B
me	be		big	did
ball	said		dog	but
sail	make		car	call

An important skill to learn is substituting known letter sounds in unknown words. Assume the children know the words *take* and *make,* then encounter the unknown word *rake.* They should be able to combine the *r* sound that they know from words like *run, rain,* and *ride* with the sound of *ake* in *take.* By this process, they unlock the new word (Yopp, 1992).

In beginning reading, it is common to teach a number of monosyllabic words containing frequently used phonograms. Practically all workbooks use these word families to teach new words. Work on the substitution of initial consonants parallels early levels of most basal series. Moving through early levels, the child sees words such as *came, fame, same, name,* and *game* and words containing other common phonograms. Each of these words contains a familiar, often recurring, phonogram. Students should not receive isolated drills on these word endings. Nevertheless, students can understand a number of important words independently when they know some sight words containing commonly used letter combinations and can substitute initial letter sounds.

INSTRUCTIONAL ACTIVITIES

■ **Using Pictures to Teach Letter-Sound Combinations.** Use pictures in teaching letter-sound substitutions. The pictures should present words that are part of students' experiential and conceptual backgrounds. In the following examples, some children may perceive the hen as a chicken. Direct students to name the picture, listen to the first sound in the picture name, and write the letter that represents this sound in the blank. Do the first two with them to make sure they understand what they are to do.

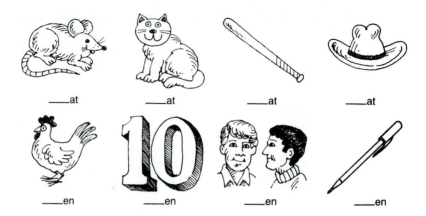

___at   ___at   ___at   ___at

___en   ___en   ___en   ___en

■ *Applying Letter-Sound Substitution Skills in Meaningful Sentence Context.* By applying such skills in context, pupils begin to understand that phonics is a tool for getting meaning. You can use sentences such as the following in a group setting to allow pupils to apply their skills. Such instruction builds on past learnings to enhance students' chances of success. Note that many of the words used for learning the sound represented by *b* are found in these sentences.

Bobby has a _____ pet _____.

fat	cat
bat	hat
hat	mat

The _____ will be back at _____ o'clock.

pen	ten
men	hen
ten	pen

Bill took his _____, _____, and _____ to the baseball game.

hat	ball	cat
rat	fall	bat
fat	call	sat

Some teachers prefer to teach a particular consonant sound at the ends of words at the same time that they deal with it as an initial sound. Other teachers work through the initial sounds and then work on single consonant sounds at the ends of words. Either procedure teaches students to notice visually and aurally the final consonants in short words. They know words such as *men, log, pen, bold,* and *leg* and the sounds of letters, including *t.* They are then asked to substitute the sound presented by *t* at the end of the words given above to get *met, lot, pet, bolt,* and *let.*

Simple Consonant Blends. To avoid confusion in dealing with many words that children will discover early in the literacy process, you must focus their attention on more than the initial consonant. Consonant blends fall into two classes: (1) simple two-letter consonant blends and (2) a smaller group of three-letter blends.

The 24 two- and three-letter simple blends may be divided into three major groups on the basis of a common letter:

1. Those that begin with *s: sc, sk, sm, sn, sp, st, sw, str*

2. Those that conclude with *l: bl, cl, fl, gl, pl, sl, spl*

3. Those that conclude with *r: br, cr, dr, fr, gr, pr, tr, scr, spr, str*

The preceding groups are not intended to suggest a particular order in which blends should be taught. A logical sequence would probably be determined by the vocabulary found in the instructional materials actually used in beginning reading.

Teachers and early readers differ according to when they deal with blends, which they teach/learn first, and how rapidly they cover the blends. Most materials suggest teaching initial blends before blends and special consonant sounds at the ends of words (such as *rest, nest, best, bark,* and *mark*). Although teaching consonant blends can take numerous approaches, the objectives of all methods are to lead the student to:

- See the printed letters involved.
- Understand that in every instance the letter sounds combine into a blended sound.
- Discriminate auditorily among the sounds of individual letters and blends such as *dug, rug, drug* and *sold, cold, scold*.

Any procedure for teaching initial consonant sounds can help teach each of the different consonant blends.

INSTRUCTIONAL ACTIVITIES

■ *Identifying Blends in Object Names.* Secure a number of pictures of familiar objects whose names begin with a blend. Show the pictures one at a time and have students write or say the blended letters. (They are not to simply name the picture.) Examples are *sk*ate, *tr*ain, *br*idge, *pl*ate, *gr*apes, *sl*ed, *fr*og, *cl*ock, *st*ar, *bl*anket, *sn*ake, *st*ore, *pl*ow, *cl*own, *sw*ing, and *sch*ool.

■ *Adding Letters.* In step 1, list words on the chalkboard that begin with *p* to which *s* can be added as a first letter to form the blend *sp.* Pronounce these words with students.

In step 2, write the *sp*-blend word to the right of each original word. Have students note the visual pattern of *sp* at the beginning of each word. Guide them in pronouncing the two words in each pair in rapid succession and in noting the blended sound in the second word in each pair (such as *pot-spot, pin-spin,* and *pill-spill*).

Step1	Step 2
pot	spot
pin	spin
pill	spill
peak	speak
pool	spool
poke	spoke
park	spark

Following is a variation of the previous activity. Instruct the students to add a letter such as *c, g, p* or *t* in front of each of the letter groups to pronounce a consonant blend. Circle the letters that blend.

_____ reat	_____ roud	_____ rain	_____ rop
_____ reek	_____ rail	_____ rice	_____ ruly
_____ rint	_____ reen	_____ row	_____ rize
_____ rip	_____ rack	_____ ree	_____ rand

■ **Identifying Blends in Sentences.**   Prepare and duplicate sentences containing a number of blends. Have the pupils underline each blend. For example:

The black crow flew away from the tree.

Pretty bright flowers grew near the bridge.

What is the price of the green dress in the store window?

We will rest when we reach the coast about dusk.

■ **Use Reading Clues in Teaching Initial Blends.**   Instruct the students, "Write the blend that spells the word that fits the clue." Examples are:

We use our __ __ain to think.

Apples and pears are __ __uits we eat.

We put our nose to a rose to __ __ell it.

A __ __amp is needed to mail a letter.

Consonant Digraphs.   A digraph is a combination of two letters that when pronounced result in one speech sound. This sound is not a simple blend of the two letters. Some digraphs have more than one sound (e.g., *ch* = *k* in *character, sh* in *chiffon,* and *ch* in *church*). The techniques used in teaching consonants and simple blends and the activities for teaching *ch* and *sh* that follow apply in teaching other digraphs.

INSTRUCTIONAL ACTIVITIES

■ **Identifying Digraphs.**   Place words beginning with *ch* on the board and direct students' attention to these initial letters. Pronounce each word, making sure students *listen* to the sound of *ch* in each word and look at the word at the same time you pronounce it. When pronouncing each word, emphasize but do not distort the *ch* sound.

chair
child
chance
chick
chill
chose

Have students pronounce each word as you point to it. Point to words randomly to encourage maximum attention. Ask students to provide other words that begin with the *ch* sound heard in *chair, child,* and *chance.* Write these on the board beneath the original words.

■ *Contrasting Single Consonants and Digraphs.*
Contrast single initial consonant sounds and
initial digraph sounds in words. Write the words
shown in column A on the chalkboard and pronounce these words with students. Next, write
the words in column B, pointing out the visual
pattern *sh* at the beginning of each word. Have
students pronounce each pair of words (such
as *hip-ship*) to contrast the different initial
sounds. Use the procedure outlined earlier with
other words that begin with *s* or *sh*. As students
contrast the initial sound in each pair of words,
they note the visual pattern *(s-sh)* and hear the
initial sounds these letters represent.

A	B
hip	ship
hop	shop
hot	shot
hark	shark
hare	share
harp	sharp
sell	shell
sort	short
sip	ship
save	shave
self	shelf
sock	shock

Use reading clues to introduce and teach initial digraphs. Read the clue and
then ask students to spell the word by using one of the digraphs provided in par-
entheses. Discuss how the letters chosen determine the meaning of a word in context.

used in bread __ __eat (wh, ch)   not open __ __ut (th, sh)

find on seashore __ __ell (sh, th)   largest in ocean __ __ale (th, wh)

can sit on it __ __air (sh, ch)   not fat __ __in (wh, th)

never do it! __ __eat (th, ch)   sun can do it __ __ine (wh, sh)

use your head __ __ink (sh, th)   must be round __ __eel (wh, th)

■ *Supplying Digraphs.*   Read the clue, and then ask the students to spell the word
by adding a digraph. Examples are:

Part of leg—rhymes with chin: __ __in

Doesn't cost much: __ __eap

At a later time, you may need to teach that *ch* = *k*, as in *chorus, chemistry,
chrome,* and *character* and that *ch* = *sh*, as in *chauffeur, chamois, chef,* and *Chicago.*
Other frequently seen digraphs include *sh, wh, th, gh, ng,* and *ph.* The sounds of
these letter combinations are as follows:

■ *Sh* is the sound heard in *shoe, shop, shell, short, wish,* and *fish.*

■ *Wh* sounds like *hw* in *when-hwen, wheel-hweel,* and *which-hwich.* When *wh* is
followed by *o,* the *w* is silent as in *whole-hole, whose-hooz* and *whom-hoom.*

- *Th* has two sounds. When voiced, it sounds like *th* in *th*em, *th*ere, *th*ey, and wi*th*. Voiceless, it sounds like *th* in *th*in, *th*ree, *th*row, and wid*th*.
- *Gh* can have the sound of *f* in lau*gh*, tou*gh*, and cou*gh*. It can be silent as in ni*gh*t, bou*gh*, ei*gh*t, and thou*gh*t.
- *Ng* sounds as in sa*ng*, wi*ng*, so*ng*, and ru*ng*.
- *Ph* usually sounds as *f* in *ph*one, ne*ph*ew, and gra*ph*.

Vowel Sounds. Difficulties exist in teaching vowel phoneme-grapheme relationships because numerous vowel phonemes exist, but only a limited number of letters and letter combinations represent these phonemes. However, a majority of these difficulties are easily taken care of as students learn the various vowel generalizations and use this knowledge in their reading and writing. The teacher should provide guidance, and most students learn phonic analysis more quickly with guidance that leads to insights. Requiring rote memorization of a myriad of generalizations hinders some students' understanding of the relationship between the generalizations and their reading. Children may become so preoccupied with learning the generalizations that they miss the application. On the other hand, verbalizing a generalization often helps learning.

Short Vowel Sounds. Techniques for teaching letter-sound relationships are unlimited. Each illustration presented deals with only one vowel-letter sound, since all of the other vowel sounds can be taught in the same manner, simply by changing the stimulus words. Practically any lesson can be presented using the chalkboard, an overhead projector, language-experience stories, recipes, big books, and so forth. The following activities illustrate the importance of teaching students to blend sounds represented by letters and letter combinations without distortion. Blending is an extremely important, yet often neglected, area in many reading programs (Anderson et al., 1985).

INSTRUCTIONAL ACTIVITIES

- ***Visual and Auditory Association Illustrated Using Short* e.**   Select a few easy words that have been used previously and contain the vowel pattern being taught. Write these words in a column and pronounce each word with students. Have them note the vowel letter in the middle of the word and emphasize the sound it represents, as in m*e*t, s*e*t, and p*e*t.

The following material may constitute different presentations on different days. Column A contains a pattern of CVC words, column B contains mixed patterns, and column C contains longer words. The sounds represented by these vowels in CVC words are highly regular. This allows you to structure learning around tasks where students can experience success. Once students have learned such CVC pattern words, you can introduce the other CVC patterns that are less regular.

A	B	C
met	leg	desk
set	men	bell
pet	bed	dress
bet	pep	sled
let	wet	best
jet	hen	help

Experiencing great success with one pattern of CVC words should enable students to succeed with mixed patterns. Instruction can then focus on longer words. Thus, you build instruction in small, related steps.

For the following activity, instruct the students, "In the blank, write a word that makes sense in each sentence. Choose the word from the right-hand column."

I like to _____ a cat.

Bobby _____ me that he could ring the bell.

Bill _____ me sail the ship.

met
set
let
bet
pet

The _____ let me play in the big boat.

The cat fell off of the boat and got _____.

Bob took a nap in _____.

leg
men
bed
hen
wet

Bill had to _____ Bobby pull the _____ up the hill.

They are _____ pals and like to play in the snow.

Mary put her book on her _____ at school.

desk
bell
sled
best
help

Provide opportunities for application of each skill in meaningful context for each area of instruction. Use meaningful examples appropriate to children's needs and capabilities and build on previous learning.

INSTRUCTIONAL ACTIVITIES

■ *Contrasting Short Vowel Sounds in Words.* In step 1, write a column of identical initial and final consonants, leaving a blank space for adding a vowel letter. In step 2, insert a vowel letter to complete the first word, and then in step 3, call on a student to name the word. Continue using a different vowel letter for each blank space. In step 4, when the column is complete, have students read the words in rapid succession to contrast the vowel sounds. In step 5, present the words in meaningful context, omitting the vowel letter. Call on each student to provide a vowel for the word that makes sense in the sentence.

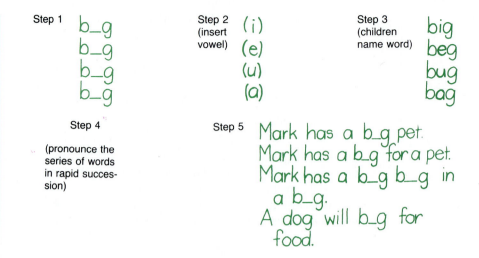

Step 1
b_g
b_g
b_g
b_g

Step 2
(insert vowel)
(i)
(e)
(u)
(a)

Step 3
(children name word)
big
beg
bug
bag

Step 4
(pronounce the series of words in rapid succession)

Step 5
Mark has a b_g pet.
Mark has a b_g for a pet.
Mark has a b_g b_g in a b_g.
A dog will b_g for food.

Other stimulus patterns are b*u*d, b*a*d, and b*e*d; p*a*n, p*u*n, p*i*n, and p*e*n; p*a*t, p*e*t, p*i*t, and p*o*t; and h*u*t, h*i*t, h*o*t, and h*a*t.

■ **Working with Final Phonograms.**   Use pictures in teaching final phonograms. Have students name the picture, then blend the initial letter (shown beneath the picture) with each of the phonograms at the right of the picture. Focus students' attention first on naming the picture and then selecting the final phonogram. Finally, have the students write the correct letter pattern in the blank spaces to complete the word. If they experience difficulties, have them say each phonogram (such as /at/, /ot/, and /ut/) and then blend the initial letter (/c/) with each. Again, be sure that students can recognize each picture and name it. The pictures of the well and the cot may not be in all students' experiential and conceptual backgrounds.

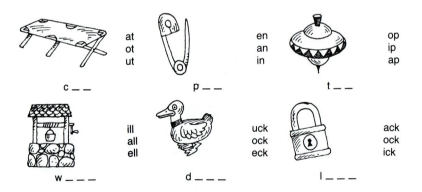

at
ot
ut

c _ _

en
an
in

p _ _

op
ip
ap

t _ _

ill
all
ell

w _ _ _

uck
ock
eck

d _ _ _

ack
ock
ick

l _ _ _

Long Vowel Sounds.   Generalizations covering vowel letter-sound relationships are numerous; however, many of these do not apply to a large number of letter patterns (Caldwell, Roth, & Turner, 1978). Therefore, separate teaching procedures are cited for two adjacent vowels (ea, ai, ee, oa patterns) and final e words.

Two adjacent vowels representing a single sound are referred to as vowel digraphs (feet, boat, sail, mean). One of the more widely quoted generalizations relates to vowel digraphs: "When two vowels come together they usually represent the long vowel sound of the first vowel," "The first vowel represents a long sound and the second is not sounded," or "When two vowels come together, the first vowel does the talking, the second goes walking." Two-vowel combinations have about as many exceptions to this rule as instances where it applies. For the specific vowel combinations of ee, oa, ea, and ai, it holds much more frequently.

INSTRUCTIONAL ACTIVITIES

■ *Contrasting Single-Double Vowel Patterns.* Prepare lists of words in which column A has a single vowel (met) and column B is identical except for an added vowel (meat).

Ask students to read the first word under column A and listen for the short vowel sound. Then ask them to read the first word under column B, note the two-vowel pattern, and listen for the long vowel sound. As a final step, have them read each pair in rapid succession to note the contrasting vowel sound (such as met-meat and led-lead).

A	B	A	B	A	B
e	ea	a	ai	e	ee
met	meat	man	main	fed	feed
led	lead	lad	laid	met	meet
men	mean	pal	pail	pep	peep
bed	bead	ran	rain	bet	beet
stem	steam	bat	bait	wed	weed
set	seat	plan	plain	step	steep

Prepare similar word lists using the o-oa, e-ea, and a-ai patterns.

Provide opportunities for application by using sentences such as the following. Focus on selecting words that make sense in the sentence:

The _____ ate _____ for dinner.
    (man, main)   (meat, met)

Bobby put the _____ in the _____.
    (bait, bat)   (pal, pail)

The _____ had to _____ on the _____.
    (men, mean)   (step, steep)   (weed, wed)

INSTRUCTIONAL ACTIVITIES

■ *The Effect of Final e.* Write a column of CVC words on the chalkboard, each of which contains the medial vowel *a* (step 1). As you pronounce these words, have students tell which vowel sound they hear in the word (ă). Explain that you will change each word by adding the letter *e* at the end.

Step 1	Step 2
can	cane
hat	hate
mad	made
pal	pale
rat	rate
plan	plane

Print the words shown in step 2. As you pronounce these words, have students note the *a___e* pattern and tell the vowel sound they hear in each of the words (ā).

Have students explain what vowel sound they hear in words with two vowels when one is a final *e*. Restate their explanations: "In many short words showing two vowels, a final *e* is not sounded while the first vowel has its long sound." Introduce the following word pairs for other final *e* series: *bit-bite, pin-pine, hid-hide, kit-kite, rid-ride, slid-slide, not-note, hop-hope, rod-rode,* and *rob-robe.*

Prepare an exercise for either chalkboard presentation or independent seatwork. List CVC words, some of which can be changed to another word by adding a final *e.* Have students read the stimulus word and determine if adding the letter *e* makes a known word. Make sure they ask themselves if the word they are making sounds like a word they have heard before. Make sure each child understands the task by completing some examples in a group. Name the word (if an oral exercise) or ask students to write the word in the space provided. For example, if the word can be changed into another word by adding a final *e,* write the new word on the line provided. If adding an *e* does not make a word, leave the line blank.

can _____		hid _____
rat _____		sob ____*____
top ____*____		mad _____
plan _____		bit _____
kit _____		not _____
hop _____		tap _____
cat ____*____		rob _____
cut _____		big ____*____

*spaces left blank

Long Vowel Sounds at the End of Short Words. Two generalizations cover single vowels at the end of words: "If a word has only one vowel that ends the word, the vowel sound usually is long" and "If a word has no other vowel and ends with *y,* the letter *y* serves as a vowel and is pronounced as long *i.*" These generalizations apply in a limited number of high-frequency words and can be taught at the chalkboard, using columns of words. Utilize activities similar to those discussed throughout the earlier sections.

be	by	try	go
me	my	sky	no
he	cry	fly	so
we	why	fry	ho
she	dry	shy	yo-yo

Vowels Affected by Particular Consonants. The long and short vowel sounds are by far the most important vowel clues in helping determine the pronunciation of words. In addition, other vowel patterns should be explained, even though they may be of less importance in phonic analysis. When a vowel precedes *r*, the sound of that vowel is affected by the *r*. Usually a blend results, which is neither the long nor the short sound of the vowel (such as *car, curl, fir, for,* and *park*). When the vowel *a* is followed by *l* or *w*, the resulting sound is a blend (such as *yawn, tall, awful, talcum, awning,* and *ball*).

Although a number of words contain a vowel followed by *r*, it is debatable whether this particular letter-sound combination causes beginning readers much trouble. That is, if children master the long and short vowel relationships, they are not likely to experience serious trouble with vowels followed by *r*. Undoubtedly, many successful readers are unaware of the difference between the vowel sounds in the words *can* and *car*.

Diphthongs. Diphthongs are two adjacent vowels, each of which is sounded, such as the *ou* in *house, oi* in *oil, oy* in *boy, ow* in *how* (but not the *ow* in *blow, grow,* or *throw,* where the sound is long *o*). Teaching diphthongs is probably not of major importance in the total phonics program. A number of words that are learned as sight words contain these sounds, and certain words can serve as keys to help students hear the sounds (such as *house, oil, boy,* and *how*).

Summary of Vowel Generalizations. The following generalizations govern vowel pronunciation:

- A single vowel followed by a consonant in a word or syllable usually has the short sound (such as *can* or *cancel*).

- A single vowel that concludes a word or syllable usually has the long sound (such as *me, ti-ger,* and *lo-co-mo-tive*).

- In the vowel digraphs *oa, ea, ee, ai,* and *ay,* the first vowel is usually long and the second is silent (such as *coat, reap, bead, wait,* and *play*). The digraphs *oo, au,* and *ew* form a single sound that is not the long sound of the first vowel (such as *food, good, haul,* and *few*).

- In words containing two vowels, one of which is final *e,* the final *e* is usually silent and the preceding vowel is long.

- Single vowels followed by *r* usually result in a blended sound (such as *fir, car, burn,* and *fur*). The vowel *a* followed by *l* or *w* usually results in a blended sound (such as *yawn, tall, claw,* and *awful*).

- The letter *y* at the end of words containing no other vowel has the letter sound of *i* (such as *my, try, sky,* and *shy*).

- Diphthongs are two-vowel combinations in which both vowels contribute to the speech sound (such as *house, boy,* and *cow*).

STRUCTURAL ANALYSIS

Structural-analysis instruction helps students identify words whose visual patterns change as a result of adding:

- Inflectional endings (such as *s, -ed, -ing,* and *-ly*).

- Prefixes (such as *pre-, ex-,* and *un-*).

- Suffixes (such as *-able, -ment,* and *-ness*).

- Root-to-root compounds (such as *sidewalk, playground,* and *basketball*).

Structural-analysis skills allow students to focus on larger units of letter patterns within known words (Rupley & Blair, 1988). Obviously, use of some of these techniques relies on previous learning. For instance, a child who uses structural analysis in unlocking words with inflectional endings must recognize the root word (such as *help*) as a familiar unit or be able to sound out the root word, solve the ending (such as *-ing*), and blend the two *(helping)*. Later, this type of analysis should not be necessary, since the student perceives the word *helping* as one familiar unit.

In applying structural analysis skills to solve unknown words, children do better if they recognize parts of words that they have studied. Instruction thus should build on what students have already mastered in reading. By building on students' prior learning, you can increase their attention to new learning, increase their chances of success with new learning, and diagnose their progress from one learning outcome to the next.

An important concept in structural analysis is syllabication. A syllable is a vowel or group of letters containing a vowel that is pronounced as a unit. Students' ability to determine the basic units of pronunciation (that is, syllables) supports effective word learning. **Syllabication** is included under structural analysis because it is the division of a word into its basic units of pronunciation. Phonic generalizations are applied to letters only after this division.

Students usually learn a number of one-syllable root words before they try to understand polysyllabic words. As they encounter longer words, they learn that most prefixes and suffixes and some inflectional endings constitute syllables. During early experience with high-frequency affixes, students break words into parts and then combine the parts into the whole, such as *re-read-ing, pre-heat-ed, bi-week-ly,* and *dis-appear-ance*. After many experiences, children reduce their reliance on this type of analysis and blend the parts into the whole more smoothly.

A series of pictures may help students develop the ability to combine syllables into words. The pictures presented should be familiar to students. They should either listen to the teacher's pronunciation of the picture's name or pronounce it themselves and indicate the number of syllables heard. Students may also clap out the number of syllables in words that the teacher pronounces.

A knowledge of vowel behavior within words is a major aid in breaking words into syllables, but the sounds of vowels and letter combinations are not as consistent as those of prefixes and suffixes. Nevertheless, many generalizations are useful. Although the following examples are not words, the letter combinations can be broken into syllables: *comration, ragmotex, obsebong,* and *fasnotel.* The likely syllabication is *com-ra-tion, rag-mo-tex, ob-se-bong,* and *fas-no-tel.* Most fluent readers would pronounce these nonsense words in substantially the same way. These readers probably would not recite rules to themselves before pronouncing these words, but they probably would be subconsciously influenced by rules they had learned.

INSTRUCTIONAL ACTIVITIES

■ *Generalizing Two Consonants Between Vowels.* When you teach generalizations applicable to syllabication, provide a number of examples. Then lead students to see for themselves what happens. Out of this experience, they can develop rules. Starting with the question, "What usually happens when two consonants come between vowels?" place a number of words on the board. For example:

af ter	win dow	rab bit	let ter
gar den	can dy	din ner	sum mer
fas ter	pen cil	lit tle	cot ton

Work toward the generalization "When two consonants come between vowels, the syllable division comes between the consonants" or "One consonant goes with each vowel." Point out that this rule does not always hold, but that it is the best guess to make when trying to pronounce an unknown word. In the case of double consonants, there are few exceptions to the rule.

■ *Generalizing One Consonant Between Vowels.* To teach what happens when one consonant comes between two vowels, place a list of known sight words on the board. For example:

be gin	fe ver	to tal	de cide
o ver	di rect	ti ger	me ter
fa tal	mo ment	pu pil	ho tel

Inflectional Endings

Inflectional endings include *-s, -es, -ed,* and *-ing* for verbs, *-er* and *-est* for adjectives and adverbs, and *-ly* for adverbs. Note that inflectional endings depend on context. Therefore, be sure to provide application exercises when you teach inflectional endings.

INSTRUCTIONAL ACTIVITIES

■ **Adding -s, -ed, or -ing to Words.** Instruct pupils, "In the space provided, add -s, -ed, or -ing to the known word. Write each new word in the column, then read the words." Note that word endings are important features of syntax. Using one or two words with the new word being formed can heighten students' attention to syntax.

Known Word	-s	-ed	-ing
play	He _____	I _____	I am _____
look	He _____	I _____	She is _____
call	She _____	She _____	He is _____
flap	She	It _____	It is _____
wait	He	He _____	I am _____
rain	It	It _____	It is _____
work	She	I _____	They are _____

■ **Adding -er, -est, or -ly to Words.** Instruct pupils, "In the space provided, add -er, -est, or -ly to the stimulus word. Then read each word."

Known Word	-er	-est	-ly
warm	_____	_____	_____
great	_____	_____	_____
high	_____	_____	_____
soft	_____	_____	_____
kind	_____	_____	_____

■ **Using s Endings.** Present the known words *look, call, clap,* and *play,* and review them when *s* is added to the end. Do this on the chalkboard and direct students' attention to the written words.

A	B
I look	He looks
I call	He calls
I clap	She claps
I play	She plays

Direct them to look at sentences as you read each one aloud, pausing briefly when coming to a blank space, then reading the rest of the sentence. Using the words from list B, have the students orally give you a word that makes sense for each sentence. For example:

Bobby _____ in the yard.

The robin _____ his wings to fly.

The dog by the door _____ mean.

Bill _____ his dog to come in at night.

■ **Choosing -er, -est, or -ly Endings.** Write clues using words that can take *-er, -est,* or *-ly* inflectional endings. Provide blanks at the right of the clues for the new words formed. Instruct students, "Read the clue. In the blank to the right, write a new word, adding the proper inflectional ending to the underlined word. The new word must fit the clue." For example:

Ending: *-er, -est, -ly*

	Clue	**New Word**
1.	sweeter than all others	_____
2.	taller than all others	_____
3.	in a quick manner	_____
4.	works more hard than Bill	_____
5.	in a quiet way	_____
6.	with swift action	_____

■ **Choosing s Endings.** Provide application by using activities such as the following. Ask students to select the word that makes sense in each sentence.

play

plays

1. He _____ ball with us.

2. I _____ ball with him.

3. They will _____ ball with us after school.

4. She _____ a game with a bat and a ball.

work

works

1. Dad _____ at home on Saturday.

2. Mother _____ at school on Monday.

3. Jan has to _____ at the game.

4. The horse _____ on the farm.

■ **Choosing -s, -er, -est, or -ly Endings.** Use sentences such as the following to provide further application of inflectional endings in meaningful context. Activities should build on what students have learned. Encourage them to think about whether their choices make sense in the sentences.

1. I like to _____ in the yard on _____ days.
        (play, plays)   (warm, warmer, warmest)

2. Today is the _____ day of the year.
        (warm, warmer, warmest)

3. This doll _____ like the _____ one in the store.
        (look, looks)   (soft, softest, softly)

- **Choosing Degrees of Comparison.** Use additional activities to point out how inflectional endings describe degrees of comparison. For example:

1. Mark is _____ than John. He is at the
      (high, higher, highest)

   _____ point on the ladder.
   (high, higher, highest)

2. This fur is the _____ fur of all.
      (soft, softer, softest)

3. Jane is a _____ person. She is _____ than
      (kind, kinder, kindest)   (kind, kinder, kindest)

   Fred, Bill, or Bob. She is the _____ person I know.
                    (kind, kinder, kindest)

4. The _____ time I ever had was at the circus.
      (great, greater, greatest)

Prefixes and Suffixes

Prefixes are added at the beginnings of words to produce new words. Examples of prefixes include *pre-, ex-, un-, in-, dis-,* and *re-*. Suffixes are added at the ends of words to produce new words. Examples include *-able, -ment, -ness, -er, -or, -ful,* and *-ish*.

INSTRUCTIONAL ACTIVITIES

- **Adding Prefixes and Suffixes.** Using root words that take prefixes and suffixes, provide lists such as the following. Instruct the students, "In each blank space, add a prefix or suffix to make a word. For prefixes, use *in-, dis-,* or *re-*. For suffixes, use *-ment, -able,* or *-ness*."

_____ agree	_____ disagree	_____ agree
_____ direct	_____ indirect	_____ direct
_____ fill	_____ refill	_____ fill

- **Choosing Suffixes.** Write clues using words that can take suffixes. Instruct students, "Read the clue. In the blank to the right, write a new word, adding the proper suffix to the underlined word. The new word must fit the clue." For example:

Suffixes: *-or, -less, -ful*

Clue	*New Word*
1. one who visits	_____
2. to be of help	_____
3. without end	_____
4. one who invents	_____
5. with hope	_____

6. without hope   _____

7. able to harm   _____

8. one who sails   _____

Suffixes: *-able, -ness, -ish, -er*

Clue	*New Word*

9. something that looks like   _____

10. can be washed   _____

11. one who paints   _____

12. having a fever   _____

13. thinking only of oneself   _____

14. being idle   _____

15. can be adjusted   _____

16. can be fixed   _____

17. one who fixes   _____

18. looking green   _____

19. someone who sings   _____

20. something that you can sing   _____

Upon completion of the clue activities, have students use the new words formed from the clues in their own sentences or stories. Write some of these on the chalkboard and use them for class discussion. As a group, discuss the meaning of the stories or sentences. Example sentences for clues 1 through 3 follow.

Uncle Frank was a <u>visitor</u> at our house.
The apple is the <u>sweetest</u> of all the apples we picked.
Our teacher is very <u>helpful</u>.
The road was <u>endless</u>.

■ *Choosing Prefixes and Suffixes.*   To help students apply their knowledge of prefixes and suffixes, use activities such as the following. Ask students to select the prefix or suffix to complete the underlined word so that the sentence makes sense.

1. I <u>agree</u> with Dan that we should buy a dog.

2. I _____ <u>agree</u> with Dan that we should name the dog Spike.
    (in-, dis-, re-)

3. Dan and I are in <u>disagree</u>_____ about the name for our dog.
    (-ment, -able, -ness)

4. I guess I am a <u>disagree</u>_____ person.
    (-able, -ment, -ness)

1. Joe drank all of the water in the bottle.

2. He will _____<u>fill</u>_____ the bottle with water.
(re-, in-, dis-)

3. The bottle is _____<u>fill</u>_____.
(re-, in-, dis-)   (-ment, -able, -ness)

Compound Words

Compound words are formed by combining root words. Examples include *side-walk, playground,* and *basketball.*

INSTRUCTIONAL ACTIVITIES

■ ***Using the Same Word in a Number of Compound Words.*** Write three compound words for each group of words. To maximize success, begin with two words to combine. Then, as pupils experience success, increase the number of combinations. For example:

air	plane	_____
book	case	_____
door	way	_____

air	plane	craft	port
_____	_____	_____	
book	case	keeper	worm
_____	_____	_____	
door	way	bell	mat
_____	_____	_____	

■ ***Combining Words to Make Compounds.*** Present lists of words that students can combine to form meaningful compound words. For example:

A		B
shoe _____		ball
sun _____		light
basket _____		maker

■ ***Choosing Compound Words.*** Write three words in a row, only one of which is a compound. Tell students, "Each line contains one compound word. Underline the compound word and write it in the blank space at the end of the line." For example:

children	dancing	fireplace _____
someone	beaches	crawling _____
alike	mousetrap	puzzle _____
downpour	happily	permitted _____
autumn	mistake	handbag _____

■ *Using Compounds in Sentences.* Write sentences, leaving a blank for students to fill in a compound word. Instruct them, "Complete each sentence by writing a compound word in the blank space." Provide practice in a group setting to make sure each student understands the task. For example:

A player can hit a home run in a game of _____.

The teacher wrote on the _____ with a piece of chalk.

The front window in a car is the _____.

The mail carrier puts mail in our _____.

In addition to providing sentences, encourage students to suggest their own sentences that include compound words. If they have difficulty, provide them with a written list of compound words to use. Either write the sentences on the chalkboard or have students write them on a sheet of paper. Discuss each sentence and its meaning. Use the activity to write group-composed stories.

CONTEXTUAL ANALYSIS

Students can use contextual clues only when they can recognize or sound out most of the words in a sentence. Phonics is only one of many skills that can aid reading for meaning. For instance, when a student does not know the meaning of a word, arriving at its exact pronunciation through phonic analysis will not help. The following sentence contains an unknown symbol:

The man was attacked by a marbohem.

Everyone reading this page can sound out *mar-bo-hem,* but no one knows what attacked the man, since saying "marbohem" does not convey meaning to the reader. If other words are substituted for marbohem, some readers may still have trouble with the meaning, even though they can analyze the speech sounds in the words. For example:

The man was attacked by a peccary.

The man was attacked by a freebooter.

The man was attacked by an iconoclast.

The man was attacked by a fusilier.

The man was attacked by a hypochondriac.

Contextual clues can help explain unknown words if the reader demands meaning. Using context plus a minimal amount of letter analysis of the beginning of the words is far better than context alone. This combination of clues is also better than intensively analyzing each word while ignoring the contextual setting of the unknown word.

In the following illustration, the blank line represents an unknown word:

The boy waved good-bye as the train left the _____.

Even with a blank line substituting, most readers have no problem supplying the correct word. The task is even simpler with the first letter supplied:

The boy waved good-bye as the train left the s _____.

Other reading situations present more difficult problems; for example:

The girl waved good-bye to her _____.

Here, a number of possible word choices make sense: friend, mother, sister, teacher, brother, parents, family, playmate, aunt, cousin, uncle, and so forth. Select any word that makes sense and insert only its first letter in the blank space. Note how that initial letter eliminates many of the words that were possibilities.

The importance of combining skills becomes more obvious in larger contexts. In the first version of the following story, it is possible to get the sense of the story even if one is not sure of the identity of a number of the missing words.

John and his cousin _____ started on their fishing trip. John said, "I have my trusty _____ pole, a _____ full of lunch, and a can of _____." After walking a long time, John said, "Not far from here there is a _____ across the stream. We can sit on the _____ and fish." When they started fishing, John said, "I'm not going to _____ from this _____ until I catch a _____ _____." Finally _____ said, "I am tired of sitting on the _____. I am going to take a walk along the _____." _____ had walked only a short way when he lost his _____ and fell into the stream. The water was not very deep, and he waded out. "Hey," said John, "You're lucky. You won't have to take a _____ when we get home."

This next version inserts the initial letter in each unknown word, which in all cases happens to be the letter *b*.

John and his cousin B_____ started out on their fishing trip. John said, "I have my trusty b_____ pole, a b_____ full of lunch, and a can of b_____." After walking a long time, John said, "Not far from here there is a b_____ across the stream. We can sit on the b_____ and fish." When they started fishing, John said, "I'm not going to b_____ from this b_____ until I catch a b_____ b_____." Finally B_____ said, "I am tired of sitting on the b_____. I am going to take a walk along the b_____." B_____ had walked only a short way when he lost his b_____ and fell into the stream. The water was not very deep, and he waded out. "Hey," said John, "You're lucky. You won't have to take a b_____ when we get home."

(Words in order of their omission are Bob, bamboo, bag, bait, bridge, bridge, budge, bridge, big bass, Bob, bridge, bank, Bob, balance, bath.)

Learning to read is very complicated. From the beginning, the learner who is attempting to identify unfamiliar words should look for and accept help from all available clues. The simultaneous use of all options helps simplify beginning reading. Occasionally, phonics is the only key to meaning that a student can utilize. More often than not, however, all of the word-identification skills—basic sight vocabulary, phonics, structural analysis, and contextual analysis—can be used together. Phonics should be used only when needed.

The two broad kinds of context clues are syntactic and semantic. The value of context clues lies not only in their ability to identify words by themselves but also in their ready application to whole-word learning, phonics, and structural analysis. As with the other decoding skills, students' ability to use context clues should be developed through both direct and informal instruction, with an abundance of practice in real reading situations. As we know, word learning is related to comprehension. Whether students are developing sight vocabularies or using phonics or structural analysis, they must have interesting, varied, and realistic practice with words in context. The use of context not only reflects the natural reading process, but also allows students to focus on meaning to aid them in determining whether the word(s) make sense in context.

Syntactic Clues

The ordering of words in a sentence is syntax. Using an example presented earlier (The girl waved good-bye to her ——————), knowledge of language helps us to determine that a person, place, or thing fits in the blank. This knowledge allows us to eliminate possibilities that do not make sense in this sentence.

When used in combination with phonics and structural analysis, syntactic clues enable students to figure out the meanings of unknown words. **Syntactic clues** include:

■ *Structure words.* Noun markers (such as *my, this,* and *any*), verb markers (such as *am, are,* and *is*), clause markers (such as *now, if,* and *before*), and question indicators (such as *why, who,* and *which*) signal what is coming next. For example:

He took *my* brother to the game.

He *is* going to the game.

My brother will go to the game *if* he is home.

Who is going to the game?

■ *Phrases.* A phrase may describe or refine a word. For example:

The boy *with the brown hair* is Mike.

The game *between the Reds and the Cubs* is sold out.

- *Language grammar.* Meaning patterns in language can indicate where certain words fit. For example:

  He took my *brother* (noun) to the game.

  He *took* (verb) my brother to the game.

  He took my brother to the game in a big, *shiny* (adjective) car.

- *Appositives.* An appositive is a word or words that explain the previous word. For example:

  Jones, *the quarterback,* was injured on the first play.

  Jubilation, *great excitement,* filled the stadium when the home team won.

Semantic Clues

Semantics refers to the reader's knowledge of word meanings and the reader's conceptual and experiential backgrounds in relation to comprehending what is read. Although syntactic clues can help explain word meaning by allowing readers to limit their choices of meaning for unknown words, semantic clues provide them with more clues to word meaning.

If a related sentence or sentences either precede or follow a sentence, the additional contextual information can help indicate the meaning. Suppose that "The girl waved good-bye to her _____" is followed by "He waved back and wiped tears from his eyes as the train began to move." In this example, the word *he* tells you that the unknown word refers to a male.

A reader who makes the connection between the male referent and the initial letter pattern or patterns of an unknown word and the sounds represented can even better determine meaning. In "The girl waved good-bye to her f_____. He waved back and wiped tears from his eyes as the train began to move," the letter *f* further narrows down the possibilities.

Johnson and Pearson (1984) classified the major kinds of *semantic clues* available to readers. A modified listing of their categories follows. Again, recognize that for semantic clues to be used efficiently, the referent for the unknown word must be in the reader's experiential and conceptual backgrounds.

- *Definitions or explanations.* Difficult words that students encounter in their reading are often defined within the text. Words such as *is, are,* and *means* signal explanations.

  Herbivores are animals *that feed on green plants.*

- *Synonyms and antonyms.* In addition to using the unknown word, writers often use synonyms or antonyms.

  The *robust* rabbit loved to visit the garden. He was so *fat* he could hardly squeeze through the fence.

- *Figurative language.* Meanings of unknown words can be obtained from metaphors and similes used in relation to preceding and following text.

It was raining *cats and dogs*. Several cars stalled in the flooded streets.

■ *Summary statements.* Based on connected story information, the meaning of an unknown word may become known.

Mark used to be a *stellar* basketball player. He could make shots from anywhere on the court. The crowd always cheered when their star player was introduced.

Contextual-Analysis Instruction

Ensuring application of word-identification skills in meaningful context allows pupils to develop an awareness of context for word meaning. Rather than repeating all of the earlier activities, following are a few examples.

Bobby put the b_____ in the water.

Bobby has a pet _____.

We use our __ __ain (br) to think.

Clue. Used in bread: _____eat.
　　　　　　　　　　　　　　(ch, wh)

Mark wants to learn how to _____.
　　　　　　　　　　　　　　(sale, sail)

Bill has a ball and a bat. The bat and ball c_____ in a set. Dad will paint Bill's n_____ on the bat and ball in green paint.

Oil comes from _____ wells.

The _____ time I ever had was at the circus.
　(great, greater, greatest)

If you can wash something, then it is _____able.

Joe drank all of the water in the bottle. Joe will re_____ the bottle with water. The bottle is _____ fill _____.

A player hit a home run in the game of _____.

The front window in a car is the _____.

DICTIONARY

Using the dictionary is another important word-identification skill associated with reading instruction. The three major goals in dictionary instruction are (1) finding a particular word, (2) determining its pronunciation, and (3) selecting the correct meaning of the word in the context in which it is used.

Dictionary skills are often neglected, even though teachers acknowledge the value of these skills. This neglect may stem from a teacher's feeling of inadequacy about certain relatively difficult facets of dictionary use, such as diacritical markings or pronunciation keys. On the other hand, the teaching may fall short when dictionary skills are considered something extra rather than as an intrinsic part of literacy instruction.

Both teachers and pupils should use the dictionary as a source for word meanings, not as a form of rote drill or a penalty for making certain errors (Lehr, 1980). Certain knowledge is essential for successful use of the dictionary. This knowledge includes:

- Alphabetical order.
- That letters and combinations of letters have different sounds in different situations and that some letters are silent.
- That *y* on the end of most words is changed to *i* before adding *es* for plurals.
- Root words and the various inflected and derived forms of root words.
- That a word can have many different meanings.

Skill in using the dictionary paves the way for greater independence in reading because it:

- Unlocks the sounds or pronunciations of words.
- Discloses new meanings of words that may be known in only one or a limited number of connotations.
- Confirms the spelling of a word when the reader can only approximate its correct spelling.
- Expands vocabulary through mastery of inflected and derived forms.

Teachers must refine and expand these skills as students move upward through the grades. The success that students feel and the utility they derive from dictionary usage can be most important factors in how they react to the dictionary as a tool for helping in all facets of communication. Students must realize that dictionary skills are needed throughout life; failure to master these skills can negatively influence their attitudes and learning development for many years to come.

Dictionary usage involves a number of developmental tasks. Educators generally agree on these tasks and the order in which they should be presented. They are:

- Recognizing and differentiating letters.
- Associating letter names with letter symbols.
- Learning the letters of the alphabet in order.
- Arranging a number of words in alphabetical order by their initial letters.
- Extending the last skill to second and third letters of words, eventually working through all letters of a word, if necessary.
- Developing facility in rapid, effective use of dictionary, that is, knowing where letters (such as *h*, *p*, and *v*) fall in the dictionary, and opening the dictionary as near as possible to the word being studied.
- Developing the ability to use accent marks in arriving at word pronunciations.
- Learning to interpret the phonetic spellings used in the dictionary.

- Using the pronunciation key that appears on each double page of most dictionaries.

- Working out different pronunciations and meanings of words that are spelled alike.

- Determining which is the preferred pronunciation when several are given.

- Selecting the meaning that fits the context.

- Using the guide words found at the top of each page to tell at a glance if the page contains the word being sought.

- Using special sections of a dictionary intelligently (such as geographical terms and names, biographical data, and foreign words and phrases).

Although particular skills are characteristically taught at given grade levels, the individual student's skills should determine what is taught. Fortunately, dictionaries are available at all difficulty levels, from simple picture dictionaries to massive unabridged editions. The individual students' needs and abilities should dictate what type of dictionary to study.

SUMMARY /

To become independent readers, students must learn to use a variety of word-identification skills and strategies. Sight vocabulary, phonics, structural analysis, and contextual analysis are the basic word-identification skills that enable readers to comprehend what they read. Competent and flexible readers do not rely heavily on any one skill; they use various clues in combination. In teaching word identification skills, remember the following principles:

- Students' language background should form the basis for word-identification instruction. Small, related instructional steps increase the likelihood that students will attend to the instruction and succeed. The teacher should closely monitor each student's progress.

- Instruction should build on what children know and are successful with.

- Opportunities to apply word-identification skills in meaningful context should be part of all word-identification instruction.

- Contextual analysis should be integrated with all other word-identification instruction. By combining sight vocabulary, phonics, and structural analysis with context, children maximize their chances of determining meaning.

- Word-identification skills can be taught in a number of ways. Any technique that proves successful for a child is justifiable, provided that it does not inhibit later growth and the instructional approach is reasonably economical in time and effort expended.

- Students should not be taught to rely heavily on any one word-identification technique. Overemphasis on phonics causes children to sound out the same words hundreds of times and attempts to sound out words that do not lend themselves to letter-sound analysis, such as once, knight, freight, some, one, eight, love, know, head, move, none, have, and laugh.

- Students require varying amounts of instruction while they are learning word-identification skills. Assessment that reveals what a child knows and does not know is essential for good instruction. In the final analysis, the optimum amount of word-identification instruction for each individual is the minimum that he or she needs to become an independent reader.

YOUR POINT OF VIEW /

Discussion Questions

1. Early reading instruction inevitably causes children to develop a set relative to reading. What reading set might children develop when they receive no opportunities to apply word-identification skills in meaningful context?
2. Is it possible to teach children to rely too much on any word-identification technique? Does learning to read involve the simultaneous application of all word-identification skills? Is each a part of a unitary process called reading?
3. How do mature readers differ from beginning readers in their use of word-identification strategies?
4. What is the optimum amount for any type of word-identification instruction?
5. What role does ongoing assessment play in word-identification instruction?

Take a Stand For or Against

1. The spelling patterns found in the English language constitute a major obstacle in learning to read English.
2. Teaching sight words, letter-sound analysis, and contextual analysis at the same time inevitably leads to confusion.
3. Since a student must learn word-identification skills before becoming an independent reader, these skills should be taught before reading for meaning is stressed.

BIBLIOGRAPHY /

Adams, M. J. (1990). *Beginning to read: Thinking and learning about print.* Cambridge, MA: MIT Press

Anderson, R. C., Hiebert, E. H., Scott, J. A., & Wilkinson, I. A. G. (1985). *Becoming a nation of readers: The report of the commission on reading* (Contract No. 400-83-0057) Washington, DC: National Institute of Education.

Dolch, E. W. (1948). *Problems in reading.* Champaign, IL: Garrard Press.

Downing, J. (October-December 1979). Linguistic awareness in learning to read. *Reading Today,* International Reading Association Newsletter, p. 2.

Durrell, D. D., & Murphy, H. A. (1978). A prereading phonics inventory. *The Reading Teacher, 31,* 385–390.

Eeds-Kneip, M. (1979). The frenetic frantic phonic backlash. *Language Arts, 56,* 909–917.

Fowler, A. E. (1992). How early phonological development might set the stage for phoneme awareness. In S. Brady & D. Shankweiler (Eds.), *Phonological processes in literacy* (pp. 97–118). Hillside, NJ: Lawrence Erlbaum Associates.

Heilman, A. W. (1992). *Phonics in proper perspective* (7th ed.). New York: Merrill/Macmillan Publishing Co.

Johnson, D. D., & Pearson, P. D. (1984). *Teaching reading vocabulary* (2nd ed). New York: Holt, Rinehart & Winston.

Juel, C. (1991). Beginning reading. In R. Barr, M. L. Kamil, P. B. Mosenthal, & P. D. Pearson (Eds.), *Handbook of reading research* (Vol. II) (pp. 759–788). New York: Longman.

Lehr, F. (1980). ERIC/RCS: Content reading instruction in the elementary school. *The Reading Teacher, 33,* 888–891.

Palmer, B. C. (1986). Is the Dolch list of 220 sight words still relevant? *Reading Improvement, 23,* 227–230.

Pollard, R. S. (1889). *Pollard's synthetic method.* Chicago: Western Publishing House.

Rupley, W. H., & Blair, T. R. (1988). *Teaching reading: Diagnosis, direct instruction, and practice* (2nd ed.). New York: Merrill/Macmillan Publishing Company.

Rupley, W. H., & Blair, T. R. (1989). *Reading diagnosis and remediation: Classroom and clinic* (3rd ed.). New York: Merrill/Macmillan Publishing Co.

Samuels, S. J. (1979). The method of repeated readings. *The Reading Teacher, 32,* 403–408.

Stahl, S. A. (1992). Saying the "p" word: Nine guidelines for exemplary phonics instruction. *The Reading Teacher, 45,* 618–625.

Taylor, B. M., & Nosbush, L. (1983). Oral reading for meaning: A technique for improving word identification skills. *The Reading Teacher, 39,* 234–237.

Walker, B. J. (1992). *Diagnostic teaching of reading: Techniques for instruction and assessment.* (2nd ed.) New York: Merrill/Macmillan Publishing Co.

Yopp, Y. K. (1992). Developing phonemic awareness in young children. *The Reading Teacher, 45,* 696–707.

5

Meaning Vocabulary

For the Reader

As you read this book, you probably encounter words that are either new to you or different in meaning from those with which you are familiar. You may figure out the meanings of these words by using context or a dictionary, or by asking someone. The meanings of words in written language are essential for comprehension. Meaning vocabulary can be thought of as hooks for our background knowledge and our concepts about the world. Thus, the broader our vocabularies, the better able we are to interact with and understand text.

The importance of vocabulary in reading has long been a major concern of researchers. Yet questions about how best to teach and expand vocabulary have not been fully answered (Beck & McKeown, 1991). Some researchers believe that vocabulary cannot be directly taught because students encounter so many new words in their reading (Anderson & Nagy, 1991). Other researchers believe that vocabulary instruction helps foster vocabulary development (Beck, McKeown, & Omanson, 1990; Stahl & Fairbanks, 1986) and that direct instruction can improve reading performance.

This chapter recognizes both viewpoints. It advocates direct/explicit instruction (see Chapter 6), wide reading (see Chapters 3, 7, and 9) and language-building activities (see Chapters 6, 7, and 9) to reinforce and extend students' meaning vocabularies.

Key Ideas

- Vocabulary is a major factor contributing to reading comprehension.
- Associating experiences and concepts with words contributes significantly to reading comprehension.
- Effective vocabulary instruction helps students relate new words to their background knowledge.
- Providing varied opportunities to encounter and practice new words is a key factor in promoting vocabulary growth.
- Engaging students in active discussion of new words is critical to promoting vocabulary growth.
- Semantic-features analysis can help students understand relationships among words and relate their background knowledge to new words.

Key Terms

meaning vocabulary   words whose meanings and concepts are represented by words already understood.

definitional knowledge   word knowledge based upon a definition from a dictionary or glossary.

contextual knowledge   word knowledge derived from context.

affixes   prefixes, suffixes, and inflectional endings.

modeling   demonstration of strategies and behaviors to enhance their conceptualization.

polysemous words   words having different meanings (such as *air* in *air ball* and to *air one's views*).

homonyms   words that sound alike but are spelled differently.

VOCABULARY KNOWLEDGE

As discussed throughout this book, reading is an interactive process of constructing meaning. Meaning derived from reading depends upon the reader's automatic word-recognition capabilities, purpose, strategies for monitoring performance, setting, and experiential and conceptual backgrounds. Vocabulary is a major factor contributing to reading comprehension (Anderson & Nagy, 1991; Stahl, Hare, Sinatra, & Gregory, 1991). The words that readers know represent the concepts and information available to help them make sense of what they read. As Nagy (1988) stated, "Vocabulary knowledge is fundamental to reading comprehension; one can't understand text without knowing what most of the words mean."

THE ROLE OF VOCABULARY IN THE INTERACTIVE VIEW OF READING

Identifying words automatically and using background knowledge to construct meaning for the text are important features of the interactive view of reading. Word meanings are the most important background knowledge for comprehension (Stanovich, 1986). Readers can use whole-word recognition, pronunciation of words through the use of phonics, and structural analysis and knowledge of word order (syntax) but still not determine text meaning unless they know meanings for the individual words.

Language Development and Word Meanings

The foundation of word-meaning development is the continuous development of language ability. Readers and writers share meanings. We acquire meanings through concrete experiences with people, places, objects, and events that build and refine vocabulary. Vicarious experiences, including pictures, films, filmstrips, reading, and writing, serve similar purposes in vocabulary development.

Increasing one's vocabulary is much more than learning names to associate with experiences. The development of a student's *meaning vocabulary* closely reflects the breadth of the student's real-life and vicarious experiences. Without prior knowledge of concepts the words represent, students cannot construct meaning. Essentially, the author and the reader share vocabulary.

Knowing Words

Knowing words can range from a simple level to a complex level (Miller & Gildea, 1987). A simple level of word knowledge may be definitional. *Definitional knowledge* is word knowledge based upon a definition from a dictionary or glossary. Often, however, definitions found in dictionaries and glossaries do not help a reader understand the contribution of an unknown word to meaning. To comprehend, a reader needs some idea of not only a word's meaning but also the ways the meaning contributes to the concepts represented (Miller & Gildea, 1987). The simple level of word knowledge may also be contextual. *Contextual knowledge* is word meaning derived from context. However, contextual clues have limitations, because using them requires some knowledge of the context and how the meaning of the words combines to facilitate author and reader interaction. As pointed out by Beck, McKeown, & Omanson (1990) in a review of vocabulary acquisition, "Simply put, knowing a word is not an all-or-nothing proposition: it is not the case that one either knows or does not know a word. Rather, knowledge of a word should be viewed in terms of the extent or degree of knowledge that people can possess" (p. 791).

Although knowing a word at a simple level can help readers construct meaning for text, such knowledge has limited value in promoting vocabulary growth. Both definitional and contextual features of vocabulary instruction can be part of an effective program, but in isolation, they have limited potential in increasing students' word knowledge. However, combining definitional and contextual approaches does help students develop a meaning vocabulary.

Knowing a word in its fullest sense goes beyond simply being able to define the word or get some gist of it from the context (Pearson, 1985). Associating experiences and concepts with words contributes significantly to comprehension (Nagy, Anderson, & Herman, 1987).

Vocabulary and Concept Development

Readers' experiential and conceptual backgrounds are extremely important in vocabulary development. Background experiences enable readers to develop, expand, and refine the concepts that words represent. Vocabulary knowledge is developmental and is related to background experiences. Tennyson and Cocchiarella (1986) note two phases in the learning of concepts. The first phase is the formation of concepts in relation to attributes (which they refer to as prototypes), making connections with existing concepts. The second phase is using procedural knowledge, which is "the classification skills of generalizing to and discriminating between newly encountered instances of associated concepts" (p. 44). In phase 1, individuals may undergeneralize or overgeneralize due to their limited experiences with the concept. This is often evident in young children when, for example, they call horses cows and all liquids for drinking are milk or juice. In phase 2, the individuals can distinguish between cows and horses and various liquids for drinking.

Vocabulary grows when the student has numerous opportunities to encounter new words and examples that are representative of the word in rich contextual settings. Individuals do not use restricted definitions of words as they engage in literacy activities, but construct meaning in terms of word meanings for the concepts that represent their background knowledge.

DIRECT/EXPLICIT VOCABULARY INSTRUCTION

The effectiveness of direct/explicit vocabulary instruction has been questioned. Teaching vocabulary versus incidental learning of words through wide reading should not be viewed as competing philosophies. Some students may not benefit from incidental learning but do benefit from instruction that initially teaches word meaning in application in meaningful text (Kameenui, Dixon, & Carnine, 1987; McKeown, 1993). Much of the criticism leveled at vocabulary teaching concerns practices in which students define words using a dictionary and write sentences for those words. Such practices must be called into question because they fail to teach words so that students encounter the words in meaningful text. Teaching vocabulary within the context of real books can promote vocabulary development.

Vocabulary emphasis should include direct/explicit instruction and appropriate practice in specific skills along with the opportunity for wide reading, writing, and other language activities. We are not recommending that practice activities be unrelated to authentic reading and writing opportunities. Rather, some students—particularly those having difficulty in literacy learning—need to practice vocabulary. As noted earlier, context does not guarantee word learning, because students must be able to recognize enough of the words to construct meaning and to use context effectively as a clue to word meaning. Wide reading and writing will provide students with many opportunities to learn new words in contextual settings; however, direct teaching of vocabulary has a place.

Beck and McKeown, (1991), Blachowicz and Lee (1991), and Maranzo and Maranzo, (1988) recommend basic guidelines for teaching vocabulary.

1. Choose words for vocabulary instruction that come from contextual reading (literary and content texts) to be done in the classroom.

2. Use direct vocabulary instruction to take advantage of the many forms (such as mental pictures, kinesthetic associations, smells, and tastes) used to store word knowledge.

3. Build a conceptual base for word learning. Use analogies, language features, characteristics (sets, e.g., a horse is an animal), and relationships to known words (such as relating newspapers, magazines, and catalogs as information sources that can be read or looked at selectively) to activate students' background knowledge of concepts and to relate new words.

4. Provide opportunities for students to engage in language-based activities (e.g., recreational reading, writing, and creative dramatics). This should be the primary means of vocabulary learning. Foster the learning of new words that are not taught directly. Provide opportunities for students to use new words in the classroom in their speaking, listening, reading, and writing activities.

5. Generate learning of new words by helping students develop strategies associated wtih structural features of words (combining roots and adding prefixes and suffixes).

Vocabulary emphasis should include direct/explicit instruction and appropriate practice in specific skills along with broad reading opportunities and other language activities. Vocabulary instruction is most effective when it relates new words or derivations of words to existing vocabulary and background knowledge. For example, a student who thinks that all animals are pets would have a difficult time with the concepts of farm animals and zoo animals. Sending this student to a dictionary or listing words on the chalkboard would be ineffective in

Wide reading and writing will provide students with many opportunities to learn new words.

teaching the vocabulary words associated with milk cows, farm life, or zoo animals. Imagine the possible comprehension problems the student might experience when encountering such words as Hereford, hedgehog, or grizzly bear.

Semantic Mapping

Semantic mapping incorporates many of the guidelines for vocabulary teaching and enables students to expand their vocabularies, understand relationships between existing and new concepts, understand multiple meanings of words, and learn actively. Semantic mapping structures information categorically so that students can more readily see relationships between new words and concepts and their existing background knowledge.

Semantic mapping can be used for preteaching essential concepts and information for content area text before students read. Upon completion of the semantic map, the teacher discusses with the students how the new vocabulary words relate to words that they already know. Students thus understand better the content of the topic they will cover or the story they will read. Figure 5.1 presents an example of a semantic map for the topic of precipitation and illustrates how teaching certain words prior to reading can help students activate their background knowledge, relate existing knowledge to new concepts, and under-

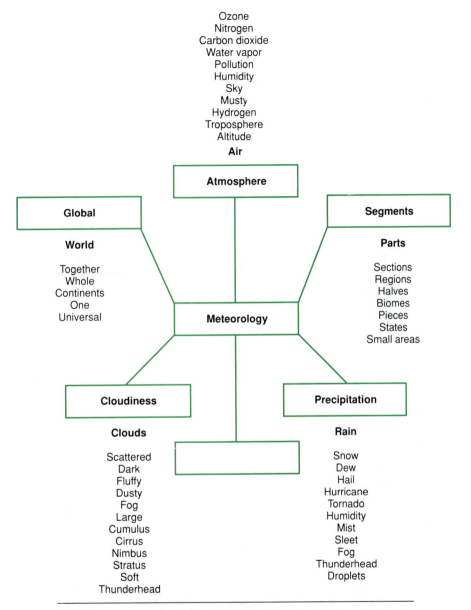

Ozone
Nitrogen
Carbon dioxide
Water vapor
Pollution
Humidity
Sky
Musty
Hydrogen
Troposphere
Altitude
Air

Atmosphere

Global

World

Together
Whole
Continents
One
Universal

Segments

Parts

Sections
Regions
Halves
Biomes
Pieces
States
Small areas

Meteorology

Cloudiness

Clouds

Scattered
Dark
Fluffy
Dusty
Fog
Large
Cumulus
Cirrus
Nimbus
Stratus
Soft
Thunderhead

Precipitation

Rain

Snow
Dew
Hail
Hurricane
Tornado
Humidity
Mist
Sleet
Fog
Thunderhead
Droplets

Words in boxes were taught directly. Bold faced words were given to students. Light faced words were contributed by students during discussion in the full map treatment; some had been taught in the preceding lesson on Clouds (*cumulus, cirrus, nimbus, stratus, water vapor, humidity*). The blank box was for students to fill in a new category during their reading.

FIGURE 5.1

A completed semantic map for precipitation

(From S. A. Stahl and S. J. Vancil, "Discussion Is What Makes Semantic Maps Work in Vocabulary Instruction," *The Reading Teacher, 40* [Oct. 1986], p. 63. Reprinted with permission of Steven A. Stahl and Sandra Vancil and the International Reading Association.)

stand how new words and concepts are related. Teachers should encourage class discussion by relating students' past reading and direct experiences to the semantic map. In discussing the semantic map, students must think about the relationships between the target word and their experiences.

The procedure for developing a semantic map for vocabulary instruction includes:

- Selecting a word that is central to a topic or story.
- Writing the central word on the chalkboard or a chart.
- Brainstorming words related to the central theme or topic and writing these words.
- Grouping the words into categories and labeling these categories.
- Noting additional words essential to the topic and placing these additional words in the appropriate categories.

A variation of semantic mapping is a procedure that Schwartz and Raphael (1985) devised to help students develop a concept of definition. They recommend direct instruction considering three questions about a concept being studied: (1) What is it? (2) What is it like? and (3) What are some examples? The procedure is for students in grades 4 and above. Conducted over several instructional periods, its basic features include introduction and refinement of the strategy, further refinement, and writing a definition.

Introducing the Strategy. Introduce students to the idea that they can develop a new strategy to aid them in the reading process. Focus on what they will learn, why it is important, and what they will be doing. Following the general introduction, introduce the word map (see Figure 5.2) and organize familiar information in terms of the three questions. Model the procedures for organizing the information by thinking aloud. Then have students complete independent activities, mapping given words and a word of their choice. After mapping, have the students use the information to verbalize a definition with the class.

Refining the Strategy. Following the introduction, give the students sentences that provide at least one class (What is it?), three properties (What is it like?), and three examples. Discuss the sentences with the students and mark (check, circle, or underline) the types of information necessary to map the information. Following this mapping, have students provide oral or written definitions for the given concepts. Help them realize that they need not always identify three properties or three examples; they may use fewer or more in understanding the word.

Further Refining the Concept. Use context that is less complete than that used in step 2. Encourage students to use sources of word meanings (such as dictionaries, encyclopedias, and textbooks) to complete their word maps. Encourage them to discuss the concepts, using their background knowledge and the other sources of information.

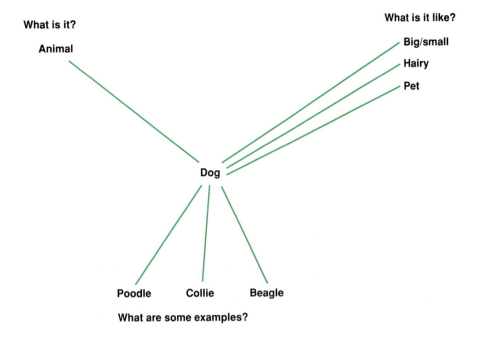

What is it?

Animal

What is it like?

Big/small

Hairy

Pet

Dog

Poodle   Collie   Beagle

What are some examples?

FIGURE 5.2

A concept-of-definition word map

(Adapted from R. M. Schwartz and T. E. Raphael, "Concept of Definition: A Key to Improving Students' Vocabulary," *The Reading Teacher, 39* [1985], p. 201.)

Writing a Definition. Use all of the mapping components without using a map. This is an internalization. Ask the students to evaluate the completeness of given definitions. If definitions are incomplete, have the students write whatever additional information is needed.

Schwartz and Raphael (1985) found that the students in their study could write more elaborate definitions than students who did not receive the concept-of-definition instruction. Furthermore, the students understand better how to figure out the meaning of a new word. The procedure helps teachers provide students with opportunities to discuss new concepts, and discussion appears to be a key in promoting active thinking about words.

Webbing

Webbing is similar to semantic mapping and word mapping. It graphically illustrates how to associate words meaningfully. Words or concepts selected for use in webbing can come from materials students have read, or webs can be used to introduce students to new concepts in both literary and content texts. Figure 5.3 presents a teacher-directed lesson using webbing to introduce first graders to a unit on machines that help us do our work. Students can be introduced to the different kinds of machines they will read about through a teacher-directed dis-

■ **Area of Needed Reading Instruction**

Ability to develop and understand meaningful vocabulary.

■ **Intended Learning Outcome**

Students will construct a web of meaningful word associations from a word source selected by the classroom teacher.

■ **Past Learning**

Students understand that words can be associated with groups of related words to construct a web of meaningful information.

Students can draw inferences and meanings from words and word associations.

■ **Building Background**

Demonstrate word associations by writing a familiar phrase on the chalkboard and asking students to help you construct a web of word associations that center on a particular theme.

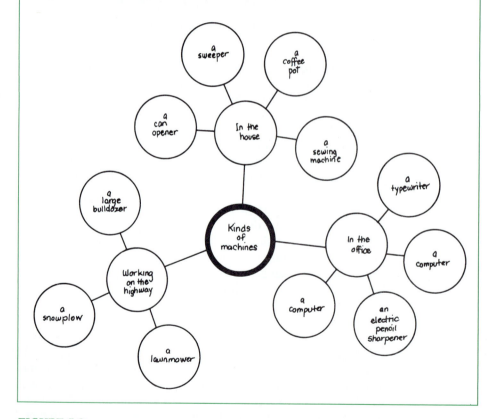

FIGURE 5.3

A teacher-directed lesson using webbing

(Reprinted with the permission of Macmillan Publishing Company from *Teaching Reading: Diagnosis, Direct Instruction, and Practice,* Second Edition by William H. Rupley and Timothy R. Blair. Copyright © 1988 by Macmillan Publishing Company.)

Use the web as an example to show how to associate words with other words and word meanings. Guide discussion to add more meaningful word associations to the web. Discuss with students how the web of word associations is one way to show relationships among word meanings. Remind students that they will have an opportunity to construct their own web of related word associations following the lesson.

■ Teacher-Directed Instruction

Provide students with a second web of word associations dealing with a familiar theme. In this instance, do not write the theme in the center of the word-association web. Have students use the word associations listed in the web to infer the theme of the web.

For example, construct the following word association web and allow students to infer the theme—colors.

Stress that words in a web of word associations must relate to the word phrase in the center of the web if the web is to make sense. Remind them that in the webs drawn on the chalkboard in this lesson, all the words can be directly associated with the center word.

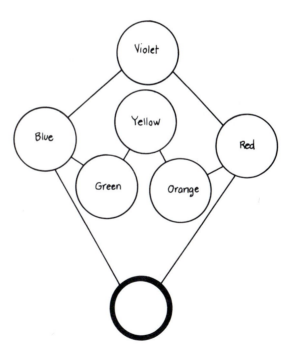

FIGURE 5.3
Continued

FIGURE 5.3

Continued

■ **Independent Student Practice**

Allow students to construct their own webs of word associations. Prepare a handout showing a word that you select at the center of the web.

Put one or two written examples on the web to make sure that all students understand the activity.

■ **Ongoing Diagnosis**

Teacher evaluation of students' individual word-association webs. Interview students about why they included certain words and why their choices were associated with the other words in the web. (Such information will provide insight into how students use their experiential backgrounds and reasoning strategies in identifying words.)

■ **Modifying Instruction**

The activity can be used as an independent instructional activity for groups of students who have difficulty constructing webs. For example, hand out a web that has several of the circles already filled in and has a few blank circles for students to complete. This procedure maximizes students' chances of success. Webbing words and word phrases can be used in content-area reading as well and can encompass historical events, science terminology and activities, social studies concepts, and so forth. Webs can also be given to students before they read to give them an overview of important text elements and essential relationships found in their reading materials.

An additional variation of this activity is to provide students with webs and to direct them to write short stories that expand on the relationships illustrated by the webs.

cussion about home, highway, and office machines. Follow-up activities can also be done by referring back to the web and discussing how machines make work easier, writing stories about machines the students could invent, and constructing their own webs of association after reading the text. To ensure that students understand the features and purposes of webbing, the teacher can use a web with an empty center. Students can better begin to understand the relationship of words in the web by selecting and discussing words that might complete the center word. For example, the color web could be related to leaves, crayons, automobiles, fruits, flowers, and so forth.

Semantic-Features Analysis

Semantic-features analysis can help students understand relationships among words and relate their background knowledge to the new words (Johnson & Pearson, 1984). Figure 5.4 is an example. Semantic-features analysis is most appropriate for words related by class or common feature.

	Enjoyment	Information	Buying	Current Events	Sports
Books	+	+	0	−	0
Newspapers	+	+	+	+	+
Magazines	+	+	0	+	0
Catalogs	+	+	+	−	0
Brochures	+	+	0	+	0

Key: present (+), absent (−), sometimes (0).

FIGURE 5.4
A semantic-features analysis

To analyze, list several familiar words that are related (such as books, newspapers, magazines, catalogs, and brochures) on the chalkboard or a chart. Direct the students to discuss features associated with the words listed. As the students suggest features, write them across the top of the board or chart, creating a matrix that the students can complete in terms of present (+), or absent (−), and sometimes (0). As the students broaden and define their concepts, the teacher adds words and features to the list and analyzes them. Semantic-features analysis can be used with narrative reading materials to analyze characters, settings, plots, and so forth. It is also effective in the content areas when introducing new topics, reviewing topics, and integrating topics across different content areas. The matrices can be refined and expanded as students' experiential and conceptual backgrounds grow (Anders & Bos, 1986).

Teaching Relationships Among Words

To help students understand the relationships among given words, use words that differ in degree (such as tiny, minute, and small) and ask students to discuss them and generate other words that fit the examples (Nagy, 1988). A variety of procedures can teach relationships among words. A good source for choosing words for this activity is shared-literature study (Iwicki, 1992). A discussion of shared literature is presented in Chapter 3. By building connections between "old" vocabulary words and words found in their new books, students begin to understand relationships among words they encounter in reading. For example, students are not just asked to supply words that fit the example but rather to describe how the word fits in the stories they have read. Donald just finished reading *The Last Dinosaur* and used *enormous* to describe the size of the dinosaur. His teacher asked Matthew if he thought that Paul Bunyan could be described as enormous, too. Matthew responded by saying, "He was enormous because he was a giant, larger than anyone else." Such practice activities that relate new words and concepts to past readings and discuss them in relation to authentic text are helping to expand students' vocabularies meaningfully.

INSTRUCTIONAL ACTIVITIES

■ *Understanding Relationships Among Words.* Give students several words that are related and ask them to identify others appropriate to the given words. The words supplied by the students can be similar or opposite in meaning and should be based on their reading of stories and books, as noted earlier.

Similar meanings can include:

big, huge, . . . (giant, large, enormous)

small, tiny, . . . (minute, wee, little)

Opposite meanings can include:

big, huge, . . . (small, tiny, minute)

Shout, yell, . . . (whisper, soft, quiet)

Combinations of meaning can include:

big, small, . . . (giant, little, enormous)

shout, whisper, . . . (yell, soft, quiet)

Ask students to provide context and write their context sentence for each of the words. After the students understand the relationships between the words, have them provide additional words that retain similar meaning in the sentences. The following example is based on a story the children had read that focused on the concepts associated with big and small:

In the story, *Our Little Wonder,* Rich and Robbie got a pet tiger kitten. It was so _____ that they could hold it in their hands. They thought about the mother tiger and wondered how such a little thing could grow up to be so _____.

Students can supply words that relate to other stories they have read about size. For example, Donald might use the word *enormous* to describe the mother cat, while Matthew might choose the word *giant* to describe her. Teachers can direct students to think about words that are opposite of those supplied for either sentence. Words such as *minute, tiny, little,* and so forth could be used to complete the first sentence.

Develop additional activities around the concept of related words. For example, write the word *release* on the board. Ask the students to discuss words that are related in meaning and list them on the board. Then, ask students to discuss words that are different in meaning and list them. Have them discuss why they listed a word in a particular column. For example:

Related	*Different*
free	grasp
dismiss	hold
	clutch
	capture
	keep

Use sentences to illustrate the different meanings. Note the changes in meaning for the words substituted for *release.* Again encourage students to use their knowledge of stories they have read to construct sentences for the words. Discuss with them how the meaning changes depending on which word is used in the sentence.

John decided to *free* the bird.

John decided to *grasp* the bird.

John decided to *capture* the bird.

John decided to *keep* the bird.

Compare related words for sentence comprehension. Ask the students to read sets of sentences and determine if they have similar meanings. Have them write S on the line to indicate that sentences communicate similar meaning, and have them write *D* to show that they have different meaning. Complete one or two examples with the students to make sure that they understand the task and will succeed at it.

_____ 1. Bill took his dog for a ride in the car.
Bill took his dog for a ride in the park.

_____ 2. The park is not far from Bill's house.
The park is close to Bill's house.

_____ 3. The park has an enormous field where Bill's dog can play.
The park has a minute area where Bill's dog can play.

Additional practice activities and games can be found in the Appendix.

Generative Reading Vocabulary Instruction

Generative reading vocabulary instruction is designed to enable students to learn the meanings of several related words (Fillmer, 1977). This approach enables students to add to their existing knowledge backgrounds and to understand relationships between the concepts that words represent.

This approach can be followed in teaching synonyms, antonyms, context clues, roots, prefixes, suffixes, and concept classifications (such as animals, size, actions, and story themes). This strategy applies to all school subjects. Following are a few suggested activities to help promote meaningful word growth.

INSTRUCTIONAL ACTIVITIES

■ ***Associating Words with Known Concepts in Context.*** Keep an accurate list of new words that students encounter and learn. Words from their reading of literature, content texts, or interest areas; words that contain the same root, prefix, or suffix; and words in concept classifications can form the basis for expanding meaning vocabularies. Teach new words by relating them to similar words the students already know.

In content areas, such as mathematics, relate new words to known concepts in meaningful context, using examples in the students' background knowledge. For example, relate as in the following:

plus	1. 4 *plus* 4 equals 8.
equals	
sum	2. 8 is the *sum* of 4
add together	plus 4.
total	
	3. We *add* 4 and 4
	together to get a
	total of 8.

In interest areas, such as basketball, relate new words to the concept in a meaningful context. For example, relate *court, score, second, scoreboard, bounce, shot, shoot, dribble, foul, rebound, time out,* and *rim*.

■ **Using Categories for Classification of Words.** Relate new words to words already known for new word categories. For example, using basketball, illustrate word relationships with the same roots, prefixes, and suffixes.

Roots	*Prefixes*	*Suffixes*
basket*ball*	*re*bound	dribbl*ing*, dribbl*ed*
base*ball*	*re*take	jump*ing*, jump*ed*
foot*ball*	*re*make	scor*ing*, scor*ed*

Classify words that students know from their reading of literature and basal stories in terms of similar properties and introduce new words that relate to the known properties. For example, a thematic unit on farm life might use the following:

Animals	*Farm Animals*	*Pets*	*Animal Sounds*	*Animal Sizes*
pig	pig	—	pig—oink, grunt	enormous pig
cow	cow	—	cow—moo, low	huge cow
sheep	sheep	—	sheep—baa, bleat	large sheep
goat	goat	—	goat—baa, bleat	big goat
cat	cat	cat	cat—meow, hiss	small cat
dog	dog	dog	dog—bark, growl	tiny dog, little dog, great dog

INSTRUCTIONAL ACTIVITIES

■ **Structural Analysis.** Develop instructional activities for the area of structural analysis. Teach **affixes** (prefixes, suffixes, and inflectional endings) to help students relate the new to what they know. Using word families (derivations of known words such as depend—dependable, undependable, dependent, independent) can enhance understanding of the meaning relationships among derived words within a family and promote independent word learning.

Introduce prefixes and their effects on meaning by presenting sentences containing prefixes. Focus students' attention on what happens to the meaning of a known word when a specific prefix is used. Once the students understand the task, have them read the rest of a given story or use one that they have read and select the words that make sense in context. The following story illustrates the use of the prefix un-:

Jason met a kind man on his trip to town. The kind man was named Farmer John. Farmer John was kind to everyone, even Jack, who was not very friendly or kind.

Jason had never met anyone who was as unkind and unfriendly as Jack. Jason helped Farmer John load his wagon with hay. Jason and Farmer John took the wagon to town to sell the hay.

Farmer John's _____ friend went with them. Jason had to
           (kind, unkind)

walk beside the wagon. He thought that it was _____ that he
                                  (fair, unfair)

had to walk and Farmer John and his _____ friend rode in
                            (kind, unkind)

the wagon. Jason knew that the _____ Jack would not help
                        (kind, unkind)

them _____ the wagon when they got to town.
    (load, unload)

When students express an interest in word building using roots, prefixes, and suffixes, construct activities to extend their understanding of word families and the effect that affixes have on word meaning. To build words, read the definition for a word that you already know (it is important that students have meaning for the base word). Then think about what you know about the prefixes and suffixes. Give short definitions to make new words. Do one or two examples with students to make sure that they will be able to do the task. For example:

depend: to rely on (clues: *in-, un-, -able, -ent*)

depend
_____: trustworthy, reliable

        depend
_____: not trustworthy, not reliable

        depend
_____: self-reliant, doing things oneself

depend
_____: relying on someone else, unable to do things oneself

agree: to consent to (clues: *dis-, -able, -ment*)

       agree
_____: a quarrel or argument

agree
_____: pleasing, pleasant

_____ agree _____: not pleasing, unpleasant

agree
_____: a contract or an understanding

Provide opportunities for students to apply different prefixes in meaningful context. Progress from sentences to longer passages to ensure a high degree of success. Depending on students' needs, the teacher can introduce the activity with sentences and then proceed to using connected text from stories that the children have read.

Bob isn't able to go to the football game with me.

Bob is _____ to go to the football game with me.
          (able, unable)

The teacher said to read the story again.

The teacher said to _____ the story.
          (read, reread)

Susan gave Billy a glass of milk. Billy drank all of it and asked for more.

Susan _____ his glass and said, "This is all of the milk."
          (filled, refilled)

Billy yelled, "It's _____ that Donald got three glasses of milk
          (fair, unfair)
and I got just two."

Donald said, "It's _____ of you to yell at Susan."
          (kind, unkind)

Susan _____, "You are a(n) _____ person, Billy,
      (agreed, disagreed)   (kind, unkind)
when you yell at me."

Contextual Approaches

Often, a single sentence has inadequate context for students to use their prior knowledge to comprehend the meaning of a word. Consider the following sentence: _Fennecs were crouched behind several small bushes waiting for any type of prey to come along the path to the water hole._ Are fennecs people or animals?

Most likely, you must guess what a fennec is because the sentence does not provide enough information to allow you to use your background knowledge. If they know fennecs are animals, readers can use their knowledge of animals. If they know fennecs are wild animals, readers can use their knowledge of wild animals. Knowing that they are wild, fawn-colored animals with large ears may help readers form an even better understanding of fennecs. Furthermore, readers who are aware that fennecs are African foxes can use their knowledge of foxes to make sense of the sentence. Sufficient natural context is often essential in teaching word meaning. To be effective, vocabulary instruction must enable students to formulate an adequate definition from a natural sounding context (Nagy, 1988).

Teachers frequently use contextual analysis to help students independently identify unknown words. As Nagy (1988) notes, "There is no doubt that skilled word learners use context and their knowledge of prefixes, roots, and suffixes to deal effectively with new words" (p. 23). Skilled readers integrate what they have read to construct meaning. If context is not enough to explain an unknown word, skilled readers may use their knowledge of prefixes, suffixes, and root words to determine the meaning. They perform these operations so rapidly and automatically that they are not aware of them. If they cannot determine the meaning of a word, they may reason that it is not important to know the word and continue reading the text.

Knowledge of what skilled readers do when encountering unknown words has direct implications for teachers. In learning to use context, students must understand how their knowledge of content can help them determine meanings of unknown words. However, context does not always provide total understanding, and often it may mislead.

Contextual analysis is best taught by guided practice in which the teacher models the procedure and uses familiar written examples. **Modeling** means that the teacher thinks out loud, thus providing instruction in strategies to use in real reading situations. Class discussions with students about how they derive word meanings from context and what they do if context does not work help them understand the strengths and limitations of the process.

An illustration of modeling the use of context clues follows. Assume that we read a sentence containing an unknown word: Jack was sure his _____ would let him go. This is the opening line of a story, and the author has yet to unfold the plot or background. Many words might complete the idea when this is all we know. Is Jack being held prisoner? The word could be *captors.* Is he thinking of getting permission? The word might be *mother, father, friends,* or *teacher.*

If we note something about the unknown word, we may get a valuable clue. For instance, in "Jack was sure his p_____ would let him go," *mother, father, teacher,* and *friends* can be eliminated because of the initial letter clue, but several possibilities remain, such as *pal, playmates,* and *parents.*

When the sentence does not provide contextual clues, we can read further to see if additional text provides the information. As we read on, we discover the context: *Mother* and *father* both agreed that they would let Jack go to the game. Thinking about the unknown word in the earlier sentence leads us to recognize it as *parents,* because the later sentence refers to *mother* and *father,* who are parents.

Rarely does a sentence alone provide sufficient context to unlock the meaning of unknown words. For example, "Although their sojourn was brief, it was enjoyable," "It was a moot point and the judge did not allow it," and "Most teachers today use an eclectic approach for teaching reading." If we consider the context supplied both before and after the unknown word, the meaning is more likely to be revealed.

In " 'It's my _____,' said Donald," a number of possibilities occur—my *idea, turn, opinion* or possession such as *bike, bat, ball,* or *saxophone.* As we consider the following context, the unknown word falls into place.

Discussions with students about how they derive word meanings help them to develop strategies.

The boys searched everywhere, but they did not find the lost puppy. "I hope Zach doesn't get hit by a car," said Billy. Donald was very worried. He had been thinking all afternoon about not closing the gate when he went to play ball. The puppy must have gotten out when he left the gate open. "It's my *fault*," said Donald. Then he told about leaving the gate open.

Such examples can help students better use contextual analysis to get meaning from unknown words.

Different Meanings for the Same Word

Some words have more than one meaning. Such words are called **polysemous words**. In early language development, students master the concrete levels of understanding before the abstract. Students may know such words as *air, blue, mine, broadcast,* and *fence,* but they can know several meanings for each word and still not be familiar with many others.

Students probably will have no difficulties with the following meanings for the word *air:*

My daddy puts *air* in the tires.

We hang our clothes outside to *air* them.

We breathe *air*.

The same students, however, may be confused by the following meanings:

. . . that Mrs. Jones is disliked because she puts on *airs.*

. . . if asked to *air* her view.

. . . that was an *air* ball.

Students may understand *blue* means in "The boy had a *blue* coat" but not be familiar with "The boy felt *blue* when his aunt left." They may understand "Grandfather rode the *horse*" but not "The coach warned the boys not to *horse* around," "That's a *horse* of a different color," or "The mayor accused the council of beating a dead *horse.*"

The relationships of words to each other and the subtle meanings that the same word conveys depend upon the context in which a word appears and the reader's background experiences. Broad reading and language-based experiences can broaden meaning vocabularies. Following are several activities for promoting students' interest in vocabulary development. They illustrate the importance of context in defining words.

INSTRUCTIONAL ACTIVITIES

■ *Deriving Word Meanings Through Use in Context.* Learning meanings can be fascinating and highly motivating. Help students realize that many words have several different meanings according to how they are used. Illustrate this concept with simple words (such as *can, stick, run,* and *set*). As you ask for different usages, write the students' responses on the board or a chart. At the same time, attempt to fix the various meanings by using other words and concepts from stories the students have read and their experiential/conceptual backgrounds. For example:

I *can* spell my name. *(Can* means *able.)*

I bought a *can* of soup. *(Can* means *a container.)*

Mother is going to *can* some peaches. *(Can* means *to preserve.)*

Use some other examples for the word *can,* depending upon students' background knowledge:

Can it Joe. *(Stop talking.)*

If you are late one more time the boss will *can* you. *(Dismiss from a job)*

Why don't you trade in that old tin *can* and get a new car? *(A battered old car)*

After several group activities stressing different meanings, not simply different sentences, present written activities. Give words to illustrate different usages. Develop this activity around a word map, as discussed earlier.

This activity can provide information about students' background knowledge, writing capabilities, and ability to generalize word meanings. Furthermore, it is highly motivating; it can promote interest in expanding word knowledge.

Homonyms

The relationships between homonyms are not so apparent as are those between words that are similar or opposite in meaning. **Homonyms** are words that sound exactly alike but are spelled differently. Many common homonyms look very much alike (such as *their/there, see/sea, hear/here,* and *course/coarse*), so young readers have problems with both whole word recognition and meanings.

INSTRUCTIONAL ACTIVITIES

■ ***Using Contextual Analysis with Homonyms.*** To expand both sight and meaning vocabularies, list homonyms in columns. On the left, put the word that the students are most likely to be familiar with. Discuss the meanings of the words in the right column to determine the students' understanding. Context plays an important role for homonyms because it provides information for comprehension.

Use the cloze-maze technique for instruction activities. Give students written sentences appropriate to their language backgrounds and ask them to identify the words that make sense in the sentences. For example:

The _____ made the grass shine in the sunlight.
     (do, dew)

Mother had to _____ the apples at the store before she
       (way, weigh)
bought them.

The basketball team that _____ the game was from our town.
       (one, won)

Working with homonyms can be enjoyable and motivating for students. It can help them understand the influence that context has on word meaning. It also can help them use context to understand the contributions that words make to meaning. Once students have grasped the concept of homonyms, point out other examples in their reading of authentic text and focus discussion on how the context provides them with a strategy for determining the meaning of the word.

LANGUAGE-BASED APPROACHES

Providing varied reading, writing, and language-based activities can contribute significantly to vocabulary development. Language-based activities help develop automaticity in word-recognition strategies using word knowledge and experiential and conceptual backgrounds.

Independent Reading Programs

Teachers can use numerous techniques to promote independent reading. The essential point is to allocate time for students to read on their own. Ways to promote independent reading include bookselling sessions, class book fairs, reading aloud to students on a regular basis, creating a book corner in the classroom, using children's literature, and having free-reading sessions daily.

Noah Webster's Blue-backed *Speller* was one of the most widely used texts for beginning reading instruction between 1780 and the early 1800's. The *Speller* did not contain as much religious material for reading as earlier readers did and children could better relate to the reading content because of the inclusion of content that was appealing to them. Furthermore, the language and content were more appropriate to their background knowledge than that found in earlier reading instructional materials.

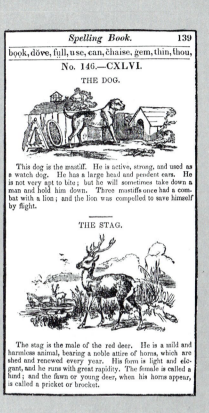

UPDATE

Today, the importance of wide reading and vocabulary instruction are recognized as important to enhancing children's vocabulary learning. However, just as Noah Webster recognized in the 1700s, teachers today realize that children need wide and varied opportunities to read text with which they can associate their experiences to expand their concepts and vocabulary. Meaning vocabulary can be thought of as the hooks on which we hang ideas and construct meaning for our reading and writing.

Providing students time to read independently is crucial to motivating them to read for pleasure. A particular time set aside each day for silent reading of self-selected materials by students and teachers is sustained silent reading (SSR), or uninterrupted sustained silent reading (USSR). This activity should stress enjoyment of reading materials, so students should not be required to report on this reading. SSR can stimulate students' independent reading, but just allowing time to read is not enough. Students need access to a variety of reading materials. The materials can include literature books, magazines, newspapers, and travel brochures. Some students may need help in locating interesting reading materials, and others may need direction in terms of their responsibilities during the reading period. Teacher guidance and assistance are extremely important in the beginning reading program.

In the beginning reading program, teachers can motivate independent reading in a variety of ways. One way is to use audiotape recorders to tape children's books. Students can help select the books to be taped if they are given a brief overview of each book before it is recorded. When taping, teachers should read relatively slowly to ensure that pupils can make the connection between what they hear and the print that represents the language.

Once a book has been taped, students can listen to it and follow along in the text at a listening center. The teacher should help students understand what they are to do and get them started. Without proper instruction, they may just listen to the stories.

Commercially taped books and stories are also readily available. Talking books that are taped commercially can introduce students to content or the experience of literature, but teacher-prepared tapes are better for developing literature appreciation than are commercially prepared tapes.

Predictable books (see Chapters 3 and 7) help students begin to use prediction strategies as they read. This frees them from focusing on individual words. In predictable books, students can easily grasp what the author is going to say next. Such books contain much repetition of content and language structure.

Additional ways to encourage reading in the early grades include the use of big books, poetry, storytelling, reading aloud to students, learning and play centers, and creative dramatics. Discussed at length in Chapters 3 and 7, these techniques can help promote a language-rich classroom that motivates young students to enagage in literacy.

Broad reading is an integral part of the application phase of the reading program, and it is one of the basic characteristics of effective reading instruction. Opportunities for independent reading provide means for expanding vocabulary knowledge, refining and building experiential and conceptual backgrounds, and developing an interest in reading.

Writing Activities

Writing activities can motivate students to become more actively engaged in learning new words and internalizing the meanings of words. Donna Norton (1992) has identified several ways that teachers can provide rich opportunities for students to use their developing vocabularies. Among the ways she suggests to expand vocabulary knowledge are poetry writing and individualized dictionaries.

Writing poetry is an excellent means to encourage students to expand their vocabularies. Several different forms of poetry stress varying types of vocabulary. For example, haiku (discussed in Chapter 7) can be used to expand students' meaning vocabularies. Teacher assistance is important in writing haikus, which enables the teacher to present a variety of words for the same poem.

> The brown dancing bear,
> Dancing around in his cage,
> Dancing on his toes.

The teacher could help the student find other words for dancing and encourage her to think of her own. Words such as *gliding, prancing, swaying,* and *teetering* could replace dancing. The images that the different words convey can be discussed with the child, and she can illustrate them with pictures.

Another form of poetry that stresses descriptive words and action words is *cinquains.* Norton (1992) notes that students should first listen to or read numerous cinquains. Then the teacher should discuss the structure of cinquains and illustrate them for students. Following these activities, students can write their own poems. The structure of cinquins are as follows:

Line 1:   A *single word* for a title.

Line 2:   Two words to describe the title.

Line 3:   Three words to express action.

Line 4:   Four words to express feeling.

Line 5:   The title again, or word like the title.

Norton recommends that teachers and students draw a diagram for the cinquain:

> title
> describe title
> action, action, action
> feeling about the title
> title

Cinquains can be written in groups or by individual students and can characters from their reading to experiment with descriptive and action words.

Norton presented several examples of students' cinquains for books that they had read:

After reading *The Story of Ferdinand,* a group of second graders wrote this cinquain:

> Ferdinand
> Happy, strong
> Sitting, smelling, growing
> Loves to smell flowers
> Independent (p. 68)

A sixth-grade class wrote the following after reading *Johnny Tremain:*

Johnny
Brave, patriotic
Daring, delivering, riding
Made a strong commitment
Apprentice (p. 69)

Another form of poetry that encourages students to use contrasting words is *diamante.* The requirements for each line of diamante are:

Line 1:   Noun

Line 2:   Two adjectives

Line 3:   Three participles

Line 4:   Four nouns or phrases

Line 5:   Three participles noting change

Line 6:   Two adjectives

Line 7:   Contrasting noun

Norton (1992) recommends that the diamante be illustrated to denote the structure and that the teacher discuss the stucture, illustrate the terms, and read several written examples. Again, she urges the use of a written diagram to help students recall the form of the diamante:

noun
describing, describing
action, action, action
transition nouns or phrases
action, action, action
describing, describing
noun

A fourth-grade class produced the following diamante after reading *The Velveteen Rabbit:*

Toy
Stuffed, velveteen
Sitting, lying, riding
Love made him real
Walking, running, leaping
Real, furry
Rabbit (p. 70)

Additional writing forms that can promote and encourage the development of students' meaning vocabularies are journal writing, diary writing, response journal writing, and indvidual dictionaries. Because journal writing is intended for the teacher to read (see Chapters 3, 7, and 11), it provides an excellent opportunity for the teacher to use response journal writing to further students' vocabulary. Students can either select their own topics or teachers can provide students with ideas for journal writing. Topics and ideas can focus on characters, settings, events, and language features (words chosen by authors). Teachers can respond in writing and subtly introduce words that relate to what students have written. For example, Matthew wrote in his journal, "I really liked reading *The Marble Cake Cat* because the cat kept looking for a home where he could be just a cat and Tommy liked him and treated him just the way a cat likes to be treated." Mrs. Hansen responded to Matthew's journal entry by writing:

> Matthew,
> *The Marble Cake Cat* is one of my favorite books. He was really a unique cat, one of a kind, but all he wanted was to be treated like a cat. You and I liked the book and it sounds like it's one of your favorite books, too.

The word *unique* appears throughout this book and is most likely a word that Matthew is beginning to associate meaning with. Mrs. Hansen took the opportunity to reinforce the meaning of the word and made a mental note to emphasize its use in her language interaction with Matthew.

Teachers have long used student-compiled dictionaries to help children develop their meaning vocabularies. Dictionaries can vary from picture versions for emerging readers to content-area versions with graphs, examples, and written definitions for upper elementary students. Lower elementary grade children can compile indvidual dictionaries for significant events in their lives that teachers can capitalize upon to further vocabulary growth. Billy's kindergarten teacher read a story to the class about a man who sells balloons. Billy drew a picture of his family as a "balloon family." He described his picture to his teacher in terms of the size of the balloons: "The biggest one is daddy." "The littlest one is Matthew." "The bigger one is mommy." His teacher wrote the words *littlest, biggest,* and *bigger* under the appropriate balloon. Billy added this page of artwork to his picture dictionary and was well on his way to understanding the graphic representation and meanings associated with the words.Entries for individual dictionaries can come from stories that the children read; from discussion of topics in science, social studies, and math; from listening to stories read to them; and from field trips. The students can select their own words to include in the dictionaries or teachers can choose words that they believe are important to developing concepts.

INSTRUCTIONAL ACTIVITIES

■ *Using a Semantic Map.* Following the completion of a semantic map, have the students write stories or plays to represent the concepts and words used in the map. Using the semantic map in Figure 5.1, encourage students to write a story about traveling in space, riding in an airplane, being a weather forecaster, or traveling across the United States. Discuss the words and concepts in the semantic map, and provide assistance as the students write their stories.

■ *Using Word Maps.* Using a word map (see Figure 5.2), ask students to write several definitions for a given word or concept. Have them exchange definitions, then have each student try to identify the word that is defined.

Engaging students in discussions about new words they learn promotes their vocabulary growth.

Use word maps as the framework for a story. Develop several related word maps (such as for *dog, park,* and *games*), and have the students integrate the concepts represented in the maps in a story that they write.

■ *Using Webs.* Have the students use webs to organize and develop the stories and reports that they write. For example, if a student wants to write about a trip to the zoo, assist the student in developing a web of experiences to organize the information. If another student wants to write about space flight, help develop a web to organize this information.

■ *Using Semantic-Features Analysis.* Basing writing activities around a semantic-features analysis, such as that in Table 5.1, have the students write riddles and exchange them with each other. For example, "You can find me almost everywhere. I am read for enjoyment, information, and current events."

Have students use their analyses for content area subjects to help them organize and write reports.

■ *Word Derivation.* Studying words of recent origin can motivate both word learning and writing. English is a living language, and as such is always growing and changing. Introduce students to recently coined words. Then place the words in categories, using semantic maps, webs, and semantic-features analysis. Following are some newly coined words. Have the students work in small teams, relying on their own knowledge and on materials available in the classroom and library.

rapper, scud missile, fax, desktop, cellular telephone, CD, in-line skates, ergonomics

In the process of placing words in categories, students may discover that some categories are too broad, such as science or technology, because they cut across almost every heading. Have the students analyze words such as *ergonomics* for insights into the logic of coining new words.

Working on a unit devoted to new words in English leads to an understanding of how language works and develops. Motivation is high during such study, particularly among students who have become overdrilled on reading skills instruction. Many writing experiences can grow out of the study of newly coined words. For example, have students coin their own words and write definitions for them as a follow-up to studying affixes (such as *rewhisperment, uncar,* and *diseating*).

Have students write creative stories using newly coined words or words they constructed themselves. Have the students keep their own dictionaries of newly coined words to share with classmates and use in other language activities.

Using a language-based approach can encourage students to incorporate new words into their writing. Have the students develop word banks for the words they encounter in their oral language, reading, and writing. Words selected for their word banks have special meaning for the students. Words can be grouped in terms of activities (such as field trips, films, and guest speakers) and integrated into writing activities.

SUMMARY /

Vocabulary is a major factor in reading comprehension. The words that readers know represent the concepts and information that they have available to help them make sense of what they read. Knowing a word in its fullest sense means that readers can associate experiences and concepts with the word. Students' vocabulary knowledge is developmental. As students expand their experiential and conceptual backgrounds, they expand and refine their knowledge of words.

Researchers disagree about the effectiveness of direct vocabulary instruction. Some argue that students encounter far too many words in their reading for direct instruction to be beneficial and that wide reading and a variety of quality language activities promote vocabulary growth most effectively. Others believe that direct vocabulary instruction can increase vocabulary knowledge. This position supports teaching words that are usable, that generate the learning of other new words, and that are keys to understanding given text.

We support a position that recognizes both wide reading and direct/explicit vocabulary instruction to (1) relate new words to background knowledge, (2) provide opportunities to encounter and learn new words, and (3) focus on words that have utility in learning new concepts. Procedures for teaching vocabulary include semantic mapping, word mapping, webbing, and semantic-features analysis. To enhance vocabulary learning, engage students in discussions about the words they are learning from their reading of literary and content texts.

Discussion Questions

1. Review the guidelines of vocabulary instruction. Apply the guidelines to the recommendations found in the teacher's edition of a basal reader series for teaching vocabulary. Determine which of the guidelines are not reflected in the recommendations. Identify ways that teachers would need to adjust their vocabulary instruction.

2. Assume that you have to develop the concept of "university or college life" for a group of incoming students. Develop a semantic map that would indicate what it is like to attend your university or college. Share your semantic map with your classmates and discuss the concepts represented.

3. Assume that you are teaching the water cycle to a group of fifth graders. Contrast having the students look up words such as *evaporation, condensation*, and *drought* and writing definitions with relating the students' existing knowledge to new words and concepts. Discuss some procedures for teaching new words and concepts that might be more effective than writing definitions and sentences for the new words.

4. Identify one or two words in a dictionary that you think your classmates will not know the meaning of (such as *heinous, hiatus, sojourn, moot*, and *redoubtable*). Present the dictionary definition and ask for sentences in which the word is used correctly. Discuss the limitations of using only a dictionary to understand new words.

Take a Stand For or Against

1. Teachers are wasting their time teaching new words to students.
2. Vocabulary knowledge is not very important in getting meaning from written text.
3. Engaging students in discussions about new words promotes learning of these words.

BIBLIOGRAPHY /

Anders, P. L., & Bos, C. S. (1986). Semantic features analysis: An interactive strategy for vocabulary development and text comprehension. *Journal of Reading, 29,* 610–616.

Anderson, R. C., & Nagy, W. (1991). Word meanings. In R. Barr, M. L. Kamil, P. B. Mosenthal, & P. D. Pearson (Eds.). *Handbook of reading research (Vol. II)* (pp. 690–724). New York: Longman.

Beck, I., McKeown, M., & Omanson, R. (1990). The effects and uses of diverse vocabulary instructional techniques. In M. McKeown & M. Curtis (Eds.), *The nature of vocabulary acquistion.* Hillsdale, NJ: Lawrence Erlbaum Associates.

Blachowicz, C., & Lee, J. J. (1991). Vocabulary development in the literacy classroom. *The Reading Teacher, 45,* 188–195.

Fillmer, H. T. (1977). A generative vocabulary program for grades 4–6. *Elementary School Journal, 78,* 53–58.

Iwicki, A. L. (1992). Vocabulary connections. *The Reading Teacher, 45,* 736.

Johnson, D., & Pearson, P. D. (1984). *Teaching reading vocabulary.* New York: Holt, Rinehart & Winston.

Kameenui, E. J., Dixon, R. C., & Carnine, D. W. (1987). Issues in the design of vocabulary instruction. In M. G. McKewon & M. E. Curtis (Eds.), *The nature of vocabulary acquistion,* (129–146). Hillsdale, NJ: Lawrence Erlbaum Associates.

Maranzo, R., & Maranzo, J. (1988). *A cluster approach to elementary vocabulary instruction.* Newark, DE: International Reading Association.

McKeown, M. G. (1993). Creating effective definitions for young word learners. *Reading Research Quarterly, 28,* 16–33.

Miller, G., & Gildea, P. (1987). How children learn words. *Scientific American, 257,* 237–270.

Nagy, W. (1988). Teaching vocabulary to improve reading comprehension. Champaign, IL: Center for the Study of Reading, unpublished manuscript.

Nagy, W., Anderson, R. C., & Herman, P. (1987). Breadth and depth of vocabulary knowledge: Implications for acquisition and instruction. *American Education Research Journal, 24,* 237–270.

Norton, D. (1992). *The impact of literature-based reading.* New York: Merrill/Macmillan Publishing Co.

Pearson, P. D. (1985). *The comprehension revolution: A twenty-year history of process and practice related to reading comprehension.* Urbana, IL: University of Illinois, Reading Ed. Rep. No. 57.

Schwartz, R. M., & Raphael, T. E. (1985). Concept of definition: A key to improving students' vocabulary. *The Reading Teacher, 39,* 198–205.

Stahl, S., & Fairbanks, M. (1986). The effects of vocabulary instruction: A model-based meta-analysis. *Review of Educational Research, 56,* 72–110.

Stahl, S., Hare, C., Sinatra, R., & Gregory, J. (1991) Defining the role of prior knowledge and vocabulary in reading comprehension: The retiring of number 41. *Journal of Reading Behavior, 23,* 487–508.

Stanovich, K. (1986). Matthew effects in reading: Some consequences of individual differences in the acquisition of literacy. *Reading Research Quarterly, 21,* 360–406.

Tennyson, R., & Cocchiarella, M. (1986). An empirically based instructional design theory for teaching concepts. *Review of Educational Research, 56,* 40–71.

6

Comprehension

For the Reader

We have all read material that was beyond our background knowledge, and as a result, we just couldn't make sense of it. Can you recall having read something, thinking that you comprehended it, but being frustrated when asked to demonstrate your understanding on an exam? It was not that you didn't comprehend. Instead, your purpose for reading, your perception of important information, your level of understanding, or your background knowledge differed from the expectations of the person who wrote the exam.

The reading process is dynamic, requiring active, meaningful communication between the author and the reader. Reading without meaning is unsatisfying and inconsequential. As a teacher of reading, your reading program should further students' comprehension abilities. This chapter examines the comprehension process and the factors that affect it. It recommends teaching strategies for improving comprehension. No other topic is more important in establishing a literate society.

Key Ideas

- Students' background knowledge of the content and the language functions of reading affect comprehension.

- Reading instruction should be comprehension based.

- Quality instruction can enhance and develop reading comprehension.

- Comprehension instruction based on a cognitive view focuses on teaching strategies that students can use as they read text; these strategies are adaptable to any text they read.

- Effective questioning and teacher response are essential to promoting reading comprehension and understanding.

- Direct/explicit comprehension instruction emphasizes students' understanding the *when* and *why* of comprehension strategies.

- The curriculum of comprehension instruction should focus on teaching students strategies to help them determine importance, summarize information, draw inferences, generate their own questions, and monitor their understanding.

- Connecting reading and writing is a chief feature of comprehension instruction that helps students develop strategies for reading and interpreting text.

- Comprehension depends on a variety of factors, including background knowledge, text content, the context in which reading occurs, sociocultural background, purposes for reading, and the reader's motivation and strategies.

Key Terms

schema theory   a theory that attempts to explain how we learn, modify, and use knowledge acquired through our experiences.

schemata   the meaningful organization of knowledge based on one's experiences. We have schemata for places, events, and roles.

slots   attributes of a schema that must be recognized for a reader to activate that schema.

metacognition   a reader's awareness of how to construct meaning and adjust strategies when he or she is not comprehending something.

literal questions   questions based on information explicitly stated in text.

inferential questions   questions that combine background knowledge and text information to make predictions about story content.

modeling   demonstrating for students how to do learning tasks. Talk-alouds help students understand the steps of a strategy. Think-alouds include the steps as well as the reasoning that readers use when performing a task.

scaffolding   teacher support that enables students to complete comprehension activities that they would have difficulty completing on their own.

story schema   readers' mental representation of story parts and their relationships. Story schema is also referred to as story grammar and story structure.

CONCEPTUALIZATIONS OF READING COMPREHENSION

Although we cannot observe comprehension directly, numerous research studies, theories, and models provide probable explanations about its components and development. Most of these explanations view reading comprehension as a number of interdependent skills and abilities.

Chapter 1 presented an interactive conceptualization of the reading process. The interactive view of reading has come about as a result of researchers and teachers (1) reconceptualizing what reading comprehension is and (2) focusing on cognitively based views of reading.

The Interactive View

The cognitively based view of reading comprehension emphasizes both the interactive nature of reading and the reader's role in constructing meaning (Dole, Duffy, Roehler, & Pearson, 1991). The interactive view recognizes the roles of both the reader and the written text in reading comprehension. It depends neither on only what the reader brings to the text nor what is written on the page. Essentially, readers simultaneously use many different areas of knowledge as they read, ranging from print features (such as letters, word parts, and words) to facts, to strategies.

The interactive view of reading considers the importance of both written text and background knowledge in comprehension of print. We believe it is most applicable to reading instruction. The following view of reading comprehension reflects much of the current understanding of the process:

> A reader's background knowledge, including purposes, has an overriding influence upon the reader's development of meaning, and reading comprehension involves the activation, focusing, maintaining, and refining of ideas toward developing interpretations that are plausible, interconnected, and complete. In addition, there is a sense in which the reader's comprehension involves two other facets: the reader knowing (either tacitly or consciously) that his or her interpretations for a text are plausible, interconnected, and completely make sense, and, ideally, the reader's evaluation of the transfer value of any acquired understanding. (Tierney & Pearson, 1985, pp. 864–865)

We can view background knowledge as an individual's experiential and conceptual backgrounds for (1) written text (word recognition, concept of print, understanding of word order, and understanding of word meanings) as well as for (2) the content of what is being read.

Schema Theory

A concept directly related to the interactive view of reading comprehension has had a major impact on both reading research and instruction since the mid-1970s. This concept is **schema theory,** which describes how knowledge is represented and "how that representation facilitates the use of the knowledge" (Taylor, Harris, & Pearson, 1988, p. 4). Anderson (1985) described the essential features of schema theory in relation to reading:

> According to schema theory, reading involves more or less simultaneous analysis at many different levels. The levels include graphophonemic, morphemic, semantic, syntactic, pragmatic, and interpretive. This means that analysis does not proceed in a strict order from the visual information in letters to the overall interpretation of a text. (p. 376)

A powerful feature of schema theory is that it helps explain how new learning is integrated with an individual's existing knowledge. It explains how we learn, modify, and use information we acquire through our experiences.

A major concept of schema theory is that our experiences and knowledge are organized by meaning (as in a thesaurus) rather than by word (as in a dictionary). For example, we have **schemata** (plural of schema) for places (e.g., grocery store, home, and school), events (football game, political convention, and wedding), roles (parent, teacher, and student), emotions (love, hate, and fear), and language concepts (story, menu, and sentence structure).

Figure 6.1 illustrates the semantic features of schemata. It is a partial semantic network for *chair*. It shows how *chair* is a schema as well as a member of other classes related to each other (functional furniture).

An adaptation of Taylor, Harris, and Pearson's (1988) description of this semantic network will help explain the nature of schemata. An important feature of this theory is that it refers to the attributes of a schema as **slots.** Slots (e.g, *seat, back,* and *legs*) must be filled or recognized for an individual to activate a schema and recognize *chair*. The chair schema illustrates both an upward and downward organization. The upward organization shows the relationship of *chair* to functional furniture. The downward organization points out the different types or examples of chairs to fill a slot.

Schemata are considered to be abstract in nature. That is, they do not represent fixed concepts (specific events, objects, or emotions), but idealized concepts, which in fact may not even exist (Taylor, Harris, & Pearson, 1988). Anderson (1985) indicates differences between schemata for concepts versus for actions and events. Schemata for concepts and for actions and events differ mainly in the ways their slots are filled. Action and event schemata have episodic or sequential dimensions (Taylor, Harris, & Pearson, 1988).

Figure 6.2 is a schema for an action—buying something. Slots for a buy schema may be selected. For example, the buyer and medium slots could be anyone from a small child with one dollar to a tycoon with millions of dollars. The possible slots for a buy scenario are episodes generally associated with buying something. How the slots in the buy schema are filled (a child with one dollar or a tycoon with millions) influences how the episodic slots are filled for the scenario. Taylor, Harris, and Pearson (1988) note:

> [T]here is a great deal of cross-referencing among schemata. For example, if a buy schema is selected and the buyer is a criminal, then the separate schema for criminal is called up and added to the buy schema. The values (actors) that fill variable slots (roles) in one schema are themselves schemata in other parts of a person's semantically organized memory. (p. 27)

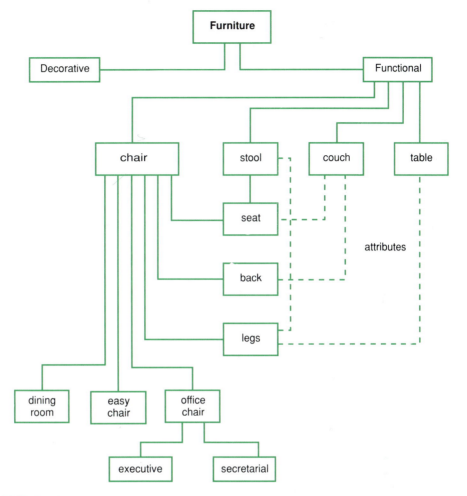

FIGURE 6.1

A partial representation of a schema for chair

(Reprinted with permission from B. Taylor, L. A. Harris, and P. D. Pearson, *Reading Difficulties: Instruction and Assessment* [New York: Random House, 1988], p. 13.)

Schemata are considered to be incomplete; that is, empty slots are always waiting to be filled as a result of new experiences. Consider a group of first graders preparing to play a game of basketball. They meet on the basketball court and choose two teams. These children have only a partial schema for the game of basketball. When a teacher assists them in getting the game started by demonstrating a tip-off, a slot for their schema of basketball is filled. However, they fill additional empty slots (e.g, what constitutes a foul, how to keep score, and when to end a game) as they more fully develop a basketball schema.

In fact, readers may change, elaborate on, or discard a schema as they proceed through text. Readers comprehend by using existing knowledge, which can change when they encounter new information. Although changes in schemata

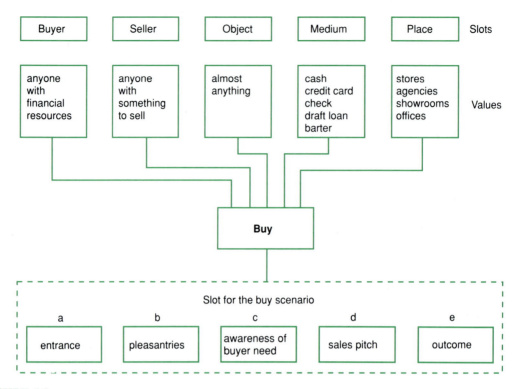

FIGURE 6.2
Partial representation of a possible buy schema
(Reprinted with permission from B. Taylor, L. A. Harris, and P. D. Pearson, *Reading Difficulties: Instruction and Assessment* [New York: Random House, 1988], p. 15.)

happen slowly, they can be considered new learning. New learning may result from modifying an existing schema or from creating a new one (Rupley & Blair, 1988).

An important feature of schema selection (or constructing meaning from the text) is inference (Anderson, 1985; Rumelhart, 1984). Inference also plays a major role in filling slots, and once a slot is filled, inference influences the filling of other slots. Furthermore, schema theory has shown that "reading is only incidentally literal. Product measures can tap recognition or recall of explicitly stated information; however, in the process of working one's way through a text, tens, hundreds, even thousands of inferences are necessary" (Taylor, Harris, & Pearson, 1988, p. 16).

How Schemata Influence Comprehension. Schema theory explains how readers use prior knowledge to comprehend and learn from text. Students' reading comprehension or lack of comprehension can be evaluated in terms of the basic features of schema theory. Rumelhart (1984) suggests several features of schemata that may influence comprehension:

- Students may not have the necessary schemata in relation to the content of the text. They may lack schemata for such topics as world politics, world economics, and farm life. As a result, students have no way to hypothesize about text content.

- Students may have appropriate schemata for text content but lack schemata for the language of the text; therefore, they cannot access schemata for understanding the content. For example, "The magistrate chastised the assembly of onlookers for the brouhaha that erupted when the verdict was rendered" is more easily understood when written as "The judge scolded the people in the courtroom for the disruption that took place when he gave his decision."

- Students may have well-developed schemata for the content and language, but the author may not have provided enough clues to suggest them. In such instances, students need assistance in filling in the gaps.

- Students may find their schemata activated and perceive meaning; however, their meaning may be different from that intended by the author. Students who often think that they know more than the author in their reading of text are most likely to demonstrate such comprehension.

How Social and Cultural Factors Affect Schemata. Schema theory highlights the importance of readers constructing meaning as they process text. In addition to helping to change the concept of reading comprehension to enhance instruction, schema theory has helped explain the effects of sociocultural variations on reading. Research conducted by Steffensen, Joag-Dev, and Anderson (1979) shows that readers from distinctly different cultures give differing interpretations of reading materials deemed culturally sensitive. Individuals who read materials related directly to their culture spend less time reading and recall more information.

Similar results were reported by Erwin (1991), who found that when elementary students were read a passage containing cultural information for which they had background knowledge, they could successfully answer questions without instruction. When hearing a story containing unfamiliar cultural information, however, they had extreme difficulty answering questions about the story. Even when the teacher added direct instruction to help the children build some knowledge of the different culture, they still had trouble both answering questions and discussing the content of what they read and studied.

A study by Reynolds, Taylor, Steffenson, Shirey, and Anderson (1981) supports the idea that reading material with identifiable cultural content directly influences an individual's comprehension. When the reader's culture and the text's cultural content are mismatched, the reader constructs different meaning. Linguistically and culturally diverse students may be unfairly evaluated if the teacher focuses on how closely their comprehension matches the text of what they are required to read. If the materials used for reading instruction contain culturally loaded content, students may not have the appropriate schemata to construct meaning that even approximates the author's intent.

Implications of Schema Theory. Schema theory can help teachers develop better strategies to enhance reading comprehension. Several important considerations:

- Make sure that the materials students are asked to read are within their experiential and conceptual backgrounds in terms of content and language.

- Help students activate their background knowledge prior to reading. Providing students with specific information to activate and build their background may be most beneficial when the goal of instruction is comprehension of a given text (Dole, Valencia, Greer, & Wardrop, 1991). Mapping strategies similar to those used in vocabulary instruction, discussions, student- and teacher-identified reading purposes, study guides, and prereading questions can help readers activate their prior knowledge relevant to the reading task.

- Help students develop background knowledge for materials that contain new information. Field trips, films, filmstrips, pictures, guest speakers, and so forth can help students build background knowledge to construct meaning for new information. Discussing new vocabulary, exploring the relationships among new and known concepts, and directly experiencing new ideas help build schemata for learning. These activities are of major importance in the content areas of science and social studies, where the suggestions in the teachers' manuals are not extensive and the previous text read by the students is by itself insufficient to build background for text containing new information (McKeown, Beck, Sinatra, & Loxterman, 1992).

- Demonstrate for students how to use strategies for constructing meaning. That is, if students are to understand information in the text, model how to do this, using familiar materials. If they are to go beyond what is found in the materials, think aloud (model this) for them, relating the text to their background knowledge.

- Monitor students' performance closely to determine if they have an appropriate schema but fail to activate it or if they lack a schema to construct meaning. This requires that teachers know their students well. Teachers must be sensitive to sociocultural factors that impede students' comprehension of the cultural aspects of reading matter.

In schema theory, readers build connections between old knowledge and new knowledge through repeated interactions with content. These interactions result in hypotheses that the readers confirm or reject in relation to the text and their background knowledge. Comprehension is the synthesis of these hypotheses that results in constructing meaning.

Metacognition. In addition to using background knowledge to construct meaning, readers must monitor their comprehension and know when the process is breaking down. This monitoring of comprehension is ***metacognition.*** Good readers are aware of how they construct meaning and can apply corrective strategies when they are not comprehending. Metacognition requires knowing how to achieve the goal that has not been accomplished and knowing when a goal has been reached. Readers therefore must have the ability to monitor their comprehension. Good readers know when they have achieved their purposes for reading, when they understand and do not understand what they are reading, and how to correct and regulate their comprehension of text.

Teachers should help students become aware of what they are doing and why they are doing it. In addition, teachers should model how to check, monitor, and test hypotheses. Metacognitive training makes students aware of what good readers do when reading for meaning. It enables them to employ strategies to monitor their own reading and focus on comprehension.

A cognitive view of reading comprehension based on schema theory has direct implications for classroom reading-comprehension instruction. Decoding and comprehension are both essential elements of a literacy instruction program. Teaching strategies for constructing meaning from text, monitoring comprehension, and providing opportunities to apply metacognitive strategies to learning are major features of teaching literacy.

WHAT TO TEACH

Early research in reading comprehension viewed it as a set of skills that students were to master. Learning each skill was assumed to result in a synthesis of skills, reading comprehension. Today, we realize that many factors influence comprehension and a list of skills should not determine comprehension instruction. New views of reading comprehension recognize it as an interactive, cognitive process. Readers use their background knowledge, text information and cues, and the context in which they are reading to construct meaning. Comprehension instruction based on the cognitive view would focus on teaching strategies that students can use as they read text; these strategies would be adaptable to any text that they read.

Dole et al. (1991) identified what should be taught in a reading-comprehension curriculum that is based on teaching reading strategies.

Determining Importance. The majority of reading comprehension in school requires students to determine the author-dictated importance of what they read rather than what they as readers perceive to be important. How good readers do this has been investigated and the findings suggest that (a) good readers use their background knowledge to access and evaluate what they are reading; (b) good readers use their knowledge of the author's bias, goals, and intentions to sort out what is important from what is unimportant in what they are reading; and (c) good readers are knowledgeable about text structure, which helps them identify and organize important information in what they read. Dole and his colleagues said, "In summary, the ability to separate the important from the unimportant leads to effective comprehension, and the ability to accomplish this task seems readily amenable to instruction" (p. 244).

Summarizing Information. Readers who can effectively summarize information can also sort through large pieces of text, distinguish important from unimportant ideas, and bring the ideas together so that the new text represents the original. The ability to summarize appears to be developmental. Young children

Quality instruction can enhance and develop reading comprehension.

can successfully summarize the plot of simple stories, but they appear to have more difficulty summarizing more complex tasks such as determining how story sections contribute to the story's theme.

Drawing Inferences.   As noted in the discussion of schema theory, inference provides the foundation for reading comprehension. Readers use inferences to fill in gaps, relate their background knowledge to the text, and to make sense of what they read. A large amount of research supports teaching inference from the beginning of reading instruction.

Generating Questions.   Students who learn and have opportunities to generate their own questions prior to reading have improved comprehension compared to students who answer teacher-asked questions. Young and Daines (1992) determined from their research with kindergarten through fifth-grade children that students are capable of asking predictive questions to set their own purposes for reading. Teachers must provide examples and structure on how to generate questions, however.

Monitoring Comprehension. As we noted earlier, comprehension monitoring (metacognition) is another important factor associated with good readers. "Comprehension monitoring and fix-it strategies appear to be important for developing expertise in reading comprehension. It is not only that good readers monitor; it is also that their monitoring appears to be the key to restoring lost comprehension" (Dole et al., 1991, p. 248).

Instructional procedures and recommendations for teaching each of these strategies are presented in forthcoming sections.

QUESTIONING STRATEGIES TO PROMOTE COMPREHENSION AND UNDERSTANDING

Teacher-identified questions are the most common method of comprehension instruction. Such questions are important to focusing students' learning on building understanding of a particular text content (Pearson & Fielding, 1991). Teachers must carefully identify questions that enable students to establish meaningful purpose for reading and to understand the text in an integrated fashion. Teacher-identified questions should help students attend to the important features of a story, not trivial information that may misdirect their thinking. In addition, teacher questions should help students relate their backgrounds to story content, develop strategies for interacting with text, and learn to understand written language.

Literal Questions

Both literal and inferential questions are important in teaching reading. *Literal questions* focus on explicitly stated information and require the reader to recall or recognize such information. Effective literal questions should help students to build or complete a schema for comprehension of the total story (summarizing information). "What did John see in the woods?" is an important question if the fact that he found an unusual set of footprints leads him to spend a summer in the woods searching for a creature. However, a question such as "What is the dog's name?" is trivial if the answer does not contribute to students' understanding of the story.

Prereading questions should encourage students to focus their attention on the text information related to the desired understanding. If the students are to know the content of what they read, then teacher-identified prereading literal-level questions are important.

Inferential Questions

Inferential questions require students to fill in information by using their background knowledge to infer text meaning. A question such as "Why do you think so?" is an inferential question that should activate background knowledge appropriate for a story. "What do you think will happen?" can stimulate students to make predictions about story content.

Asking both literal and inferential questions before reading a story can help students set purposes for reading, activate their background knowledge, and predict story information. Again it is important to remember that teacher-identified questions typically focus on knowledge of the text content.

Activating Students' Background. How questions are asked can either limit students' inquiry or expand it. For example, asking students, "Did you think about the story before you read?" does not promote activation of their background knowledge. However, asking, "What do you already know about this story and what do you think will happen?" will better assist students in understanding how they can use their background knowledge to understand what they read. The following comprehension-questioning strategy (Nessel, 1987) illustrates how teachers can engage students in better understanding of what they read and uses both teacher and student questions to activate students' experiential and conceptual backgrounds:

1. Identify one or two major turning points in the story.

2. Stop the reading at these points and ask, "What do you think will happen?" Encourage differences of opinion.

3. Have the students give support for their predictions by asking, "Why do you think so?" or "What have you experienced that makes you think so?"

4. As the students read further in the story, ask them to evaluate their original predictions in light of what they have read. Ask, "Do you still think that will happen or have you changed your mind?" Ask them to give reasons for retaining or changing their predictions. Ask, "Why do you want to keep (change) your prediction? What did you read that helped you decide?"

5. Design follow-up activities to encourage reflection on story content and language, to elicit creative responses (such as enacting, writing, and drawing), and to improve the students' ability to both make and justify predictions.

This strategy for teacher questioning has several advantages (Nessel, 1987). First, it focuses on the students' background for the story, not just their related experiences. Second, the stops for story discussion provide opportunities to share information and to add to prior knowledge. Discussions also help students develop their metacognitive abilities as they keep, change, and discard earlier predictions about a story. Third, the teacher can monitor students' comprehension and reasoning ability. The predictions and supporting arguments provide insights into students' ability to connect prior knowledge with story content to make sense of what they read.

Question-and-Answer Relationships (Helping Students Draw Inferences)

Teaching question-and-answer relationships (QAR) helps provide students with a strategy for reading and answering questions (Raphael, 1984, 1986). Use of QAR with young students has been shown to be effective in helping them to determine whether a question can be answered with background knowledge alone or in combination with information in the text. The procedure improved students' comprehension, particularly in their answers to inferential questions (Dole, et al., 1991).

QAR identifies two basic sources of information for answering questions: (1) in the book and (2) in my head (see Figure 6.3). Raphael (1986) notes that most students can make this distinction after discussions using a short text and one or two related questions as examples. To introduce the relationships, present the sample text on an overhead projector or chart, read the text, and then ask the first question. This question should be one that has an answer in the book. As the students respond to the question, locate the information in the text rather than focus on the accuracy of the responses.

The second question should require an in-my-head response. Focus on the source of the answer in addition to its appropriateness. Once students understand the differences between in the book and in my head (Raphael notes that this takes minutes for upper-grade students and several weeks for early primary students), focus on developing each type. You should try to expand only one of the categories at a time.

Developing the in-the-book category includes helping students to realize when the answer to a question is either (1) explicitly stated in the text in one or two sentences or (2) explicitly stated in the text but requires putting together information from several parts. Raphael suggest that teachers refer to the synthesis of explicit text as *putting it together.* This instruction stresses strategies for locating information.

Expand the think-and-search category when working with upper elementary and middle school students (see Figure 6.3) by including strategies for identifying information in terms of text structure. Knowledge of text structure can help students understand how text information is organized and how such knowledge helps them locate information to answer questions.

Once students are competent in the in-the-book QARs, expand the in-my-head component. The two categories for this component are: (1) author and you and (2) on my own. The primary distinction between these two is whether or not the student needs to read the text for a question to make sense. If the answer requires interaction of the text and the student's background, then the question is related to the author-and-you component. If the response to a question depends only on the student's background knowledge, then it is the on-my-own component. For example, if students are asked to answer a question such as, "Why did Sally run home and change her clothes?" it is important for them to know that Sally was playing in the sand pit even though her mother had told her to stay home. This information—coupled with the reader's knowledge that by changing clothes Sally might be able to prevent her mother from knowing where she had been—provides an answer for the question. An on-your-own question might be "How do you feel when your mother punishes you for misbehaving?" which the reader can respond to without reading or understanding the story.

A valuable feature of QAR is that it can be used as a framework for comprehension instruction. Teachers can use it to identify the types of questions that are most important for guiding students in the reading of a story. On-my-own questions can activate students' background knowledge and stimulate students

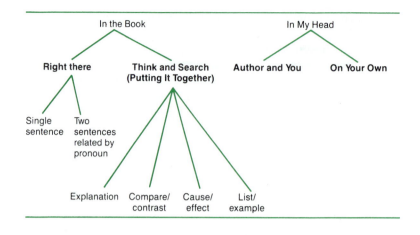

In the Book — In My Head

Right there — **Think and Search (Putting It Together)** — **Author and You** — **On Your Own**

Single sentence — Two sentences related by pronoun

Explanation — Compare/contrast — Cause/effect — List/example

In the Book QARs

Right There
The answer is in the text, usually easy to find. The words used to make up the question and words used to answer the question are **Right There** in the same sentence.

**Think and Search
(Putting It Together)**
The answer is in the story, but you need to put together different story parts to find it. Words for the question and words for the answer are not found in the same sentence. They come from different parts of the text.

In My Head QARs

Author and You
The answer is *not* in the story. You need to think about what you already know, what the author tells you in the text, and how it fits together.

On My Own
The answer is not in the story. You can even answer the question without reading the story. You need to use your own experience.

FIGURE 6.3
Relationships among the four types of question-and-answer relationships and ways to explain them
(From T. Raphael, "Teaching Question-Answer Relationships, Revisited," *The Reading Teacher, 39* [May 1986], pp. 517 and 519. Reprinted with permission of Taffy E. Raphael and the International Reading Association.)

to think about how it relates to a given story prior to reading. On-my-own and author-and-you questions can extend and encourage student interaction with the text and promote their drawing inferences.

Teacher Responses

Although the quality of questions is important, the teacher's responses to students' answers are equally important. To develop students' thinking and to improve the quality and quantity of class discussions, teachers should be aware of their reactions to student responses.

Research on wait-time (Rowe, 1974) has significant implications for teachers today. Waiting for approximately three to four seconds after asking a question, with no further comment, has the following positive benefits:

- The length of response increases.
- The number of unsolicited but appropriate responses increases.
- Failure to respond decreases.
- Confidence in responses increases.
- Student-to-student comparisons of information increases.
- Evidence-inference statements increase.
- The frequency of student questions increases.

The benefits of wait-time indicate that it is a powerful yet simple strategy to enhance students' interactions with questions posed by the teacher. Increasing wait-time benefits all students, shifts the responsibility for the dialogue to them, and encourages speculative and reasoning responses. Essentially, wait-time gives students the chance to activate their background knowledge and to relate the experiences to the questions asked. This is an important point for teachers to consider, especially when asking inferential questions.

Responding to Students. Coupled with wait-time, responding effectively to students' answers and comments encourages them to make predictions, elaborate on the text content, and draw inferences. A teacher's response may involve asking questions that encourage students to clarify and expand upon their responses, redirecting students' thinking and strategy, or monitoring students' strategies to correct and provide alternatives. The teacher's response can also provide insights about how students derived an answer and can promote interaction among students about how an answer was derived. When students share their strategies with each other, it shifts the focus from getting a right answer to how the answer was derived. The following examples (Duffy & Roehler, 1987) illustrate the use of teachers' responses:

Responding to Misunderstandings. A third-grade teacher's response to a student's answer revealed that he used only part of a paragraph's information to construct a main idea. The teacher was directing him to use all of the paragraph.

S: [Giving incorrect main idea] Getting new words from Indians.

T: Well, let's test it. Is the first sentence talking about new words from the Indians?

S: Yes.

T: Is the next?

S: Yes.

T: How about the next?

S: No.

T: No. It says that Indians also learned new words from the settlers, right? Think about how this fits into your main idea.

S: The Indians taught the settlers words, and the settlers taught the Indians words.

T: Good. You see, you have to think about all the ideas in the paragraphs to decide on the main idea. (p. 517)

Responding to Mental Processing. A third grade teacher's discussion after the students read a story. The teacher is responding not to the correct answers but to the strategies students can use in making predictions.

T: What do you think is going to happen next here? I mean, you're reading the story. What'll happen next? Candy?

S: [Gives a response]

T: Oh, okay. What do you think, Moss?

S: [Gives a response]

T: Interesting. Why do you think what you think? How can you make these predictions like this? How can you predict what's going to happen next in the story?

S: I thought about the story and Roberto and his problem.

T: Yes, but how did you use that to predict? Did you use your own experience?

S: Yeah. I thought about what I thought would probably happen.

T: That's right. Because you've been thinking about the story and you've been thinking about Roberto and his problem. And that's part of what reading is. It's making predictions about what's going to happen next. (p. 519)

DIRECT/EXPLICIT COMPREHENSION INSTRUCTION

Enabling students to interact with and construct meaning for text is the goal of literacy instruction. The concept of reading comprehension has been expanded to include background knowledge, text structure, flexible use of knowledge, reader habits, fluency, automatic word recognition, automatic word knowledge, and the orchestration of skills that support each other in varying ways. This expanded view of comprehension should cause teachers to view themselves as people who facilitate students' understandings about text content, developing strategies to understand the text, and learning how the process of reading functions (Dole et al., 1991).

Direct instruction once was thought of as the teacher directing and managing students' learning. An interactive view of literacy instruction often refers to direct instruction as explicit instruction. Explicit instruction emphasizes students' understanding the when and why of comprehension strategies. The importance of direct/explicit instruction was brought out in Smagorinsky and Smith's (1992) review of research addressing how best to facilitate students' literacy understandings. They argued that the job of teachers of literature is "determining what kinds of literature students need to know how to read, identifying strategies necessary for reading them, and designing instruction to teach the strategies" (p. 295).

Regardless of what it is called, direct/explicit instruction has some important features. Among the more important features are modeling, gradually turning over the responsibility of learning to students, and ultimately fading out of the picture so that students apply the strategies independently (Pearson & Fielding, 1991).

Modeling

As its name implies, **modeling** is demonstrating for the students how to do learning tasks. As Dole and his colleagues (1991) and Duffy and Roehler (1991) noted, modeling varies in relation to how much information is explicitly provided. For example, in classrooms with many opportunities for students to read books independently (see Chapters 8 and 9), the teachers' modeling is the reading of books themselves. However, students are not given explicit instruction, but must infer what the cognitive processes are and how to do them.

More explicit types of modeling are *talk-alouds* and *think-alouds*. Both of these involve teacher discussion and teacher-student interaction. Our discussion of meaning vocabulary (Chapter 5) used an example of a talk-aloud for helping students develop strategies in using context clues. An important feature of talk-aloud modeling is the teacher demonstrating the strategies while discussing the steps in the process.

Think-alouds often discuss the steps used in a strategy, but they also include a description of the reasoning that readers use when performing the task (Duffy & Roehler, 1991). Think-alouds are intended to help students "get inside the teacher's mind" and begin to understand what strategies they can use when doing similar tasks. An example of a think-aloud illustrates how teachers can use them in their literacy instruction:

> I want to show you what I look at when I come across a word I don't know the meaning of. I'll talk out loud to show you how I figure it out. Then I will help you do this. [reading] "The cocoa steamed fragrantly." Hmm, I've heard that word "fragrantly" before, but I don't really know what it means here. I know one of the words right before it though— "steamed." I watched a pot of boiling water once and there was steam coming from it. That was hot so this must have something to do with the cocoa being hot. OK, the pan of hot cocoa is steaming on

the stove; that means steam coming up and out, but that still doesn't explain what fragrantly means. Let me think again about the hot cocoa on the stove and try to use what I already know about cocoa as a clue. Hot cocoa bubbles, steams and . . . smells! Hot cocoa smells good. [reading] "The cocoa steamed fragrantly." That means it smelled good! [addressing the students] Thinking about what I already knew about hot cocoa helped me figure out what the word meant. (Duffy & Roehler, 1991, pp. 869–870)

The purpose of modeling is to teach students strategic reasoning. When teachers attempt to explain how they think, however, they tend to do it in a step-by-step manner that can oversimplify the process of strategic reasoning.

Herrmann (1992) recommends two ways that teachers can better use modeling of strategic processing in their classrooms. First, select short passages from several texts that contain unfamiliar content. Talk out loud and tape record the process used to construct meaning as the passages are read. Listen to the recordings to identify the thinking used to construct meaning for the passages. Revise and refine this initial modeling attempt. By practicing this type of modeling before teaching, teachers can avoid oversimplification of strategic reasoning.

A second way to use modeling effectively is to encourage students to think aloud about the strategies they use when reading. Herrmann (1992) thinks that this serves two important purposes: "[It] helps the students become more familiar with the complex nature of strategic reasoning, and it helps me improve my ability to verbalize reasoning processes" (p. 430).

Modeling is an effective way that teachers can help students understand reading strategies and how to apply them. It is most effective when done in reading content rather than as an isolated, infrequently used skill instruction activity.

Gradually turning over the responsibility of learning to students is another important feature of direct/explicit instruction. Instruction in an area of reading comprehension (see Figure 6.4) can begin as a series of connected lessons that move from students understanding what they are to learn (modeling that learning), to application of the learning in real text with teacher support, then to students applying the learning independently. In earlier instruction phases, the teacher would offer more guidance. The teacher would adjust instruction-based ongoing assessment (see Chapter 11) to determine instruction appropriate to students' needs.

Scaffolding

Scaffolding is teacher support that enables students to do comprehension activities that by themselves would be too difficult. Scaffolding allows teachers to transfer the responsibility for learning to students gradually and still provide expert guidance. Pearson and Fielding (1991) discuss the role of scaffolding in comprehension instruction:

In scaffolded instruction, the teacher determines the difference between what students can accomplish independently and what they can accomplish with just more expert guidance, and then designs instruction that provides just enough scaffolding for them to be able to participate in tasks that currently are beyond their reach. Providing appropriate scaffolding requires teachers to engage in an ongoing, dynamic interaction with students. Each response provided by a student or students gives teachers information about what they do and do not understand; these responses become cues to the teacher concerning the level and kind of feedback the teacher should give the step or steps that should be taken next. When scaffolded instruction operates according to plan, two things happen: first, the tasks and texts of the moment gradually come more and more under the learner's control; and second, more difficult tasks and texts become appropriate bases for further teacher-student interaction. (p. 849)

■ **Area of Needed Reading Instruction**

Reinforcement of the ability to make inferences.

■ **Intended Learning Outcome**

Students will complete an open-ended story by writing inferences to complete the story.

■ **Past Learning**

Students are aware of and have had some practice in drawing inferences from short passages and sentences.

■ **Building Background**

Review the concept of drawing inferences from reading material by writing on the chalkboard key concepts that students need to remember when they think about inferences. For example, write that inferences are used when the purpose for reading requires students to anticipate outcomes, make generalizations, and draw conclusions.

Give students some quick verbal situations in which they must make inferences and ask different students to tell you whether the purpose for reading was to anticipate an outcome, make a generalization, or draw a conclusion.

■ **Teacher-Directed Instruction**

Write several open-ended statements and questions on the chalkboard and have the class read each one silently. For example, give students a headline from a news article and ask them to infer or predict what the article is about.

Write students' responses on the chalkboard and discuss why each one inferred what they did.

Next, list open-ended story starters on the chalkboard and have each student respond. Instruct students that they are to write the outcome of the story starter. Then instruct students to list the events that caused the final outcome.

FIGURE 6.4   *continues*
Direct instruction example for teaching reading comprehension
(Reprinted with permission of Macmillan Publishing Company from *Teaching Reading: Diagnosis, Direct Instruction, and Practice,* Second Edition by William H. Rupley and Timothy R. Blair. Copyright ©1988 by Macmillan Publishing Company.)

FIGURE 6.4
Continued

Story starting examples can include:

It was a cold, snowy morning in the mountains. Jim had lost all his camping gear and food to the grizzly bears last night. He prepared to turn back when suddenly he heard . . .

Jerry had one more lap of the car race to go. He was neck and neck with the other lead car. As they began the last lap of the race, Jerry . . .

- **Independent Student Practice**

Hand out a story starter similar to the ones in the teacher-directed instructional activity. For example:

The hot July summer was making it hard to live in New York City. Several teenage youths were standing on the street corner near the jewelry store when suddenly . . .

Discuss the inferences that could be included in this story and list them on the chalkboard. Distribute an additional story starter and allow ample time for students to write an ending.

- **Ongoing Diagnosis**

Teacher evaluation of the inferences made in students' written responses.

Discuss and share written responses to the story starter with the group. Students who are experiencing difficulty with this activity can be grouped together for additional instruction. Give them written passages and short stories and guide them in making inferences.

- **Modifying Instruction**

The difficulty level for this activity can be easily varied. Easier tasks can focus on events that are extremely familiar to students: holidays, games, television programs, and so forth. More difficult tasks can be based on longer passages and more abstract concepts.

Direct/explicit instruction is an important feature of a program to help students become better readers. Direct or explicit instruction is active, reflective teaching where the teacher recognizes that reading is an interactive process and that students can be effectively taught to become strategic in their comprehension of text.

Guidelines for Effective Direct/Explicit Comprehension Instruction

Although instructional methods used depend on students' capabilities, the text being read, the purposes for reading, and the context in which reading occurs, teachers can provide effective instruction by concentrating their efforts in the following ways:

- Designing reading programs that allow students to develop meaning vocabulary by using concept-acquisition strategies based on the students' background knowledge.

- Concentrating on improved questioning abilities that include appropriate questions, appropriate feedback to students' responses, and instructional methods (such as reciprocal teaching) that encourage students to develop thinking and reasoning strategies.

- Providing direct/explicit instruction that is appropriate to the type of learning (ranging from knowledge to strategies) and students' background.

- Focusing instruction on strategies for reading comprehension rather than skill acquisition, using modeling and scaffolding to enhance students' success in learning, and applying these strategies in authentic texts.

- Helping students establish purposes for reading that encourage them to engage actively in reading.

- Giving students varied opportunities to assume their own responsibility for learning through application of reading-comprehension strategies in authentic texts.

Example of Direct/Explicit Comprehension Instruction

Direct/explicit instruction will help students interact with and understand written language. Figure 6.4 is an example of a direct/explicit comprehension lesson. Teachers' editions of both traditional basal readers and newer literature-based readers contain a variety of lessons and suggestions on teaching such lessons that both beginning and experienced teachers can use. Teachers may need to modify such lessons, however, to include modeling, moving students toward independent application in authentic texts, and scaffolding. The features of the following lesson components (see Figure 6.4) foster students' abilities to construct meaning and develop strategies for what they read:

1. *Using past learning.* This component focuses on determining students' existing experiential and conceptual background in relation to the focus of instruction. The teacher bases assessment on what the students already know that they need to relate to and understand the text used for instruction and practice application of comprehension strategies.

2. *Building background.* After determining what existing knowledge to activate, focus on how to do this in the lesson. Utilize students' existing schemata. Model, explain, and demonstrate the lesson objective; review examples for application in meaningful context; and provide purposes for learning by assisting students in asking questions and making predictions about the text and strategies they will use.

3. *Modeling, explaining, and demonstrating.* This component involves making sure students understand the tasks and how they are to apply their strategies to reading. Use familiar materials and focus on explicit strategies and flexibility in application of strategies.

4. *Practice in application of strategy.* Students can do this either independently or in small groups that the teacher monitors closely to provide appropriate scaffolding. Encourage students to monitor their own application of the comprehension task and relate its application to similar text and comprehension tasks.

This will assist them in assuming more of the responsibility for their own learning.

5. *Ongoing assessment.* Based upon students' performance in both group and independent activities, assess their learning. Focus on their application of comprehension strategies in other comprehension tasks.

6. *Modifying instruction.* Based on learning assessment, the teacher modifies instruction. You may need to provide scaffolding for some students in the initial instruction of a comprehension strategy by simplifying the task. However, since an important feature of scaffolding is to enable students to perform comprehension tasks that are beyond their existing capabilities, some tasks may need to be extended and reinforced with more difficult activities.

Teaching Strategic Reasoning Using Direct/Explicit Instruction

A direct/explicit instruction model (Baumann & Schmidt, 1986) for teaching reasoning strategies integrates three types of knowledge associated with strategic reasoning: (1) declarative knowledge, which is the strategy; (2) procedural knowledge, which is how the strategy is applied in reading; and (3) conditional knowledge, which is metacognitive awareness about why the strategy is important, and when or when not to use it. Four steps for direct/explicit reading-comprehension instruction incorporate these three types of knowledge.

1. *The what step.* Tell the students what comprehension strategy they will learn. Use familiar examples, definitions, illustrations, and descriptions to assist the students in conceptualizing what they are to learn.

2. *The why step.* Make sure that students associate value with their learning by understanding why the strategy will help them become better readers. Provide examples of or model the strategy using authentic text so that students can conceptualize its importance in reading for meaning.

3. *The direct/explicit instruction step.* Use direct/explicit instruction to ensure that the students understand how the strategy helps construct meaning. Model, demonstrate, or discuss it to facilitate their understanding of the procedure associated with the strategy. Monitor students' practice and application and provide appropriate scaffolding to maximize transfer of the strategy to other reading materials.

4. *The when-to-use-the-strategy step.* To help students realize when they should use a strategy, discuss and illustrate the conditions (such as the types of written text and purposes for reading) appropriate for using the strategy. This is the metacognitive feature of the instruction.

Determining What Is Important

Because determining what is important (the main ideas or central problems) is a major feature of comprehension instruction in elementary reading programs, teachers should use instructional procedures that promote this ability. In their summary of research on comprehension instruction, Pearson and Fielding (1991)

Y ou probably read *Weekly Reader* or a similar type of school weekly news magazine when you were in elementary school. These news magazines have been an important feature of many teachers' reading programs for several years. Such news magazines provide pupils with opportunities to apply reading skills to reading materials dealing with timely topics and current events.

		CURRENT EVENTS		COMMUNITY LIFE		
GEOGRAPHY			HELPFUL SEATWORK			BIOGRAPHY
	HEALTH	**MY WEEKLY READER** Vol. I SEPTEMBER 21, 1928 No. I			NATURE STUDY	

Issued weekly, from September to June, except Thanksgiving and Christmas weeks, by American Education Press, Inc., 40 South Third Street, Columbus, Ohio, and 1123 Broadway, New York, N. Y. Yearly subscription 75c a year. Special rates to schools.

Two Poor Boys Who Made Good Are Now Running for the Highest Office in the World!

A QUAKER BOY

A LITTLE boy sat in Quaker meeting. He had been there an hour. He began wiggling and wiggling, and whispered to his father, "Dost thou think meeting will be over soon?" After

church, he was punished, for Quakers were very, very strict.

That was in Iowa, about fifty years ago. The boy was Herbert Hoover. Today we are talking of making him President. Herbert was born in a small cottage. Next to it was his father's blacksmith shop.

Herbert went to Oklahoma to visit his Uncle Laban. His three were the only white children in town. All the rest were Indian boys and girls.

Such fun as he had playing with the Indian boys! They taught him how to build Indian fires; how to trap rabbits and squirrels, and how to catch fish.

When Herbert was nine, his mother took a very bad cold and died. The Hoover children were orphans now.

Herbert went to live on a nearby farm with his Uncle Allan. Here he fed the pigs, hoed the garden, and helped milk the cows. He went to the country school every day. Quakers were very strict about school, too. They thought that learning was next in importance to religion.

A LITTLE NEWSBOY

F IFTY-FIVE years ago, a baby boy was born in New York City. It was on the East Side, near the river, where

W eekly Reader was and still is today a popular type of reading material found in elementary classrooms. Along with various newspapers, magazines, catalogs, and quality literature, these materials represent the "real reading" component of a complete literacy program. This component emphasizes the application of literacy capabilities in meaningful reading situations. Two of the more recent magazines aimed at the elementary school are *Sports Illustrated for Kids* and *Zillions: Consumer Reports for Kids*.

noted that students benefit when teachers help them use their background knowledge to understand the story line of narrative text and relationships among information presented in informational text. This highlights the importance of enhancing students' comprehension by helping them determine what is important in what they read. Moldofsky (1984) recommended the following guidelines for teaching students to determine what is important in text:

1. *Activate the students' schemata.* Illustrate and demonstrate for the students the problems and solutions they know about from previous text they have read.

2. *Organize the students' schemata.* Categorize the problems that emerge in the story—wanting or needing, thinking differently, or thinking the wrong way. Use examples to direct the students' thinking as they read. Encourage students to develop and elaborate on their own ideas.

3. *Model the process for the students.* Use examples within the students' experiential and conceptual backgrounds, such as "The Three Little Pigs," "Jack and the Beanstalk," and "Little Red Riding Hood," to model how to identify the central story problem (what is important). Two strategies for modeling (Pearson, Dole, Duffy, & Roehler, 1991) are (1) recall and compare (this reminds me of) and (2) predict and justify (this will probably happen because of that). For example, help students recall "the Three Little Pigs" and compare their wanting to build a house with Little Red Riding Hood's wanting to visit her grandmother. Assisting students in inferring from other events in such familiar stories will enable them to understand that several possibilities may exist, but they must fit the story in a manner that makes sense.

4. *Provide for transfer and application.* Teacher guidance and scaffolding are important features of this step. Help students evaluate their story problems and redirect their thinking if necessary. You may have to use additional examples and illustrations within students' background knowledge. Further model for those experiencing problems in independent application. As students become more proficient in their application, this learning can serve as a foundation for expanding the strategy.

5. *Expand the students' strategies.* Students can compare the central problems (what is important) stories in numerous ways, such as by the type of problem, the type of solution, and multiple but related problems. Teach vocabulary in relation to story problems. Go beyond such concepts as good and bad. Use concepts associated with expressive vocabulary to label characters (such as bold, brave, cooperative, assertive, cowardly, or loyal) and build relationships between character traits, problems, and solutions. Through examination of setting and its effect on story problems, continue to expand students' development of comprehension strategies.

Modified Directed Reading Activities

Many of the recommendations for teaching stories found in commercial reading series are based on the directed reading activity (DRA). The basic features of DRAs associated with commercial reading series (see Chapter 8) are (1) introduction of identified vocabulary, (2) introduction of the story, (3) silent reading of the story, (4) questions about and discussion of the story, (5) skill activities with workbooks and worksheets, and (6) enrichment activities. Figure 6.5 presents a reorganization of these features (Reutzel, 1985).

Compared with a typical lesson, this procedure involves several differences. First, rather than using enrichment activities after students have read a story, they are used before reading and coupled with the new vocabulary. This procedure can activate students' background knowledge for the information and concepts in the story they are going to read. In addition, skill and strategy instruction are related specifically to a story before students read it. This enables students to apply the skills and strategies to the text rather than to isolated examples. Moreover, when teachers present questions before reading, students can predict content and establish purposes for reading.

After silent reading, teachers should ask, (1) Did the students comprehend? (2) How well did they predict the answers to their prereading questions and fulfill their prereading purposes? and (3) Did the prereading questions and purposes improve the discussion?

This procedure is a reversal of the standard DRA format. Such a modification addresses the concern of researchers that teachers spend little time in prereading instruction, and it changes the focus of reading instruction.

Schmitt and Baumann (1986) also recommend modification of the DRA procedure to help students develop strategies for monitoring their comprehension. They argue in favor of metacognitive instruction, which can be incorporated into basal reader lessons with minimal modification. This modification can facilitate students' comprehension monitoring throughout the prereading, reading, and postreading phases of the directed reading activity.

Schmitt and Baumann recommend prereading strategies to activate students' background knowledge and to help students monitor their comprehension as they read. Teachers should model the following strategies:

1. Activate background knowledge. This recommendation is common to both typical and modified basal instruction. Students should use pictures, titles, and

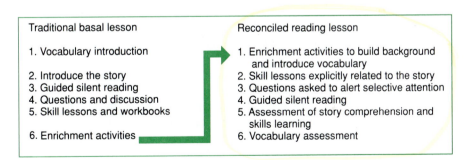

Traditional basal lesson

1. Vocabulary introduction

2. Introduce the story
3. Guided silent reading
4. Questions and discussion
5. Skill lessons and workbooks

6. Enrichment activities

Reconciled reading lesson

1. Enrichment activities to build background and introduce vocabulary
2. Skill lessons explicitly related to the story
3. Questions asked to alert selective attention
4. Guided silent reading
5. Assessment of story comprehension and skills learning
6. Vocabulary assessment

FIGURE 6.5

A comparison of a traditional basal lesson and a reconciled reading lesson
(From D. R. Reutzel, "Reconciling Schema Theory and the Basal Reading Lesson, *The Reading Teacher, 39* [November 1985], p. 196. Reprinted with permission of D. Ray Reutzel and the International Reading Association.)

other text information to help them identify what they already know about the text.

2. Make predictions about the content. Students should make predictions about a story before analyzing the structure. Stimulate group discussion and record the predictions.

3. Set purposes for reading. Students should always read with purposes in mind. The predictions that the students make can serve as sources for meaningful reading purposes.

4. Generate questions. To be more actively engaged with the text as they read and to improve their comprehension, students should generate questions before they read. The questions should relate to the basic structural features of the story (such as setting, theme, plot, and resolution).

Guiding students through the silent reading of the text can enhance their comprehension-monitoring abilities. The following strategies are more detailed than the earlier ones; however, they can easily be integrated with them:

1. Summarize at various points. Students should check for comprehension breakdowns by stopping their reading at various points. The features of story schema (see Story Schema section) are points at which to use this strategy. For example, after a setting has been established, students should stop and check their understanding of it.

2. Evaluate and make new predictions. As students read the text, they should compare their prereading predictions with the new information they encounter. They should understand that new information may cause them to change, discard, or create new predictions. Again, teachers should model this strategy and use familiar text to ensure the students' understanding and application of the strategy.

3. Relate new information to prior knowledge. Illustrate for the students how to activate their background knowledge as they read the story. For example, if students are reading about animals sold at a fair, activate their animal schema.

Schmitt and Baumann's recommendations for postreading strategies are intended to help students develop comprehension-monitoring techniques and thus become more responsible for their learning. As students become proficient in monitoring their comprehension, use briefer discussion sessions.

1. Summarize the total selection. Through the use of group discussions and individual, written summaries, teach the students to summarize story information. Summaries should focus on the main point or points in the story to help students improve their comprehension and recall of text information.

2. Return to the purposes set for the reading. Help students make a good final check on their reading by determining whether they met the purposes they set for reading. Both group and individual written activities can help students realize that the purposes they set directly influence the meaning they construct.

3. Generate questions for the total selection. Glean information about the students' comprehension by encouraging the students to ask questions about the total selection. Questions about the structure features can help students monitor their comprehension.

Teachers can easily modify the DRA to help them monitor their reading. The focus of such instruction is not on skills acquisition, but rather development of strategies that give students responsibility for constructing meaning.

STORY SCHEMA

Another important area in teaching reading comprehension is ***story schema.*** Story schema is a set of expectations about how stories are usually organized (Gordon & Braun, 1983). An internal organization of story knowledge enables readers to process print by retaining story information in memory until it makes sense and adding more information as they read. A reader's story schema also is important in recalling what is read.

Many reading researchers have investigated story schema, and they have proposed several descriptions of it. Figure 6.6 is a direct/explicit instruction lesson for a possible story schema, including setting, initiating event, internal response, attempt, consequence, and reaction.

Setting

The story setting may contain both major and minor settings. Major settings include time, place, character, and state. Time may be either implied (e.g., "Sally looked out her window") or stated (e.g., "One clear and bright summer morning"). Time may also be represented by "once upon a time" or "long, long ago," both characteristic of fables and fairy tales. Place, too, may be either implied (e.g., "Everyone sat down to breakfast") or stated (e.g., "Mark went to visit Aunt Jane's farm"). Major and minor characters are typically identified by name (e.g., Mark, Aunt Jane, or Frank), occupation (e.g., bellhop, police officer, or teacher), or relationship (e.g., friend, mother, or neighbor). State refers to what is occurring. Ongoing states found in different stories include a party where children are playing games; wishes and superstitions; and fishing, camping, or hiking.

Minor settings include the same elements as major settings and develop the story. For example, the major setting time may be summer, but a minor setting time may be one day. The major location may be Aunt Jane's farm, but a minor location may be an old barn. The major character may be Frank, the hired hand, but a minor character may be Aunt Jane. The ongoing state for the major setting may be new experiences on the farm, but a minor state may be new friendships.

Theme

Theme can be either the goal of the main character or the author's message. For example, Billy's wanting his friends to have a good time at his birthday party is a goal of the main character and is a story theme.

- **■ Area of Needed Reading Instruction**

Ability to understand story parts.

- **■ Intended Learning Outcome**

Students will be able to match sentences from a selected passage to appropriate story parts.

- **■ Past Learning**

Students have an existing sight vocabulary and word-identification skills for reading a simple story.

Students understand story analysis and its importance in getting meaning from print.

Students understand that story analysis is related to reading comprehension.

- **■ Building Background**

Review students' past experiences with the major categories of story analysis by providing a simple story on the chalkboard, listing each sentence next to its appropriate category, and guiding students through directed discussion of each category. Explain that the major categories of analyzing a story are setting, initiating event, internal response, attempt, consequence, and reaction. An analysis of the story "The Strange Tracks" might look like this:

Setting	Introduces character and provides background information	Once there was a man who lived on a mountain.
Initiating event	Begins the episode	One afternoon while climbing the mountain, he saw some huge, strangely shaped tracks in the snow.
Internal response	Decision	The man was curious and wanted to learn more about the tracks.
Attempt	A try at reaching a goal	He followed the tracks for two days. On the third day a heavy snow storm covered the tracks and made it impossible to search any farther.
Consequence	Outcome	The man discontinued his search and returned to his cabin on the mountain.

FIGURE 6.6

An example for teaching story schema

(Reprinted with permission of Macmillan Publishing Company from *Teaching Reading: Diagnosis, Direct Instruction, and Practice,* Second Edition by William H. Rupley and Timothy R. Blair. Copyright ©1988 by Macmillan Publishing Company.)

Reaction	Character's response	He realized that his attempt to find the source of the strange tracks was unsuccessful and that they would remain a mystery to him for a long time.

Use guided discussion to clarify each major category of story analysis using the written example on the chalkboard to facilitate understanding of setting, initiating event, internal response, attempt, consequence, and reaction. Use the story "The Strange Tracks" as a source to specify that *setting* includes introducing the character and providing background information, that *initiating event* refers to the first episode of the story, and so forth. Be certain that students clearly understand the terminology and can associate a meaningful relationship for each component with the story.

Remind students that if they understand story analysis they will better understand story meaning. Emphasize that story analysis is directly related to reading comprehension.

■ Teacher-Directed Instruction

Provide each student with a copy of a simple story. Write the same story on the chalkboard to use for reference in guided discussion. "The Foggy Night" is a simple story that contains the major components of setting, initiating event, internal response, attempt, consequence, and reaction:

The Foggy Night

An old woman lived in a lighthouse on the edge of the ocean shore. Late one night she noticed that a deep fog had set in and would make ocean travel dangerous for several nearby ships. She decided to turn the lighthouse lamp to its brightest wattage. So she climbed to the top of the lighthouse and turned the lamp switch to high. Now the ships could tell if they were too close to the shore. The old woman knew that she had fulfilled her mission and she was able to sleep soundly that night.

Instruct students to read the story silently. Guide them through a discussion of each story component by examining and categorizing each sentence. Use the chalkboard to list sentences and match components accordingly:

Setting	An old woman lived in a lighthouse on the edge of the ocean shore.
Initiating event	Late one night she noticed that a deep fog had set in and would make ocean travel dangerous for several nearby ships.
Internal response	She decided to turn the lighthouse lamp to its brightest wattage.

FIGURE 6.6
Continued

continues

FIGURE 6.6
Continued

Attempt	So she climbed to the top of the lighthouse and turned the lamp switch to high.
Consequence	Now the ships could tell if they were too close to the shore.
Reaction	The old woman knew that she had fulfilled her mission and was able to sleep soundly that night.

It is important that your students understand the meaning of the components used to analyze a story and that they can relate each component of story analysis to appropriate sentences. Again, emphasize the importance of story analysis to reading comprehension. Have the students notice that story components such as setting, initiating event, and so forth usually follow a sequential pattern. Ask students questions relating to story sequence: How would changing the sentence order of the story alter the meaning of the story? Would it make sense to list the old woman's *reaction* in the story analysis at the *beginning* of the story? Why or why not?

■ Independent Student Practice

Distribute a second handout for students to complete as seat work. Instruct students to match sentences from a simple story on the handout with their appropriate story components by using the correct letter that precedes each sentence as is done here:

___A___	Setting	**Jasey the Cat**
_____	Attempt	(A) Once there was a cat named Jasey who
_____	Reaction	lived on a farm. (B) One day Jasey was be-
_____	Initiating	hind the barn hunting for field mice when he
	event	heard a rustling sound in a nearby bush. (C)
_____	Consequence	He wanted to find out if the sound might be

(A) Once there was a cat named Jasey who lived on a farm. (B) One day Jasey was behind the barn hunting for field mice when he heard a rustling sound in a nearby bush. (C) He wanted to find out if the sound might be made by a mouse and so he decided to jump into the bush after it. (D) To his surprise and dismay the sound was coming from a skunk. (E) Jasey turned on his heels to run away but it was too late. The skunk sprayed Jasey from head to tail. (F) Jasey knew his trick didn't work and he had realized that the lingering odor on his fur would serve as a reminder never to jump into a bush unless first knowing what it holds.

Help students match the first component of the story with its appropriate sentence in order to assure their understanding of this activity. Refer students to the examples on the chalkboard to help them relate the meanings of the story components with the appropriate sentences.

Plot

Story plot contains five subparts that together represent an episode. First, the starter event begins the episode. It may be an action by a character or an occurrence (e.g., Billy opening his birthday gifts). Second, the character has an inner response—feelings, thoughts, goals, or plans (e.g., Billy was disappointed when he didn't get a new bicycle for his birthday). Third, action is how the story character plans to achieve his or her goal (e.g., Billy planned to work at odd jobs and save his money for a bicycle). Fourth, what happens is the outcome of the character's actions (e.g., Billy found only a few odd jobs and couldn't save enough money to buy a new bicycle). Fifth, reaction is a response to an outcome or earlier action (e.g., Billy decided to buy a used bicycle and fix it up). Episodes are tied together by relationships (e.g., Billy got a used bicycle and then began to fix it up or Billy spent all his money on a used bicycle and his parents gave him the money to fix it).

Resolution

Resolution can be thought of as the main character's achieving his or her goal or the moral of a story. For Billy and his bicycle, the resolution could be that he finally got a bicycle, which he was very proud of buying himself. A possible moral could be that a person who is willing to work hard for something can achieve his or her goal.

Gordon and Braun (1983) caution teachers to realize that this schematic representation of story structure is ideal; not all stories contain all main features, nor do all episodes contain all subcategories. They further point out that not all subparts of an episode occur in the same order. However, knowledge of story structure may help students to "infer content under the omitted story categories" (p. 118).

Teaching Story Schema

Following are some basic guidelines for teaching story schema. They are adapted from Gordon and Braun's recommendations (1983).

1. Use well-formed stories to introduce both the structure and the terminology of story grammar. Walk the students through this initial story and several others by relating the information to their experiential and conceptual backgrounds.

2. Set and illustrate reading purposes. It is important to activate students' background knowledge in relation to the story content and concept and to guide their thinking by referring to familiar examples.

3. Identify the story structure before identifying the content. Initially, discuss the structure features to enable the students to see the permanence of the structure. Just the content of the stories changes.

4. Once students can associate story structure with specific story content, ask story-specific questions. Phrase the questions so that they match the features

of the story structure being addressed. Focus on literal comprehension of the story. After the students have identified story structure with teacher direction, ask inferential questions.

5. Begin to introduce less well-organized stories to ensure that students realize that not all stories follow the ideal story structure. This supports the earlier guideline for teacher-directed instruction, proceeding from the simple to the complex.

Story Frames

Story frames focus on the structure rather than the specific content of stories. They help direct students' attention to how the content fits the structure. Cudd and Roberts (1987) found story frames useful in teaching reading comprehension to first graders. Figure 6.7 presents the different types of story frames they developed for use with a basal reader.

These educators note that developing story frames is not difficult and that in many instances, it is possible to change the basic frame (see example 1 of Figure 6.7) to fit appropriate stories. Therefore, this procedure can be used with longer pieces of text and whole books found in literature-based instruction (see Chapter 9).

1. Ask the following questions while reading the story.

   ■ Is there an identifiable problem? If there is, why is it a problem?
   ■ Are there important events that contribute to the solution of the problem? If there are, what is the sequence?
   ■ How is the problem solved? or What is the solution to the problem?

2. After reading the story and answering the questions, determine if the basic frame will work. If the basic frame does not fit the story, then add or delete the appropriate parts (see examples 2 and 3).

Based on their experiences in using these story frames, Cudd and Roberts (1987) recommend the following instructional procedures.

1. Begin instruction by drawing attention to the structural features in stories (such as setting, theme, plot, or resolution). Print the features on cards to help draw attention to the element being discussed.

2. Once students begin to understand the basic structural features, have them complete short summary frames (see example 4). Use stories that have an identifiable sequence (first, second, then, next, etc.) to help the students understand key sequence frames (see example 5). Begin the teaching of story frames with half-page frames, which are not as intimidating as full pages and can be completed in less time.

3. Introduce the frames, establishing meaningful purposes for them, to help the students understand their function. Remind students not to worry about cor-

rect spelling. Also remind them that the purpose of the activity is to understand the story.

4. As students become more capable in completing story frames, use more complex stories and organize the frame around the main episode (see example 6). Provide concrete examples and supervise completion of the more complex frames so that the students can apply the techniques independently.

Cudd and Roberts note several advantages in using story frames. Students begin to use their knowledge of story structure to organize and learn story infor

Example 1
Basic story frame

Title **The Best Birthday**

In this story the problem starts when **Maria gets sick and she can't have a birthday party.**

After that, **her friends want to make her feel better.**

Next, **they go get a clown and ask him to help.**

Then, **the clown goes to Maria's house.**

The problem is finally solved when **the clown makes Maria laugh.**

The story ends **when Maria says this is the best birthday ever.**

continues

FIGURE 6.7
Story frames that can be developed for the types of stories students read
(From E. T. Cudd and L. L. Roberts, "Using Story Frames to Develop Reading Comprehension in a 1st Grade Classroom," *The Reading Teacher, 41* [October 1987], pp. 75–79. Reprinted with permission of Evelyn T. Cudd and the International Reading Association.)

FIGURE 6.7
Continued

Example 2
Basic frame with no sequence of events

Title The New Pet

The problem in this story was Chen wanted a
puppy.

This was a problem because his apartment was too
small for a dog.

The problem was finally solved when his mother gets
him a Kitten.

In the end, Chen played with the Kitten.

Example 3
Story specific basic frame

Title The Sad Mule

In this story a mule had a problem. His problem was he was
too old to work.

This was a problem for him because the farmer was
going to sell him.

Then one day a hen had a good idea. She told the
farmer's children to ride on the mule's back.

This solved the mule's problem because the children had fun
and they wanted to keep the mule.

In the end, the farmer said yes and they were
happy.

Example 4
Short summary frame

Title __Two Cats__

A country cat came to the __city__ to see __his brother__. But he didn't like __the cars__, and he didn't like __the noise.__ . Then the city cat went to __the country.__ The city cat liked __the soft grass__, and he liked __the old barn,__ . But he didn't like __the big dogs__ He ran back to __the city__.

and stayed there.

Example 5
Story frame with key sequence words

Title __Mike's House__

A little boy made a __playhouse__ out of a box

First, he __made windows__ on the sides.

Next, he __made a door__ on the front.

Then, he __put a rug__ on the floor.

Finally, he __put a sign__ on the door.

The sign said __Mike's House__.

FIGURE 6.7
Continued

continues

mation. They also begin to ask each other questions that deal with story structure. They even ask more probing and significant questions about stories. Perhaps one of the most important advantages is that students appear to perceive stories as wholes, made up of important and recurring parts.

Understanding basic story structure appears to have a significant impact on students' concepts of what reading means. Students begin to view reading as an interactive process and to understand that constructing meaning is the primary

FIGURE 6.7
Continued

Example 6
Main episode frame

Title Red Tail Learns a Lesson

The problem in this story begins because a greedy squirrel doesn't want to share his acorns.

The other animals warn Red Tail that someday he might need their help.

After this, a big storm comes and knocks Red Tail's house down.

Then, all of the acorns are gone because the tree fell in the river.

Finally, the other animals share with Red Tail.

Red Tail's problem is solved when he learns that it is better to share

In the end Red Tail and his friends sit down and eat.

---

purpose for reading (as opposed to identifying words or reading to remember a number of details).

VISUAL DISPLAYS OF TEXTS

Visual displays of story information can be used to teach reading-comprehension strategies and assist students in understanding text content. *Webbing* is a visual display that can help demonstrate the features of story structure and help students understand the relationships among text elements (characters, plot, setting, reaction, etc.). Chapter 9 presents an elaborated discussion of using webbing in helping students develop comprehension strategies and understanding. Norton (1991) concluded from the results of a 3-year study with literature webbing that it is one of the most effective ways to teach the important characteristics of a story. Figure 6.8 presents an example of a web for "Three Billy Goats Gruff." Additional examples of story webs and ways to visually represent text can be found in Chapter 10.

Discussion Webs

The discussion web incorporates all of the language arts—listening, speaking, reading, and writing. It can be used as either a prereading or prewriting activity and as a postreading activity. In addition, the discussion web promotes the use of cooperative learning groups. Figure 6.9 is an example of a discussion based on "Jack and the Beanstalk."

Teachers and students go through five steps in completing a discussion web (Alvermann, 1991).

1. Prepare students to read the selection by activating their background knowledge, establishing purposes for reading, and discussing new vocabulary and concepts.

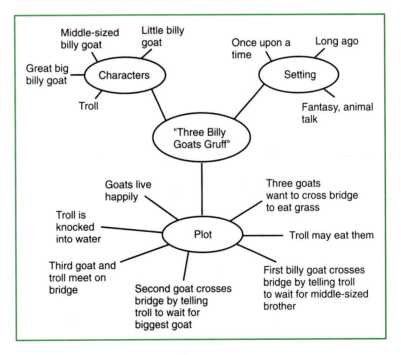

FIGURE 6.8
An example of a story web that represents characters and plot development in chronological order
(Reprinted with the permission of Macmillan Publishing Company from *The Effective Teaching of Language Arts*, Fourth Edition by Donna E. Norton. Copyright ©1993 by Macmillan Publishing Company.)

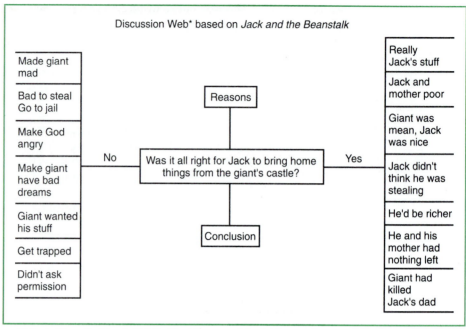

Discussion Web* based on *Jack and the Beanstalk*

Made giant mad			Really Jack's stuff
Bad to steal Go to jail			Jack and mother poor
Make God angry		Reasons	Giant was mean, Jack was nice
Make giant have bad dreams	No — Was it all right for Jack to bring home things from the giant's castle? — Yes		Jack didn't think he was stealing
Giant wanted his stuff			He'd be richer
Get trapped		Conclusion	He and his mother had nothing left
Didn't ask permission			Giant had killed Jack's dad

*Adapted from Duthie, J. (1986). *The History and Social Scence Teacher, 21,* 232-236.

FIGURE 6.9

A discussion based on "Jack and the Beanstalk"

(From D. Alvermann, "The Discussion Web: A Graphic Aid for Learning Across the Curriculum," *The Reading Teacher, 45* [1991], p. 95.)

2. Upon completion of their reading, introduce the discussion web with a question ("Was it all right for Jack to bring home things from the giant's castle?"). Students work in pairs and discuss the pros and cons associated with the question by writing key words in the *no* and *yes* columns. Although students need not write a response for each line in the columns, they should be encouraged to give an equal number of responses.

3. After students have had sufficient time to write their responses, they are paired with another set of partners, and the four students compare their responses. The focus of this step is for the group to reach a consensus; however, individuals may disagree with the conclusion.

4. When each group of four students has reached a conclusion, the teacher or group appoints a group spokesperson. Each group then has approximately three minutes to discuss which of all the reasons given most supports the group's conclusion. Each group should select only one reason to ensure that all spokespersons will have at least one new reason to present. Spokespersons report for each group as part of a whole-class discussion.

5. Individual students write answers to the discussion web question, including their own ideas as well as those expressed by other students. These individual responses are displayed in the classroom so other students can read them.

Alvermann (1991) reports that many teachers have used the discussion web across a variety of grade levels and content areas. It can serve as an alternative to end-of-story questions found in reading series and is appropriate for small groups as well as the whole class. Use of the discussion web has resulted in many students frequently constructing their own questions for the web.

RECIPROCAL TEACHING

A strategy to help students establish purposes for reading and increase their interactions with the teacher and each other is called reciprocal teaching (Brown 1988), also known as interactive teaching. Reciprocal teaching has been used primarily for teaching in the content areas, but it can be used to teach the structure of narrative text as well (Palincsar & Brown, 1988). Essentially, with this strategy the teacher and students take turns in assuming the teacher's role. The goal of reciprocal teaching is gradually transferring to the student the responsibility for thinking while reading. Briefly, the procedure involves four basic steps: (1) predicting, which requires students to activate their background knowledge to predict what they will find in a given text; (2) questioning, in which students learn to determine what a good question is, how to ask questions, and how to read to answer questions; (3) summarizing, or identifying the important content in a passage; and (4) clarifying, which requires students to address reasons that text might be difficult to understand (such as vocabulary, new concepts, and author style).

Reciprocal teaching with narrative text should focus on the features of story schema, purposes for reading, and comprehension. Predicting should consider the resolution. Questioning should identify important information on which to establish purposes for reading. Summarizing should deal with plot. Finally, clarifying should identify which strategies to employ to construct meaning. The purpose of associating the interactive procedure with story schema is to teach another strategy to construct meaning. In introducing and developing the concepts associated with story schema, model the strategy and demonstrate with familiar examples.

ORAL LANGUAGE, READERS' THEATER, AND VISUAL ARTS

Students can demonstrate understanding of what they read using drama, readers' theater, oral-language activities, visual arts, and writing. These methods can also be used as means for instruction.

Throughout this chapter and other chapters in the book we have discussed the importance of oral language in literacy development. For example, Chapters 3, 7, and 10 present numerous instructional activities and suggestions to promote oral-language interactions in the literacy program. Furthermore, in our presentation of modeling, one of the essential features was encouraging students to talk aloud about the strategies they used to construct meaning for text.

Opportunities for oral-language interaction in the classroom need to be realistic and not based on situations contrived by the teacher. One example of a good opportunity is the discussion web, which gives students an opportunity to interact and learn from each other. Such interaction facilitates comprehension, understanding of text and the recognition that individuals can have differing interpretations of text.

Additional ways to stimulate oral interaction among students are to group them together to complete projects (e.g., in science and social studies), share their reactions to books they have read, discuss features of language in books they have read (most interesting parts, most exciting parts, confusing parts, etc.), and work cooperatively in writing activities (e.g., plays, poems, stories, and articles). Such activities can be used effectively at all grade levels and can encourage students to talk about and share what they are learning with others.

Readers' Theater

Readers' theater does not depend on students' action to convey meaning, but involves using "reading rate, intonation, and emphasis on the meaning-bearing cadences of language to make the print come alive" (Hoyt, 1992, p. 582). Teachers can use either published scripts or the students' reading selections for readers' theater. However, using students' reading selections shifts the focus to their responses to literature and integrates features of story schema, writing, and classroom discussion. Integrating such features reinforces and provides an opportunity to apply past learning.

Teachers can use several variations with readers' theater. They can have only one student at a time reading the part of each character, have several students take turns reading the same part and discuss the variations in their readings, use choral reading of parts, or read parts together in small groups. Hoyt (1992) argues that reading parts chorally or together in small groups gives all students a role, which encourages repeated reading for fluency.

Modeling and scaffolding are important components of readers' theater. The teacher can model reading the various parts with feeling and illustrate how variations in language communicate meaning. Teachers can use think alouds to model how they decided to read certain parts with anger, excitement, disappointment, and so forth. Scaffolding is important to ensure that students who have difficulty have background knowledge to relate to the story content and characters. Repeatedly practicing the story with teacher assistance can help students become more confident in presenting the story to an audience.

Visual Arts

Visual arts such as drawing and painting offer students a way to express their understanding of text that doesn't require oral or written language expression. A pictorial representation of a story requires students to use both the affective and cognitive domains; they must think about the story as a whole in selecting what to represent visually. Although a visual representation may seem like a simple task, Hoyt (1992) notes that it requires a lot of evaluation, analysis, and summarization.

Hoyt notes a visual arts activity that teachers can use to facilitate students' comprehension called *Sketch to stretch*. After students have read some text (story, poem, or nonfiction), they have a limited time to create a sketch about what they learned, what they were thinking, what they liked, and so forth. The teacher also creates a sketch on the chalkboard, easel, or overhead projector. The time limit encourages students to create a general impression of the text rather than many details. The sketches serve as a focal point for discussion as students clarify, reflect, and consider relationships before verbally discussing their learning.

Visual arts activities should not take the place of actual time spent in reading and writing; however, they can provide teachers with alternative means for assessing and teaching reading comprehension. As stated by Hoyt (1992), "[Visual arts] can be a powerful vehicle for learning that deserves a place in the reading program" (p. 584).

THE READING AND WRITING CONNECTION

Many of the instructional strategies discussed in this chapter can serve to integrate reading and writing and to enhance reading comprehension. Several additional strategies follow. The use of these strategies can help students develop and refine both their reading and writing capabilities.

Probable Passages

The probable-passages strategy developed by Wood (1984) can illustrate the similarities between processes used in constructing meaning for both reading and writing. This strategy depends on a story schema that uses the story features of setting, character(s), problem(s), solution(s) to the problem(s), and ending. The steps in developing a probable passage include preparation, prereading, reading, and postreading.

Preparation.   Analyze the story selection to identify the significant concepts and vocabulary. Present these words visually along with the story features (the features may need modification to correspond to the structure of the story to be read). Present an incomplete story frame on the chalkboard to use both before and after reading. In this incomplete story frame, incorporate the story features (e.g., "This story takes place in _____" and "_____ is a character who wants _____").

Prereading.   Read the list of significant concepts and vocabulary and direct students to construct a story line mentally. After the students have mentally developed a story line, have them determine where to place each of the key words in the story frame. They should realize that some words may fit in more than one feature and that they can use words from their background knowledge that are logical choices. Have the students justify their responses, requiring them to verbalize their versions of the probable passage.

Integrating reading and writing enhances students' reading comprehension.

Upon completion and discussion of the story features, have students use this information to develop a probable passage. Write in the information for the story frame and guide students' responses by asking such questions as "How can we make that idea fit here?" "Can we reword this sentence to better communicate an idea?" and "Can we shorten this and still make it say the same thing?"

Reading. Upon completion and discussion of the story frame, have the students either read or listen to the story.

Postreading. Have students modify the story frame after reading to represent the actual story events more accurately.

Wood notes that it may take several instructional periods for students to become competent in this procedure. Once students can apply it, however, they can work together in small groups to write their own probable passages. Have them share their probable passages with the class and discuss the range of passages.

The probable-passages strategy integrates reading and writing. It also activates students' background knowledge prior to reading. It provides a structure for students to use in making predictions, reinforces the features of story schema, and engages all students in writing text both before and after reading.

Reporting About Books

Use a story schema to assist students in summarizing and reporting on books they read. Olson (1984) developed the following general guidelines to help students summarize and write about books:

1. Use a story map for a familiar story to help students understand that stories have common features, such as settings, main characters, events, problems, and goals.

2. Present the features of a story schema and use familiar stories to illustrate each feature. Use the features to specify questions that will guide the discussion of story features. To direct students to apply a story schema to these familiar stories, ask such questions as "Where does the story take place?" "Who is the major character?" "What major things happen to the main character?" "What does the main character want to do?" and "What happened to the main character at the end of the story?"

3. After the students understand how to use the questions to guide their reading and summarizing of stories, assist them in identifying a book to read.

4. To help students in writing their book reports, have them list the main characters and events and the relationships among them. Use a story map to accomplish this or have students write responses to a series of questions. Encourage them to identify their own questions as well.

5. After students have either completed the story map or written their responses to the questions, have them write a summary of the book.

This strategy to assist students in writing book reports gives them opportunities to practice and develop an understanding of story structure. It also begins to develop an understanding that reading and writing share many common features.

Thinking and Writing About What Students Read

The importance of questioning and reading comprehension were discussed earlier in this chapter. Teacher- and student-identified questions were both cited as means to promote active engagement with text and purposes for reading. Questions also can be an integral part of a literacy program that encourages students to think about what they are reading. Teachers are often caught in a dilemma when making the transition from reading instruction based solely on a basal reader series to a literature-based reading program. Angeletti (1992) shares her experiences in making such a transition and how she used question cards to help her students think about and respond to what they read in their own books. One of the major features of her instruction was encouraging students to write about the books they were reading by writing questions on cards that stimulate higher order thinking. The basic elements of her instruction were:

1. Using question cards that encouraged students to state opinions (see Figure 6.10). The teacher modeled the cards' use during oral reading of the book to students. Students asked questions of the teacher, who modeled the role of the reader.

2. Practice opportunities were provided for the whole class as students asked the questions of readers who wanted to share the book they were reading. An-

---

Comparison and contrast card 1

Choose two characters from one story. Do the characters look alike? How are they alike? How are they different? What problems do the two characters have that are the same? How are the feelings of the characters different?

Comparison and contrast card 2

Choose two stories. Were the places alike? How were the stories the same? How were they different? How were the story endings different? Which story did you like better? Why? Which character did you like better? Why?

Opinions

What did you like about the main character? What did the character do that made you like him or her? What did you think about the ending? Was anything surprising to you in the story? What was it? Why were you surprised?

Inference

Look at the pictures and at the title. What do you know about the story before you begin to read it? Read the story. Think about the ending. If the story had continued, what might have happened? Why?

Drawing conclusions

Draw a picture of your favorite character. Tell as much as you can about what kind of person your character is. Tell things he or she did in the story. Is this a nice person? Why or why not? Would you like to have this person for a friend? Why or why not?

Characters

As you read a story you learn about the characters by what they say and do. Choose a character from your story. What kind of person is your character? Do you like him or her? Why? How would they act if you were with him or her?

FIGURE 6.10
Examples of questions cards
(From S. R. Angeletti, "Encouraging Students to Think About What They Read."
The Reading Teacher, 45 [1992], pp. 295–296.)

Author's style

Every writer has his or her own style of writing. When we learn the author's style, we know what to expect from that writer. We often know whether books written by a particular author will be easy picture books or chapter books. We know what kind of characters are typical of the writer—animals that talk, or people like us. We might know whether there will be a happy ending. We know whether we would enjoy reading another book by the same author. Choose an author whose style you know and tell what you know about the author's style of writing. Give examples from books you have read by that author.

Author's purpose

Sometimes authors write a story to teach you something. Sometimes they tell a story about something that happened to them. Sometimes they just want to entertain you. Or, they may have another reason for writing. Tell in one sentence why the author wrote the story you read. Then tell how you knew the author's reason for writing the story.

Type of literature

Tell what kind of book you are reading. Look for clues that let you know. If it is fantasy or fiction, for example, there may be animals that talk, or magic things may happen. If it is realistic fiction, there may be real people in the story, and the story could have happened, but the author made it up, perhaps using ideas from his or her own life. If you find rhyming words, short lines, and writing that makes every word count, you are reading poetry. Or you may be reading facts from a book like an encyclopedia. If so, the book is factual. Think about what section of the library you would go to in order to find the book. Then put your book into one group and tell what clues let you know which type of book it is.

FIGURE 6.10
Continued

geletti recommends that the teacher provide guided practice opportunities for a long period to ensure that all students will succeed in the next steps.

3. Small group practice was used with student-formed groups of two to five students. The groups used the cards as questioning guides. Through the practice students became aware of books other students were reading, talked with each other about their books, and planned for other books they would read and talk about together.
4. Students' written responses to the question cards became a major focus of the instruction. Angeletti (1992) noted that students' writing moved from simple retelling to elaboration about what they read and included inferences, conclusions, and character's motives.

The program was extremely successful with first, second, and fifth graders. Writing revealed that students at all ability levels learned to choose their own questions and write responses that reflected understanding and appreciation of the books they had read. Students were in control of their own learning as a result of the modeling and scaffolding that the teacher provided in the early stages of instruction.

Sequence of Events

A. Ask students to bring in their favorite comic strips from the newspaper. Collect these for several days. Cut the comic strips into individual frames and place in envelopes. Give these to students and allow them to arrange the pieces to tell a story. Variations of this can integrate reading and writing: (1) delete a frame and have students infer what is missing and write a description for it, (2) delete the ending frame and have students infer and write an ending for the strip, and (3) remove some of the balloons of dialogue and have students infer appropriate dialogue.

B. Prepare short stories in which the sentences are out of order. Students are to rearrange the sentences in an order that makes sense.

Example: (1) The strange man walked to the door and knocked.
(2) He was invited into the house.
(3) The small dog barked when he heard the sound at the door.
(4) The lady walked to the door and opened it.
(5) The man hummed to himself as he waited for the door to open.

Variations of this can be used for students to predict what happens next, write an ending, and construct sequence maps.

Story Detail

A. Mount a detailed picture on a piece of cardboard. In an accompanying envelope, provide students with three-by-five cards on which individual paragraphs about the picture have been typed and numbered. Students are to read the paragraphs and determine which one provides such things as the (1) most detailed description, (2) enough information for someone who knows a lot about what the picture represents, (3) not enough information to understand the picture, and so forth. This activity can help students realize the importance of their background knowledge in relation to reading for details.

B. Provide students with a series of paragraphs in each of which a nonsense phrase or two has been inserted. Students read each paragraph and detect the absurd phrase, which can help identify students who are too reader-based in their reading. Students can replace the nonsense phrase with one that makes sense for the content of the paragraph, which requires them to activate their own background knowledge in relation to the meaning of the text.

C. Have students read several paragraphs each describing a different character. Have students select the character they like best and list the words from both the text and their own experiences that describe the character. Students can read their list to the class to see if classmates can identify the character. Encourage students to discuss why they used certain words to describe the character(s).

Cause or Effect

A. Prepare or select several paragraphs which describe several events that result in the occurrence of a final event. Ask the students to determine what happened to cause the final

FIGURE 6.11

Suggested activities for reinforcing and applying comprehension strategies and skills
(From Edward C. Turner, "Improving Comprehension Practice and Application
Activities" [University of Florida, Gainesville], by permission of the author.)

event. (This is an excellent introductory activity for story schema, and instruction can progress to longer paragraphs and stories.)

Example: Charlie left for work late one morning because the alarm clock didn't ring. Being late caused him to hurry and he slipped on the sidewalk and twisted his ankle. At work he spilled his coffee on some very important papers and the boss was angry. Charlie was caught in the rain and his new shirt faded on his pants. When Charlie got home he kicked the cat.

Question: What happened that made Charlie kick the cat? Encourage students to discuss and elaborate upon their answers for the question. As students respond, their ideas can be charted on a story map or story frame, which can be used to introduce the concept of story structure.

B. Select or prepare several short paragraphs in which there is a final act. Ask the students to explain and discuss why the act occurred.

Example: Jack slipped out of the house and ran to his favorite climbing tree. As he neared the top, a branch broke and he fell to the ground.

Question: What happened to make Jack fall?

This activity can help students realize how to identify important literal text information in relation to an outcome. Ask the question or questions before students read to direct their attention to important text information.

C. Find or make up several reasoning statements for the students and have them give the answers. Discuss with the students how they reached a conclusion and any statements about which they disagree. Encourage them to discuss what would have to change in the given statements to make their answers not be true.

Example: If there are clouds in the sky it may rain;
If there are not clouds in the sky it will not rain.
It is raining;
therefore, *there are clouds in the sky.*

A variation of this is to have students develop their own reasoning statements and exchange them with classmates who construct an answer.

Inference

A. Proverbs can be identified for which students determine the different meanings that can be inferred. The fact that proverbs are brief and to the point permits different interpretations, which relate directly to individuals' background knowledge.

Examples: Don't put off till tomorrow what you can do today.
A journey of a thousand miles begins with a single step.
He who hesitates is lost.
Procrastination is the thief of time.
Without starting you will arrive nowhere.
He who is not ready today, will be less so tomorrow.
Make hay while the sun shines.

Getting students to speculate about meaning can also be introduced and practiced with other smaller language units: quotations, nonfactual statements, and analogies.

Examples: It is the good reader that makes a good book.
Character is what you are when no one is watching.
You must have a good memory to be a successful liar.
People are lonely because they build walls instead of bridges.

FIGURE 6.11
Continued

continues

FIGURE 6.11
Continued

Students can discuss and interact about the various interpretations for such quotations.

Example: Good people are more miserable than other people.

Students can discuss why they agree or disagree with such a statement. They can write their own nonfactual types of statements and present them to the class for discussion.

Examples: Shoe is to foot as glove is to _____.
          Glove is to hand as shoe is to _____.
          _____ is to foot as _____ is to head.

Students can discuss their choices for completing the analogies, and the teacher can emphasize that differences are due to the inferences students make in relation to their background knowledge.

These activities with smaller units of language are not intended to replace the reading of text; their primary purpose is to introduce a concept or strategy (reflecting the instructional guideline that instruction proceed from simple to complex). As students discuss and provide reasons for their inferences, insights into reading are developed. Soon the students begin to see that in the final analysis these words take on the meaning that each reader gives them.

B. Begin reading a story to the class but stop before completing it. Provide students with several possible endings and discuss why each ending would or would not be an appropriate ending for the story.

C. Select or prepare several paragraphs for students. For each paragraph, provide three or four questions which are not answered directly in the text. Before reading the paragraphs provide students with brief information about the content and have them predict what it is about, what happens, where it takes place, and so forth. Record their predictions on the board and have them read the paragraphs. After reading a paragraph ask the questions you prepared and discuss students' predictions with their responses to the questions.

Example: Henry flinched as he touched his swollen eye. He was mad at himself for not being more careful yesterday during the team's first game. The first game of the season, and Henry stepped right in front of the first pitch.
        (a) What happened to Henry?
        (b) What game was he playing?
        (c) What do you think happened after he got hit?

Inferring Conclusions

A. Give each student a slip of paper on which is written a job title and the characteristics of that job. Each describes to the class the characteristics of that job.

Example: I get up early, I wear overalls. I drive a tractor. I milk cows.
Job: A farmer.

Guide students to discuss the key features of the description that were most important in identifying the job. Have them explain why some features are more important than others.

B. Have students participate in a class activity involving riddles. In these riddles only a few facts are given and students must ask yes or no questions to obtain information to infer an answer for the riddle.

Example: There lying in an open field with a pack on his back. The question is, What can you determine about this situation?

FIGURE 6.11

Continued

Inferring Main Idea

A. Have students write short news articles about world, local, or class events and then select titles for the articles which would be appropriate for newspaper headlines. Students read their headlines to the class and the class predicts what the article is about. The author of the headline and article can provide feedback (warm or cold) about students' predictions of main idea.

B. Provide students with short stories and articles. Students read the text and then represent the important information with a summary drawing. The drawings are presented to the class and the students compare and contrast the drawings and discuss why there are variations. Discussion should focus on the fact that students used different background knowledge in reading and representing story information. Have students explain why they did or did not include certain information in their pictures.

Mood

A. Provide students with large pieces of drawing paper and make available crayons. Play an instrumental record for three to five minutes while students listen. Turn off the record player and direct students to draw anything they feel like. At the end of an appropriate time, ask students to write how they feel on the back of their drawings. As students share their drawings with the class, the class tries to determine how the artist was feeling.

Fact and Opinion

A. Students collect and bring to class several advertisements from magazines and newspapers. In small groups have students select advertisements to discuss with the class. Analyze the advertisements to determine their validity.

B. After discussing with students the kinds of articles found in newspapers, have them bring to class two or three of each type discussed. Have students distinguish between articles that describe actual events and those that are the writer's ideas.

   Example: Report on a local bank robbery versus editorial about litterbugs.

C. Show students a short film or part of a film in which an incident takes place (an automobile accident, bank robbery, scene in a supermarket, etc.) Ask students to write about what they have seen. Discuss what they have written and then replay the film looking for things they have written about. Compare their descriptions with what actually happens in the film.

Author Purpose

A. Provide students with several types of books and articles (comics, cookbooks, science texts, fiction, history). Have them classify the books and articles as to why they were written.

B. Divide students into several small groups. Working together, each group prepares a short story to be read to the class. After hearing the story, members of the class try to determine the reason why the group wrote the story.

C. Provide students with several sets of paragraphs. In each set there are two paragraphs with the same main theme. One of the paragraphs in the set is written so as to provide the reader with factual information about the theme and the other tells a humorous story about the theme. Have the students read the paragraphs in each set and tell why each was written.

   Example: The theme might be raccoons. One paragraph gives facts about the raccoon and the other tells of humorous incidents when a raccoon gets into a camper's tent.

Developing the Reader-Writer Relationship

Other procedures can make students aware of the reader-writer relationship in constructing meaning. Following are several examples that emphasize the reading-writing connection in comprehension (also see Figure 6.11).

- Have students rewrite stories and text to be appropriate for students at a lower grade level.

- To establish real purposes for writing, have students write to authors, companies, classmates, and so forth. Let them interact in small groups to evaluate the communication features of their writing. When their writing is not clear, ask such questions as "What do you want the reader to know or do?" "How can this say the same thing in a shorter manner?" and "What did you mean to say here?"

- Give students objects or puzzles and direct them to write directions or descriptions for these. Have them exchange the written directions or descriptions with other students who attempt to draw the object or puzzle.

- Provide stories that have no endings. Have students read the stories and write appropriate endings for them.

- Give students examples of poorly formed stories to revise and rewrite in small groups. Have them discuss why they revised certain parts.

The preceding are just a few ways to connect reading and writing and to enhance reading comprehension. The key common element of these activities is their emphasis on communicating meaning.

COMPREHENSION ACTIVITIES

Figure 6.11 provides activities that Turner (1988) developed to help reinforce comprehension skills and strategies. Note that these activities are only supplemental and that direct/explicit instruction using the features of teaching comprehension strategies is recommended.

SUMMARY /

Throughout this book we have emphasized that students must learn strategies to use in constructing meaning from text. Teachers must provide varied opportunities for students to learn comprehension strategies and to apply the strategies in familiar and meaningful reading materials. For any instructional activity to teach reading comprehension, teachers must follow some important guidelines. Pearson and Fielding (1991) offer some essential guidelines for teachers.

1. The strategy must be instructionally relevant.
2. Instruction should proceed from simple to complex.
3. An analysis of instruction and transfer tasks should provide evidence of where breakdowns occur.
4. Direct/explicit instruction should explain when and how to use the strategies.

5. The teacher should use modeling, scaffolding, and feedback during class discussions and during or following independent work.
6. A variety of passages and authentic text should be used to facilitate students' assuming responsibility for application to new situations.
7. Monitoring procedures should be inherent parts of comprehension instruction.

The guidelines for comprehension instruction reflect what research has told us about quality reading instruction and development of reading strategies. These guidelines can be adapted to fit most instructional programs, including both basal and literature-based programs.

Instructional strategies can help students develop processes for comprehension. Teachers should combine these strategies, which include direct/explicit instruction, metacognition, story structure, questioning, activation of students' schemata, purposes for reading, and wide and varied opportunities to read books and authentic texts.

YOUR POINT OF VIEW /

Discussion Questions

1. Many commercial reading programs delineate more than 100 comprehension skills. What are possible positive and negative effects of this emphasis?
2. Some investigations of reading comprehension have reported that very little direct/explicit instruction takes place in the classroom. Why do you think this is the case?
3. Why do you think that it is more effective to teach students reading strategies for comprehension than reading-comprehension skills?

Take a Stand For or Against

1. Reading comprehension cannot be taught.
2. An emphasis on comprehension instruction should not begin before third grade.
3. Integrating reading and writing has only a minimal effect on students' reading comprehension because reading and writing are different processes.

BIBLIOGRAPHY /

Alvermann, D. E. (1991). The discussion web: A graphic aid for learning across the curriculum. *The Reading Teacher, 45,* 92–99.

Anderson, R. C. (1985). Role of the reader's schema in comprehension, learning, and memory. In H. Singer and R. Ruddell (Eds.), *Theoretical models and processes of reading* (3rd ed.) (pp. 372–384). Newark, DE: International Reading Association.

Angeletti, S. R. (1992). Encouraging students to think about what they read. *The Reading Teacher, 45,* 288–297.

Baumann, J. F., & Schmitt, M. C. (1986). The what, why, how, and when of comprehension instruction. *The Reading Teacher, 39,* 640–647.

Brown, A. L. (1988). *Interactive learning environments.* Paper presented at University of Illinois Conference on Reading Comprehension, Urbana, IL

Cudd, E. T., & Roberts, L. L. (1987). Using story frames to develop reading comprehension in a 1st grade classroom. *The Reading Teacher, 41,* 75–79.

Dole, J. A., Duffy, G. G., Roehler, L. R., & Pearson, P. D. (1991). Moving from the old to the new: Research on reading comprehension instruction. *Review of Educational Research, 61,* 239–264.

Dole, J. A., Valencia, S. W., Greer, E. A., & Wardrop, J. L. (1991). Effects of two types of prereading instruction on the comprehension of narrative and expository text. *Reading Research Quarterly, 26,* 142-159.

Duffy, G. G., & Roehler, L. R. (1987). Improving classroom reading instruction through the use of responsive elaboration. *The Reading Teacher, 40,* 514–521.

Duffy, G. G., & Roehler, L. R. (1991). Teachers' instructional actions. In R. Barr, M. Kamil, P. Mosenthal, & P. Pearson (Eds.), *Handbook of reading research* (Vol. II) (pp. 861–884). White Plains, NY: Longman.

Erwin, B. (1991). The relationship between background experience and students' comprehension: A cross cultural study. *Reading Psychology, 12,* 43–62.

Gordon, C. J., & Braun, C. (1983). Using story schema as an aid to reading and writing. *The Reading Teacher, 2,* 116–121.

Herrmann, B. A. (1992). Teaching and assessing strategic reasoning: Dealing with the dilemmas. *The Reading Teacher, 45,* 428–437.

Hoyt, L. (1992). Many ways of knowing: Using drama, oral interactions, and the visual arts to enhance reading comprehension. *The Reading Teacher, 45,* 580–585.

McKeown, M. G., Beck, I. L., Sinatra, G. M., & Loxterman, J. A. (1992). The contribution of prior knowledge and coherent text to comprehension. *Reading Research Quarterly, 27,* 78–93.

Moldofsky, P. B. (1984). Teaching students to determine the central story problem: A practical application of schema theory. *The Reading Teacher, 38,* 377–382.

Nessel, D. (1987). The new face of comprehension instruction: A closer look at questions. *The Reading Teacher, 40,* 604–606.

Norton, D. E. (1991). *Through the eyes of a child* (3rd ed.). New York: Merrill/Macmillan Publishing Co.

Norton, D. E. (1993). *The effective teaching of language arts* (4th ed.). New York: Merrill/Macmillan Publishing Co.

Olson, M. W. (1984). A dash of story grammar and . . . Presto! A book report. *The Reading Teacher, 37,* 458–461.

Palincsar, A. S., & Brown, A. L. (1988). Teaching and practicing thinking skills to promote comprehension in the context of group problem solving. *Remedial and Special Education, 9,* 53–59.

Pearson, P. D., Dole, J., Duffy, G., & Roehler, L. (1991). In S. J. Samuels & A. E. Farstrup (Eds.), *What research says to the teacher* (2nd ed.). Newark, DE: International Reading Association.

Pearson, P. D., & Fielding, L. (1991). Comprehension instruction. In R. Barr, M. Kamil, P. Mosenthal, & P. Pearson (Eds.), *Handbook of reading research* (Vol. II) (pp. 815–860). White Plains, NY: Longman.

Raphael, T. (1984). Teaching learners about sources of information for answering comprehension questions. *Journal of Reading, 28,* 303–311.

Raphael, T. (1986). Teaching question-answer relationships, revisited. *The Reading Teacher, 39,* 516–522.

Reutzel, D. R. (1985). Reconciling schema theory and the basal reading lesson. *The Reading Teacher, 39,* 194–197.

Reynolds, R., Taylor, M., Steffenson, M. A., Shirey, L. L., & Anderson, R. C. (1981). *Cultural schemata and reading comprehension.* Urbana, IL: University of Illinois, Center for the Study of Reading, Technical Report No. 201.

Rowe, M. B. (1974). Wait-time and rewards as instructional variables, the influence on language, logic and fate control: Part one—Wait-time. *Journal of Research in Science Teaching, 11,* 81–94.

Rumelhart, D. E. (1984). Understanding understanding. In J. Flood (Ed.), *Understanding reading comprehension* (pp. 86–94). Newark, DE: International Reading Association.

Rupley, W. H., & Blair, T. R. (1988). *Teaching reading: Diagnosis, direct instruction, and practice.* (2nd ed.) New York: Merrill/Macmillan Publishing Co.

Schmidt, M. C., & Baumann, J. F. (1986). How to incorporate comprehension monitoring strategies into basal reader instruction. *The Reading Teacher, 40,* 28–31.

Smagorinsky, P., & Smith, M. W. (1992). The nature of knowledge in composition and literacy understanding: The question of specificity. *Review of Educational Research, 62,* 279–306.

Steffensen, M. S., Joag-Dev, C., & Anderson, R. C. (1979). A cross-cultural perspective on reading comprehension. *Reading Research Quarterly 15,* 10–29.

Taylor, B., Harris, L. A., & Pearson, P. D. (1988). *Reading difficulties: Instruction and assessment.* New York: Random House.

Thomas, D. G., & Readence, J. E. (1988). Effects of differential vocabulary instruction and lesson frameworks on the reading comprehension of primary children. *Journal of Reading Research and Instruction, 27,* 1–13.

Tierney, R., & Pearson, P. D. (1985). Learning to learn from text: A framework for improving classroom practices. In H. Singer & R. Ruddell (Eds.), *Theoretical models and processes of reading* (3rd ed.) (pp. 860–878). Newark, DE: International Reading Association, 860–878.

Turner, E. C. (1988). *Improving comprehension practice and application activities.* Gainesville, FL.: University of Florida.

Wood, K. (1984). Probable passages: A writing strategy. *The Reading Teacher, 37,* 496–499.

Young, T. A., & Daines, D. (1992). Students' predictive questions and teachers' pre-questions about expository text in grades K–5. *Reading Psychology 13,* pp. 291–308.

III

Developing Literacy and Teaching Reading

OVERVIEW

Designing and implementing appropriate literacy opportunities congruent with student needs is a tall order for teachers of literacy. This part focuses on the various instructional strategies and materials one may use to teach literacy. Instructional procedures and materials for teaching reading synthesize the wide array of learning principles, strategies, and skills discussed throughout the text into a cohesive plan to produce independent readers and writers. Chapters in this part will cover the whole-language philosophy and its implementation in the classroom, the basal reader, the language-experience approach, the use of the computer to teach reading, literature-based reading, and content-area reading. The all-encompassing individualized reading philosophy is discussed in Part IV.

INTEGRATING PRINCIPLES OF TEACHING READING

The following principles, presented in Chapter 1, will be reinforced in this part:

- Reading and writing are language processes.

- Reading and writing are interrelated and interactive processes, and literacy instruction should capitalize on this relationship.

- The use of quality literature should be an integral part of literacy instruction throughout the entire school curriculum.

- Literacy is a developmental process.

- Motivation contributes to the development of literacy.

- Teachers of literacy must forge partnerships with the home and community to promote reading growth.

- Instruction should lead children to understand that reading is a meaningful, active, and strategic process.

- Teachers need to foster students' abilities to reason and critically evaluate written ideas.

- Literacy instruction needs to be an integral component in all content areas.

7

Emergent Literacy

For the Reader

Can you recall your first experiences with literacy? You probably had a variety of literacy experiences prior to beginning school—children in our society generally do. Individuals may read books to them. They may see adults making lists and writing messages. They encounter print in their everyday activities through trips to places such as McDonald's, Kmart, Sears, and Kroger. They often recognize brand names for their favorite cereals, soft drinks, and toys. They also may experience print through educational television programs, such as "Sesame Street," "Mr. Rogers' Neighborhood," and "Barney & Friends." Furthermore, children often begin to explore writing through scribbles, writing letters, and drawing, as well as asking others to write lists, stories, and titles for their art.

In addition to direct experiences with print, children begin to develop an awareness of stories and story structure, which is often reflected in their play and make-believe activities. Children's literacy experiences vary according to their home backgrounds and opportunities for language interaction with adults. These early experiences are the beginnings of reading and writing.

Key Ideas

- Children's early literacy experiences vary according to their home backgrounds and opportunities for language interaction with adults. These early experiences are the beginnings of reading and writing.

- Through exposure to print, children begin to establish concepts about print, experiment with its use, and develop understandings about what it means and how it functions.

- Parents' reading aloud to their children contributes significantly to children's experiential and conceptual backgrounds for developing concepts about print, understanding relationships between oral and written language, and developing phonemic awareness.

- Experiences with environmental print help children understand both the forms and functions of print, develop a sight vocabulary, recognize letters and letter names, and develop knowledge of visual details.

- Children must understand the following about print before acquiring conventional literacy: (1) knowing that print is meaningful, (2) the meaning of language used to talk about language, and (3) knowing that letters and letter combinations represent speech sounds.

- Assessment in the literacy program helps teachers adjust their instruction to address students' literacy needs.

- Emerging and beginning literacy stages are broad and lay the foundation for ongoing literacy development in a developmentally appropriate way.

- In planning an emergent literacy and beginning reading program, teachers should capitalize upon what they know about effective teaching, children, learning, and language development.

- Teacher-directed instructional activities in the early literacy program should not be discrete, isolated skills lessons. They should be woven into literature-based instruction.

Key Terms

emergent literacy   children's reading and writing behaviors that occur before and develop into conventional literacy.

environmental print   print in the environment, such as store names, menus, and signs, that has meaning to children.

functions of written language   to inform, entertain, and direct.

phonemic awareness   awareness of sounds in spoken words.

thematic units   integrating content and (science, math, social studies) using literacy to facilitate children's learning of important concepts and ideas.

big books   books with large pictures and print that children in group settings can easily see. The stories often use predictable, repetitive language.

predictable books   books in which students can grasp easily what the author is going to say next. They use much repetition of content and language.

visual discrimination   the ability to note visual similarities and differences, particularly in letters and words (such as the difference between *b* and *g* and the difference between *bat* and *bit*).

auditory discrimination   the ability to recognize the differences in speech sounds within words.

phonics   the relationship between letters and the sounds they represent in written words.

Working with young children, school, and teaching are delightful, dynamic, and captivating experiences for all of those involved. Early reading instruction is changing: It is much more exciting, personal, and child-centered. Reading materials for teaching young children are abundant and creative. Literature-based reading instruction (see Chapter 9) is popular and instruction is no longer shackled to commercial workbooks and basal readers, where the language was dry and unimaginative. Teachers have more freedom of choice today about how they wish to structure their early literacy programs and what materials they use.

A concept that has contributed significantly to this more exciting teaching of reading and writing in kindergarten and first grade (some states, such as Kentucky, no longer have a designation of kindergarten, first, second, and third grades; instead, students are in a primary block from age 5 to 10) is emergent literacy. *Emergent literacy* has been defined in a variety of ways; however, features common to most definitions are: (1) emergent literacy is the reading and writing behaviors of children that occur before and develop into conventional literacy and (2) emergent literacy is developmental (Sulzby & Barnhart, 1992). Teale (1987) considers the meaning of both *emergent* and *literacy* in his conceptualization. He notes that the term *literacy* is of major importance because it stresses both reading and writing rather than just reading development. Teale refers to *emergent* as a forward-looking term. It implies that children are developing in a positive manner in their literacy development.

Emergent literacy is a concept that can be applied to all children. As noted by Sulzby and Barnhart (1992):

> All children are becoming literate—all are emerging as writers and readers. It is clear that some children come from backgrounds in which they have been included in literacy events from birth forward as a matter of course. Other children have had few such experiences. In our research and that of other researchers we note that the kinds of [literacy] behaviors we describe . . . are shown by children from low- as well as middle- and high-income families and by children from all the ethnic and cultural backgrounds that have been studied. (pp. 122-123)

Although all children are emerging in their reading and writing development, children will have had varying literacy experiences before beginning school. Also contributing to the variation in children's level of emergent literacy development are gender and school experiences. Several researchers (Day & Day, 1991; Halpern, 1986) have found that girls typically outpace boys in early literacy development. Beach and Robinson (1992) examined the knowledge and understanding about print that children brought to a first school experience and how it changed as a function of grade in school and of gender. They administered several emergent literacy tasks to preschool through third grade children. The results indicated that:

1. Preschool children have some knowledge and understanding about written language when they come to school. For example, they recognized logos, realized that logos conveyed a message, and wrote using scribbles or letter-like

The research conducted by Mabel V. Morphett and Carleton Washburne in the 1930s and 1940s led to the almost universally accepted idea that children must attain a mental age of six and a half years before they are taught to read or even be ready for reading. As a result, reading instruction was delayed if children had not reached this mental age. Teachers focused on "reading readiness" activities that were intended to prepare children for reading. However, many of the areas of instructional focus, such as eye-hand coordination and visual discrimination of shapes, were not related to reading acquisition.

UPDATE

Today, we realize that children have a wide range of literacy experiences prior to beginning school. They reflect their knowledge of literacy in their play and make-believe activities. They are often aware of print in their environment, they explore writing through their scribbles, writing letters and lists, drawings, and titles for their artwork. They are often read to by their parents and are familiar with the features of books. These reading and writing behaviors that occur before and develop into conventional literacy are now the focus of early and beginning literacy acquisition.

forms. Many of the preschoolers could write at least the first letter of their name and respond to their own writing by telling what they had written.

2. Kindergarten children showed more knowledge about print and its meaning. They were a little better in reading environmental print and most of them knew that they read print in a book. All of them could write their names and were using many letters in their writing.

3. First graders attended more to the actual print than did pre-first grade children. All of them knew that it is the print that is read in a story. Many of them knew the terminology used to talk about print (words, letters, etc.) and wrote stories using letters. Approximately two-thirds of them were reading conventionally.

4. Finally, second and third grade children knew the concepts associated with print, used conventional and invented spelling in their writing, and were reading and rereading their writing in a conventional manner.

Beach and Robinson (1992) also found differences between boys and girls in some of their emergent literacy behavior. Girls did better than boys on the tasks that were most like school literacy tasks (e.g., reading a book, noting errors in word and letter order) in first grade, but differences narrowed in second grade and disappeared in third grade. Girls also outperformed boys on writing and rereading their writing until second grade, where there was no difference. Boys scored higher when preschool and kindergarten boys and girls were compared on environmental print in context tasks. Thus, when given tasks from their everyday environment, pre-first grade boys outperformed pre-first grade girls. Pre-first grade and first grade girls excelled in written language that was more decontextualized from real life.

In summarizing the implications of their findings for classroom literacy instruction, Beach and Robinson note:

> Both boys and girls should be provided with opportunities to interact with written language that requires both problem solving behaviors and lesson learning behaviors. Activities to foster problem solving behaviors would include reading and writing materials in play areas such as home centers or dramatic play areas such as hospital, restaurant, or post office centers as well as including functional print as part of every day literacy routines. Activities to foster lesson learning behaviors would include structured literacy experiences around books, responses to books, language experience stories, the opportunity to read books independently or with friends, and the opportunity to not only observe an adult or literate "expert" write but also to experiment with writing and reading as well. (p. 16)

Early in their lives, children are exposed to environmental print. They see it in stores, on signs, on television, in restaurants, and in their homes. They are exposed in varying degrees to print in books, magazines, newspapers, and to adults who write lists, letters, notes, and other messages. Through this exposure to print, children begin to establish concepts about print, experiment with its use, and develop understandings about what it means and how it functions. The emerging literacy behaviors that children typically demonstrate in varying de-

Through exposure to print, children begin to understand the concept of literacy.

grees are associated with their interactions with print (storybooks, writing opportunities, and art and play activities) and their environment. Through such experiences, children begin to develop concepts about print and what it means to read and write.

ACQUIRING CONCEPTS ABOUT PRINT

The experiences that children have with print and the world and the concepts that relate to these experiences contribute significantly to their emergent literacy. As discussed in earlier chapters, reading is an active process in which readers interact with a multitude of factors related to themselves, the text, and the context in which reading occurs to construct meaning. The meaning depends upon the reader's experiential and conceptual backgrounds. Knowledge that children's backgrounds develop through trips with their parents, playing with friends, watching television, and so forth determines a basis for language on which teachers can build meaningful literacy experiences.

As noted in *Becoming a Nation of Readers* (Anderson, Hiebert, Scott, & Wilkinson, 1985) how significant adults interact with children about their experiences influences children's understandings and knowledge. Interaction, where significant adults talk about experiences with children, helps children develop concepts and vocabulary. Although a background of experiences and oral language emerges from such interactions and helps establish a basis for success in reading, the abilities essential for reading rely more on written language experiences—parents and adults reading to children, children's experiences with environmental print, and children's art and play activities.

Parents' Reading to Children

Reading experts have long recognized the value of parents' reading to children. In the mid-1960s, however, scientific studies established support for the benefits of this practice in contributing to children's reading development. Since that time, additional support has accumulated. Anderson et al. (1985) identified reading to children as:

> the single most important activity for building the knowledge required for eventual success in reading. . . This is especially true during the preschool years. The benefits are greatest when the child is an active participant, engaging in discussions about stories, learning to identify letters and words, and talking about the meanings of words. (p. 23)

The value of parents' reading aloud to their children supports the language-development concepts and phonemic-awareness concepts of emergent literacy. Essentially, this activity contributes significantly to children's experiential and conceptual backgrounds for establishing ideas about print, understanding relationships between oral and written language, and developing phonemic awareness.

Reading aloud to children has some direct benefits that contribute to their emerging literacy. They learn that print is read left to right, what a page is, where to begin reading on a page, that pages are read top to bottom, differences between pictures and print, what constitutes a word, and how oral language is represented in written form, among other things. Listing these benefits does not imply that parents and adults who read to children make a conscious effort to "teach" such concepts. Children acquire much of this understanding indirectly through parent's modeling and informal discussions.

Environmental Print

Children acquire background knowledge for literacy through interaction with print in their environment. **Environmental print** is print in the environment that is encountered in meaningful settings. Examples of such print are labels and signs on objects (e.g., McDonald's restaurants, Coke and Pepsi cans, a Kmart bag, Crest toothpaste), signs (e.g., Stop, Yield, Post Oak Mall), and functional print (e.g., telephone books, newspapers, catalogs, *TV Guide*, lists, and menus).

Experiences with environmental print help children understand both the forms and functions of print, build a sight vocabulary, recognize letters and letter names, and develop knowledge of visual details. Lomax and McGee (1987) found that young children's performance on environmental print tasks reveals that they can visually discriminate many letters.

Parents and adults who point out and talk about print in the child's environment are facilitating the development of print concepts. For example, the parent who responds to a child's question, "Is that McDonald's?" by saying, "Yes, look at the sign. It starts with a big golden M and says McDonald's." is promoting the child's understanding of how print functions.

Art and Play Activities

Children's art and play activities are also important features related to their experiential and conceptual backgrounds for literacy development. Experiences with art, paper, and pencils are related to children's early reading and writing development. Drawings and scribbles are early forms of writing. Although these are not perceived as conventional writing, children use these forms to tell a story or represent an event. After going to see the circus, Rose Marie drew a series of pictures about her experience. She then asked her mother to write the words "balloons, clowns, elephants, lions, and cotton candy" under the appropriate pictures. Rose Marie then simulated reading by looking at each picture as she told a story to her mother. Rose Marie proudly announced, "I can read!" Later in the day, this 3-year-old was making wiggly lines beneath each of the circus pictures and said "I'm writing a story for Matthew," who is her 1-year-old brother.

Children as young as 3 years of age can differentiate drawings from writing (Harste, Woodward, & Burke, 1984). This ability is apparent in their early writing activities. For example, Rose Marie's pretend writing was linear and she moved from left to right as she "wrote" her circus story. She also, as do many children, used some individual letters in her writing and put in some dots. When asked to read her story the next day, she was consistent in her rereading and it was almost identical to her reading of it on the day she wrote it. Most young children are consistent in rereading their stories (Sulzby, Barnhart, & Hieshima, 1989).

Opportunities for young children to draw and experiment with paper and pencil establish background knowledge for later reading and writing tasks that are more instructional in nature. Children often request that their artwork be labeled or titled, that their names be written on it, and that a story about it be written. Such requests show that they are beginning to acquire many of the print concepts associated with emerging literacy and connecting oral language with literacy.

Print Concepts Associated with Decontextualized Language

Chapter 3 presented the concept of decontextualized language, which is central to acquiring literacy abilities that go beyond language in familiar contextual setting; it focuses only on communication with others. Many of the literacy experiences children have before formal schooling determine how well they understand features of decontextualized language. Such experiences are related to storybook reading, for example, knowing that stories have structure, reading from left to right and top to bottom, and knowing the difference between print and pictures. Three concepts about print often develop more slowly, however, but are essential to acquiring conventional literacy capabilities.

Print Is Meaningful

Although most young children can tell the difference between print and pictures and distinguish print from other graphic symbols, an essential understanding for continued literacy growth is the concept that print represents meaningful language. While some children understand the meaning features of print when they come to school, others do not see any connection between oral language and literacy. As noted in Chapter 3, children will not benefit from literacy activities that do not reflect their speaking and listening capabilities. Teachers who provide opportunities for children to focus on the concepts that (1) print represents a message and (2) this message must be as sensible as spoken language will enhance the development of the concept that *print is meaningful*.

Language Used to Talk About and Teach Literacy

Adults often take for granted that young children understand what reading is, including the left-to-right progression of print, the meanings of basic language terms used in teaching literacy, the relationship of our writing system to features of oral language, and the basic *functions of written language* (to inform, entertain, and direct). For example, the term *word* is essential in most beginning reading instruction. The teacher may tell children that they will look at words, learn how to figure out words, and write words. Before beginning school, few children have been asked to think about words, and even fewer children have been asked to think about written words. Kastler, Roser, and Hoffman (1987) point out that for children between the ages of 3 and 6, there is a major gap between understanding of language and understanding of the language we use to talk about language (*word, sentence, letters, paragraphs*, etc.) Furthermore, children's concepts about print are developmental (Sulzby & Barnhart, 1992; Beach & Robinson, 1992). They are influenced by attention to environmental print, attention to visual details of print, phonemic awareness, and decoding ability.

Emergence of concepts about print directly reflects early literacy experience in the child's environment. Parents and others who read to children and provide a literacy-based environment contribute significantly to knowledge of the function and form of written language. However, children's conceptual understanding of reading and writing instruction terminology and the functions of print are not simply the result of defining the terms and discussing the functions of print. Rather, a language-based literacy program emphasizing oral and written activities best helps children refine and apply their emerging abilities in these areas. Activities should expose children to print in the form of oral reading, environmental print, various art forms (such as music and art), writing, and play activities.

Phonemic Awareness

Juel (1987) identified an issue that has direct implications for beginning reading programs. The issue is "whether phonemic awareness is a necessary precursor to successful acquisition or is merely a consequence of learning to read" (p. 240). Several recent studies (Adams, 1990; Juel, 1991; Ehri & Wilce, 1987) support the importance of letter-sound awareness for success in early literacy.

As noted throughout the text, children must be able to recognize words and use their background knowledge to construct meaning. They can accomplish this in three major ways. First is visual memory (recognizing whole words), second is letter-sound correspondence (phonics), and third is context (semantics and syntax). Mature readers use all three of these, depending on the text they are reading. Beginning readers, however, need to develop automatic decoding skills (Chall, 1983; Stanovich, 1986; Stahl, 1992), which are facilitated by *phonemic awareness,* or awareness of sounds in spoken words. Juel (1987) gives considerable support for this position:

> The combination of findings from experimental training studies and from longitudinal studies when taken together seem to offer almost overwhelming evidence

Parents and others who read to children contribute significantly to their knowledge of the function of written language.

for the importance of phonemic awareness for success in early literacy. The training studies demonstrate a cause-effect relationship, while the longitudinal data indicate that this relationship is not just an artificial one induced by experimental training. (p. 242)

The issue regarding phonemic awareness appears to be resolved: Phonemic awareness facilitates beginning reading development. The feature of phonemic awareness that promotes children's beginning reading development is the ability to blend sounds in words. The concept of emergent literacy suggests that phonemic awareness further develops as children interact more with print and develop automatic decoding capabilities.

ASSESSING EMERGENT LITERACY

Many commercially prepared tests are available for use in early literacy programs; however, many of these tests do not provide teachers with information they need to make informed decisions about their instruction. Furthermore, assessment results obtained from such tests often focus on comparing a child's performance with other children and thus provide little diagnostic information for the teacher. Assessment in the literacy program should help teachers adjust their instruction to address students' needs. If, for example, a teacher discovers that some children can recognize environmental print but have had limited experiences with actual storybooks, then the teacher could use opportunities to build on the students' environmental print knowledge in exposing them to storybook reading.

Assessment of children's early literacy experiences is important in an effective reading and writing program. Assessment should focus on the experiential and conceptual areas associated with success in beginning literacy, such as language, concepts of print, language of instruction, and phonemic awareness. Clay (1979) identified four cueing systems for readers: (1) visual attention to print, (2) directional rules about position and movement, (3) talking like a book, and (4) hearing sounds in words. In her presentation of reading stages (see Chapter 1), Chall (1983) identified many of the early literacy behaviors that children acquire before beginning first grade. These emerging literacy behaviors provide the foundation for children moving toward acquiring traditional literacy. Included among such early learning is: (1) knowing that books are for reading, (2) understanding that certain words begin with certain sounds, (3) hearing rhyming in words, (4) recognizing some environmental print, (5) pretending to read by retelling stories while looking at the pages, (6) playing with and knowing uses of books, pencils and paper, and (7) engaging in early writing attempts.

The most useful and valuable assessments of early literacy are observational, informal techniques that focus on children's experiences with print. The purpose of informal assessment is to adjust instruction based on the results. Teachers must evaluate carefully the appropriateness of their instruction in light of students' progress. Each teaching situation is also an assessment situation.

Information from Parents

Home background plays a significant role in children's emerging literacy. A survey conducted by the Roper Organization (1988) identified several home factors that contribute to children's early literacy. Included among the factors were reading to children, letting children see parents reading, having children read and pretend read to their parents, and making books available to children (buying books and taking trips to the library). In addition to these factors, the report of the Commission on Reading (Anderson *et al.,* 1985) recommended that parents provide their children a solid foundation for literacy by encouraging them to learn letters and words and teaching them about the world in which they interact.

Child's Name: _____

Parent's Name: _____

Language(s) Spoken in the Home: _____

Names and Ages of Brothers and Sisters: _____

_____

Family Trips, Interest, and Hobbies: _____

_____

_____

Child's Special Abilities and Interests (Hobbies, Sports, Music, etc.):_____

_____

_____

_____

> Please respond to the list of questions and statements below. Please write in responses where requested.

1. Does your child enjoy being read to? _____
2. Does your child have a favorite book? _____
3. Does your child ever pretend to read the favorite book to others? _____

   _____
4. Does your child ever demonstrate the following behaviors with reading situations? Please place a check mark for the behaviors you have observed.
   a. Turn the pages of a book from front to back? _____
   b. Point to where you or he/she is reading? _____
   c. Read along when read aloud to? _____
   d. Show you where to begin reading? _____
   e. Point to words he/she knows in the stories? _____

FIGURE 7.1
Home information questionnaire on emerging literacy

Obtaining information from parents about children's home backgrounds is extremely important. Such information can indicate students' level of emergent literacy. Many teachers ask parents to complete a questionnaire about their child. Although each teacher may wish to develop a parent questionnaire that parallels the instructional program, the example in Figure 7.1 has been used successfully by several school districts.

The questions in Figure 7.1 are only representative of the kinds of information teachers may wish to gather about their students, and questions may be added or deleted. Valuable information gathered from such questionnaires can be used in adjusting literacy instruction. For example, knowing the names of children in the family and information about them enables the teacher to engage the child in meaningful oral language and literacy activities by talking, reading,

---

f. Tell you what he/she thinks will happen in stories? _____

g. Name the characters pictured in stories? _____

h. Know how to recognize some words, such as store names (McDonald's, Kmart, and Kroger), brand names (cereals, toys, and clothing), and his/her name? _____
Please list some of the words your child can recognize/read: _____
_____

i. Know the functions of lists, television guides, phone books, catalogs, and newspapers? _____

j. Scribble and tell you what he/she is writing? _____

k. Write letters in his/her scribbles? _____

l. Write some words, such as his/her name, family member names, and common words (is, the, and, etc.)? _____

m. Know some of the letters of the alphabet on sight? _____
If so which ones? _____

n. Know some of the sounds represented by letters? _____

o. Try to sound out words? _____

p. Know that words can rhyme and rhymes words? _____

5. Is your child already reading? If so, please list some of the books, magazines, and other materials that he/she reads.
_____
_____
_____

6. Please list any information about your child's reading and writing that would be of interest to his/her teacher.
_____
_____
_____
_____
_____
_____

FIGURE 7.1
Continued

and writing about things that are familiar. The teacher also can use information about the children's special abilities and interests to encourage their participation in literacy situations based on familiar settings and information.

Observing Children's Literacy Behaviors

Teachers can construct checklists to facilitate observation of early literacy. Such checklists should focus on major instructional areas, and should reflect the literacy program goals. Major areas of emerging literacy can form the basis for such checklists, such as those listed in the reading behavior inventory presented in Figure 7.2. In addition to the major categories of book awareness, comprehension, reading-like behavior, directionality, print and word awareness, use of cueing systems, and texts, teachers may wish to add writing-related categories. Checklists should be based on the literacy curriculum of the school and the teachers' classroom. Information from checklists such as Figure 7.2 can be used to develop appropriate instructional activities that build on children's existing capabilities.

Classification Scheme for Assessment of Emergent Reading and Writing

Sulzby (1991) developed a simple assessment strategy to be used with children's favorite storybooks. She recommends that for classroom use, teachers select storybooks with characters and plots that children have responded to enthusiastically over repeated rereadings.

To conduct a formal assessment, the teacher should select a quiet place in the classroom and ask the child to "Read your book to me." For informal assessment, the teacher can eavesdrop while one child reads to another child (see discussion of paired reading in chapter 3) or to a group of children. To prompt the child's reading, the teacher can use phrases such as, "It doesn't have to be like grown-up reading—just do it your own way." If this is unsuccessful, the teacher can read with or to the child, pausing at the end of sentences for the child to complete the sentence or phrase. After completing a few pages of reading with the child, the teacher can again ask the child to read: "It's your turn now, Please read to me." During the reading, the child holds the book and turns the pages.

The teacher can evaluate students' reading and writing using the classification scheme in Figure 7.3. Teachers can make notes as the child reads based upon the behaviors noted in the classification scheme. Sulzby (1991) says, "The classification scheme is a direct measure of emergent reading and of initial conventional reading. It can be extended into the early conventional period by using other assessment strategies such as informal reading inventories and running records" (p. 499). She also notes that it has been found to be successful in assessing emergent reading and writing behaviors among middle- and low-income children from both Anglo and Hispanic backgrounds.

Results from the storybook-reading classification scheme can be used to plan appropriate reading and writing instruction. For example, if a child is attending to pictures and forming oral stories, the teacher can begin to provide more literacy activities that focus on reading and storytelling-like language. Opportunities

Child's name:			

Age: _____   D.O.B.: _____

Book awareness The child: • listens to stories • shares reading with others (unison reading) • begins looking at books as a self-initiated activity • holds the book right side up • turns pages in sequence from right to left, front to back • examines pictures in a book • enjoys having stories read to him or her	Beginning	Secure	Date
Comprehension The child: • recalls the main idea of the story • recalls details from the story • can name events in the story • understands cause and effect in the story • predicts	Beginning	Secure	Date
Readinglike behavior The child: • attempts to read the selection (oral response may or may not reflect the exact text or pictures) • attempts to read using pictures as the cue to story line (attends to pictures) • attempts to read by retelling a remembered text (attends to memory and pictures) • attempts to read matching the retelling to particular pages (page matching using pictures and memory as clues)	Beginning	Secure	Date

continues

FIGURE 7.2
Reading behavior inventory
(From Gail Heald-Taylor, "Predictable Literature Selection and Activities for Language Arts Instruction," *The Reading Teacher, 41* [October 1987], pp. 10–12. Reprinted with permission of Gail Heald-Taylor and the International Reading Association.)

FIGURE 7.2
Continued

Directionality The child: • consistently turns pages from right to left • recognizes where print begins on a page • recognizes where print ends on a page • begins to move his/her eyes and finger left to right across the print while attempting to read (finger does not stop at individual words) • develops awareness of line directionality (child's finger moves left to right across line of print and then moves to the far left of the page and down to track the next line of print)	Beginning	Secure	Date
Print and word awareness The child: • begins to point to clumps of letters and assigns an oral response (each oral response may not accurately match the text) • begins to accurately word match: —beginning of sentences —names of people and things —end of sentences • holistic remembering—uses memory, picture and text to recall the story line • accurately word matches a repetitive pattern in the story • tracks (word points) to find a specific word • word points according to oral language syllables • recognizes common words in stories • integrates many strategies to get meaning (picture clues, memory, tracking, word recognition, context and syntax)	Beginning	Secure	Date

FIGURE 7.2
Continued

Print and word awareness	Beginning	Secure	Date
• begins to accurately word match familiar literature pattern books (uses picture clues, memory, word recognition, context and syntax) • begins to self-correct for meaning			
Use of cueing systems The child: • uses memory, picture clues, tracking, syntax and semantic systems well • becomes aware of letter and sound/symbol relationships • recognizes letter names in familiar words • talks about his or her own reading behaviors ("That's 'dog'. I know because it begins like my name—David.") • begins to use the phonetic cueing system with familiar materials • integrates picture, memory, tracking, syntax, semantics and phonetics to read familiar material • begins to transfer reading behavior from known material to unknown material • uses a variety of cueing systems to read new material	Beginning	Secure	Date
Texts The child: • reads familiar predictable texts • reads unfamiliar pattern texts • reads unfamiliar texts (without pattern) • reads factual texts • reads a variety of texts (functional, fantasy) • chooses to read for enjoyment	Beginning	Secure	Date

Broad Categories	Brief Explanation of Categories
1. Attending to Pictures, Not Forming Stories	The child is "reading" by looking at the storybook's pictures. The child's speech is *just* about the picture in view; the child is not "weaving a story" across the pages. (Subcategories are "labelling and commenting" and "following the action.")
2. Attending to Pictures, Forming *ORAL* Stories	The child is "reading" by looking at the storybook's pictures. The child's speech weaves a story across the pages but the wording and the intonation are like that of someone telling a story, either like a conversation about the pictures or like a fully recited story, in which the listener can see the pictures (and often *must* see them to understand the child's story). (Subcategories are "dialogic storytelling" and "monologic storytelling.")
3. Attending to Pictures, Reading and Storytelling mixed	This category for the simplified version was originally the first subcategory of (4). It fits between (2) and (4) and is easier to understand if it is treated separately. The child is "reading" by looking at the storybook's pictures. The child's speech fluctuates between sounding like a storyteller, with oral intonation, and sounding like a reader, with reading intonation. To fit this category, the majority of the reading attempt must show fluctuations between storytelling and reading.
4. Attending to Pictures, Forming *WRITTEN* Stories	The child is "reading" by looking at the storybook's pictures. The child's speech sounds as if the child is reading, both in the wording and intonation. The listener does not need to look at the pictures (or rarely does) in order to understand the story. If the listener closes his/her eyes, most of the time he or she would think the child is reading from print. (Subcategories are "reading similar-to-original story," and "reading verbatim-like story.")
5. Attending to Print	There are four subcategories of attending to print. Only the *final* one is what is typically called "real reading." In the others the child is exploring the print by such strategies as refusing to read based on print-related reasons, or using only some of the aspects of print. (Subcategories are "refusing to read based on print awareness," "reading aspectually," "reading with strategies imbalanced," and "reading independently" or "conventional reading.")

FIGURE 7.3
Simplified version of the Sulzby storybook-reading classification scheme
(From Elizabeth Sulzby, "Assessment of Emergent Literacy: Storybook Reading,"
The Reading Teacher, 44 [March 1991], p. 500. Reprinted with the permission of the
International Reading Association.)

for the child to hear others read (e.g., teacher reading orally, taped books, paired reading, and shared reading as presented in Chapter 3) could be used to promote continued development of early literacy.

Language-Based Assessment Techniques

In addition to checklists, several language-based procedures are successful in assessing children's early literacy. Coupled with observation of students' engagement in both formal and informal literacy opportunities—such as during instruction and during the time they spend at language-based centers—these techniques provide a wealth of assessment information. Teachers should:

- Hand children a book and observe how they hold it. Do they turn the book so the cover is right side up? Do they turn the pages? Ask them to point out or tell where it begins; how to turn the pages; where to begin reading on a page; and what words, letters, and sentences are.

- Tell short stories that have parts that do not fit with the story and ask children to say what is wrong with the stories. If they understand the concept that oral language must make sense, they usually respond by indicating that they don't understand the story or that it is silly.

- Engage in discussions that help children expand and refine their use of language. For example, if a student says "That's nice," the teacher can respond, "You mean my gold watch is nice?" or "Why do you think my watch is nice?"

- Provide a sentence strip and ask children to cut off a word, a letter, two words, the beginning word, the ending word, and so forth. This will give you some indication of their knowledge about ordinal and spatial features of print, such as word boundaries, and their understanding of beginning and ending words within the context of written sentences.

- Tell short, unfinished stories appropriate to children's experiential and conceptual background and direct them to complete the stories orally. Evaluate whether their endings relate to the beginnings of the stories. Also evaluate whether children are attempting to provide endings that make sense.

- Present children with a situation where a new student who doesn't know anything about reading and writing is coming into your classroom. Direct the children to share with you what they would tell this student about reading and writing.

- Provide students with writing opportunities and note their attempts to communicate meaning. Note how they use invented spellings (e.g., *brthda* for *birthday* and *kresms* or *krms* for *Christmas*). The focus is on attempts to construct meaning rather than sentence structure, correct spelling, grammar, and word usage.

Using Assessment Information

How teachers use information from their observation and informal assessment will depend on their literacy instructional program. As noted earlier, however, the purpose of assessment is to adjust instruction to address students' needs.

Chall's (1983) stages of reading and Sulzby's (1991) storybook-reading classification scheme can provide help in interpreting assessment information and planning appropriate instruction. One way to use assessment information is to consider how children's literacy capabilities are growing and changing. By looking at students' strengths, teachers can begin to consider the demands of subsequent learning and how the strengths can be used to meet the demands. For example, if a child in first grade has had limited experiences with print in the home and the environment, then expecting this child to succeed at conventional literacy activities will lead to failure. Providing the child with abundant opportunities to engage in print activities associated with emergent literacy and offering literacy instruction that builds on these will prompt literacy growth.

INSTRUCTIONAL FEATURES OF EARLY LITERACY AND BEGINNING LITERACY PROGRAMS

In Chapter 1 we presented general areas of the literacy curriculum that apply to various grade levels. The areas included developmental reading, application-transfer, independent or recreational reading, content reading, and functional reading. Early and beginning literacy programs form a foundation for the literacy curriculum and include all of the significant components found at higher grade levels, such as word recognition, vocabulary, comprehension, study skills, independent reading, literature and so forth. As Schell (1992) noted, the early and beginning reading stage is not narrow but rather broad; for literacy to develop later, the early literacy instructional program should lay the foundation in a developmentally appropriate way. Children in a beginning literacy program have widely varying reading and writing abilities. As noted in Chall's stages (1983), Sulzby's research (1991), and Adams' (1990) summary of research on reading acquisition, some children enter kindergarten and first grade already reading and writing conventionally, while others may have limited understanding about and experiences with literacy. Instruction at the appropriate level is important for kindergarten and first grade teachers, because these levels lay the foundation for future literacy growth.

In planning an emergent literacy and beginning reading program, teachers should capitalize upon their knowledge of effective teaching, children, learning, and language development. To maximize the probability that children will learn to read and write, teachers should:

■ Design activities around a language arts base (listening, speaking, reading, and writing) to build on and extend the language background of children. The language-rich classroom provides the environment in which such activities would flourish and nurtures children's literacy growth.

■ Develop in children the concept that literacy is communication and that constructing meaning is essential.

■ Teach and expand children's vocabularies through the use of both oral and written context.

- Provide children varied opportunities to read and to be involved with meaningful reading and writing activities, including reading literature books, writing stories and books, participating in creative dramatics, and sharing books orally.

- In an integrated fashion, teach essential reading terminology (e.g., *word, letter, sound, sentence,* etc.) and concepts (e.g., left-to-right progression, page, letter names, etc.)

- Stimulate and support interest in reading by reading aloud a variety of stories that capture children's interest.

- Incorporate arts (such as music, drama, drawing, cutting, and pasting) to increase motivation and foster language growth.

- Prepare activities to foster and teach listening skills associated with literacy.

- Set short-term goals based on assessment results that build on children's strengths and that they can readily achieve.

- Give children tasks that they understand and can complete with a high degree of success.

- Give responsibility to all children and not just those who are already confident.

- Select goals for your program according to children's needs—not according to what a commercially prepared program states.

Language-Based Reading and Writing Instruction

Children who lack literacy-related experiences benefit from language-based initial literacy instruction. Such instruction includes numerous opportunities to experience and interact with print. For example, teachers should use writing activities, read books aloud, use story telling, label objects in the room, use read-along books. They also should make predictable books, big books, learning and play centers, catalogs, and magazines available to children. The appropriate beginning point is a language-rich classroom environment that helps children acquire and refine basic concepts that are emerging in their literacy knowledge.

The following representative instructional activities coupled with those presented and discussed in Chapter 3 can encourage students' success in beginning reading. Many of the activities appropriate for early literacy instruction, such as oral reading, story telling, diary writing, and language and learning centers have been discussed earlier and are important instructional components of emergent and beginning literacy instruction.

Play and Learning Centers

Although Chapter 3 emphasized the importance of and some features of learning centers in kindergarten and first grade classrooms, this section focuses on some additional features and suggested uses of such centers.

Teachers are an important part of classroom play and learning centers. Morrow and Rand (1991) found that adult guidance in using various materials during play time in learning centers results in children participating in more literacy activities. Adults guided students in the use of literacy materials by reminding them to perform tasks specific to the play area (e. g., fill out forms for prescriptions, fill out forms for patients, and read to pets in a veterinarian's office play area). Adults also modeled behaviors for children by participating in play with them. The role of the teacher in using classroom play centers is extremely important in guiding and modeling literacy behavior that children can emulate. Morrow and Rand recommend that when selecting a setting for dramatic play areas, teachers choose those that relate to a theme being studied in the classroom that literacy materials can further enrich. They suggested the following themes and literacy materials for dramatic play areas:

- Fast food restaurant, ice cream store, or bakery. Literacy materials would include menus, order pads, cash registers, specials of the day, recipes, and lists of flavors or products.

- A newspaper office with writing paper, telephones, computers, directories, maps, typewriters, and areas that focus on sports, travel, general news, and weather.

- A supermarket or local grocery story would include cans of food, cereal boxes, packaged foods, cash registers, shopping receipts, coupons, checkbooks, newspaper ads, and telephones.

Teachers can develop other play and learning centers focusing on situations familiar to all children, such as the local discount store, pet store, post office, and so forth. Neuman and Roskos (1990) also advocate using play and learning centers to foster literacy. They argue that "[literacy] enriched play centers foster more sustained and involved literacy interactions" among young children. They also encourage teachers to make literacy props available in all of their play centers. Literacy props would include telephone books, cookbooks, food coupons, grocery store ads in a kitchen play center; calendars, appointment books, signs, magazines, assorted forms in an office play center; and library book return cards, children's books, stamps and ink pads, bookmarks, and sign in/sign out sheets in a library play center.

In addition to using thematic centers to support literacy activities, teachers should include a reading center and writing center in their classrooms. The features of these centers were discussed in Chapter 3.

Thematic Units for Writing and Reading Activities

For writing and reading to be an integral part of early literacy instruction, children need a wide range of experiences and activities to motivate them to read and write. **Thematic units** built around play centers can be expanded to thematic units that create an environment that promotes children's reading and writing.

Isom and Casteel (1991) described the success of two kindergarten teachers in promoting reading and writing by designing their yearly program around central themes. The teachers focused on three goals to build their literacy environment.

Create an Environment Around a Topic.   The teachers created a spectacular display for their topical unit to get children motivated. For example, the teachers made the outside of their classroom look like the front of barn when using a farm unit. They made their classroom into a jungle when the jungle was the theme. For the jungle theme, paper vines, monkeys, a life-size tiger, and a life-size gorilla were used.

Provide for Language and Concept Development.   The teachers used oral reading, discussion, questioning, art projects, and individual inquiry to facilitate children's language and concept development. They used a variety of books, pictures, tapes, and models about the jungle.

Provide for Group and Individual Writing.   As a result of daily classroom discussions and activities, children produced group-dictated stories often followed by individually dictated stories and illustrations. Children also were stimulated to write at the classroom writing center, which contained blank books in the shape of the theme. They also dictated big book stories and illustrated them. Children shared their writing with each other and their books became "worn with use."

Some teachers have built units to promote reading and writing development by using cereal boxes. Cereal boxes are environmental print that appeal to all young children. Kettering and Graybill (1991) used the boxes to connect home and school in a way that demonstrated to the children that reading is purposeful and relevant to everyday life. They used cereal boxes for developing literacy with graphs by having children place their favorite cereal boxes in columns on the floor and asking questions about which cereal most students liked, how many more Fruit Loop boxes there were than Cheerios boxes, and which cereal had the fewest boxes. Later, they had the children make bar graphs that represented students' favorite cereals.

Cereal boxes were also used in a study of nutrition by graphing the grains from which the cereals were made using columns for corn, oats, wheat, and rice. Stories such as *The Little Red Hen* were used to help children understand how grain is made into food. Other stories, such as *The Terrible Eater* and *What a Good Lunch,* were also employed in the unit on nutrition.

Writing activities included listing cereals by grain, writing ads for favorite cereals, designing new boxes, describing how to make breakfast, creating new cereals, and so forth. Children's writing can be combined into classroom books, displayed around the classroom, and shared with parents.

Writing and reading activities based around thematic units create both experiences for children to write about and motivate them to participate in reading and writing activities. Teachers can create a classroom environment in which writing and reading emerge as a consequence of students' interest and active participation.

Literature and Book Activities

Early reading instruction can use children's literature in a variety of ways. Audio tape recorders can be used to tape children's books, and commercially taped books and stories also are available. Talking books that are taped commercially can introduce youngsters to the content of children's literature or help them gain experiences with it. Books taped by the teacher should be read in a normal manner, with the children following along in the book as they listen to the recorded text. Without instruction to follow along, children often just listen to the stories, which defeats the purpose of taping the book—to help them connect what they hear with the print that represents language. Teacher-prepared tapes also are better for developing literature appreciation than commercially prepared tapes. Children can help select the books to be taped if they are given brief overviews of the books.

Big Books. *Big books* have large pictures and print that children in group settings can easily see. The stories often use predictable, repetitive language and focus on content appealing to young children. Big books are used frequently in a shared-reading setting, where the teacher reads the story aloud and children join in the reading. Because the language is repetitive, teachers can let children finish reading parts of sentences and phrases. Teachers point to the words as they read with feeling and expression. Using big books helps children to develop an appreciation for reading, make connections between print and oral language, understand directionality of print (reading left to right), and see relationships between graphemes and phonemes in meaningful context.

We have observed wide variation in the effective use of big books in kindergarten and first grade classrooms. Some teachers working with children who have limited literacy experiences focus on helping them understand the features of books, such as front, back, page, left to right progression, top to bottom, title, author, and words. During shared reading, teachers emphasize each of these features without interfering with appreciation and enjoyment of the story. They often have children come up and turn to their favorite page, show them the top of the page, where they would begin reading, and so forth. Big books are also placed in the reading center, where children can use them individually or with each other. We have often observed children "playing school" by using big books to read to two or three other children, modeling many of the things that their teacher emphasized during reading of the big book.

Teachers can purchase big books through commercial publishers or make their own. Many of the large paperback picture books that can be purchased inexpensively at discount stores can be used to construct big books. Teachers would need to buy two copies of the book, cut out and paste the pictures on tagboard, and write the story beneath the appropriate picture using large print. Books selected for use in making big books should reflect children's interests and background knowledge and be well written. Other sources for big books include using song lyrics, old calendars, and children's drawings.

Big books can be made from cereal boxes and used with either a thematic unit on nutrition or in shared reading. Box fronts from children's favorite cereals

Teachers can create a classroom environment in which literacy emerges as a consequence of students' interest and active participation.

can be glued to large sheets of tagboard and large print used to write predictable text: "Trix, the cereal that the rabbit loves to munch," "Fruit Loops, the cereal where colors come in a bunch," "Cheerios, the cereal that you can eat for lunch." Children can construct other big books by dictating group-experience stories about their favorite cereals.

Big books are available for areas such as science and social studies. These books are excellent for introducing new concepts and vocabulary. Children can also help the teacher create big books in content areas that relate to direct experiences they have both in and out of the classroom. For example, we recently visited a kindergarten class that created a big book about the rabbit, mice, and gerbil kept as pets in the classroom. The children dictated information about the size of each animal, their living conditions, and the types of food they eat. The teacher recorded the children's dictation in large print and used photographs taken with an instant camera to illustrate the text.This activity preceded a visit by a veterinarian who specialized in exotic animals. After the veterinarian's visit, the children dictated additional information to add to their "Care and Feeding of Animals" big book. The children made similar big books for a unit on farm animals. These activities are similar to those associated with the language-experience approach discussed in Chapter 8. As a result of shared experiences, children dictate to the teacher how they want their experiences to be represented in print. They can draw their own pictures to represent their experiences, or the teacher can help select appropriate illustrations, such as photographs or magazine pictures. Language-experience activities can result in construction of big books, shared experience charts, or individual student books.

Predictable Books. ***Predictable books*** help children begin to use prediction strategies as they read. This frees them from focusing on individual words as they read. A predictable book is one in which students can grasp easily what the author is going to say next. A basic feature is much content and language repetition. To begin using predictable books, follow these steps (Tompkins & Weber, 1983):

1. *Introduce the book.* Read the title and show the cover illustration. Ask children to make predictions about the story content. Direct them to use both word and picture clues in making their predictions.

2. *Read the book aloud.* Read the book through the first set of repetitions into the second set. Ask students to make predictions by telling you what they think will happen next.

3. *Discuss the predictions.* Following the students' predictions, ask them to explain why they made such predictions.

4. *Read the next set of repetitive patterns.* Confirmation of the predictions is the focus here.

5. *Continue reading, and repeat steps 2 through 4.* Monitor students' predictions closely as they make and confirm their predictions. If the students experience difficulty, they may lack the experiential or conceptual background for the content, language structure, or both.

Once children begin to experience success with teacher direction, they can begin to read predictable books on their own. Be willing to accept approximations of story language and to support students' attempts to complete reading of predictable books. Provide ample opportunities to model and transfer their prediction strategies to other reading activities, such as shared and paired reading.

Basic characteristics of predictable books (strong rhythm and rhyme, repeated language patterns, logical sequence, supportive illustrations, and traditional story structure) allow them to be used in a variety of ways to support emergent literacy. Examples include identifying rhyming words, making sounds associated with animal characters, talking as the characters might talk, dramatizing how the characters might act, making picture dictionaries for items presented in the stories, creating murals and clay figures, identifying and classifying characters by similar and different traits, and writing different endings. Such activities with predictable books create a language-based instructional program that enhances literacy development.

Poetry in the Literacy Program

Literature in the early reading program should include poetry, and the best way to introduce it is to read it aloud. Many other activities can further acquaint children with poetry, including writing, creative dramatics, art, reading, and language awareness.

Children enjoy listening to poetry that is predictable and will often join in reading it aloud with the teacher. For example, one of Billy's favorite poems was about a frog; and after the teacher read it to him several times, he took much delight in reading it to himself and his friends. What made the poem so appealing to him was the repetition of the line "Hop, hop, hop," which made up about seven stanzas of the poem.

The teacher can also read appropriate poems to children as they listen with their eyes closed to the melody of the poem. Children can be encouraged to form mental images of the contents and discuss their perceptions of the melody and mental images with each other. By reading the same poem several times with a different language melody each time, teachers can help children begin to appreciate and understand the language features of poetry.

Teachers can use language activities to compose poems individually or in a group. An excellent poetry form for introducing such activities is haiku. Colorful pictorial materials, such as paintings, photographs, and drawings can stimulate children to form the word pictures for haiku. Haiku is a 17-syllable pattern in three lines, with five syllables in the first and third lines and seven in the second line. For example, a picture of a dancing bear inspired Donald to dictate the following to his teacher, who assisted him with identifying words to fit the haiku pattern (this assistance is important, and the teacher can help children identify words by discussing features of the picture with them and offering word possibilities):

The brown dancing bear,
Dancing around in his cage,
Dancing on his toes.

Pictures that the children draw can be used to stimulate poetry writing. Janet drew a picture of some ghosts and monsters for a Halloween activity and dictated the following poem to her teacher:

Ghosts are floating in the air,
Floating, floating, floating.
Look out there's a monster over there.

Other poetry-writing experiences can relate to music and art activities. For example, a kindergarten class composed the six lines of the following poem with guidance by their teacher.

Music, music in the air.
Music, music everywhere.
We went skipping,
    sliding
    jumping,
    running,
    bouncing,
    hopping,
    dancing,
Round and round the room.

Poetry can be used to encourage students' reading and writing. In addition, children can learn concepts associated with phonemic awareness using the context of poems to focus on spelling patterns and the sounds represented. The teacher could use the "Hop, hop, hop" part of the poem that so intrigued Billy to teach the sounds the letters *op* represent in words such as *stop, flop, mop, pop,* and so forth. Children can then use these words to generate more stanzas for the poem, replace words in the poem, and write new poems.

Reading Aloud and Telling Stories

Reading aloud to children and its role in a language-rich classroom were major points of discussion in Chapter 3. We reemphasize the importance of reading aloud to children to encourage all teachers to make it an integral part of their daily literacy program. Children need to understand early in their reading development that the purpose of reading is communication. Reading stories and other written materials that captivate their minds and stimulate their interest in reading helps youngsters conceptualize written language and the basic features of written text. Specifically, the daily oral sharing of books is important for emerging literacy development. Children learn basic concepts from this practice, including story language, expectations for story characters, and storytelling. In essence, they learn to talk like a book. Also, reading aloud to them expands their vocabularies and background knowledge and is an enjoyable experience.

Storytelling is another important practice that can help children understand the relationship between oral language and literacy. All kids love to hear a story that is well told. Sources that teachers can use for identifying stories to tell include family traditions or events, parts of favorite books that appeal to children, stories about traditional holidays or made-up holidays, characters familiar to the children, and so forth. Lundsteen (1989) recommends that teachers prepare for telling the story by (1) planning a brief introduction that relates the story to the children; (2) relating the story incidents in the intended sequence and being spontaneous; (3) making characters come alive by effective use of voice, gesture, and/or posture; (4) using interesting speech patterns to represent characters and mood; and (5) using verbal, mechanical, or musical sounds to accompany the telling of the story.

Teachers can use several variations in telling stories. They can tell the story and stop at appropriate places to ask children to predict what will happen next. They can also stop and ask children questions about their feelings or why certain events might have happened in the story. Sometimes interrupting the story will diminish youngsters' interest in it; however, on other occasions such discussions can heighten their interest. Teachers should monitor children's interest closely and adjust the discussion during storytelling to maintain a high level of children's interest.

Another variation of storytelling is to have children illustrate the story that was told. This requires them to relate the story directly to their comprehension of language. Promote discussion of the pictures by the children and write their comments at the bottom of each of their picture pages. Use the drawings to discuss major story events, sequence, character traits, and as prompts if they wish to retell the story.

A third variation is to start a story and direct children to add to it. As each child makes a contribution, write the response on a flip chart for everyone to see. This reinforces the relationship between oral and written language and illustrates the concepts associated with literacy language, such as words, letters, sentences, and communication of meaning.

In still another variation of storytelling, let children dramatize stories told to them. This can be combined with the concept of readers' theater (see Chapter 6), whereby children create a script for a book or part of a book. Students can write the script individually, in pairs, or in small groups. Once written, the writers and others can dramatize the script. Dramatizing stories helps youngsters develop understanding of story parts. In preparing the script, children must translate the story parts into an integrated whole. Dramatization also reinforces the communicative function of print by helping the teacher better understand students' comprehension of stories told to them and read to them.

DIRECT/EXPLICIT INSTRUCTIONAL ACTIVITIES

The majority of the activities presented so far place the teacher in the role of facilitator and promoter of literacy activities for children. However, some areas of early literacy programs require direct/explicit instruction (see Chapters 6 and 9). Facilitating acquisition and development of listening capabilities, auditory discrimination, visual discrimination, phonics, comprehension, and vocabulary requires teacher-directed instruction. These are not taught as discrete, separate activities that resemble isolated skills lessons, but are woven into literature-based activities. Instruction in these areas still aims to develop capabilities within the context of meaningful text and language, but the teacher's role is more central in initiating, guiding, and directing students' learning.

Listening Capabilities

In developing listening skills, one deals with a much broader area than just auditory discrimination of speech sounds. Listening is involved in all facets of the curriculum. Listening is required for following directions, developing and expanding concepts, maintaining discipline, planning curricular activities, and the like. Listening is closely related to many literacy behaviors, such as developing auditory memory and processing language presented orally in stories and discussions.

Children differ noticeably in their listening abilities. Some children come to school with poor listening habits, while others develop inadequate habits early in school. These deficits have an impact on classroom activities and deter learning. Listening involves more than just being physically present while someone is speaking. Providing a variety of experiences in listening is as important as providing experiences in literacy learn.

Many learning activities in school depend on listening. These include listening to stories, listening to the teacher, and listening to other students. Following are a few activities to involve children in listening to and interpreting language.

They call upon the learner to attend to, process, retain, and respond to language stimuli.

Riddles.   Most youngsters are intrigued by riddles. They enjoy both telling them and listening to them. Often they will come up with many variations of the same riddle. Both factual and nonsense riddles are appropriate to use in developing children's listening capabilities. In addition, children will often come away from an activity that uses riddles motivated to write their own and construct a book of riddles. Sharon brought home her book of riddles, which consisted of seven pages. Each page was a variation of one riddle that her teacher used to encourage listening—"Why did the hippopotamus cross the road?" (answer: it was the chicken's day off). Examples of Sharon's riddles were: "Why did the cat cross the road?" "Why did the giraffe cross the road?" and "Why did the bug cross the road?" Of course, each riddle had the same answer, "It was the chicken's day off." The teacher had written this and several other riddles on the chalkboard; Sharon copied the text and asked her teacher to help her write each of the different animal words. She also drew a picture for each variation of the riddle. Her parents knew she must have been listening, because she also asked them several other riddles— "What chases the moon away every morning?" (the sun); "What goes away when you stand up?" (your lap); and "What holds up trains?" (train robbers). This activity clearly promoted careful listening by Sharon and motivated her to create, write, and read her own riddles.

Teachers can write short, descriptive passages on the chalkboard—about objects, characters from a story, shared experiences, and events from stories—read the passage to the children, then direct them to listen carefully and draw a picture of what is described. As the teacher reads the story aloud, he or she should direct students to focus on the written text as well. For example:

> I wanted to catch a lot of fish.
> I stuck my tail through a hole in the ice.
> I didn't catch any fish.
> I now have a short tail.
> Who am I?

> I grow outdoors.
> In the summer I am full of leaves.
> Sometimes I have baby birds living in me.
> In the fall I am full of colors.
> What am I?

Not only does listening to these descriptions help children develop listening skills, but children can also discuss what clues were the most important in helping them figure out what is being described.

Telling and Reading Stories.   The activities described earlier for storytelling and reading aloud are excellent ways to encourage listening in a meaningful context. When telling or reading stories, the teacher plants the ideas that good listening is the key to enjoyment of the story and print is meaningful.

Visual Discrimination

By the time children come to school, they have had thousands of experiences in seeing and noting likenesses and differences. They have developed ability for fairly high-order *visual discrimination,* in many cases based on relatively small clues. Visual discrimination is the ability to see similarities and differences. For example, at the age of 3 years, a child can identify and claim her tricycle from a group, even though she was not able to explain exactly how she did it.

Later, children can identify common trademarks on the basis of size, color, shape, and function. They can sort a group of objects by size and shape without much difficulty based on visual discrimination.

Children's need for fine visual discrimination in reading is self-evident, since the symbols that they read are visual stimuli. Many words look alike and a child who cannot differentiate among the various words in a passage cannot possibly understand that passage. The widely accepted definition of reading as "getting meaning from printed symbols" slights the sensory skills that are essential to getting meaning.

We have found from working in many lower grade classrooms that one of the most effective ways to help children develop the ability to visually differentiate letters and words is through wide exposure to meaningful text. Furthermore, as children begin to recognize whole words, they become better able to visually discriminate words that are spelled differently. Many times teachers must point out the features of words to facilitate development of visual discrimination. They can do this using meaningful text—big books, predictable books, library books, and children's writing, for example. This practice was observed recently in a local kindergarten. Jason had checked out *The Whole Book of Wheels* from the school library. His teacher asked him which two words in the title start with the same letter. Jason did not respond. The teacher rephrased her question: "Show me the two words that start with the letter W." Jason immediately pointed to *whole* and *wheels.* This example illustrates the importance of integrating visual discrimination activities into a literacy program rather than treating them separately as skill lessons that may not be meaningful for children.

Auditory Discrimination/Phonemic Awareness

The major objective of fostering *auditory discrimination* is to help children become conscious of speech sounds within words. This ability is also known as phonemic awareness. The importance of phonemic awareness was discussed in Chapter 3, where it was noted that it is an important precursor to acquiring conventional reading capabilities. Stahl (1992) pointed out that in learning to read, children need to view words in terms of the sounds they represent. By understanding that spoken words contain phonemes (sounds), children can learn the relationship between letters and the sounds they represent.

Many children come to school playing language games with rhyming words. Rhyming words are an excellent starting point for teaching and reinforcing phonemic awareness. However, for rhyming activities to be effective, teachers must ensure that children understand the concept of rhyming words. Examples of activities using rhyming words are presented next.

INSTRUCTIONAL ACTIVITIES

■ *Rhyming Color Names.* Review some familiar color names with children (e.g., red, blue, green, orange, black, white, yellow, brown). Write the color names on the chalkboard and direct students to listen carefully to the ending sounds in the two words you will pronounce. Ask students to think about which color word rhymes with (has the same ending sounds as) the two words pronounced. Model one or two examples for them before calling on students to give a response.

> *Said* and *Fred* rhyme with?
> *Down* and *frown* rhyme with?
> *Night* and *bright* rhyme with?

■ *Rhyming Lines and Jingles.* Jingles and rhyming lines can demonstrate intonation and rhyming elements. These involve longer language units that also provide experiences for auditory memory. The following example uses number words and asks children to discriminate the word that is stressed and complete the statement with a number word that rhymes with that word. Follow the same procedures used for the color name activity.

> I saw a number on the door
> The number that I saw was _____

> The door led into a den
> The snakes I counted numbered _____

> I left the room and I did see
> A boy who said his age was _____

> To keep this rhyming game alive
> We have to say the number _____

Many of these activities are similar to those that Griffth and Olson (1992) proposed for developing children's phonemic awareness. In addition to such activities, they recommend that teachers read books that play on language (alliteration, repetition of vowel sounds within words, and rhymes), provide writing opportunities that allow children to use invented spellings, and draw boxes around sounds represented by letters in written words ([d] [u] [ck]).

Visual and Auditory Integration

Visual and auditory integration is combining visual and auditory capabilities with print. It usually occurs after children have learned to recognize letters and some words. A series of instructional activities can build on students' reading and writing experiences to help youngsters acquire these capabilities.

Once children have developed phonemic awareness and visual discrimination of letters and words, teachers can use words from big books, predictable books, children's writing, and environmental print to teach visual and auditory integration. The earlier example of Billy's fascination with the poem that repeated the phrase hop, hop, hop in several stanzas suggests ways to teach auditory and visual integration. The word *hop* could illustrate how the words *stop, pop, mop, flop,* and others require visually discriminating the different beginning letter, hearing the sounds represented, and integrating both to determine that *hop* and *pop* are different words. Using different endings could reinforce visual and auditory integration *(hop-hot, pop-pot)*. Changing words and inserting them into the text could prompt a discussion of changes in meaning and whether the language makes sense.

Phonics

Chapter 4 presented the content of phonics. ***Phonics*** is the relationship between letters and letter combinations and the sounds they typically represent in words. The focus here is on presenting some instructional guidelines that treat phonics not as an isolated skill, but rather weave it into classroom literacy activities. Combining what is presented here with the variety of activities presented in Chapter 4 can help teachers select those that match their students' needs.

Literature and literacy activities that are happening in the classroom can provide materials for teaching phonics. These sources can furnish words to illustrate phonic generalization: The words are taken out of text and then placed back in the text to illustrate application of phonics in reading. This still allows for the systematic study of words in terms of their graphemic/phonemic features (letter(s) and sounds typically represented); however, phonics is integrated into the literacy program, not isolated from it.

Stahl (1992) identified some guidelines for phonics instruction that can apply in literature-based classrooms and classrooms using a basal text as the core text.

■ Phonic instruction builds on children's phonemic awareness. Stahl says, "Only by understanding that spoken words contain phonemes can one learn the relationships between letters and sounds" (p. 621).

■ Phonic instruction is clear and direct. By using words familiar to students from their reading and writing activities, teachers can illustrate letter sound relationships in a more meaningful fashion. Stahl recommends that teachers present written word(s), such as *bear,* and stress that it starts with the letter *b* and makes the sound /b/. Or teachers can present the letter *b,* then show words that begin with the sound that letter represents. Following these activities, children would practice reading other words beginning with the letter *b.*

■ Phonics is an integral part of the reading program, not a dominant feature of instruction. Teachers can use text that students have read or written to teach a high utility phonic element (e.g., a beginning consonant digraph, such as *sh*). Written examples of words from the text can be applied to help in reading another text containing several examples of the phonic element.

- Phonics should focus on reading words, not learning rules. Stahl recommends using rules to point out a particular spelling pattern, but not requiring children to memorize or recite the rule.

- Phonics instruction may include the use of onsets and rimes. Onsets are the part of the syllable before the vowel. Rimes are the part from the vowel onward. Approximately 500 words can be derived from the following rimes:

-ack	-ain	-ake	-all	-ame	-and
-ank	-ap	-ash	-at	-ate	-aw
-ay	-eat	-ell	-est	-ice	-ick
-ide	-ight	-ill	-in	-ine	-ing
-ink	-ip	-ir	-ock	-oke	-op
-or	-ore	-uck	-ug	-ump	-unk

Children can be taught to compare unknown words with known words and then ask themselves if their predictions or identifications of unknown words "make sense in the story." Again, familiar literacy activities can supply words to highlight the use of onsets and rimes: for example, if students know *clap* and *duck,* then they can figure out *cluck* using their knowledge of onsets and rimes.

- Phonics instruction may include invented spelling practice. Although invented spelling is no substitute for direct phonics instruction, Stahl notes that practice with invented spelling does improve children's awareness of phonemes.

- Phonics instruction is intended to develop children who use independent word-recognition strategies, focusing on the internal structure of words. Phonics makes children aware of orthographic patterns in words and helps them use this knowledge to recognize words. Recognizing these letter patterns makes children efficient at identifying words.

- Phonic instruction should develop automaticity in word recognition. Children who can automatically recognize words spend less time decoding the text and more on comprehension. Automatic word recognition comes about through practice in reading words. This is the purpose of Chall's (1983) stage two, where children develop fluency in reading. Continuing to use meaningful literacy activities that allow children to apply their knowledge of phonics will provide them the practice needed to improve both their word recognition capabilities and comprehension.

A classroom environment that supports children's acquisition of phonic knowledge will provide for application of phonic generalizations. Phonic charts that the students and teacher develop cooperatively can be displayed for the students' reference when reading. Words that illustrate particular letter-sound relationships on the charts can come from children's writing, predictable books, big books, and literature-based reading series. For example, teachers could develop large classroom charts such as the following using onsets and rimes:

```
_____ake


    bake          shake

    rake          lake

    make          cake
```

The teacher can make such charts for individual students or for the whole class. Those used with individual students can be bound into a booklet that the child refers to when reading and writing. Children can add their own words to those listed as they encounter words that fit the spelling pattern. The teacher can add more words found in the children's reading and writing.

Children can also make and add to their own phonic big book that is available for the whole class to use. For example, after Mrs. Smalling's first grade went on a field trip to the zoo, each child selected an animal, drew a picture of it, and then drew pictures representing words that began with the same letter as the animal's name. Shawn drew pictures of a bear and boat, bottle, box, ball, Batman, and Batmobile. Mrs. Smalling then printed the names of three of the objects beneath them and asked Shawn to print the beginning letter for the remaining objects. He printed the letter *b* and, with the teacher's help, printed the rest of the words. Mrs. Smalling assembled all of the children's products into a big book that not only represented their trip to the zoo, but also served as a support for phonic knowledge and application.

Building Background Knowledge

Helping children increase their background knowledge is essential in promoting vocabulary and comprehension of text. Children cannot understand things for which they have no prior knowledge, whether it is the language structure, the words that represent ideas, or the content of what they are reading. Chapter 5 focuses on vocabulary and presents many instructional activities for developing children's meaning vocabulary. Comprehension is presented in Chapter 6 along with strategies for teaching comprehension and making instruction effective. This section presents some examples of how teachers can better prepare children for literacy activities by expanding their background and vocabulary knowledge.

Using Pictures, Videos, Films, and Filmstrips. Visual materials are excellent ways to expand and refine concepts associated with children's background knowledge and literacy. For example, a picture of an eroded hillside is much more effective in fixing the concept of erosion than is a word definition or term.

The same picture can be used at different levels for teaching words and meanings. Imagine a picture available to almost any teacher: a downtown scene in an average-size city. It shows a bus, a boy on a bicycle, various store fronts and offices, a police officer directing traffic, a fire hydrant, and a bank. Without going into more detail, we might build a hierarchy of concepts. The degree of teacher direction will vary according to students' existing capabilities.

"Point out the police officer."

"Where is the police officer standing?"

"Yes, he is really standing where two streets cross—what is that called?"

"That's an intersection." (The students' capabilities and interest will determine whether or not the teacher further explains the term intersection.)

"How many kinds of travel or transportation do we see?"

"Some people are walking."

"Some are riding in a bus. It is a city bus."

"How do we know that it is a city bus?"

"A boy is riding a bicycle."

"There are lots of cars."

"Do you see any boats?"

"Why do you think there aren't any boats?"

The teacher points to a building with a symbol on it for the phone company and asks, "What is this building?"

"Must be the telephone office."

"How do we know that?"

"Has a sign for the phone company."

"What is this building?"

"McDonald's!"

"How do we know?"

"Has a McDonald's sign."

The teacher negotiates a discussion with the children about concepts related to background knowledge, vocabulary, and language. The picture we have visualized could be used in a variety of ways. Through its use the teacher can stress concepts and direct children to notice:

- Details.
- Symbols standing for things.
- Many different names for the same thing (such as McDonald's, restaurant, and fast-food restaurant).
- The same word having different meaning according to usage (such as *meter* for parking meter, gas meter, or electric meter).

Children can begin to understand the relationships between speaking, reading, and writing by creating stories from pictures.

Example 1: Introducing a Student to *The Great Big Enormous Turnip*

Setting the topic, theme, and characters

Teacher: Let's look at our new book. This story is about a big turnip, isn't it? *The Great Big Enormous Turnip.*

Prompting constructive activity

Teacher: Let's see what happened. Here's a little old man and he's . . . (Pausing) What's he doing?
Child: He's telling it to grow.
Teacher: And then what's he trying to do?
Child: Pull it out.
Teacher: Pull it out! Can he pull it out?
Child: (Shakes his head.)
Teacher: No! Who does he ask to help him?
Child: The little old woman.

Increasing accessibility or presenting new knowledge

Teacher: (Turning the page) They're asking the granddaughter to help, aren't they?

Accepting a partially correct response

Teacher: Who do they ask next?
Child: The dog.
Teacher: The black dog, that's right.

Providing a model (of anticipating the outcome)

Teacher: And does it come up? Does it? I think it might. And they all . . . (turns the page). Oh, no, not yet! Who do they have to ask?

FIGURE 7.4
Example of storybook introduction

(From Marie Clay, "Introducing a New Storybook to Young Children," *The Reading Teacher, 45* [December 1991], pp. 268–269. Reprinted with permission of the International Reading Association.)

Example 2: Introducing a Student to *Trug and Leaf*

The teacher clearly thought this story might be difficult for this child to understand, but for some good reason she selected it at this stage of the child's progress.

Setting the topic, title, and characters

Teacher: I've got another book about Trug for you. It's about Trug and Leaf this time and poor Leaf is ill.

Probing to find out what the child knows

Teacher: Do you know what it means when you are ill?
Child: (No response)
Teacher: It means you are sick, and Trug's going to try to look after her. Look, she's in bed.

Asking the child to work with new knowledge

Teacher: Trug's going to get some water for her. What do you think water might start with?
Child: *W.*
Teacher: I bet you can show what word says water.

Accepting partially correct responses

Teacher: That word does start with *w.* It says *will.*

Tightening the criteria of acceptability

Teacher: Can you find another?
Child: (Locates *water.*)
Teacher: That's got *w,* hasn't it? Right, he's going to get some water.

Prompting constructive activity (to understand the plot)

Teacher: He's trying to carry it in his hands. Is that working? It drips on the mud, doesn't it? That's not much good. Look, it's still dripping! Has he got any water left? I wonder how he is going to get the water? What does he see? What can he use?
Child: The egg.
Teacher: Where has the baby bird come from?
Child: The egg.
Teacher: He's come out of the egg, hasn't he? What's Trug going to do with the egg?
Child: Put water in it?

Providing a model (of reflecting on the story)

Teacher: He had a good idea, didn't he? And he can take the water to Leaf. She might get better now she's got a drink of water, mightn't she? Do you think so? Because she's ill, isn't she?

FIGURE 7.4
Continued

The value of visuals is their wealth of detail and their ability to convey conceptual information in a concrete manner (e.g., seeing a picture of a longhorn steer). What children can see stays in their minds so it can be referred to after a discussion has progressed to other things. During a unit on the human body, we observed a first grade teacher present part of a 60-minute video on the human body to her class. She used only the portion of the video (the skeletal system) appropriate to her unit of instruction. Days later, when the class was studying insects, Heather asked where a lady bug's skeleton was. As the teacher began to explain the ectoskeleton of insects, she made many references back to the video the children had seen on the human skeletal system. Every child appeared to have a look of understanding as they talked about the skeletal system of insects and humans.

Introducing New Storybooks to Children. Marie Clay (1991) sees much value in introducing new storybooks to young readers. Storybook introduction ensures that children have a "successful first reading early in the lesson before the teacher develops lesson activities." (p. 264) New storybooks also activate children's existing background knowledge and introduce new knowledge. Existing concepts are extended for both the storybook's content and the language. The steps in introducing new storybooks are enumerated here and illustrated in Figure 7.4.

- The teacher uses illustrations to encourage students to respond to the storybook and relates the story to other stories they have read.
- The teacher gets students to discuss experiences related to the new story and then identifies areas that may confuse students. The teacher can then clear up these areas of confusion.
- The teacher can sketch out the plot or the sequence of events up to the climax. The purpose is to create an overview of the story structure that will provide a framework for the children's anticipation of what will come.
- The teacher stimulates children to relate personal experiences or other stories they have read to the theme or topic of the new story. Such discussions identify and clear up conceptual problems related to the plot.
- The teacher uses novel language features (unusual name, unfamiliar syntax, and meaning for multiple meaning words) in talking about the story. The discussion of the story would focus on these deliberately.
- The teacher uses a particularly difficult or new sentence pattern two or three times and may have the students repeat it. This helps them to have a language model (build background knowledge) that they can use in reading the text. Clay notes: "It is not memorizing the lines of the book but rather readying the mind and ear to grapple with novelty" (p. 267).

SUMMARY /

Emergent literacy is the reading and writing behaviors of children that precede and develop into conventional literacy. While all children experience emergent literacy, children's experiences before beginning school vary. Such variations may be due to parents' reading aloud to them, opportunities to interact with environmental print, and experiences with art and play activities.

Before acquiring conventional literacy capabilities, children must (1) know that print represents a message and that this message must be as sensible as spoken language; (2) understand the concepts about the language used to talk about print; and (3) develop phonemic awareness, which is an awareness of sounds in spoken words. Children learn these concepts through a variety of written-language experiences, which suggests that a language-based literacy program best helps children refine and apply their emerging abilities in these three areas.

Assessment of children's early literacy experiences is important in an effective reading and writing program. Assessment should focus on the experiential and conceptual areas associated with success in beginning literacy: language development, concepts of print, language of instruction, and phonemic awareness. Teachers can use several assessment techniques. Information from parents, observation, checklists, and classification schemes are informal procedures that focus on growth and change in children's literacy capabilities.

The literacy program in the early grades lays the foundation for later development. In planning an emergent and beginning reading program, teachers should take into account what they know about children, effective teaching, learning, and language development. The appropriate beginning point is a language-based classroom to help children acquire and refine basic concepts that are emerging in their literacy knowledge. Such an environment would include play and learning centers, thematic units for reading and writing, big books, predictable books, poetry, storytelling, and reading aloud.

Some areas of an early literacy program, however, require direct/explicit instruction. Facilitating children's acquisition and development of listening capabilities, phonemic awareness, visual discrimination, background knowledge, vocabulary, and phonics requires teacher-directed instruction. These are taught not as discrete, separate activities that resemble isolated skills lessons, but rather are woven into the literature-based activities happening in a language-rich classroom.

YOUR POINT OF VIEW /

Discussion Questions

1. Assume that you are responsible for helping kindergarten and first grade teachers set up play and learning centers in their classrooms. Discuss what types of centers you would set up, what materials you would include, and how they would be used in literacy instruction.
2. Assume that you have worked closely with a group of 6-year-olds who learned to read before entering school. Discuss the literacy capabilities you think they would possess and the types of instruction that would be appropriate for continued literacy development.
3. Refer to the section on thematic units for writing and reading and discuss the important concepts that would bind together a unit on *nutrition.*

Take a Stand For or Against

1. Most parents don't have time to read to their children and should encourage them to watch educational television programs to take the place of reading to them.
2. First graders don't need instruction in phonics because they will learn for themselves how to use letter-sound relationships to figure out unknown words.
3. Combining reading and writing instruction is too difficult to accomplish in the classroom, and if youngsters can read, they will also learn to write.

BIBLIOGRAPHY /

Adams, M. J. (1990). *Beginning to read: Thinking and learning about print.* Cambridge, MA: MIT Press.

Anderson, R. C., Hiebert, E. H., Scott, J. A., & Wilkinson, I. A. G. (1985). *Becoming a nation of readers: The report of the commission on reading.* Washington, D.C.: The National Institute of Education.

Beach, S. A., & Robinson, R. J., (1992). Gender and grade level differences in the development of concepts about print. *Reading Psychology, 12,* 309–328.

Chall, J. S. (1983). *Stages of reading development.* New York: McGraw-Hill Book Co.

Clay, M. M. (1991). Introducing a new storybook to young readers. *The Reading Teacher, 45,* 264–273.

Clay, M. M. (1979). *The patterning of complex behaviour.* Auckland, New Zealand. Heinemann Educational Books.

Day, K. C., & Day, H. D. (1991). The concurrent validity of four tests of metalinguistic awareness. *Reading Psychology, 12,* 1–11.

Ehri, L. C., & Wilce, L. S. (1987). Does learning to spell help beginners learn to read words? *Reading Research Quarterly, 22,* 47–65.

Griffith, P. L., & Olson, M. W. (1992). Phonemic awareness helps beginning readers break the code. *The Reading Teacher, 45,* 516–525.

Halpern, D. F. (1986). *Sex differences in cognitive abilities.* Hillsdale, NJ: Lawrence Erlbaum Associates.

Harste, J. C., Woodward, V. A., & Burke, C. L. (1984). Examining our assumptions: A transactional view of literacy and learning. *Research in Teaching of English, 18,* 84–108.

Isom, B. A., & Casteel, C. P. (1991). Creating a writing-rich environment in the preschool classroom. *The Reading Teacher, 44,* 520–521

Juel, C. (1987). Support for the theory of phonemic awareness as a predictor in literacy acquisition. In J. Niles (Ed.), *Solving problems in literacy: Learners, teachers, and researchers* (pp. 239–243). Rochester, NY: National Reading Conference.

Juel, C. (1991). Beginning reading. In R. Barr, M. L. Kamil, P. B. Mosenthal, & P. D. Pearson (Eds.), *Handbook of reading research,* (Vol I) (pp. 759–788). New York, NY: Longman.

Kastler, L., Roser, N., & Hoffman, J. (1987). Understandings of the functions of written language: Insights from children and parents. In J. Readence & S. Baldwin (Eds.), *Research in literacy: Merging perspectives* (pp. 85–92). Rochester, NY: National Reading Conference.

Kettering, L., & Graybill, N. (1991). Cereal boxes foster emergent literacy. *The Reading Teacher, 44,* 522–523.

Lomax, R. G., & McGee, L. M. (1987). Young children's concepts about print and reading: Toward a model of word reading acquisition. *Reading Research Quarterly, 22*, 237–256.

Lundsteen, S. W. (1989). *Language arts: A problem solving approach.* New York: Harper & Row.

Morrow, L. M., & Rand, M. K. (1991). Promoting literacy during play by designing early childhood classroom environments. *The Reading Teacher, 44*, 396–402.

Neuman, S. B., & Roskos, K. (1990). The influence of literacy-enriched play settings on preschoolers' engagement with written language. In J. Zutell & S. McCormick (Eds.), *Literacy theory and research: Analysis from multiple paradigms* (pp. 179-188). Chicago: National Reading Conference.

Roper Organization. (1988). *The Jell-o desserts family reading survey.*

Schell, L. (1992). Personal communication.

Stahl, S. A. (1992). Saying the "p" word: Nine guidelines for exemplary phonics instruction. *The Reading Teacher, 45*, 618–625.

Stanovich, K. (1986) Matthew effects in reading: Some consequences of individual differences in the acquisition of literacy. *Reading Research Quarterly, 21*, 360–406.

Sulzby, E. (1991). Assessment of emergent literacy: Storybook reading. *The Reading Teacher, 44*, 498–500.

Sulzby, E., & Barnhart, J. (1992). The development of academic competence: All our children emerge as writers and readers. In J. W. Irwin & Doyle, M. A. (Eds.), *Reading/writing connections: Learning from research* (pp. 120–144). Newark, DE: International Reading Association.

Sulzby, E., Barnhart, J., & Hieshima, J. (1989). Forms of writing and rereading from writing: A preliminary report. In J. Mason (Ed.), *Reading and writing connections* (pp. 31–50). Boston: Allyn and Bacon.

Teale, W. H. (1987). Emergent literacy: Reading and writing development in early childhood. In J. Readence and S. Baldwin (Eds.), *Research in literacy: Merging perspectives* (pp. 45–74). Rochester, NY: National Reading Conference.

Tompkins, G. E., & Weber, M. (1983). What will happen next? Using predictable books with young children. *The Reading Teacher, 36*, 278–303.

8

Instructional Procedures for Teaching Literacy

For the Reader

If you will, imagine an entire class of students taking a course on speaking and writing the French language. Would everyone learn at the same rate and achieve the same success with one instruction method? The chances are that some students would do well, some would do average work, and others would fail. These differences can be the result of several factors, among them the teacher's failure to adapt to students' needs.

This same analogy applies to literacy instruction. The use of materials and instructional procedures without consideration of the students' needs will likely result in some having difficulty in learning to read and write. Chapter 7 discussed emergent literacy and implementation of the whole-language philosophy. This chapter continues the discussion of how students learn literacy. Basal reader materials are popular and are fully explained in this chapter. Additional materials and procedures for teaching reading are the literature-based and individualized reading approaches. Chapter 9 presents literature-based teaching and Chapter 12 covers individualized reading approaches. Supplemental materials and instructional procedures for teaching literacy are presented in this chapter as well as in Chapters 6, 7, and 13.

Key Ideas

- The successful use of materials and instructional procedures depends on the classroom teacher.
- Effective teachers use a combination of reading approaches to meet the needs of their students.
- Quality literature and real-life literacy experiences should be incorporated into the literacy program at all levels.

Key Terms

basal reader   reading materials that are organized and sequenced readers. The instructional sequence of skills and strategies depends on the readers and the accompanying manuals and materials.

directed reading activity (DRA)   an organized, sequenced strategy for teaching a reading selection. The typical steps include vocabulary, silent reading, comprehension checking, purposeful oral reading, skill development, and enrichment activities.

directed reading-thinking activity (DRTA)   an organized, sequenced strategy for teaching a reading selection that focuses on reading as a thinking process. Three overall steps include readiness and prediction, active reading, and reaction.

language-experience approach (LEA)   the approach for teaching reading that is built on children's experiences. Children dictate their experiences and the teacher writes them down or the children write their own stories as the basis for instruction.

sustained silent reading (SSR)   A scheduled period of silent reading in the classroom. During this time, both teacher and students may read a book or any form of print without interruption.

computer-assisted instruction (CAI)   instruction that interacts with a microcomputer.

LITERACY INSTRUCTION

A discussion of teaching literacy inevitably turns to how teachers teach. The materials and instructional procedures used to teach literacy have been the subjects of a large number of research studies, debates, and discussion. Unfortunately, research comparing reading materials and instruction has been inconclusive. No single approach to teaching literacy works best for all students. In a sense, no set of materials or instructional procedures is foolproof. By knowing when to modify or use different materials and instructional procedures to address strudents' needs, the teacher is the major factor in determining the success of a literacy program.

The following materials and instructional procedures for teaching literacy are discussed in the text: (1) basal readers, (2) literature-based programs, (3) the whole-language philosophy, and (4) individualized reading. Different materials and instructional procedures for teaching literacy are based on different philosophies regarding how children learn and different interpretations of literacy processes. However, all philosophies overlap each other to a certain degree, borrowing various procedures, strategies, and materials. Because of its unique relationship to the area of emergent literacy, the whole-language philosophy and its implementation were discussed in the previous chapter. Basal readers and literature-based procedures are by far the most popular materials used in U.S. schools. This chapter focuses on the basal reader in detail. Chapter 9 is devoted entirely to literature-based instruction, and Chapter 12 presents individualized reading. While each of these four is discussed separately, it must be emphasized that this treatment is for the sake of presentation. Effective reading teachers integrate features associated with different philosophies and materials to match the needs of their students.

Teachers also can use numerous beneficial supplemental materials and instructional procedures to teach literacy (Thompson, 1991). These procedures are supplemental in the sense that they are usually used in conjunction with other materials and procedures. Two widespread supplemental reading approaches are the language-experience approach and computer approaches. The language-experience approach and computers are discussed in this chapter due to their close relationship to and use with basal reader materials. Figure 8.1 lists some of the major features and assumptions associated with materials and instructional procedures for teaching literacy.

BASAL READERS

Elementary schools rely heavily on basal reader programs. As stated in *Becoming a Nation of Readers* (Anderson, Hiebert, Scott, & Wilkinson, 1985), "The observation that basal programs 'drive' reading instruction is not to be taken lightly. These programs strongly influence how reading is taught in American schools and what students read" (p. 35). Effective teachers make good use of reading materials, especially the basal reader.

Materials/Instructional Procedures	Assumptions and Characteristics
1. Basal reader materials	■ Students learn best with an eclectic method.
	■ Includes provisions for teaching word identification, word meanings, comprehension, study skills, and literature appreciation.
2. Literature-based reading materials	■ Students learn best with literature as the main vehicle for reading instruction.
	■ Integrates reading skills with literature selections.
3. Whole-language philosophy	■ Instruction focuses on developing both writing and reading in a natural way.
	■ Emphasizes whole-text writing and reading.
4. Individualized reading	■ Students learn best when they select their own books to read, pace themselves in reading a book or learning a skill, and receive specific skill or strategy instruction based on individual need.
	■ Emphasizes interest in reading and motivation to read on one's own with a variety of materials.
5. Language experience	■ Students learn best through reading materials based on their own language and experiences.
6. Computer	■ Based on operant conditioning principles, students will respond favorably to step-by-step sequential presentation of information.

FIGURE 8.1
Assumptions and characteristics of materials and procedures for teaching literacy

Design and Content

Each basal reader program differs in its rationale, sequence of skills and strategies, story content, instructional recommendations, and supplemental materials. However, most basals set meaning as the paramount goal from the outset. Also, most basals cover the major strands of the elementary school reading curriculum as mentioned in Chapter 1—decoding, comprehension, word meanings, reading-study skills, literature, and independent reading—in their own particular way.

Through a series of books of increasing difficulty (a separate book for each level), **basal readers** are designed to bring children to a high degree of reading proficiency. Each level functions as a prerequisite for success at the next level. The focus of basal programs is to develop the reader's competence in vocabulary, word identification, word meanings, comprehension, and study skills. The basal program should not be viewed as the total reading program. *The Reading Teacher* publishes an excellent index to the many American basal reader series. Greenlinger-Harless (1987) compiled the latest cross-referenced index covering kindergarten through grade 8.

Heath Reading (Alvermann, Bridge, Schmidt, Searfoss, Winograd, & Paris, 1991) is a basal reader series of kindergarten through grade 8. This is a literature-driven program that systematically teaches skills and strategies in six major areas: (1) decoding, (2) vocabulary, (3) comprehension, (4) language, (5) literature, and (6) study skills. All instruction and classroom activities focus on children's literature (both fiction and nonfiction) organized in clusters that explore favorite themes. This basal program attempts to develop all the language arts throughout various curriculum areas in a meaningful way. To promote strategic reading, the lesson plan for each story models effective strategies for before, during, and after reading. In the "Think Ahead" section, students review prior knowledge on the topic, preview, predict, and set purposes for reading. The "Think While Reading" section encourages the teacher to model various questioning strategies to monitor comprehension. In the "Think Back" section, students think about the story by evaluating and critically thinking about what they have read, integrate the other language arts in various activities, and develop skills and strategies. Skills instruction follows a whole-to-part philosophy: Once students understand a story, the teacher provides direct instruction on the skill with subsequent meaningful practice related back to the story. Figure 8.2 shows the *Heath Reading* titles and their appropriate grade levels. This basal reader program covers all the major strands in the elementary school curriculum and the major areas of a complete reading program as outlined in Chapter 1.

Grade Levels	Title of Readers
Kindergarten	The Cat and the Fiddle
Readiness	The Mouse in the House
Preprimer 1	Yellow Fish, Blue Fish
Preprimer 2	My Friends the Frogs
Preprimer 3	Grab That Dog!
Primer	Little Duck Dance
First Reader	My Best Bear Hug
Grade 2-1	Cats Sleep Anywhere
Grade 2-2	Come Back Here, Crocodile
Grade 3-1	A Soft Pillow for an Armadillo
Grade 3-2	Never a Worm This Long
Grade 4	Turtles Like to Sleep In
Grade 5	Rare as Hens' Teeth
Grade 6	I Touched the Sun
Grade 7	Through the Starshine
Grade 8	Roads Go Ever On

FIGURE 8.2
Heath Reading *basal series*

All basal programs include a tremendous number of materials for both teacher and students. For teachers, programs may include:

- A teacher's edition for each level, giving detailed lesson plans for each story in the student's book, a complete listing of strategies and skills for developing reading, writing, listening, and speaking processes at each level, and assessment procedures
- Detailed descriptions of supplemental literary libraries and recommendations for literacy development in various content areas
- Various instructional supplements for application of strategies and skills
- Prepared pictures of characters, teaching charts, posters, transparencies, and word cards for specific stories
- Various films, filmstrips, recordings, videos, videodiscs, audiocassettes, and compact discs
- Teachers' editions of student workbooks
- A management system, including an informal reading inventory or placement test, criterion-referenced pretests and post tests for each level, phonic inventories, alternative assessments for both reading and writing, portfolio assessment, and various record-keeping devices.

For students, basal programs may include:

- A student book for each level
- A workbook for each level
- Literature libraries including high interest–low vocabulary paperback books
- Readiness posters and big books
- Writing portfolios
- Computer software programs
- Supplemental games and activities to practice skills and strategies being taught.

Advantages of Basal Series

Although the abundance of materials in basal programs can be overwhelming, the crucial point to remember is they do not guarantee an exciting and worthwhile program. An effective teacher of reading must orchestrate the materials based on learner needs. Some of the advantages of using a basal series include:

- Basal readers have excellent photographs and artwork.
- Books are sequenced in increasing difficulty to provide systematic instruction from the emergent literacy phase through the upper elementary grades.
- Graded materials permit teacher flexibility in dealing with individual differences.
- Teacher guides are available for each book or level. These provide suggestions for a step-by-step teaching program.

- If used properly, basal reader series deal with all phases of the reading program, guarding against overemphasis of some aspects and neglect of others.
- Basal series introduce practice of new skills and strategies in a logical sequence.
- Review is provided.
- Vocabulary is controlled to prevent frustration for beginning readers.
- Prepared materials allow teachers to save time.
- Formal and informal assessments that the series provides reflect the materials that teachers will use.
- Basal programs provide an overall management system for coordinating the elementary school reading program.

In addition to the preceding features, most basal programs have changed drastically in the last decade. Changes have reflected the significant advances in our understanding of the reading process, how students learn, and what teachers should teach. As such, most basals today feature the following characteristics:

- Integrated language arts is emphasized not only during reading instruction but also in the content areas.
- Quality literature is viewed as the driving force in the elementary school reading program, with thematic units designed to facilitate student learning and appreciation.
- Reading and writing are linked specifically as mutually supportive processes.

Quality literature should be an integral part of the literacy program.

- Appealing, high-quality literature is carefully selected for both the regular basal readers and supplemental libraries.
- Quality literature is emphasized for independent or recreational reading.
- Multicultural focus is increased.
- Lesson recommendations reflect the idea that reading is an interactive, constructive, and strategic process. Lessons give explicit attention to teaching decoding skills and strategies and comprehension strategies. Instruction includes use of authentic literature and prior knowledge in story preparation. Thinking and problem-solving abilities are taught through literature.
- Cooperative and partner grouping is encouraged.
- Assessment is viewed as ongoing and is linked directly to instruction using a variety of informal and formal measures.
- A real partnership is fostered between the school's elementary reading program and the home.

Economy of teacher time is a major factor in the widespread use of basal series. No teacher would ever have the time to match the meticulous planning that goes into a good basal series. Prepared materials leave teachers more time to develop supplementary exercises as needed. Teachers still must prepare these exercises for certain pupils, since the basal program cannot meet all individual needs; however, preparing supplementary lessons for a few is easier than building the entire program.

Teacher's Editions

One of the advantages of using a good basal series is the teacher's edition. These editions contain a variety of instructional procedures, lesson plans, and rationales for using certain materials and instructional procedures. Beginning teachers can benefit from becoming familiar with the rationales and concrete suggestions that basal readers contain. Experienced teachers might find the detail of these manuals a bit tedious, but they know that they can take what is offered and adapt it in light of their own experience and their students' learning needs. A teacher's edition is beneficial only if teachers use it properly, however. Teachers should not be awed by these impressive volumes, nor should they follow them word for word—that is not teaching. Teachers should know their students' learning needs better than any teacher's guide. Remember, basal materials work best for a knowledgeable, flexible teacher. Use the suggestions when they match your students' learning needs, and supplement and adapt suggestions at all other times. Teachers should view manuals as a compilation of suggestions that they can use, modify, or discard (Durkin, 1993).

Workbooks

Basal reader series generally contain workbook supplements. The educational value of using workbooks has been debated for years. It is true that workbook exercises can deteriorate into nothing more than busywork. Yet, with proper, teacher-directed instruction, students can use workbooks for meaningful practice.

Properly used, workbooks can have considerable educational value. Since they deal with a wide variety of skills, some exercises will likely provide needed and meaningful practice in essential literacy skill areas. Workbooks also can serve as ongoing diagnostic instruments, since they identify individuals who do not understand a particular reading strategy or skill. A study of miscues will show the alert teacher where to provide further instruction. Workbook exercises are brief —usually one page—which makes them especially appealing to students with short attention spans.

Workbooks, like all other instructional media, are neither all good nor bad. How the teacher uses workbooks determines whether they contribute to a quality instructional program. Osborn (1984) identified important guidelines for workbook tasks. Carefully consider these guidelines for using workbooks and worksheets that accompany basal reading series:

- Workbook activities should match the instruction and learning taking place in the unit or lesson.

- Some workbook tasks should provide systematic, cumulative, and meaningful review of what students have been taught.

- Workbooks should match the most important learning taking place in the reading program. Activities of lesser importance should be voluntary.

- Workbooks should provide relevant tasks for students in need of extra practice.

- Both the vocabulary and concept features of workbook tasks should be within students' experiential and conceptual backgrounds and should relate to the rest of the program.

- The language features of a workbook page should be consistent with those in the instructional lesson and the rest of the workbook.

- Instructions for completion of a workbook activity should be clear and easy to follow. Teachers should direct one or two practice examples to ensure that students understand the tasks.

- Page layout should combine attractiveness and utility.

- Content should be sufficient to ensure that students are learning and not just being exposed to something.

- Discrimination activities should follow a sufficient number of tasks to provide practice of the components of the discriminations.

- Content of workbook activities should be accurate and precise to ensure that it presents neither incorrect information nor incorrect generalizations.

- Some workbook tasks should be fun.

- The manner in which students respond should be consistent from workbook task to workbook task.

- Response modes should match normal reading and writing as closely as possible.

- Cute and nonfunctional workbook activities, which may be time-consuming (i.e., busywork), should be avoided.
- Workbook assignments should include teacher discussions about their purposes and their relationships to reading.

Directed Reading Activities

An integral part of the teacher's edition of a basal reader is a systematic description of how to teach a reading and/or writing lesson. The ultimate purpose of each lesson in a basal reader is to teach the strategies needed to read and write independently, comprehending and learning from both. Thus, each lesson is a vehicle for increasing youngsters' literacy abilities. The following set of suggested procedures is commonly referred to as a *directed reading activity* (DRA). The DRA provides a framework for systematic and sequential growth of reading and language abilities. Although each basal series has its own concept of the DRA, most contain the following components:

- Readiness, including prior knowledge, previewing, key vocabulary and concepts, and purpose-setting questions (either teacher set or student set, or both), and student prediction about the content of the selection.
- Silent reading.
- Comprehension development.
- Purposeful oral reading.
- Skill and strategy development, including word identification or decoding, comprehension, study, and vocabulary.
- Enrichment, including creative assignments related to the story.

Similar in nature to the DRA is the *directed reading-thinking activity* (DRTA) (Stauffer, 1975). The three overall stages of the DRTA are readiness, active reading, and reaction to the story. This instructional procedure focuses on reading as a thinking process. Students are encouraged to predict; form a purpose for reading; read to verify, reject, or modify that purpose; then continue that process.

Pieronek (1979) provided a model for teaching an integrated reading lesson based upon the assumption that reading is a thinking process. Steps for teaching a reading lesson include (1) concept development, (2) vocabulary recognition, (3) setting overall goals for comprehension, (4) directed reading and thinking activity, (5) purposeful oral reading, (6) follow-up activities, and (7) enrichment activities.

There is no set way to teach a reading lesson. Modern basal reader programs follow a similar instructional format to directed-reading and directed reading-thinking activities focusing on teaching strategies before, during, and after reading. Teacher's manual recommendations may be modified, expanded, deleted, or reordered according to students' existing abilities. A DRA begins by preparing students for reading.

A DRA often refers to concept development as building background. The manual may recommend using pictures, real objects, or discussion of the theme

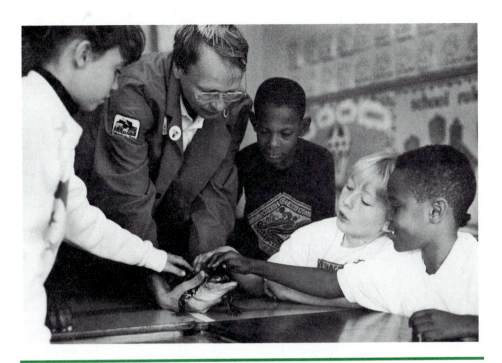

Prereading experiences with live objects are excellent motivators in preparing to read a story.

of the story to motivate students. Some manuals include this step in the purpose-setting phase or the story introduction. The concept-development step of a DRA is extremely important in activating students' experiential and conceptual backgrounds in relation to the story content. To help students identify with the lesson, the teacher may need to modify or break down procedures into simpler but related parts. Essential to concept development is the teacher understanding that background knowledge central to comprehending important text concepts should be the focus.

The vocabulary-recognition step is closely related to concept development. Teachers may have to supplement or expand the recommendations found in a manual. Just telling students is not as effective as using concrete examples and illustrations.

According to Singer, Samuels, and Spiroff (1973–1974), "the objective of teaching comprehension is to have students learn to ask their own questions and guide their own thinking so that they can become independent in the process of reading and learning from text" (p. 904). Therefore, in addition to setting goals for comprehension, teachers should model various strategies for comprehension in DRTAs.

Purposeful oral reading of selected portions of a story is optional. If oral reading is to be included in the lesson, selections must be meaningful to students, such as the funniest part, the saddest part, the answer to a particular question, or parts of the story to be acted out in class. Although some stories are meant to be read aloud, reading every story aloud day after day is both a waste of time and a probable cause of such difficulties as word-by-word silent reading and development of poor self-esteem.

The next step in a DRA involves follow-up, or practice, activities. Using either the story or the workbook as a vehicle, students should learn, practice, or apply specific skills and strategies, depending upon their needs. Such activities may be teacher supervised or done independently.

The final step in teaching a DRA is to provide enrichment activities related to the story. Although this step fosters independent and creative learning, teachers often omit it because of pressure to concentrate on basic skills and to cover a certain number of lessons. However, teachers should capitalize on this step to share the joy of reading with students. Ways of providing enrichment for a particular story are endless, including cross-curriculum activities, reading of good literature, panel discussions, puppet shows, choral speaking, music and art activities, dramatization, creative writing, and independent reading.

The teacher acts as the key to an effective DRA by selecting activities appropriate to students' needs. No teacher's manual can make reading meaningful and enjoyable. A thinking teacher who views the lesson plans in a manual as guides and not mandates is more likely to provide effective reading instruction.

To help reduce the gap between research on reading comprehension and practice, Reutzel (1985) proposed a revised DRA that focuses on reviewing past knowledge and background experiences. Reutzel's proposal, called the reconciled reading lesson, essentially reverses the traditional steps in a DRA.

The steps are (1) enrichment activities to build background, (2) a story-related skill lesson, (3) questions to guide reading, (4) silent reading, (5) comprehension assessment, and (6) vocabulary development. Reutzel's procedure is an excellent example of how teachers can adapt commercial materials to reflect current research on the reading comprehension process. (See Chapter 6 for additional discussion of revised DRAs.)

A Critical View

Critics have attacked basal readers through the years. They have alleged basals to be inferior because of boring content, cultural bias, absence of literary merit, and unrealistic and repetitive language. Responding to these and other criticisms, authors and publishers have made significant changes in basals to reflect current reading research and teacher effectiveness studies (McCallum, 1988).

Other critics have attacked basal readers for the ways that teachers use them. These criticisms should not be aimed at the materials themselves, however. The practices criticized are neither suggested nor condoned by any basal program, even though certain critics contend that these practices are inevitable outcomes of using the basals. For instance, when using basals, teachers sometimes do the following:

■ Have a group of students read every story in a round-robin manner.

■ Use three groups within a classroom, and retain the same groups throughout the year.

- Make no provision for individual differences beyond the three-group pattern.
- Restrict the more capable readers to the basal material, forcing them to move at a pace far below their capacities.
- Prohibit students from selecting and reading other books in which they are interested.

Research by Durkin (1984) provides some insights into the use of basals in teaching reading. Durkin observed 16 teachers during their reading instruction to better determine how they used basal manuals. She observed first, third, and fifth grade classes. Her findings are not very encouraging; however, if teachers become aware of them, perhaps it will help them improve the quality of basal reading instruction. Following is a summary and discussion of her findings.

Introduction and Presentation of New Vocabulary Words. Most basal manuals suggest introducing new words in written context and illustrating them in familiar, written sentences. Few of the teachers followed this recommendation and rarely did they give any attention to teaching and practicing new vocabulary words.

Discussion and Presentation of Background Information. Basal manuals often provide background information about concepts and themes found in stories that are intended to activate pupils' experiential and conceptual backgrounds. Durkin found that none of the teachers reviewed or developed background information for their pupils.

Presentation and Discussion of Prereading Questions. Rarely did the observed teachers present and discuss questions before their students read a story from their basal. Most manuals present questions to ask students before they read a story for the first time to guide students' reading.

Silent Reading of the Story. Durkin reported that silent reading was uncommon in the first grade. Although third and fifth grade teachers used silent reading more often, they typically ignored the recommendations found in the manual. Basal manuals often recommend that teachers supervise students' silent reading by questioning them after they have read a few pages or discussing their reading immediately following silent reading of the whole story.

Meaningful Oral Reading or Rereading. Basal manuals do not typically recommend oral reading or rereading of every story assigned to students; however, the observed teachers spent considerable time on oral reading.

Instruction. Today considerable emphasis is given to instructional procedures that foster comprehension and provide meaningful, supervised skill practice. All teachers, except one fifth grade teacher, used the manual sections on practice assignments. The focus, however, was on completing written practice assignments rather than using many of the manual's suggestions for instruction.

The hornbook was the earliest form of reading activity that children were to use by themselves. It received its name from the thin layer of horn that was placed over the text to prevent it from becoming dirty. Most hornbooks were in the shape of a paddle and measured about 2½ by 5 inches. The alphabet, Arabic numerals, and the Lord's Prayer were usually written or printed on a piece of paper. The paper was then pasted onto the paddle and covered with the thin layer of horn. Hornbooks were used in America into the nineteenth century.

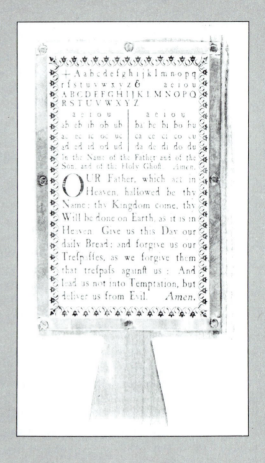

LESSON V.

Răb	Ann	hăt	cătch	sēe
		ē	ch	s

See Rab! See Ann!
See! Rab has the hat.
Can Ann catch Rab?

From McGuffey's *Eclectic Reader,* published in the mid 1800s, children were taught to read and recite. The readers used primarily an alphabetic-phonetic approach along with a controlled vocabulary. Although the language of the beginning level readers was choppy and uninteresting, the readers were extremely popular for many years. The story content often was intended to teach religious, moral, and patriotic values.

"Look here," said Father.
"Look at Mother and me.
Here we come."

Sally said, "Away we go!
Dick and Jane.
Father and Mother.
Tim and me."

"And Spot and Puff," said Dick.
"Away we go!"

63

Dick, Jane, Sally, Spot, Father, Mother, and Puff are familiar to many of us as the characters of a popular reading series used in the mid 1900s. These readers were characterized by controlled vocabularies, near total emphasis on a narrative style of writing, and stories dealing with middle-class white families living in single-family homes.

Practice Assignments. Suggested assignments are often abundant in basal manuals, but manuals seldom suggest that teachers use every one of these. All but one of the observed teachers assigned all of the written practice activities found in the skill-development portions (workbook pages and worksheets). None of these teachers used the manual when giving assignments, and the teachers did not appear to make assignments in terms of students' needs. The teachers also failed to provide students with a purpose for reading, to review the format and directions, to complete practice examples, or to establish a relationship between the assignment and the ability to read.

Provisions for Individual Differences. With most stories in the basal, manuals include provisions intended to help teachers differentiate their instruction and address the needs of individual students. Durkin found that one third grade teacher used these recommendations with the whole class, and a first grade teacher used some of them for her whole class. The other teachers did not use the recommendations in their teaching.

Durkin's findings are limited because they deal with a small number of teachers observed for a short time; however, these findings are no different from those reported in other classroom observation studies (Durkin, 1984). Teachers do not use the suggestions and recommendations in basal reader manuals for two common reasons: (1) they do not have the time to do everything the manual recommends, and (2) they often do not think the manual recommendations are important. Durkin thought teachers should connect these two concerns. That is, if teachers don't have the time to follow all of the recommendations, they should heed those that develop and enhance students' reading abilities. Durkin offers the following advice for using the basal manual to improve the quality of reading instruction:

> Giving more time to new vocabulary, background information, prereading questions, instruction on essential topics, and better but fewer assignments, and . . . spending less time on oral reading and comprehension questions, is a possible change that is not likely to promote any more problems than were seen in the classroom. What the different allotment of time may promote, however, is better readers. (p. 744)

Bacharach and Alexander (1986) also found teachers to be selective in using the basal manual. As in the Durkin study, teachers did not give the prereading step the attention it should have in teaching a lesson. Teachers in this study viewed the vocabulary suggestions as most helpful, followed by comprehension instruction, skill instruction, and background and prereading questions. Least helpful were enrichment activities.

Important Considerations in Using a Basal

Basal manuals offer many suggestions for teaching reading, but teachers should not follow these suggestions blindly. Teachers should use their knowledge of students' needs and capabilities to determine which recommendations to use, which

Effective teachers sometimes work directly with students to modify and extend the basal reader to ensure students are taught what they need to learn.

to modify, and which to ignore. Mason (1983) identified three important features that teachers should consider in evaluating and preparing lessons in manuals. First, a lesson may need to be reorganized to focus on the story's topic, illustrate its purpose or value, and relate to students' existing knowledge and to other texts. Second, the teacher should choose activities that relate to the workbooks and worksheets selectively; not all of them recommended in the manual need be assigned. The teacher can omit activities that are of questionable value, too lengthy, or unrelated to the lesson at hand, which allows for more teacher-directed instruction. Third, the teacher must develop alternatives for independent student work and practice. Independent activities such as library reading, research projects, and creative writing are essential to foster comprehension abilities and provide application of literacy in real-life situations.

A final important consideration is how much teacher time and effort are needed to learn how to effectively use any basal reader program. Tulley's (1991–1992) research on how first-year teachers employed a new basal program indicated that "(1) for many of these teachers at various grade levels and with differing amounts of experience, learning to use a new basal reading program was a relatively lengthy and difficult process, and that (2) loyalty to proven and effective instructional techniques and methods, coupled with the absence of any systematic training scheme, may lead teachers to depend upon self-designed and capricious approaches when learning to use a basal" (p. 20). Such findings underscore the importance of not only knowing the basal program but continually monitoring one's application of the approach to ensure student learning.

Going Beyond the Basal

The overall goal of teaching literacy is to develop students who can (and do) read and write on their own for a variety of reasons. Teachers at every level must be sensitive to a range of instructional goals—mastery of basic skills, facility in using comprehension strategies, development of critical and creative responses to various forms of text, and growth of appreciation and enjoyment of language used in reading and writing. However, the transfer of reading skills and strategies to recreational reading is not automatic: Skills and strategies are mastered through wide reading of literature (Aiex, 1988).

Although one may suspect that mastery of literacy skills automatically leads to increased recreational reading and learning, a study by Blair and Turner (1984) indicates otherwise. As part of a status study of reading interests and attitudes, they assessed the perceptions of middle school students regarding how well basic reading instructional materials fostered recreational reading. Surprisingly, almost half of the students thought their regular reading materials neither helped them learn in other school subjects nor develop recreational reading habits.

The findings of this study strongly support the integration of literature into the regular basal program. A common strategy for elementary teachers using a basal is to encourage students to read library books related to a basal story or to bring in copies of the book excerpted in a basal for students to read. This practice integrates literature more fully into the basal reader program.

In addition to individual classroom strategies to implement a literature-based reading approach, the following are strategies for the school environment:

- Reading and literature, including *silent sustained reading* (SSR), book fairs, and multimedia projects.
- Magazines, including opportunities to read a variety of magazines independently, group discussions of various stories, and student oral reports.
- Reading-related projects, including a literature emphasis based on writing (for example, on plays) and a semester project (for example, on China or energy).
- Careers, including extensive reading and writing about careers and assembly programs on various occupations with guest speakers.

As the preceding discussion indicates, basal readers cannot be viewed as the complete reading program. No matter how comprehensive a basal program might appear to be, it must be combined with other materials for students to learn what they need to know. Clements (1991) agrees and suggests "that we go beyond the basal and the workbook to supplement reading programs with extensive reading, enrichment, and follow-up" (p. 59). Clements' undergraduate students compiled the following excellent listing of ways reading teachers can go beyond the basal:

storytelling	letters
menus	recipes
music	cereal boxes
games	read along cassettes
projects	comic books
filmstrips	computers
plays	puppet shows
language experience	paired reading
	(p. 62)

Finally, an excellent source for not only a complete view of the basal but for specific ways to supplement and extend the basal is the text *Improving Basal Reading Instruction* by Winograd, Wixson, and Lipson (1989).

INSTRUCTIONAL PROCEDURES

The Language-Experience Approach (LEA)

A valuable supplemental reading approach is the **language-experience approach** (LEA). Regardless of what other materials schools or other teachers may have adopted, most teachers of beginning literacy include teacher-written charts and stories in their literacy programs. Using student experiences as the content for writing charts and stories is a long-standing practice. Throughout the years, modifications and extensions have placed renewed emphasis on this procedure. The LEA is used predominately with primary grade children but is also adaptable for slower learners of all ages and for ESL students. Hall (1981) summarized the rationale and philosophy of the language-experience approach.

The language-experience approach for teaching literacy, Hall said, is based on the relationship of language to the learner's experiences as the core from which language communication radiates. Language-experience literacy is viewed as a communication process closely related to communication in speaking and listening. The approach uses students' oral language and experiences to create personal reading and writing sources. This approach integrates the teaching of literacy with all of the language arts; as students listen, speak, write, and read about their personal experiences and ideas, their speech determines the language patterns of their reading materials, and their experiences determine the content. The language-experience approach assumes that literacy has the most meaning to students when the materials being read are expressed in their language and are rooted in their experiences.

Features of the LEA

Although the language-experience approach has many variations, teachers should understand some basic features when using this approach. They include:

- A shared experience for the students.
- Shared talk about the experience.

- Decisions about the written product, including a group chart or story or an individual student story.
- Shared reading of the charts or stories by the students.
- Follow-up activities.
- Group experience charts and stories.

Group experience charts and stories are means of capturing students' interests by tying their personal experiences to their literacy activities. The charts and stories, which tell about shared activities, are prepared cooperatively by the teacher and the class. They are often extensions of earlier and less difficult experiences, wherein the teacher wrote single words, short sentences, days of the week, names of the months, the seasons, and the dates of students' birthdays and holidays on the chalkboard. Group experience charts and stories provide practice and application in a number of developmental areas closely related to literacy, including:

- Using oral language in group planning prior to a trip and in recounting the experience after a trip.
- Giving and taking ideas as the experience is discussed.
- Sharpening sensory acuity, particularly visual and auditory, while on excursions.
- Developing and expanding print-related concepts, such as directionality (left to right), space between letters and words, punctuation, capital letters, and the relationships between oral and written language.
- Expanding concepts and vocabulary.
- Learning words as wholes in meaningful contexts, thus building a sight vocabulary based on one's language.
- Focusing on reading and writing as a process of constructing meaning.
- Reading and writing about one's own experiences.

In preparing group experience charts and stories, the teacher should plan a meaningful shared experience, such as taking a field trip, viewing a film or filmstrip, hearing a story, reacting to a picture, observing an experiment, or participating in a class or school activity. Let us assume that the teacher arranges a trip to a nearby farm. This teacher organizes the necessary transportation and visits the farm in advance to determine specifically what students will experience. As a result of the visit, this teacher identifies what they need to know to benefit from the experience. Several days of instruction help prepare students for their visit.

Following the trip to the farm, the teacher guides the students through a discussion and sharing of the highlights of their experiences. This discussion serves to get all of the students involved and attending to the task to follow—writing the experience chart. After each student's response, the teacher writes it on the chalkboard or on large poster paper. Students are encouraged to respond and to discuss their responses. The group-composed chart follows:

Our Trip to the Farm

We went to Mr. Johnson's dairy farm.
We saw lots of cows.
We saw a machine that milks the cows.
The cows' heads are put in bars.
In Mr. Johnson's big barn, he milks five cows at once.

After the teacher and children read the complete chart, the teacher may ask a student to point out (1) the line that tells what kind of farm they visited, (2) the line that tells the name of the owner of the farm, (3) his/her favorite or most exciting event, and so forth.

The same chart may be used in other ways. The teacher may duplicate each line in the chart on a strip of heavy paper, hand a sentence to a student, and ask him or her to find this line on the chart. The teacher may print individual words on oaktag or cardboard, hold them up, and ask a student to point out that particular word on the chart. The teacher may prepare word cards for a particular line, hand them to a student in mixed order, and ask him or her to arrange them in proper order to correspond with the line on the chart. A group experience chart can be used with a class as a whole and also with various groups of students. After its use with a unit, the teacher may refer to it when certain words used on the chart arise in other contexts and activities.

Individual Experience Stories. Children enjoy talking about their experiences, particularly about incidents that involve them, their families, their pets, special events, and the like. One of the best ways to take advantage of such motivation is to write individual experience stories. These language productions are usually brief, ranging from one to several sentences about one incident. In the early stages of literacy, students usually dictate the stories and the teacher usually transcribes them. Since these brief stories relate to students' own experiences, they encourage involvement in literacy. The stories are always meaningful and should be written using words that parallel students' own language usage.

Expansions and Variations of the Language-Experience Approach

In addition to the features and uses of LEA mentioned earlier, teachers can use this instructional approach in a variety of ways. Reimer (1983) suggested several ways to expand and vary use of the LEA:

Direct and Indirect Discourse. Use different-colored pens to identify different speakers when recording a group experience story. Students can identify who said what by noting the color of the writing. The teacher should use the same color consistently for each individual so that the class can associate that color with a particular student. As a variation, use a photograph of each student and attach a discourse balloon to help everyone understand who contributed what to a group story. Later, write these stories with the youngsters and replace the color or picture with the words, "Mary said," or "Billy said," to help students understand how these words function in direct discourse. Teach indirect discourse by removing the punctuation marks and introducing the word *that* (such as Sue said *that* the horse is big).

Various Forms of Writing. Use group LEA to introduce different forms of writing. Demonstrate a science experiment and have the group tell what happened, have students report a shared experience by responding to reporter questions (who, what, where, when, why, and how), or have students learn about letter writing by composing a group letter.

Shape Stories. Guide children to write stories about an experience that is represented by a shape—a fish, clown, car, dog, and so on. As children dictate the story, write it on the paper cut into a particular shape.

Written Dialogue. This procedure works well with many youngsters at all elementary levels. Rather than talking with students, exchange notes. These notes may range from extremely simple phrases ("Good job!") to paragraphs. Match the complexity of the notes to the students' abilities to read and respond in writing. This variation of LEA helps students to understand the relationships between oral and written language and realize that written language must make sense to the reader.

The concept of language experience has been extended far beyond the group chart and writing individual stories. Today, the term *language experience* applies to practically every type of self-expression through language and every experience that involves manipulation of language.

The role of teachers has undergone considerable change also. Teachers now assume responsibilities far beyond those of scribes who write down stories students tell. Teachers still reinforce students' egos by writing personal stories, but by using additional language stimuli, they also help students expand their concepts and improve their language proficiency.

Language activities that promote both learning about language and using language as a tool for further learning are becoming major features of instruction (Dole, 1984). Students write poetry, read poetry, and solve riddles (and make up some of their own). Working with homonyms, they learn that different spellings may have the same pronunciation. Working with homographs, students learn that words may be spelled the same but have different meanings and pronunciations. They learn about relationships through analogies, combining sentences, and arranging sentences into larger units. In working with language, students learn that a word may have dozens of meanings, that plurals take many forms, that new words are constantly added to our language, and that over time, the meanings of words change.

Language experience is, thus, experiencing language. The teacher's role is to help children understand that

Writing a word is an achievement
Writing a story is a larger achievement
Combining stories into a book is quite a production.

Saying something one way is an achievement
Saying it another way and
    noting what you did the second time
    permits you to control language!

When you can control language
you can mold words like clay
    mix words like paints
    use words to draw pictures.

The next step is to let children try it. Let them tell or write the answer to the following question:

How many ways can a leaf fall?

"Down" you say.

Surely there's another way.
  A leaf can
  just fall—
    fall gracefully
  glide—
    glide like a glider
    glide and swerve
  sail—
    sail like a rudderless ship
    sail like it had a mind of its own
  dip—
    dip and glide
    dip and rise and bank gracefully to a landing
  dance—
    complete its solo dance
    dance with the wind
  fall with no map to guide it—
    map its own course
    try many detours
    twist slowly in the wind.

How many ways can a leaf fall that we didn't write today?

"No other way," you say?

Don't you think leaves like to play?
  playfully! (of course)
    If in a hurry?
  plummet
    with memories of summer?
  reluctantly

Any procedure has both merits and limitations, and this is true of the language-experience approach to teaching reading. The major strengths of experience charts and stories have already been discussed. Relying too heavily on teacher-written materials may have drawbacks of its own, including:

- Difficulty in controlling the vocabulary—too many words may be introduced at one time.
- Not enough repetition of basic sight words to ensure mastery.
- When used exclusively as a method, too much of a burden on the teacher, demanding too much time and too high a level of training.
- Difficulty in adapting this type of instruction to the needs of all students.
- Encouragement of memorization rather than mastery of sight words.

The strengths and weaknesses of the experience method are a factor of the teacher's application and are not inherent in the method itself. Under certain conditions, overemphasis, misuse, or lack of understanding may cancel out all the advantages of the method. The language-experience approach is vulnerable when used as the total reading program. Most teachers prefer to use the approach as a supplement to other materials and instructional procedures (see Figure 8.3).

Language-experience activities can enhance basal reading instruction and vice versa: Aspects of LEA can be used to do the following:

- Provide for both individual and group reading instruction.
- Allow for practice, transfer, and application of word-identification and comprehension skills and strategies in meaningful context.
- Build on and emphasize students' life and language experiences.
- Emphasize the relationship between oral and written language to help students understand that reading and writing are constructing meaning.
- Engage students in meaningful instruction based on their own interests.
- Encourage vocabulary development by having students try new words and use these new words in meaningful context.
- Develop better writers and children who will experiment with writing. (Rupley & Blair, 1989)

As emphasized throughout the text, the process of reading and writing development are complementary. LEA is a wonderful springboard for both processes. Karnowski (1989) proposes linking the process-writing approach and LEA by combining process-writing steps (i.e., prewriting discussion, actual writing, revising, and publishing) in a modified language-experience approach. Karnowski explains: "By using a modified LEA in which students decide what topics to explore, what ideas to include, and what modifications to make, young readers and writers begin to realize the work and the job of becoming published authors" (p. 465).

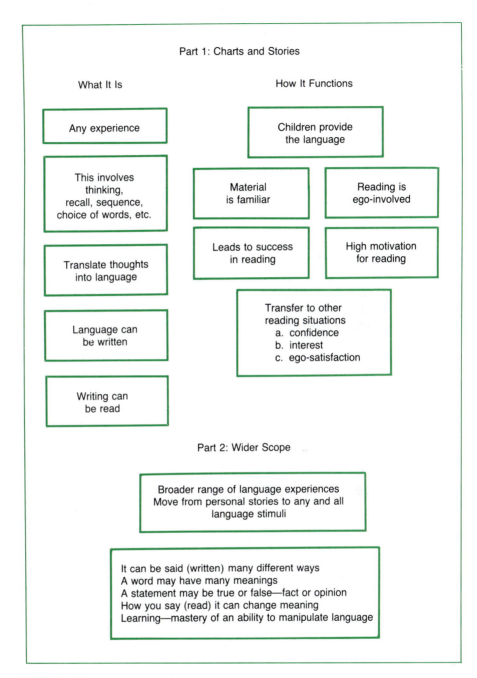

Part 1: Charts and Stories

What It Is

How It Functions

Any experience

Children provide
the language

This involves
thinking,
recall, sequence,
choice of words, etc.

Material
is familiar

Reading is
ego-involved

Translate thoughts
into language

Leads to success
in reading

High motivation
for reading

Language can
be written

Transfer to other
reading situations
a. confidence
b. interest
c. ego-satisfaction

Writing can
be read

Part 2: Wider Scope

Broader range of language experiences
Move from personal stories to any and all
language stimuli

It can be said (written) many different ways
A word may have many meanings
A statement may be true or false—fact or opinion
How you say (read) it can change meaning
Learning—mastery of an ability to manipulate language

FIGURE 8.3
The basic features of the language-experience approach

Computers

Virtually every school district in our country is using microcomputers in one way or another. Computers are also becoming more and more a part of literacy instruction in our classrooms. Any display of reading approaches, materials, and activities today includes myriad microcomputer applications, so a key concern is how schools and teachers are using the computer's marvelous capabilities. Like other tools, computers and programs can help teachers. The challenge for all teachers is to harness computers' power and versatility (Blanchard, Mason & Daniel, 1987).

The first thing teachers should realize is that computers cannot replace good teaching. Second, microcomputers may or may not assist individual teachers in achieving their instructional goals. Indiscriminate use of computers (or any materials) in the classroom can be detrimental to learning. However, when used properly, computers are effective. Among their advantages are (1) the motivation they provide, (2) their flexible presentation formats, (3) the immediate feedback they give students, and (4) their capacity to provide an abundance of individually tailored reinforcement.

Computers have the potential to expand and enhance the teaching of literacy. To effectively use computers, teachers need not know how to program, but they do need to know basic computer terminology, possible computer applications, the proper way to use the computers themselves, the importance of evaluating various software programs (e.g., drill and practice lessons on long vowel sounds), and ways to incorporate computers during literacy lessons (Pitts, 1983).

Uses

Futurists see classrooms in which students interact with computers in all phases of learning: They read and write and hold sophisticated conversations with the computers on all levels of thinking. Computer applications in the classroom are very powerful, and future applications will depend greatly on pedagogical considerations determined by educators, not on computer technology (Richardson, 1984).

In today's classrooms, most of the computer usage in reading is in the form of *computer-assisted instruction* (CAI) (Schaudt, 1987; Harrison, 1987). CAI involves a student in particular skill. When the system is in operation and an individual is sitting at the terminal, CAI may have the following capabilities:

- To show anything that may appear in any material ordinarily presented via chalkboard or overhead projector.
- To permit the learner to respond on a typewriter-like keyboard.
- To provide explanations, give directions, or present supplementary data through an auditory (voice) component.
- To respond almost instantly. This instant feedback can be visual, auditory, or both.
- To record and store all responses a learner makes. If a student is absent for a time, the system can resume exactly where he or she left off. If the student

has forgotten a crucial principle, the program can ascertain this through the student's error pattern and can send him or her back through a review or to easy material that fits the present need.

Software Programs

CAI software comes in a variety of modes: For example, drill and practice exercises, tutorial dialogues, simulations, learning games, and creative writing. Drill and practice programs are very popular, but they are also the most unimaginative of the computer applications. In essence, many of the programs are merely electronic workbook exercises. However, such applications have good potential for helping students practice and reinforcing basic word-identification and comprehension skills in terms of individual student needs. Although many educators have criticized the quality of the programs, it is hoped that the quality will improve as teachers become more involved in software development.

The typical sequence in a drill and practice program is (1) presentation of a question, (2) student response, and (3) computer response (usually "correct," "incorrect," or "let's try again"). The cycle begins again. The student receives very little, if any, explanation of the task.

Drill and practice programs allow students to practice skills independently and provide the practice necessary to make basic skills automatic. Some programs even give teachers a report of student tries per item and an analysis of student performance on particular skills. With quality software, these programs can be most beneficial for both teacher and students in carrying out the independent practice step of the direct instruction format.

Tutorial dialogues are more sophisticated than drill and practice programs. The computer provides more explanation of a drill and reteaches, if necessary. Instead of just providing feedback of "correct" or incorrect," these programs give students more detailed explanations. If a student response is incorrect, an explanation appears along with more examples similar to the one missed. If the student responds correctly, the computer branches to more difficult material.

Simulations are programs that allow students to role play an experience. In a typical program, the computer displays an experiment or hypothetical situation, and the student responds with new information. The computer runs the experiment, and the student responds with new information as needed. The computer then displays the new results.

In reading and writing, a variety of learning games provide interesting practice in reading skills. Many of these games (such as hangman and Scrabble) reinforce spelling and vocabulary development. The instructional cycles are similar to those of the drill and practice programs.

The underlying assumption of CAI is programmed instruction theory. The programs are based on operant conditioning principles and are similar in presentation to commercially programmed materials. In literacy, most of the computer programs now available are the drill and practice type. Although research on CAI is in its infancy, initial reports indicate that the drill and practice programs have a positive effect on student achievement (Blanchard, Mason, & Daniel, 1987).

Much more research is needed before CAI can be hailed as having a significant impact on reading achievement, however.

In addition to CAI, a growing application of the computer in teaching reading is computer-managed instruction (CMI). In CMI, computers administer diagnostic tests, score the tests, record and store the results, and prescribe appropriate instruction (Weisberg & Balajthy, 1989). Computer-managed instruction offers excellent possibilities for aiding teachers in these areas.

New Computer Applications in Literacy

New uses of the computer are continually being developed and tested (Rickleman & Henk, 1990). One such application integrates reading and writing through word-processing programs. This application allows students to type a story or any text and to edit the text by inserting words, deleting words, or rearranging paragraphs and sentences. This application is popular with writers in all fields, but its use at the elementary level is only beginning to grow. In beginning reading, as part of the language-experience approach, a teacher can type a student's story and play back the story in print and voice. Smith (1985) summarized the research on using word processing to teach writing and incorporating it in the language-experience approach: "Good reading/writing instruction that occurs without the computer can be still better with it" (p. 559).

An exciting new computer application is *Apple Early Language Connections* (1992). This is a literature-based multisensory language arts program for kindergarten through grade 2 featuring an array of hardware, software, books, and audiotapes. More than 200 literature books are available on the Macintosh computer which brings the stories to life. Students can progress at their rate and interact with each story using various senses. The quality literature is thematic in nature and the units contain lesson plans with literature, music, math, art, and science activities.

Computer software programs are also being developed to support literature-based reading. Wepner (1991) reports on eight software packages for enhancing reading in different genres (fairy tales, realistic fiction, science fiction, and biography and historical fiction in social studies). Using word-processing packages, students can interact at various levels with the books. Wepner highlights the advantage of this technology to foster a joy of reading and states "software that serves as an open-ended forum for self-expression and discovery offers students real-world opportunities to communicate with and about books" (p. 70).

Software Evaluation

The ultimate success or failure of computer-assisted instruction depends on two conditions: (1) the quality of the educational software (the programs containing the steps and procedures for the computer to follow) and (2) the ability to use the computer to meet instructional goals. Software programs for elementary reading are proliferating. A quick glance at any magazine rack indicates that this market is growing more competitive. In fact, teachers attempting to select a few reading programs among the hundreds on the market may easily begin to feel confused. "Which program is best?" is the wrong question. The correct question is "Which program will best match my students' learning needs?"

Just as effective teachers select other supplemental materials in relation to student needs, so too must they select computer programs. Underlying this concern is determining the quality of the programs. Do the steps in a lesson and the related procedures follow the tenets of effective instruction? Does the software allow students to interact with the computer? Unfortunately, a majority of software programs offer poor rather than good instruction. Yet, remember that many current programs are written by computer experts, not educators. Many of today's programs purport to teach a skill but do not fulfill this expectation. Also, although software production is expanding at an unbelievable rate, software development is still in its infancy. If teachers eventually have greater influence on software development, the quality will improve.

Remember, the best hardware (the computer) is only as good as the software the teacher selects. Demand quality software for your students. The cardinal rule in software evaluation is: Never buy or use a program until you try it for yourself. This allows you to experience how "user friendly" it is, as well as whether directions are clear, help is easy to obtain, you can control the pacing, and you can enter and exit easily. A trial run can help you evaluate these and other important aspects of the program. Figure 8.4 should help you evaluate reading software by examining the program's ease of use, instruction design, content accuracy, and special features.

In addition to actually running through the software program and systematically using an evaluation form, you must have your students try out the program. Their perceptions of the effectiveness of a program are most crucial—after all, they are the ones who will need to spend their time completing the program.

With quality software a continual problem, Issak and Joseph (1989) recommend that teachers consider writing their own instruction software. Recent advances in software-writing systems can help teachers create computer applications specific to their students' needs. Composing software can accomplish the following:

1. Create materials for instruction in emergent literacy, spelling, word recognition and analysis, fluency, and vocabulary development.

2. Provide direct instruction in reading comprehension and metacognition via modeling, guided practice, and independent application.

3. Enhance the potential concreteness of any reading material, however unfamiliar, through the use of media integration that can provide graphics and sound to clarify text portions requiring elaboration.

4. Heighten at-risk readers' appreciation of literature through the use of expressive audio support.

5. Develop "local" interactive text adventures that place students vicariously in the stories.

6. Create parallel lessons of the same content text assignments in which the readability levels vary according to the ability of the reader.

	Good	Adequate	Poor
Type of Program			
_____ Drill and practice	____	____	____
_____ Tutorial	____	____	____
_____ Simulation	____	____	____
_____ Learning game	____	____	____
Ease of Use			
Clear directions	____	____	____
Exit capabilities	____	____	____
Control of pacing	____	____	____
Provision for help	____	____	____
Instructional Design			
Clear objectives	____	____	____
Introductory explanations of skills	____	____	____
Sample exercises	____	____	____
A number of practice exercises	____	____	____
Immediate and varied feedback	____	____	____
Branching capability	____	____	____
Built-in assessment of progress	____	____	____
Monitoring of student responses	____	____	____
Corrections made by reteaching, giving clues, or explaining skill	____	____	____
Summary statements	____	____	____
Program length	____	____	____
Appropriate difficulty level	____	____	____
Content Accuracy			
Direct correspondence between lesson objectives and lesson procedures	____	____	____
Accuracy	____	____	____
Procedures reflecting what a reader has to do in the process of reading	____	____	____
Correct sequence in presenting skill	____	____	____
Special Features			
Animation	____	____	____
Speech	____	____	____
Music	____	____	____
Laser videodiscs	____	____	____
Touch screen	____	____	____
Graphics	____	____	____
Audio	____	____	____
Color	____	____	____

FIGURE 8.4
Reading software evaluation guide

7. Generate dynamic test formats by using a parsing feature that allows for more than one possible answer.

8. Use the parsing feature in combination with videodiscs to show readers the results of their text predictions.

9. Train preservice and practicing teachers in instructional design, especially the step-by-step delivery of a precise reading lesson.

10. Create interactive environments for practice in reading diagnosis and lesson delivery. (p. 255)

Instructional Principles

In addition to quality software, the effectiveness of CAI ultimately depends on its proper implementation. While teachers do not need to learn new teaching techniques, they do need to apply sound educational principles to integrate CAI into the total reading program. Teachers should consider the following principles as they begin to make decisions regarding the use of microcomputers in the classroom:

- Teachers must devote considerable time to planning CAI applications in their classroom.
- Students should have a great degree of control and interaction with the computer.
- Teachers should use CAI only with students who respond positively to it.
- Teachers should hold weekly conference with all students to review their progress.
- Managing use of the microcomputer should not inordinately disrupt normal teaching routines.
- Teachers should introduce students to the microcomputer by explaining how and why they will use it in their class.
- Teachers should always share a program's objectives with students.
- Teachers should be certain to use software that corresponds to their instructional goals.
- Teachers should monitor pupil involvement to ensure a high degree of time on task.
- Teachers should vary the use of CAI so that students will not get bored doing the same thing each time they work with the microcomputer.
- Teachers should never view CAI as being more than one part of the total reading program.
- When appropriate, teachers should assign students to work in pairs on a microcomputer.
- Teachers should use CAI lessons in a logical sequence.
- Teachers should always evaluate the application of CAI after examining test results, observing the students, and obtaining student evaluations.

Effective teachers of literacy know how to use a variety of materials and instructional procedures to teach literacy and to match students' needs. Four major materials and instructional approaches to teaching literacy are basal readers, literature-based programs, individualized reading, and whole language–based instructional approaches. While each approach has its own unique characteristics, effective teachers integrate various aspects of the different approaches to reflect their students' learning needs.

The basal reader program was highlighted in this chapter. By far the most popular approach in our schools today, this approach incorporates much of the current research on the reading process, reading comprehension, and teaching reading. Modern basals also stress an integrated language arts curriculum with an emphasis on quality literature. Even with the multitude of materials in a basal program, however, no basal program should be viewed as complete; rather, the teacher must supplement them with a variety of materials to satisfy student needs. Effective teachers use a blend of instructional activities to fulfill the major components of a complete reading program, including developmental reading, application transfer, independent or recreational reading, content reading, and functional reading.

In addition to the four major approaches, supplemental reading approaches abound to help in teaching reading. Two significant supplemental approaches discussed in this chapter were LEA and computer-assisted instruction.

Besides understanding the characteristics and assumptions of each of these approaches, teachers should develop a critical questioning attitude in implementing them. Since all approaches have strengths and weaknesses, teachers must become thoroughly familiar with the features of an approach and how they address students' needs. Approaches and materials should be viewed as aids in the teaching of reading, since the teacher, not the approaches and materials, teaches reading. Adapting approaches and materials to learner needs is absolutely necessary for successful literacy instruction.

YOUR POINT OF VIEW /

Discussion Questions

1. Why are basal readers viewed as representative of the eclectic method?
2. Why must teachers modify some features of a basal manual regardless of students' literacy capabilities?
3. Which of the features of the basal reader lesson example (DRA) would Durkin's findings suggest deserves the most attention from teachers?

Take a Stand For or Against

1. Someday reading researchers will find one reading approach that will work with all students.
2. All reading instruction materials that follow the structures and patterns of English usage can be said to be linguistic.

3. The time it takes for teachers to integrate the features of the language-experience approach with basal readers is not worth the effort.

4. Teachers who do not use the basic recommendations of a basal manual are probably better than are teachers who use such recommendations blindly.

BIBLIOGRAPHY /

Aiex, N. K. (1988). ERIC/RCS: Literature based reading instruction. *The Reading Teacher, 41*, 458–461.

Alvermann, D., Bridge, C. A., Schmidt, B. A., Searfoss, L, Winograd, P., & Paris, S. G. (1993). *Heath Reading.* Lexington, MA: D. C. Heath and Co.

Anderson, R. C., Hiebert, E. H., Scott, J. A., & Wilkinson, I. A. G. (1985). *Becoming a nation of readers: The report of the commission on reading* (Contract No. 400-83-0057). Washington, DC: The National Institute of Education.

Apple Early Language Connections (1992). Cupertino, CA: Apple Computer, Inc.

Bacharach, N., & Alexander, P. (1986). Basal reader manuals: What do teachers think of them and how do they use them? *Reading Psychology, 7*, 163–172.

Blair, T. R., & Turner, E. (1984). Skills instruction and independent learning. *Middle School Journal, 15*, 6–7.

Blanchard, J. S., Mason, G. E., & Daniel, D. (1987). *Computer applications in reading* (3rd ed.). Newark, DE: International Reading Association.

Center for the Study of Reading. (1986). *A guide to selecting basal reading programs.* Urbana, IL: Center for the Study of Reading, University of Illinois.

Clements, N.E. (1991). Maximizing time on task: Supplementing basals and workbooks. In R. A. Thompson (Ed.), *Classroom Reading Instruction.* Dubuque, IA: Kendall/Hunt.

Dole, J. A. (Spring 1984). Beginning reading: More than talk written down. *Reading Horizons, 24*, 161–166.

Durkin, D. (1984). Is there a match between what elementary teachers do and what the basal reader manuals recommend? *The Reading Teacher, 37*, 734–744.

Durkin, D. (1993). *Teaching them to read* (6th ed.). Boston: Allyn and Bacon.

Greenlinger-Harless, C. S. (1987). A new cross-referenced index to U.S. reading series, grades K–8. *The Reading Teacher. 41*, 293–303.

Hall, M. (1981). *Teaching reading as a language experience* (3rd ed.). New York: Merrill/Macmillan Publishing Co.

Harrison, N. F. (1987). *The relationship between opportunity to learn basic reading skills and student achievement via computer assisted instruction.* Doctoral dissertation, Texas A & M University, College Station.

Issak, T., & Joseph, J. (1989). Authoring software and teaching reading. *The Reading Teacher, 43*, 254–255.

Karnowski, L. (1989). Using LEA with process writing. *The Reading Teacher, 42*, 462–465.

Mason, J. M. (1983). An examination of reading instruction in third and fourth grades. *The Reading Teacher, 37*, 906–913.

McCallum, R.D. (1988). Don't throw the basals out with the bath water. *The Reading Teacher 42*, 204–209.

Osborn, J. (1984). Workbooks that accompany basal programs. In G. G. Duffy, L. R. Roehler, & J. Mason (Eds.), *Comprehension instruction: Perspectives and Suggestions.* New York: Longman, 163–186.

Piernek, F. T. (1979). Using basal guidebooks—The ideal integrated lesson plan. *The Reading Teacher, 33,* 167–172.

Pitts, M. R. (1983). *The educator's unauthorized microcomputer survival manual.* Washington, DC: Council for Educational Development and Research.

Reimer, B. L. (1983). Recipes for language experience stories. *The Reading Teacher, 37,* 396–404.

Reutzel, D. R. (1985). Reconciling schema theory and the basal reading lesson. *The Reading Teacher, 39,* 194–197.

Richardson, J. (1984). *The three A's: Influencing teachers' awareness, attitudes, and anxieties about using computer assisted instruction for reading classes.* Richmond: Virginia Commonwealth University.

Rickleman, R. J., & Henk, W. A. (1990). Reading and technology in the future. *The Reading Teacher, 44,* 262–263.

Rupley, W. H., & Blair, T. R. (1989). *Reading diagnosis and remediation: Classroom and clinic* (3rd ed.). New York: Merrill/Macmillan Publishing Co.

Schaudt, B. A. (1987). Selected research on computer-assisted instruction. In M. J. Burger & R. J. Kansky (Eds.), *Technology in education: Implications and applications.* College Station, TX: Instructional Laboratory, College of Education, Texas A & M University.

Singer, H., Samuels, S. J., & Spiroff, J. (1973–1974). The effect of pictures and contextual conditions on learning responses to printed words. *Reading Research Quarterly, 9,* 355–367.

Stauffer, R. (1975). *Directing the reading-thinking process.* New York: Harper & Row.

Thompson, R. A. (Ed.) (1991). *Classroom reading instruction* (2nd ed.). Dubuque, IA: Kendall/Hunt Publishing Co.

Tulley, M. A. (1991–1992). Learning to teach with a new basal reading program. *Journal of Reading Education, 17,* 12–28.

Weisberg, R., & Balajthy, E., (1989). Reading diagnosis via the microcomputer. *The Reading Teacher, 42,* 636.

Wepner, S. B. (1991). Linking technology to genre—basal reading. *The Reading Teacher, 45,* 68–70.

Winograd, P. N., Wixson, K. K., & Lipson, M. Y. (Eds.). (1989). *Improving Basal Reading Instruction.* New York: Teachers College Press.

Yeager, B. (n.d.). *Data management and decision making in the PLATO elementary reading project.* Urbana: University of Illinois.

9

Literature-based Reading Instruction

Donna E. Norton

For the Reader

Our nation is currently emphasizing an increase in the use of literature in its reading programs. According to *Reading Today* (1988), the newspaper of the International Reading Association, "Everywhere you look, there seems to be a renewed interest in the use of children's literature in the school reading program. This trend is evident in increased coverage of the topic in conference presentations, journal articles, and books" (p. 1).

The same article identifies both concerns and realizations that encourage this emphasis. Many communities believe that students are neither learning to read adequately nor choosing to read independently. Of equal concern are the criticisms that many basal readers are limited in their scope and contain neither classic nor contemporary literature. On the other hand, literature-based reading programs appear to promote the fun and joy of reading; enrich students' lives; provide material that is inspiring, interesting, and informative; and increase reading ability.

In the literature-based view, reading is not the acquisition of a set of isolated skills. Instead, reading is the ability to read all types of literature with understanding, appreciation, and enjoyment. In this viewpoint, literature can be used to support the reading curriculum, to teach or reinforce reading skills, and to introduce students to a wide variety of good and enjoyable books. Students discover that reading is more than skill lessons, workbook pages, and short, disconnected stories. Through literature, students discover that reading can become a lifelong habit that brings both knowledge and enjoyment.

Key Ideas

- In the reading program, the use of literature should develop in the students an understanding of literature and an appreciation for it.

- Teachers can develop reading capabilities through the use of literature.

- Literature-based reading programs include objectives related to understanding and appreciating the different literary genres and elements.

- Developing an understanding of and appreciation for literature requires that teachers help students recognize the literary elements and the ways that authors use those elements to create exciting and credible stories.

- Strategies for teaching reading through literature include using predictable books, analyzing plot structures, semantic mapping, and modeling.

Key Terms

core literature   books that should be taught in the classroom through close reading and intensive consideration. These books can serve as important stimuli for writing and discussion.

extended literature   works that teachers may assign to individuals or small groups as homework or supplemental classwork.

literature-based reading program   a program that emphasizes the ability to read all types of literature with understanding, appreciation, and enjoyment.

classics   extraordinary books that last beyond their authors' lives and continue to attract readers.

theme   the central idea that ties the plot, characterizations, and setting together in a meaningful whole.

style   an author's choice and arrangement of words to create plot, characterizations, setting, and theme.

point of view   the viewpoint that authors choose when they tell a story, including the details they describe and the judgments they make.

recreational reading groups   students grouped on the basis of their interests to discuss the same book, books by the same author, or books with similar characteristics.

LITERATURE-BASED READING PROGRAMS

Literature may support the basal reading curriculum or it may be the core of the total reading program. When teachers use literature to support the reading curriculum, they identify reading skills taught in the basal approach and assign literature selections that reinforce those skills. As a result, students see that the major goal of the reading program is to understand, appreciate, and enjoy, not merely to complete workbook pages.

Programs in which teachers use literature as the core of the reading and language arts curriculum are multiplying rapidly. The California State Department of Education (1986) published a list of recommended readings in literature, identifying a literature-based core curriculum. The California list recommends over 1,000 titles categorized according to genre, grade span, cultural group, and the place of the literature in the curriculum. *Core literature* includes books that should be taught in the classroom. With close reading and intensive consideration, they are likely to be important stimuli for writing and discussion. *Extended literature* includes works that teachers may assign to individual students or small groups of students as homework or supplemental classwork. Recreational-motivational literature includes works for students to select for individual, leisure-time reading from classrooms, schools, and community libraries. This literature-based curriculum uses the primary sources of the literature (as opposed to anthologies). This approach promotes literacy, developing an understanding of and appreciation for literature.

Hiebert and Colt (1989) identify the varied instructional formats that can be found in effective literacy programs that focus on children's literature. These formats range from teacher-led instruction using teacher-selected literature for teaching critical strategies to teacher- and student-led interaction using teacher-and-student-selected materials to independent reading from student-selected literature.

According to Hiebert and Colt (1989), effective literature programs include a variety of these formats because

> When teachers focus only on independent reading of student-selected material, they fail to consider the guidance that students require for becoming expert readers. A focus on teacher-led instruction fails to develop the independent reading strategies that underlie lifelong reading. A total reading program should contain various combinations of teacher and student interaction and selection of literature so that children develop as thoughtful, proficient readers. (p. 19)

Whether a total literature approach or a support for the basal reading curriculum is used, teachers must be aware that use of literature in the reading curriculum should develop understanding of literature and an appreciation for it. To choose literature that motivates students to read and that stimulates an appreciation for literature requires knowledge about literature, awareness of students' interests, and knowledge about instructional approaches that stimulate interest and appreciation. Ruddell (1992) argues that motivation is extremely important. He states, "Creating high reader motivation depends on the teacher's understanding of the student and his or her intimate knowledge of literature selections. The development of high reader motivation depends heavily on the teacher's ability to connect the student with the literary work by using student background knowledge and personal interests that are directly relevant to the content, language form and style, and format and illustrations of the literary work" (p. 616). Likewise, to teach reading through literature requires knowledge about appropriate literature and instructional approaches that encourage the broad development of reading skills as well as the understanding of literary elements used by the authors of literature.

In addition to reading for goals such as the main idea, important details, and cause-and-effect relationships, we can emphasize the strengths of good literature by encouraging students to develop understanding and appreciation for characterization, setting, conflict, plot, theme, author's style, and point of view. Within the author's style are such complex areas as symbolism, metaphor, simile, personification, allegory, and allusion. In addition, genre has specific reading and writing demands. Thus, folklore, fantasy, poetry, realistic fiction, historical fiction, biography, autobiography, and informational literature have unique reading requirements. It is appropriate to heed Fishel's (1984) warning: "Of the content areas, English is one of the most demanding in terms of the reading skills required to understand the various genres. In addition, appreciation of the genres is a teaching goal" (p. 9).

The development of an excellent *literature-based reading program* requires extensive teacher knowledge. Teachers need to know how to select literature. They also must have considerable knowledge of instructional strategies that both highlight the best features of literature and excite students. Gardner (1988) warns that literature approaches must not become basal approaches. Instead, programs should "help students select wisely, respond to literature in creative, personally meaningful ways, or help readers raise ethical issues" (p. 251). Gardner also expresses the importance of teacher preparation in this approach when she asks, "Will sufficient time be devoted to teaching children's literature in the teaching institutions?" (p. 252).

This chapter emphasizes the selection of literature, the development of an understanding of and appreciation for literature, and the instructional strategies that focus on the strengths of literature. It highlights approaches that encourage oral and written interactions with literature and that inspire readers to develop excitement about what they read.

Objectives

Literature-based reading programs include objectives related to understanding and appreciating the different literary genres and elements. The National Council of Teachers of English (1983) states that students should (1) realize the importance of literature as a mirror of human experience, (2) be able to gain insights from their involvement with literature, (3) become aware of writers who represent diverse backgrounds and traditions, (4) become familiar with past and present masterpieces of literature, (5) develop effective ways of discussing and writing about various forms of literature, (6) appreciate the rhythms and beauty of the language in literature, and (7) develop lifelong reading habits.

Objectives from the guidelines published by various states also emphasize the interaction of appreciation and understanding. For example, the third grade objectives of the Illinois *State Goals for Learning and Sample Learning Objectives: Language Arts* (1985) state that students should read and enjoy appropriate literary works. At the same grade level, objectives related to genre state that students should recognize the nature of prose, biography, and poetry, and be able to compare versions of folktales. By the sixth grade, students should recognize historical fiction, fantasy, science fiction, realistic fiction, and folk literature.

The Illinois third grade objectives for literary elements include recognizing plot sequences and actions; identifying setting; identifying important character traits; explaining how and why characters change throughout a story; recognizing the main idea of a selection; and identifying similes, personification, and onomatopoeia. By the sixth grade, the list of objectives for literary elements expands to understanding an author's tone, point of view, symbolism, and other types of figurative language.

Literature-based reading programs accomplish additional goals. Using folklore collections, writings of Robert Louis Stevenson and Louisa May Alcott, and poems by Langston Hughes and Robert Frost, they help us understand and value

When the storm was over they explored the island. When they weren't looking, they fell into an enormous hole. They tried to get out but the owner came in (which was the Zerc)!

He was mad because he thought they wanted his food. They tried to stab the Zerc but he was to strong. Ulysses thought up a plan, but it did not work. So a man got the Zerc's attention, and Ulysses tied a rope around the Zerc's legs and he fell!

When Ulysses was climbing out of the hole, he said, "Did you have a nice trip Zerc?" He then kept on climbing.

When they got out, they started to look for a tall, straight tree. Ulysses told a man to go to the ship to get the ax. When he came back with the ax, Ulysses chopped down the tree. When he chopped down the tree, the whole crew carried it back to the ship. When they got back to the ship, they sewed a sheet on it for a sail. Then they put it over the hole where the old hollow mast was. After they got that done, they pushed the Penearo in the water.

One way of furthering children's literature appreciation is to have children create original stories based on stories they have read.
(Excerpt from *Ulysses Fights the Zerc* used with permission of Ian King.)

our cultural and literary heritage. Using historical fiction and nonfictional books that chronicle the early explorations and the frontier expansion, they allow us to vicariously live through world history. Using books on scientific breakthroughs, they open doors to new knowledge and expand our interests. Using fantasy, science fiction, and poetry, they nurture and expand our imaginations and allow us to visualize worlds that have not yet materialized or to see common occurrences with insight. Using realistic fiction, biography, and autobiography, they allow us to explore human possibilities and to develop personally and socially. Interactions with many types of literature allow us to expand our language and to enhance our cognitive development (Norton, 1992).

The Literature and Reading Connection

Sawyer (1987) reviews studies that support literature-based reading curriculums. He argues that we can no longer separate learning to read and reading to learn, because the two are interwoven. Sawyer contends that the story structures chosen to teach reading are important because the structures themselves teach the rules of narrative organization.

Meeks (1983), a British educator, adds strong support for using literature in the reading curriculum. She contends that students who fail to learn to read have not learned "how to tune the voice on the page, how to follow the fortunes of the hero, how to tolerate the unexpected, to link episodes" (p. 214).

Studies show that using literature, whether it is read to students or by students, improves reading comprehension, develops understanding of story structures, and increases appreciation of reading and literature. For example, Feitelson, Kita, and Goldstein (1986) report that first grade students who listened to and discussed literature for 20 minutes each day outperformed comparable groups in decoding, reading comprehension, and active use of language. Feitelson (1986) attributes the success to the adults who helped the students interpret the literature, understand the language that was unfamiliar to them, enrich their information bases, increase their knowledge about various story structures, encounter various literary devices, and extend their attention spans. Norton and McNamara (1987) report that a literature-based reading program that uses modeling and emphasizes cognitive processes and story structures significantly increases reading comprehension and improves attitudes toward reading by students in the fifth through eighth grades.

Educators who use and recommend literature-based reading instruction emphasize the dynamic nature of the environment and the desirability of both understanding of and appreciation for literature. For example, Taxel (1988) describes the literature-based classroom "as fluid and dynamic . . . a place where educators see literature as central to the curriculum, not as an occasional bit of enrichment undertaken when the real work is completed" (p. 74). May (1987) describes a literature-based program in which understanding and enjoyment are the major goals.

Five (1988) uses brief lessons that focus on such literary elements as characterization, setting, flashbacks, and book selection. Following each lesson, students read related literature, discuss the books, and complete writing activities. Five emphasizes that the program dramatically increases independent reading, peer discussions of literature, and student evaluation of such concerns as believable characters and effective language and dialogue.

Reading research provides strong rationales for teaching literature and guidelines for how to teach it. Early and Ericson (1982) identify nine findings to consider when developing a literature-based curriculum. First, readers use their knowledge of texts and contextual cues to create meaning during reading. (Schema theory also suggests that successful readers use their knowledge of various kinds of texts, the world, and contextual cues to create meaning.) Literature provides one of the best sources for acquiring and reinforcing this knowledge. Second, readers learn to read by reading. This implies that students need many opportunities to read a variety of literature. Third, readers need to experience whole texts to increase understanding. Literature is an obvious choice for encouraging students to develop meaning from longer texts.

Fourth, good readers understand when their reading makes sense, are aware when their reading processes break down, and use a variety of corrective strategies. Different genres and literary elements encourage students to use a variety of reading strategies. Fifth, readers improve their comprehension if teachers use such techniques as modeling, direct explanation, and questioning. These strategies work especially well with literature. Sixth, good readers use cues in the text and their prior knowledge to make predictions.

Seventh, students benefit from direct teaching of strategies for reading literature. Literary discussions can focus on many details in literature, such as characterization, setting, plot and theme. Eighth, students need help in looking for details to use in making inferences. Ninth, the range of students' reading achievement grows wider at each successive grade level. Consequently, a wide variety of literature helps meet this variety of needs.

SELECTING LITERATURE

When selecting the literature for a school curriculum, teachers should consider students' development, reading abilities, listening abilities, and interests as well as literary standards, curricular needs, and genre and cultural balance. It is beyond the scope of this chapter to cover the vast amount of information usually covered in children's literature courses. Instead, the chapter provides a brief review of the sources and criteria that you may use to help you select and evaluate literature.

Sources

Major children's literature texts are the best sources to use to help you select literature that meets the needs of your students. For example, Norton's *Through the Eyes of A Child: An Introduction to Children's Literature* (1991) provides evaluative criteria, recommendations for literature, and classroom applications for picture books, traditional literature, fantasy, poetry, contemporary realistic fiction, historical fiction, multicultural books, biography, and informational literature. The books discussed range from those for younger children to those for students through the middle school. Norton's *The Impact of Literature-Based Reading* (1992) suggests books and strategies that may be used with the books. *Children's Literature* (1993) by Huck, Hepler, and Hickman contains chapters on the major literature genres. Sutherland and Arbuthnot's *Children and Books* (1991) discusses the major authors who write in each of the genres.

Other books look at specific areas or specific needs of students. For example, Rudman and Pearce's *For Love of Reading: A Parent's Guide to Encouraging Young Readers from Infancy Through Age 5* (1988) explores various stages in young children's development and recommends books that enhance that development. Rudman's *Children's Literature: An Issues Approach* (1984) discusses and recommends books in areas such as sibling relationships, death, special needs, adoption, and gender. Matthews' *High Interest, Easy Reading* (1988) recommends books with high interest and lower vocabulary for junior and senior high school students. Wilms' *Science Books for Children* (1985) provides reviews of informational books recommended by *Booklist*, a literature journal. Gillespie and Gilbert's *Best Books for Children* (1985) provides brief annotations for books according to subject. Trelease's *The Read-Aloud Handbook* (1985) provides guidelines for selecting and reading books to students up to age 12.

Literature journals are fine sources for current books as well as for specialized lists. *Booklist, Horn Book,* and *School Library Journal* include reviews. They star reviews of books that the editors believe are of exceptional quality. *Booklist* also

Award-winning books and classics encourage students and teachers to explore and discuss selections considered to be the best in their fields.

publishes specialty lists of books such as "The U.S.A. Through Children's Books, 1988" (1988) and "Poetry for Young Children" (1988). *School Library Journal* publishes a "best books" list for each year as well as lists of specific subjects. Other helpful journals include *The Reading Teacher, Language Arts,* and *The New Advocate.* "Children's Choices" is published each year in *The Reading Teacher.* The journal *Book Links,* a publication of the American Library Association, is also extremely helpful when selecting books that are related to specific type of literature, theme, or author.

Award-winning books and classics, whether they are read to or by students, are of special interest in reading programs. These books encourage students and teachers to explore and discuss selections considered the best in their fields. For example, the Caldecott Medal and Honor Awards, presented since 1938, are awarded annually to the illustrators of the most distinguished books published in the United States. The Newbery Medal and Honor Awards, presented since 1922, are awarded annually for the most distinguished contributions to children's literature published in the United States. The Children's Book Award, presented since 1975, is awarded by the International Reading Association to a children's author whose work shows unusual promise. These and additional awards are listed on pages 687–695 in Norton's *Through the Eyes of A Child: An Introduction to Children's Literature* (1993).

Many of the older award-winning books are now considered classics. Many other books, however, were published before the awards were given. According to Rudman and Pearce (1988), **classics** are extraordinary books that last beyond their authors' lives and continue to delight and reach the minds and hearts of readers for many generations. The folktales of the Brothers Grimm and Charles Perrault, the picture books of Kate Greenaway *(A Apple Pie)* and Robert McCloskey (1941) *(Make Way for Ducklings),* the fantasies of A. A. Milne (1926) (the "Pooh" books) and E. B. White *(Charlotte's Web),* the poetry of David McCord *(One at a Time)* and Edward Lear *(Book of Nonsense),* the realistic fiction of Frances Hodgson Burnett *(The Secret Garden)* and Robert Louis Stevenson *(Treasure Island),* and the historical fiction of Esther Forbes *(Johnny Tremain)* and Laura Ingalls Wilder (1932) (the "Little House" series) deserve to be shared with all students. These books and other noteworthy classics have been identified by the Children's Literature Association as touchstones in children's literature. These books are considered so good that they should be used to evaluate all literature. A list of "Touchstone Books" is available from the Children's Literature Association, publisher of *Children's Literature Association Quarterly.* Breckenridge (1988) complied a list of modern classics in 1988. These lists offer many good examples of children's literature. They include books that teachers and students should read, discuss, and evaluate.

Evaluation Criteria

The various book sources emphasize different and valuable aspects of evaluation. Teachers must be aware of how books are evaluated when they read book reviews and choose literature from those reviews. Older students may also use these different criteria when they discuss or write about books.

The Caldecott Medal is awarded annually to the artist of the most distinguished American picture book of the year. The text also must be of a high quality and worthy of the pictures. The award is named after Randolph Caldecott, an English artist in the mid 1800s. Caldecott's picture books for children were beautifully illustrated nursery rhymes and old ballads.

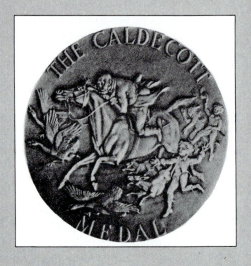

A major topic of discussion at the 1921 American Library Association meeting was children's reading in the library, home, and school. Frederic C. Melcher, who was the founder of Children's Book Week, felt that librarians could encourage the writing of quality children's books. He proposed that a medal be awarded for the most distinguished children's book written by a citizen or resident of the United States. The proposal was overwhelmingly supported. Mr. Melcher suggested the award be named the "John Newbery Medal," in honor of the bookseller who was keenly aware of children's reading interests and sought to find authors to write quality children's books.

/ / / /
/ / / /
/ / / /
■

UPDATE

Awards for outstanding children's books are usually selected by a committee made up of adult members. As a result, many of the books that children would find interesting and fun to read may be omitted. Since 1975, however, *The Reading Teacher* has published annually "Children's Choices," a listing of books that children themselves like. The list is based on the responses of 10,000 children from five different regions of the United States.

Kennemer (1984) identified three classifications of book reviews: (1) descriptive, (2) analytical, and (3) sociological. Descriptive reviews provide factual information about the story, plot, characters, theme, and illustrations. These reviews look at the who, what, where, and when of a story. Analytical reviews discuss, compare, and evaluate such literary elements as characterization, plot, setting, theme, and style. Analytical reviews may also discuss illustrations and relationships to other books. These analyses encourage their readers to see literature in new ways, to consider what makes the story believable or worthwhile, to note the techniques authors use, and to discover why they are successful or unsuccessful. Sociological reviews emphasize social context, concerning themselves with the characterizations of particular social or ethnic groups, the moral values, possible controversy, and potential popularity. They consider the social impact of the book. For example, a review might consider how the author depicts specific groups and what, if any, are the stereotypes.

Most of the textbooks in children's literature include review elements from all three types. There is, however, a greater emphasis on analytical reviews related to literary elements. Kennemer (1984) reported that the reviews in *Bulletin of the Center for Children's Books* are mostly descriptive. Reviews in *Booklist, The Horn Book, Kirkus Reviews,* and *The School Library Journal* chiefly analyze literary elements. *The School Library Journal* also emphasizes sociological analysis.

Reviews in content-area journals emphasize important elements in that specific content area. For example, in each April/May issue of *Social Education,* the book review subcommittee of the National Council for the Social Studies–Children's Book Council Joint Committee (1992) publishes a bibliography, "Notable Children's Trade Books in the Field of Social Studies." The books selected for this bibliography "(1) are written primarily for children in grades K–8; (2) emphasize human relations; (3) represent a diversity of groups and are sensitive to a broad range of cultural experiences; (4) present an original theme or a fresh slant on a traditional topic; (5) are easily readable and of high literary quality; and (6) have a pleasing format and, when appropriate, illustrations that enrich the text" (p. 253).

Reading and discussing the facts of literature are obviously easier than analyzing the literary or sociological aspects. A good literature program enables students to go beyond the factual level. Reading and discussing good children's literature increases one's awareness, enables one to discover the techniques an author uses to create a believable plot or memorable characterizations, and provides standards for comparison. Reading and discussing good literature help every student become a worthy critic, what Kingsbury (1984) defines as one "who offers us new perspectives on a text, who sees more in it than we saw, who motivates us to return to it for another reading" (p. 17).

This chapter refers to the literary elements that students should understand and appreciate. It briefly reviews the literary elements of plot, characterization, setting, theme, style, and point of view.

Plot. The plot of a story is the plan of action or sequence of events. A plot must have a beginning, a middle, and an end. A good plot allows students to become involved in the action, feel the conflict developing, recognize the climax, and respond to a satisfactory ending. The plots in most books for younger children follow a chronological, or sequential, order of the character's life, whether the story occurs over a day, several days, or a longer period. Cumulative action, such as that found in "The House That Jack Built," is popular in books for younger students, as the actions and characters are mentioned again when new action or new characters are introduced. Books for older students sometimes use flashbacks in addition to chronological order.

Excitement in the plot occurs when characters experience struggles or overcome conflict. The major types of conflict found in children's literature include person against person, person against society, person against nature, and person against self. With believable conflict, the readers understand the conflicting circumstances. For example, in *Hatchet* (1987), Paulsen describes nature in such a way that readers visualize the power and the danger. We know that the main character is in a life-or-death struggle and that he must learn about nature if he is to survive alone in the Canadian wilderness.

Many books for more advanced readers develop person-against-self conflict. In Strachan's *The Flawed Glass* (1990), the plot develops as the main character struggles against her physical handicap and eventually discovers her true worth.

Characterization. Believable characters, especially in books for older students, should be three dimensional—characters with pasts, futures, hopes, fears, parents, and siblings. Most memorable characters develop throughout the course of the story. To develop the many sides of a character, an author can reveal the character's strengths and weaknesses directly or by describing the character's thoughts, showing the character in action, and recording the character's dialogues. Characters such as Burnett's Mary Lennox in *The Secret Garden* (1911) are memorable because, like real people, they are neither all good nor all bad. Like real people, they must overcome believable problems as they progress through life.

Contemporary characters such as Fox's 11-year-old boy in *Monkey Island* (1991) frequently relate more closely to modern problems. The author develops vivid characterization as the boy is forced to live on the streets of New York City after his mother disappears.

Setting. Setting is where the story takes place. It identifies the time as past, present, or future. Whether the setting is developed through illustrations or text, it must provide details that reinforce the plot and characterization. Setting in historical fiction is especially important, because the details must be true to the time period. In science fiction and fantasy, the author must provide enough detail to make the readers believe in a world that is yet to materialize or in a place that is impossible from what we know of our world. As in Brown's *Shadow* (1982) or Rylant's *Appalachia: The Voices of Sleeping Birds* (1991), setting may create the mood of a story. As in Sperry's *Call It Courage* (1940), setting may create the antagonist. As in Freedman's *Lincoln: A Photobiography* (1987) or Vos's *Hide and Seek* (1991), setting may create the historical background. Finally, as in *The Secret Garden* (1911), setting may create a symbolic location for human growth and healing as well as natural growth.

Theme.   *Theme* is the central idea that ties the plot, characterizations, and setting together into a meaningful whole. The theme is frequently the authors' purpose for writing the story, the message. Authors of books for younger children frequently state the theme, while authors of books for older students usually imply the theme through characterizations and conflict resolution. A memorable theme usually relates to the reader's needs. For example, Grifalconi's *Darkness and the Butterfly* (1987) develops two themes: (1) it is all right to experience fears and (2) we can and must overcome our fears.

Style.   *Style* is an author's choice and arrangement of words to create plot, characterizations, setting, and theme. The sounds may appeal to the senses. The word choices and sentence lengths may create a leisurely or frightening mood. Figurative language may allow us to visualize concepts in new ways. Symbolism, such as that found in Voigt's *Dicey's Song* (1982), may allow us to understand characterization and appreciate a well-crafted novel. Effective style is usually most noticeable when reading a book orally.

Point of View.   Authors choose a viewpoint to use when they tell a story, including the details they describe and the judgments they make. Frye, Baker, and Perkins (1985) state, "[T]he narrator, or teller of the story, may stand within the story or outside it, narrating as it occurs, shortly after, or much later, providing in each instance a different narrative perspective in space and time" (p. 302). Consequently, the same story would change drastically if told from another ***point of view.*** For example, Potter's *The Tale of Peter Rabbit* (1902) would certainly change if told from the viewpoint of Mr. McGregor.

Avi's *Nothing But the Truth: A Documentary Novel* (1991), a fictional novel written in documentary format, allows readers to interpret each of the incidents, draw their own conclusions about the truthfulness of the documents, and decide which characters are changed the most by the incidents and the conclusions. As a consequence, students may gain insights into how emotions define and distort the truth and how important understanding of point of view is when reading a book.

Authors may use first person, which allows them to speak through the "I" of one of the characters; an objective point of view, which lets actions speak for themselves; an omniscient point of view, which allows the author to tell the story in third person and be all-knowing about the characters; or a limited omniscient point of view, which allows the author to concentrate on one character but to still be all-knowing about other characters. First-person narratives are frequently used in books for younger students, such as in the various "Ramona" stories. Books for older students frequently use the omniscient or limited omniscient point of view. Whatever point of view is used, it should be consistent.

DEVELOPING LITERARY ENJOYMENT AND APPRECIATION

One of the primary goals of any reading program is to develop readers who turn to literature for both pleasure and knowledge. Providing many opportunities for students to listen to, read, and discuss literature entices them to love and appreciate books. This section focuses on two activities that are beneficial to the reading teacher who is trying to increase enjoyment of reading: (1) oral reading to students and (2) recreational reading groups.

Oral Reading to Students

Reading to students develops understanding of various story structures, increases knowledge of language patterns, expands vocabularies, and introduces genres of literature that students might not read independently (see Chapters 3 and 7). Consequently, the book selected for reading aloud should be worthy of the time spent by both the reader and the listeners. Children's ages, attention spans, and levels of reading ability are important considerations. The books chosen should increase students' appreciation of outstanding literature. The numerous easy-to-read books should usually be left for younger students to read independently.

Reading aloud should not end in the lower elementary grades. Older students also benefit from being exposed to literature too difficult for them to read independently. Books such as Esther Forbes' *Johnny Tremain* (1943) and Kenneth Grahame's *The Wind in the Willows* (1908) should not be missed because the language is too difficult for students to read. Kimmell and Segel (1983) compiled an annotated list of books appropriate for reading aloud to older students.

After selecting a book, the teacher should read it silently to understand the story, identify the sequence of events, recognize the mood, identify any concepts or vocabulary that may cause problems, decide how to introduce the story, and consider the appropriate type of discussion. Next, the teacher should read the book aloud to himself or herself in order to practice pronunciation, pacing, and voice characterization. Teachers should *never* read stories aloud to an audience before reading the stories themselves.

Lamme (1976) provides the following observations concerning effective oral reading to students:

1. Child involvement, including predicting what will happen next and filling in missing words, is the most influential factor during oral reading.

2. Eye contact between the reader and the audience is essential.

3. Adults who read with expression are more effective than those who use a monotonous tone.

4. Good oral readers put variety into their voices; pitch should be neither too high nor too low, and volume should be neither too loud nor too soft.

5. Readers who point to meaningful words or pictures in a book as they read are better than those who merely read the story and show the pictures.

6. Knowing the story, without needing to read the text verbatim, is more effective than straight reading.

7. Readers who select picture books large enough for the students to see and appealing enough to hold their interest or elicit their comments are most effective.

8. Grouping students so that all can see the pictures and hear the story is important.

9. Adults who highlight the words and language of the story by making the rhymes apparent, discussing unusual vocabulary words, and emphasizing any repetition are better readers.

It is impossible to have an effective oral reading experience without adequate preparation. Also notice that many factors, such as highlighting the language of the story and encouraging students to predict what will happen next, are related to important reading skills.

Recreational Reading Groups

Reading widely and frequently encourages literary appreciation and reinforces the development of reading skills. Reading activities based on literature help students synthesize information from several sources, clarify their developing literary skills, and share revelations about their discoveries. Uninterrupted sustained silent reading (USSR) and *recreational reading groups* encourage the reading of literature.

Recreational reading groups are especially appropriate for literature-based reading programs because they encourage discussion of books. The criteria of selection allow discussions that relate to specific objectives for the reading groups.

If students select their own materials, divide the class into about three groups, with a leader designated for each group. Have students bring their books to one of the three circles, read silently for about 30 minutes, and then tell something

Recreational reading groups are especially appropriate for literature-based reading programs.

interesting about their books. During the first experience, it is advisable to form one group in which you model independent reading behavior and begin telling something about the book. Later, you may move from group to group. By placing competent readers next to less efficient readers, you encourage students to get help with unknown words. The reading groups may contain different students each time, or the groups may remain together until their books are finished.

If the groups are formed according to topic, literary genre, or characteristics of literature, leave them together until the subject has been thoroughly explored. Focus discussions on that element of the literature, the authors' development of the element, and what students liked or did not like about the authors' development. Focus groups should provide opportunities to reinforce specific reading skills or to explore topics of interest.

For example, form a group around personification. Choose literature from picture storybooks, poetry, and longer novels, depending on the students' interests and reading levels. Choices of literature may include picture storybooks, such as Anthony Browne's *Gorilla* (1983), Virginia Lee Burton's *The Little House* (1942), Emily Arnold McCully's *School* (1987) (a wordless book in which personification is interpreted through the illustrations), and Margery Williams' *The Velveteen Rabbit* (1958); poetry, such as Stephen Dunning's *Reflections on a Gift of Watermelon Pickle . . .* (1967), Jamake Highwater's *Moonsong Lullaby* (1981), and Henry Wadsworth Longfellow's *Hiawatha* (1893); and longer novels, such as W. J. Corbett's *The Song of Pentecost* (1983), Kenneth Grahame's *The Wind in the Willows* (1908), Brian Jacques' *Redwall* (1986), Robert Lawson's *Rabbit Hill* (1944), and E. B. White's *Charlotte's Web* (1952).

If personification is the focus, have students look for and discuss evidence of personification by identifying how the authors personify animals, nature, and objects; by discussing the meaning of personification; and by deciding on the appropriateness of the personified images for the story.

If symbolism is being studied, have students discuss the symbolism in books such as Frances Hodgson Burnett's *The Secret Garden* (1911), Sid Fleischman's *The Whipping Boy* (1986), Sharon Bell Mathis's *The Hundred Penny Box* (1975), and Cynthia Voigt's *Dicey's Song* (1982). Other effective literary topics include characterization, setting, conflict, theme, point of view, and style. Focus discussions on specific literary characteristics that are also important reading objectives. Focusing on specific genres of literature helps students broaden their reading interests and increase their understandings of the characteristics of folklore, fantasy, poetry, realistic fiction, historical fiction, biography, and nonfiction.

Topics for recreational reading groups are as varied as the students' interests and the available literature. Humorous literature, animal stories, space science, stories by specific authors, and stories about children who are the same ages as the class are just a few. Focus the reading and discussion on such topics as how the author develops humorous stories and the effectiveness of the techniques, and how the readers respond to the humor in the stories. Looking at the various books of one author or poet is interesting. Authors such as Maurice Sendak, Dr. Seuss, Russell Hoban, and Tomie de Paola have written numerous stories for younger students. Likewise, authors such as Betsy Byars, Beverly Cleary, Helen

Creswell, and Marguerite Henry have written many stories for middle elementary students. Authors such as Lloyd Alexander, John Christopher, Susan Cooper, Jean Craighead George, Virginia Hamilton, Madeleine L'Engle, Scott O'Dell, Katherine Paterson, and Cynthia Voigt have written numerous stories for older elementary and middle school students.

DEVELOPING READING SKILLS THROUGH LITERATURE

Literature and literature-related activities are important for improving and developing reading skills. Predictable books help students predict language and plot structures. Studying literature and developing semantic maps to accompany literature improve vocabulary.

Using Predictable Books

Books that encourage students to predict language and plot structures are recommended for teaching reading and language skills to younger students. Books with repetitive language and plot development may be used for readiness or beginning reading. Predictable books are frequently introduced for oral-language activities and then used for reading activities. Tompkins and Weber (1983) and McCracken and McCracken (1986) have developed guidelines for this sequence.

Tompkins and Weber describe the following five-step teaching strategy to direct students' attention to repetitive and predictable features of a book:

1. The teacher reads the title orally, shows the cover illustration, and asks students what they believe the story is about.

2. The teacher reads through the first set of repetitions, stopping where the second set of repetitions begins and asking students to predict what will happen next or what a character will say.

3. The teacher asks students to explain why they made their specific predictions.

4. The teacher reads the next set of repetitive patterns to allow students to confirm or reject their predictions.

5. The teacher continues reading the selection, repeating steps 2, 3, and 4.

For example, to use this technique with Mem Fox's cumulative tale *Hattie and the Fox* (1987), read the title, pointing to each word. Point to the cover illustration and ask students what they think the story will be about. Through discussion, encourage the students to predict that Hattie is a hen because a hen's picture is on the cover, that the story is about a fox and a hen because the word *fox* is in the title, and that the story includes a confrontation between the fox and the hen because we know from other stories that the fox and hen are usually enemies. Expand the predictions by recalling other stories that give hints to the possible characterizations of fox and hen, such as "The Cock and the Mouse and the Little Red Hen" (a folktale found in Anne Rockwell's *The Three Bears and 15 Other Stories*, 1975). To help confirm these initial predictions, turn to the title page within the text. On this page, a fox is lurking behind a tree.

During the second step, read the first three pages of the text. These pages introduce the main character, a big black hen named Hattie, the beginning of a cumulative description of the hidden fox, and the repetitive responses of the various farm animals. Read the beginning of the fourth page of the text, "And Hattie said, . . ." Stop here and ask students what they think Hattie will say. Tell the students to look at the illustrations because the illustrator is providing hints about what Hattie will say. Turn the page and ask the students to predict the responses of the goose, pig, sheep, horse, and cow.

During the third step, ask students to provide reasons for their predictions. They should notice that the illustrator helps with the predictions by showing only a hidden nose in the first series of illustrations and increasing the view to a nose and eyes in the second series. Likewise, if students have had frequent experiences with repetitive text, they will expect that the animals will use the same language during the second series.

Next, read the text to allow students to confirm or reject their predictions. Continue the process, as with each repetition Hattie sees a little more of the fox's body. Students enjoy this book, because they quickly catch on to the cumulative action and the repetitive responses of the animals. They easily predict the conclusion, in which the fox acts in a predictable manner and the animals change their complacent responses.

Hattie and the Fox is equally successful with the beginning reading approach recommended by McCracken and McCracken (1986). After reading a predictable book several times to students, they encourage students to join in the reading. They use pictures to help the students follow the sequence. Then, they introduce the students to the text by printing the repetitive portion on the chalkboard or word cards in a pocket chart. They point to the words as the students say the lines.

Next, the students match the words on the word chart or chalkboard with a second, identical set of word cards. If the words form a refrain, they either place the whole refrain on the chart while the students match the words by placing identical words on top of the cards, or they create the first line of the refrain while the students produce the next lines. They repeat this activity several times, to provide many opportunities for students to read the text.

Finally, they place the story on phrase cards in the pocket chart, then have the children match the phrases to pictures that represent each phrase. They continue this type of activity as the students build and rebuild the entire story, providing many opportunities for individual and group reading practice.

Additional books that may be used for these activities, because they contain either predictable plots or repetitive language, include:

- Arnica Esterl   *The Fine Round Cake*
- Nancy White Carlstrom   *Baby-O*
- Arnold Lobel   *A Rose in My Garden* (cumulative illustrations reinforce this cumulative poem)
- Tracey Pearson   *Old MacDonald Had a Farm*

- Merle Peek — *The Balancing Act: A Counting Song*
- Nadine Westcott — *Peanut Butter and Jelly: A Play Rhyme*
- John Ivimey — *The Complete Story of Three Blind Mice*

Increasing Vocabulary Knowledge Through Literature

Reading or listening to literature encourages vocabulary development and expands vocabulary comprehension. Through literature, students discover the impact of carefully selected words. Many of the vocabulary techniques developed elsewhere in this text are equally effective with literature.

Picture books that contain extensive details or that provide motivational excitement are excellent sources for oral or written vocabulary expansion. Students may examine pictures and describe objects, animals, colors, shapes, and actions. Two books by Chris Van Allsburg are very successful with students in first through fifth grades. *The Z Was Zapped* (1987) encourages interaction between the reader and the text by presenting the alphabet in the form of a 26-act play. In each act, a letter is treated to an action that begins with that specific sound.

For example, introducing the play, the letter *A* is bombarded with falling rock. The reader must look carefully at the page to develop a script to accompany the first act. Prediction enters into the discussion, because readers must turn the page before they discover that the author describes Act 1 as "The *A* was in an avalanche." The readers can then compare their titles with the one identified by the author and consider how to change their scripts and alter their vocabularies if they consider the author's title. They can ask, What words describe an avalanche? What words emphasize the causes of an avalanche? What words tell where an avalanche takes place? What words detail the consequences of an avalanche on an unsuspecting letter?

Van Allsburg's almost wordless book, *The Mysteries of Harris Burdick* (1984), presents 14 full-page illustrations, a title, and a one-line caption to accompany each illustration. In the introduction to the book, Van Allsburg asks readers to provide the missing stories. Teachers report that the illustrations contain enough elements of mystery and fantasy to motivate excellent oral and written stories.

Concept books enhance categorizing vocabulary according to specific functions. For example, Anne Rockwell's *First Comes Spring* (1985) may be used to categorize vocabulary related to clothes, work, play, and environmental characteristics that accompany each season of the year. Janet and Allan Ahlberg's *The Baby's Catalogue* (1982) may be used to classify vocabulary according to such categories as breakfast, toys, shopping, pets, gardens, and games. Gail Gibbons' *Trains* (1987) encourages expansion of specific vocabulary. Books such as Tana Hoban's *Shapes, Shapes, Shapes* (1986), *Circles, Triangles, and Squares* (1974), and *Round & Round & Round* (1983) stimulate identifying and categorizing vocabulary according to shapes. Hoban's *All About Where* (1991), Hutchins's *What Game Shall We Play?* (1990), and Noll's *Watch Where You Go* (1990) foster categorizing vocabulary according to spatial concepts such as above, behind, and under.

Older students benefit from responding to wordless books that have geographical, historical, or literary connections. For example, John Goodall's *The Story of a Main Street* (1987) and *The Story of an English Village* (1979) depict changes over time. Detailed illustrations in *The Story of a Main Street* trace the evolution of an English street from medieval, to Elizabethan, to Restoration, to Georgian, to Regency, to Victorian, to Edwardian, and to current times. Describing the architecture, costumes, customs, trade, or transportation, students may compare similarities and differences across periods as well as increase their technical vocabularies.

Mitsumasa Anno's detailed wordless books contain literary, historical, and geographical details. Some are in the correct time and place, while others are not; therefore, students must search the illustrations for literary, artistic, and historical details. The detailed drawings in *Anno's Britain* (1982), *Anno's Italy* (1980), *Anno's Flea Market* (1984), and *Anno's USA* (1982) encourage extensive vocabulary development; analysis of time and place; and application of literary, artistic, and historical knowledge.

Semantic mapping or webbing procedures, identified as effective for vocabulary development by Toms-Bronowski (1983) and Johnson and Pearson (1984), are especially effective when used with literature. Semantic mapping can help students identify words with similar meanings, expand a precise vocabulary, understand multiple meanings for words, develop concepts, and perceive relationships among words and ideas.

Semantic Mapping and Vocabulary Development

To use a semantic-mapping approach to increase vocabulary development, first read the literature selection and identify vocabulary words or concepts that are crucial to understanding that book. Next, draw a web on the board with the title of the book in the center of the web (see Figure 9.1). On the arms extending from the center, place the important words from the story. During a brainstorming session, have students add words, such as synonyms and definitions that expand their comprehension of the key words. Complete this activity as a prereading vocabulary introduction, an exploration to discover students' previous knowledge, or an introduction to important information.

Use the same web to build students' understandings of each vocabulary word. Have them consider the meaning developed by the author, select the term that is closest to that developed in the story, add new words or even phrases gained from the story, and use the vocabulary word identified in the web to increase their story comprehension. Vocabulary webs are appropriate at any grade level and may accompany books either read by students or to them (see Chapter 5).

The following is an example of how to conduct this activity with upper elementary students reading a legend, Selina Hastings' *Sir Gawain and the Loathly Lady* (1981). On the chalkboard, draw a web similar to that shown in Figure 9.1. Place the title of the book in the center of the web. Extend the vocabulary words *knight, armour, charger, challenge, foe, enchantment, loathly, honor, bargain,* and *quest* from the center. During the prereading activity, introduce these vocabulary

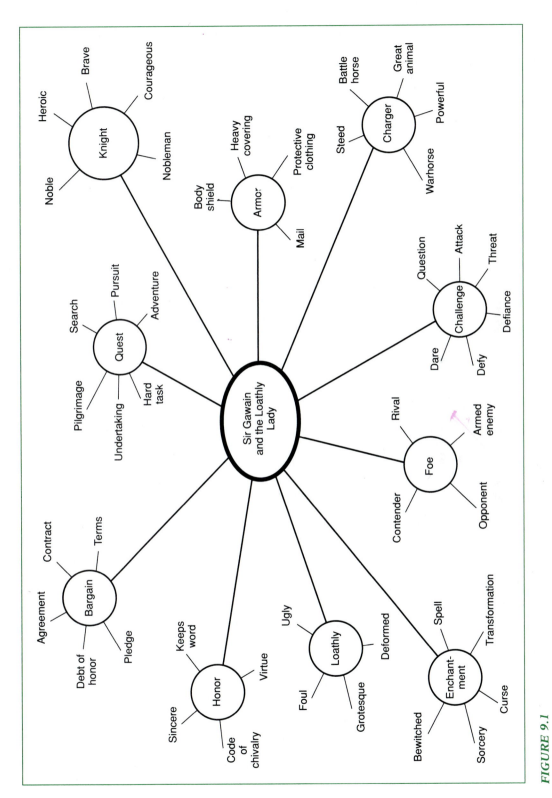

FIGURE 9.1
Vocabulary web for a literature selection

words and have students define them or identify synonyms. Next, have students read the literature. Finally, have them add vocabulary terms to the web and identify the best meanings for the vocabulary within the context of the literature.

DEVELOPING UNDERSTANDING OF LITERARY ELEMENTS

Reading literature with understanding and appreciation requires readers to recognize various literary elements and the ways that authors use those elements to create exciting and credible stories. This section describes some of the techniques teachers may use to develop understanding of the literary elements.

Semantic Mapping

Semantic mapping or webbing is effective for identifying the literary elements in a book and extending discussions around those literary elements. Prior to the webbing experience, introduce and discuss the literary elements of setting, characterization, conflict, plot, and theme by reading and discussing folktales with the students. Tales such as "The Three Little Pigs" and "Cinderella" are good for this introduction because the good and bad characters, the conflict, and the theme are easy to recognize.

For the first webbing activity around literary elements, demonstrate the technique to the entire group. On the board, draw a web around the title of the story, with the literary elements extending from the center. As you read the story, have students listen for the various categories. After you complete the story, lead a discussion encouraging students to fill in the various categories on the web or only one element. If necessary, reread sections to help students identify the specific element(s) and choose appropriate wording for the web.

After demonstrating this activity several times, let the students try the webbing approach with other types of literature or with more complex literature. Either read the literature to the students or have them read it themselves. Have students develop their own webs before you lead the discussion or have them develop the webs concurrently with the discussion. If students developed their own webs beforehand, have them add to the webs during the discussion to focus their attention on the task and involve them in the discussion.

Figure 9.2 is a literary web developed by a fifth grade class around Hastings' Arthurian legend, *Sir Gawain and the Loathly Lady*. Portions of the web may be expanded. See Figure 9.3 for a web of the different types of conflict found in the book. *Sir Gawain and the Loathly Lady* contains person-versus-person, person-versus-self, and person-versus-society conflicts.

Expansion of characterization and theme are also valuable with this book. Another idea is to expand on the characteristics of legends found in this book and to identify other books that contain the same characteristics. Older students could compare the plot development and the literary elements found in *Sir Gawain and the Loathly Lady* with Chaucer's "The Wife of Bath's Tale." Such comparisons encourage higher thought processes, analysis of text, synthesis of ideas,

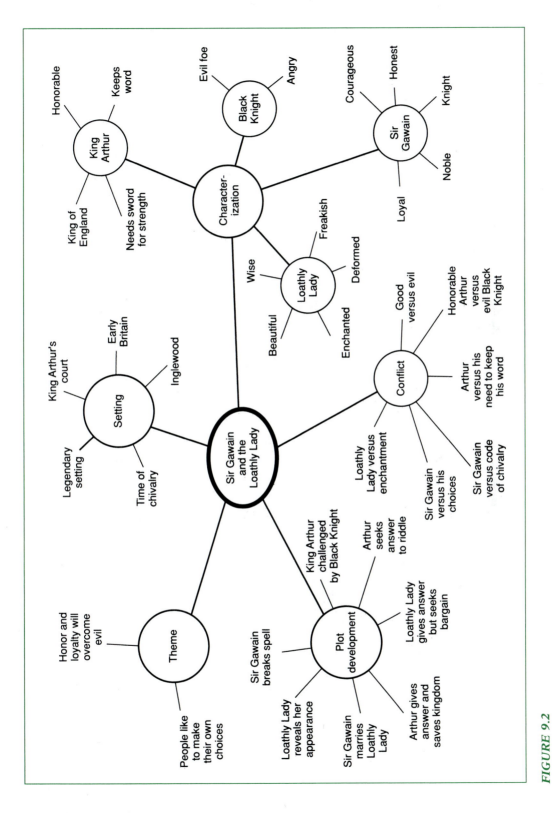

FIGURE 9.2
Literary elements web for a literature selection

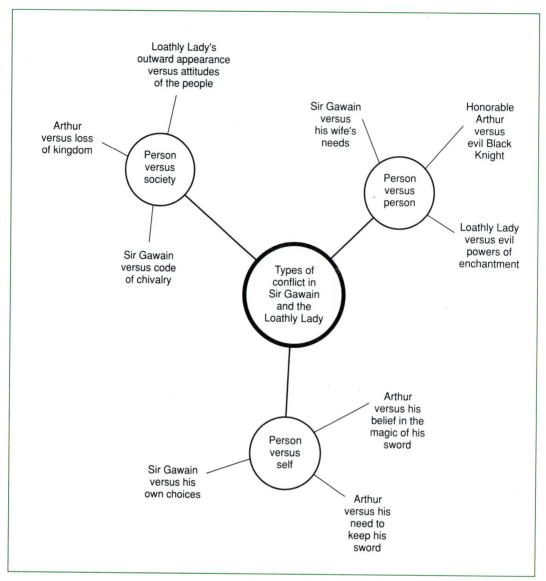

FIGURE 9.3
Conflict web in a literature selection

understanding of literary elements, and comprehension of story structures. The activities encourage interaction among the students and the text and among the students and the teacher. As students expand their ability to identify and analyze various literary characteristics, they may add new insights to the literature discussion. Additional literary webs are found in Norton's *Through the Eyes of a Child* (1991), *The Effective Teaching of Language Arts* (1993), and *The Impact of Literature-Based Reading* (1992).

Plot Structures

As noted, a story must have a beginning, a middle, and an end. Diagrams of plot structure help students understand plot development and the inherent conflicts. Two plot structures are especially important in children's literature: (1) those with external conflict and (2) those with person-versus-self conflict.

Most plots in stories for younger students follow a structure that introduces the characters and conflict at the beginning of the story, increases the conflict until a climax, identifies the turning point, and ends the conflict. This structure is usually found when the main character faces external forces. You can help your students recognize and understand this structure by diagraming the key incidents from such a story. Figure 9.4 diagrams a structure with such external conflict. Using this structure, Figure 9.5 diagrams the plot structure of *Sir Gawain and the Loathly Lady*.

In a second plot structure, the conflict is basically within the main character (see Figure 9.6). Cohen (1985) states that person-versus-self stories follow a structure that introduces the character and conflict, follows the conflict within the character, moves to a climax (the point where the character realizes the problem and accepts it), and concludes when the character finally achieves peace. Figure 9.6 depicts this plot structure. Figure 9.7 applies this person-versus-self structure to Marion Dane Bauer's *On My Honor* (1986), a contemporary realistic fiction story.

Modeling Literary Analysis

Modeling is one of the most important strategies to use when developing students' comprehension of literature (Dole, Duffy, Roehler, & Pearson, 1991). Researchers Roehler and Duffy (1984) and Gordon (1985) developed an instructional approach that places the teacher in an interactive role with the students (see Chapters 2 and 6). In this approach, the teacher analyzes literary concepts before expecting the students to accomplish a similar task. The modeling helps students understand important cognitive processes. As the modeling progresses, the approach proceeds from total teacher modeling, to gradual student interaction, to total student analysis. This section considers how to use modeling when developing students' literary understanding.

Modeling is especially effective when developing understanding of literature, because the longer literature texts encourage a synthesis of ideas and provide more opportunity for teachers and students to draw evidence. The reasoning stage of literary analysis encourages teachers and students to think about some of the more difficult aspects of the literature and to draw on their previous experiences. Modeling is especially effective with complex tasks, such as inferring characterization, identifying theme, and speculating about allusions and symbolism.

Teachers who are developing and teaching modeling lessons should follow the recommendations for effective modeling identified by Dole and colleagues (1991):

1. Modeling that provides explicit, unambiguous information is more effective than one that provides vague or jumbled information.

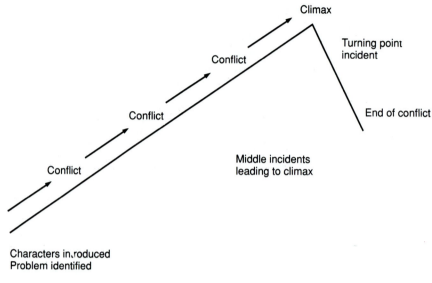

FIGURE 9.4
Plot structure for external conflict

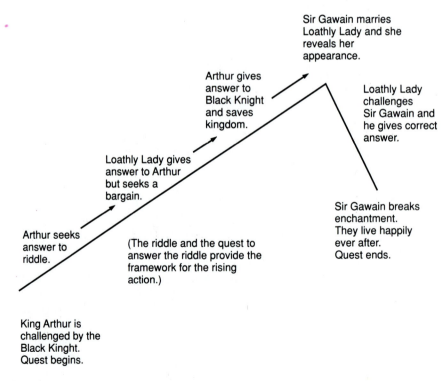

FIGURE 9.5
External conflict structure for **Sir Gawain and the Loathly Lady**

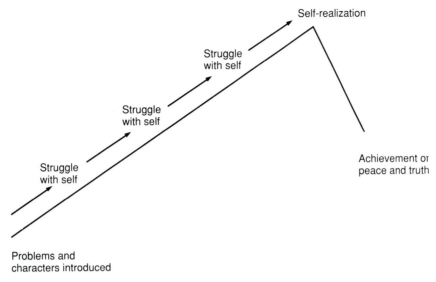

FIGURE 9.6
Plot structure for person-versus-self conflict

2. Modeling that demonstrates flexible adjustment to text cues is more effective than modeling that emphasizes rigid rules.

3. If teachers merely ask questions without explaining the reasoning employed to answer those questions, many students will have difficulty understanding how the questions were answered.

If students do not understand how the questions were answered, they will not gain control of the process associated with answering the questions. Consequently, the process suffers.

Gordon (1985) uses a five-step approach to help students understand important cognitive processes associated with comprehension of text. First, the teacher identifies the skill to be taught, analyzes the requirements for effective reasoning within that skill, identifies text samples that require the skill, and identifies questions to stimulate the students to use that skill or thought process. During this preparatory phase, the teacher also considers how to introduce the skill to students.

Second, the teacher completely models the strategy by reading the text, asking a question, answering the question, citing evidence that supports the answer, and then verbally following the reasoning process used to acquire the answer.

Third, the teacher involves the students in citing the evidence. During this step, the teacher reads the text, asks a question, and answers it. Then the teacher asks the students to cite evidence for the answer. Finally, the teacher leads a discussion that explores the reasoning. The strategy is more clear to students if they make notes concerning the various parts.

Fourth, the teacher involves the students in answering the question. During this step, the teacher reads the text and asks a question; the students answer the

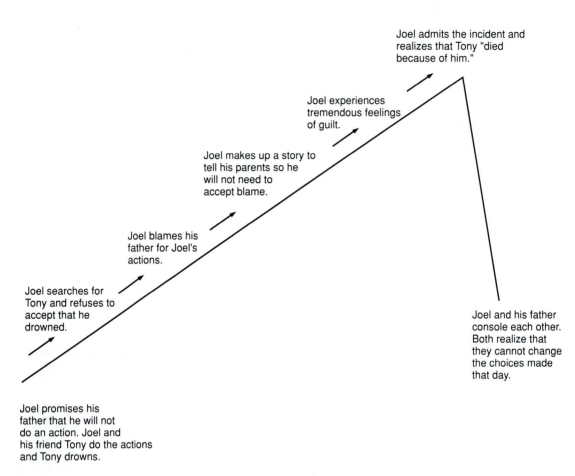

Joel admits the incident and realizes that Tony "died because of him."

Joel experiences tremendous feelings of guilt.

Joel makes up a story to tell his parents so he will not need to accept blame.

Joel blames his father for Joel's actions.

Joel searches for Tony and refuses to accept that he drowned.

Joel and his father console each other. Both realize that they cannot change the choices made that day.

Joel promises his father that he will not do an action. Joel and his friend Tony do the actions and Tony drowns.

FIGURE 9.7
Person-versus-self structure for **On My Honor**

question; the teacher cites the evidence; and then the teacher leads a discussion that explores the reasoning process.

Fifth, students have primary responsibility during most of the strategy. The teacher reads the text and asks a question, but the students answer the question, cite the evidence that supports the question, and explain the reasoning involved in reaching their answers.

This approach is especially effective with children's literature in which the author uses inferences to develop characterization; uses figurative language to create mood, suggest characterization, or enhance conflict; uses conflict and interactions among characters to develop theme; or uses historical settings to develop background, create an antagonist, or develop person versus society conflicts, because such literary concepts are difficult for students to understand. Books that contain these characteristics stimulate exciting discussions as students recognize the author's techniques and discover the impact of well-developed literature.

Teachers may model with picture storybooks that are completed in one lesson or with books that take several days to complete. Modeling is especially effective when the teacher identifies techniques used by an author and then demonstrates how to read and understand the techniques. Modeling may introduce a book that the students will read later. In this way, the modeling stimulates interest in the literature and encourages students to read with understanding and appreciation.

Consider how to use modeling to introduce the understanding of figurative language in Rudolf Frank's *No Hero for the Kaiser* (1986). In this historical fiction book for older students, Frank uses figurative language to depict the wartime setting, enhance characterization, clarify the conflict, and suggest theme.

In step 1, identify a skill, such as inferring the author's meaning from figurative language. Analyze the requirements for effective inferences, which are:

- To identify nonliteral comparisons.
- To realize that figurative language is meant to clarify and enlighten by developing new relationships.
- To identify the similarities or differences between two things.
- To go beyond the information the author provides in the text.
- To use clues from the text to hypothesize about the relationships between figurative language and setting, characterization, conflict, and theme.
- To use background knowledge gained from other experiences.

Then identify text examples of figurative language. For example, similes appear on pages 2, 12, 44, and 46. Many more similes are in the text, but these few should produce interesting modeling and discussions. Contrasts appear on pages 45, 46, and 65. Symbolism appears on pages 2 (plum tree), 18 (Wild Goat), and 59 (Lance Corporal Poodle). Allusions to Napoleon appear on pages 42 and 49–51. Allusions to a myth about the skull of an African sultan that supposedly influenced the beginning of World War I appear on pages 21 and 70–71. Notice that the students may have comprehension problems in these areas.

In step 2, introduce the text. Review the place by identifying Germany, Russia, and Poland on a map. Discuss these places, the student's knowledge of the historical time (1914–1918), the seasons, and the fact that war causes desolation and destruction. Review figurative language, such as simile, contrast, symbolism, and allusion, using examples. For example, be sure that the students know that a simile is a direct comparison in which the author uses *like, as,* or *as if.*

Begin reading, stopping on page 2 to emphasize and discuss the meaning of the similes in this passage:

> The distant thud of cannon came closer, like a thunderstorm brewing. And as if the storm had already broken, women, boys, girls, and soldiers began to rush around in confusion; trumpets sounded, and suddenly the Russians had swept out of the village like the wind. Now they were firing down from the low hills into the village. It sounded like the high-pitched whine of mosquitoes as they fly

past your ear looking for a place to settle and bite: zzzzzz—a thin, sharp noise, full of malice. (p. 2)

Ask an inferential question or questions, such as "What is the author telling us about the setting in the Polish village?" "What is the author telling us about war?" "How does the author's use of simile increase your ability to visualize the setting and the war that will follow?" "Do you believe that these are good comparisons?" "Why or why not?"

Answer the question or questions. Tell the students, "The town is, or will be, the setting for a noisy and destructive battle. Soldiers who once enjoyed the town are running to take their places on the battlefield. People in the town are also running. The author tells us that war is terrible and destructive. The author's use of similes helps us hear the battle, see the movement, and feel the danger. I believe that the similes are good comparisons."

Cite evidence for your answers. Say, for example, "The author describes the normal activity and appearance of the town and describes changes. The sound of cannon is compared to a thunderstorm. The rapidly advancing Russian soldiers are compared to wind sweeping through the town. The sound of bullets is compared to the whine of mosquitoes."

Explore your own reasoning process. For example, "The author describes the village and then shows what happens to it when two forces are about to fight. I know from my own experience that a thunderstorm and a cannon sound alike. I also know from my experience and from other reading that a thunderstorm can bring destruction in the form of lightning and high winds. I believe that this is a good comparison for an approaching battle. I can close my eyes and see and hear the battle.

"I also know from experience that when wind sweeps through the streets, it moves everything in front of it. I can close my eyes and see people rushing away from the army as it sweeps through town without thinking of the consequences of its actions. In this way, the army is also like the wind.

"I also know that bullets and mosquitoes sound somewhat alike. I know that mosquitoes have a nasty bite. When the author uses expressions such as "sly malice," I think that he is saying that the bullets are much worse than mosquitoes.

"The author also may be saying that mosquitoes and bullets are alike in another way. They both hit innocent victims. I believe from these comparisons that the author is telling us that war is terrible for all people, including innocent bystanders." Notice that this last statement may also encourage a discussion about what the students believe to be the theme of the book.

Continue the modeling approach, using other examples, until the students can provide evidence for their answers and can rationalize them. Encourage discussion and varied viewpoints. This approach helps students check their reasoning and does not suggest that there is only one correct answer. In fact, modeling lessons usually broaden rather than narrow the students' answers.

Asking students to jot down their answers, their evidence, and their reasoning before discussion encourages them to focus on the task, interact during the discussion, and develop their thought processes. Additional good subjects for modeling and discussion include:

- *Additional similes,* such as, "What does the author mean when he states, 'Like huge wolves the four cannon of the Seventh Battery went into the field'?" (from page 46).
- *Contrasts* of the peaceful and war meanings for words and phrases, such as *bullseye* (from page 45) and "in the fields" (from pages 45–46). Ask, "What is the author saying when he uses these comparisons?" and "How does the author use these comparisons to reinforce the antiwar theme of the book?" Encourage the students to cite evidence that supports their answers and to describe the reasoning they used to reach their answers.
- *Symbolism.* Model and discuss the significance of symbolism for things and names. Ask, for example, "What does the symbolism of the plum tree (on page 18) reveal about the author's attitude toward war?" "What does the author's symbolism of Wild Goat (on page 54) and White Raven (on page 18) reveal about the characterization of the two German officers?" and "What is the author telling us about war when he names the dog Lance Corporal Poodle on page 59?"
- *Allusions.* Model and discuss the author's choice of allusions to Napoleon (see pages 42 and 49–51), the skull of the African sultan (see pages 21 and 70–71), and the Flood (see page 56).

SUMMARY /

Literature-based instructional programs, in which teachers use literature as the core of the reading curriculum, are increasing rapidly. In such programs, reading is considered the ability to read all types of literature with understanding, appreciation, and enjoyment. Creating students who both understand and appreciate literature has specific requirements.

Choosing literature that motivates students to read and stimulates an appreciation of literature requires knowledge about literature and an awareness of the students' interests. Likewise, teaching literature requires knowledge about literature and instructional approaches that encourage the broad development of reading skills. In addition to developing literary understanding and appreciation, literature-based programs encourage students to realize the importance of literature as a mirror of human experience, be able to gain insights from their involvement with literature, become aware of writers who represent diverse backgrounds and traditions, become familiar with past and present masterpieces of literature, develop effective ways of discussing and writing about various forms of literature, appreciate the rhythms and beauty of the language in literature, and develop lifelong reading habits.

As students expand their abilities to read literature for understanding, appreciation, and enjoyment, they are confronted with such terms as *plot, characterization, setting, theme, style,* and *point of view.* Literary enjoyment and appreciation are enhanced through oral reading to students and recreational reading groups. Reading skills are strengthened through literature using predictable books, increasing vocabulary knowledge, and developing understanding of literary elements.

Discussion strategies that encourage students to respond to and interact with literature are especially effective. This chapter develops several of these strategies, including semantic mapping of literary elements and vocabulary, plot structuring for conflicts outside or within a character, and modeling of the thought processes associated with analyzing literary elements.

YOUR POINT OF VIEW /

Discussion Questions

1. Identify the reading objectives stated in a unit of a basal reading series. Develop a list of literature selections that would reinforce and strengthen those objectives. Share your rationales for choosing the books.

2. Assume that you will be teaching a literature-based program at a specific grade level. What are the literature selections that you consider important for that grade? Take into consideration the quality of the literature, the appropriateness of the literature for the grade level, and the reading objectives that you want to teach. Develop a core list of books. Give your reasons for selecting the books.

3. Choose an instructional approach, such as modeling, semantic mapping, or plot structuring. Develop a lesson plan that uses one of these strategies to increase understanding of literature.

4. Assume that you will be using recreational reading groups to enhance students' enjoyment of literature. Develop a list of books that follow a genre approach, an author approach, or a literary elements approach. Try one of the recreational reading groups in your college reading class. Analyze the responses of the class. What types of information did they share? Did you want to read any of the books discussed by other members of the group? Now, what do you believe are the strengths of recreational reading groups?

Take a Stand For or Against

1. Some reading authorities want literature to supplement the basal reading curriculum. In contrast, other reading authorities want literature to form the total reading curriculum. Consider the advantages and disadvantages of each approach. Share your responses with your class.

2. Several groups have identified the literature selections that should be the core of the school literature program. Read and analyze several of these lists, such as *Recommended Readings in Literature: Kindergarten Through Grade Eight* (1986) and "Education Secretary Bennett's Suggested Reading List for Elementary-School Pupils" (1988). What is your opinion of each list? Are there books that should be added or deleted? Is there a core of books that every educated person should read? Why or why not?

Ahlberg, J., and Ahlberg, A. (1982). *The baby's catalogue.* Boston: Little, Brown & Co.

Anno, M. (1980). *Anno's Italy.* Ontario, Canada: Collins.

Anno, M. (1982). *Anno's Britain.* New York: Philomel.

Anno, M. (1982). *Anno's USA.* New York: Philomel.

Anno, M. (1984). *Anno's flea market.* London: Bodlet Head.

Avi. (1991). *Nothing but the truth: A documentary novel.* New York: Orchard.

Bauer, M. D. (1986). *On my honor.* New York: Clarion.

Book Review Subcommittee of the National Council for the Social Studies–Children's Book Council Joint Committee. (April/May 1992). *Social Education,* 253–264.

Breckenridge, K. (April 1988). Modern classics. *School Library Journal, 34,* 42–43.

Brown, M. (1982). *Shadow.* New York: Charles Scribner's Sons.

Browne, A. (1983). *Gorilla.* New York: Watts.

Burnett, F. H. (1911). *The secret garden.* New York: J. B. Lippincott Co.

Burton, V. L. (1942). *The little house.* Boston: Houghton Mifflin Co.

California State Department of Education (1986). *Recommended readings in literature: Kindergarten through grade eight.* Sacramento, CA: State Department of Education.

Cohen, C. L. (August 1985). The quest in children's literature. *School Library Journal, 31,* 28–29.

Corbett, W. J. (1983). *The song of Pentecost.* New York: E. P. Dutton.

Dole, J., Duffy, G., Roehler, L., & Pearson, P. D. (1991). "Moving from the old to the new: Research on reading comprehension instruction." *Review of Educational Research, 61,* 239–264.

Dunning, S., Lueders, E., & Smith, H. (Eds.) (1967). *Reflections on a gift of watermelon pickle. . .* New York: Lothrop, Lee & Shepard.

Early, M., & Ericson, B. (1982). The act of reading. In B. F. Nelms (Ed.), *Literature in the classroom: Readers, texts, and contexts.* Urbana, IL: National Council of Teachers of English, 31–44.

Education Secretary Bennett's suggested reading list for elementary-school pupils (September 1988). *The Chronicle of Higher Education,* B3.

Feitelson, D., Rita, B., & Goldstein, Z. (1986). Effects of listening to series stories on first graders' comprehension and use of language. *Research in the Teaching of English, 20,* 339–355.

Fishel, C. T. (1984). Reading in the content areas of English. In M. M. Dupuis, *Reading in the content areas: Research for teachers.* Newark, DE: International Reading Association.

Five, C. L. (1988). From workbook to workshop: Increasing children's involvement in the reading process. *The New Advocate, 1,* 92–102.

Fleischman, S. (1986). *The whipping boy.* New York: Greenwillow.

Forbes, E. (1943). *Johnny Tremain.* Boston: Houghton Mifflin Co.

Fox, M. (1987). *Hattie and the fox.* New York: Bradbury.

Fox, P. (1991). *Monkey island.* New York: Orchard.

Frank, R. (1986). *No hero for the kaiser.* New York: Lothrop, Lee & Shepard.

Freedman, G. (1987). *Lincoln: A photobiography.* New York: Clarion.

Frye, N., Baker, S., & Perkins, G. (1985). *The Harper handbook of literature.* New York: Harper & Row.

Gardner, M. (1988). An educator's concerns about the California initiative. *The New Advocate, 1,* 250–253.

Gibbons, G. (1987). *Trains.* New York: Holiday.

Gillespie, J., & Gilbert, C. (1985). *Best books for children.* New York: R. R. Bowker.

Goodall, J. (1987). *The story of Main Street.* New York: Macmillan Publishing Co.

Gordon, C. (1985). Modeling inference awareness across the curriculum. *Journal of Reading, 28,* 444–447.

Grahame, K. (1908). *The wind in the willows.* New York: Charles Scribner's Sons.

Greenaway, K. (1979). *A apple pie.* Secaucus, NJ: Castle Books.

Grifalconi, A. (1987). *Darkness and the butterfly.* Boston: Little, Brown & Co.

Hastings, S. (1981). *Sir Gawain and the loathly lady.* New York: Lothrop, Lee & Shepard.

Hiebert, A., & Colt, J. (1989). Patterns of literature-based reading instruction. *The Reading Teacher, 43,* 14–20.

Highwater, J. (1981). *Moonsong lullaby.* New York: Lothrop, Lee & Shepard.

Hoban, T. (1991). *All about where.* New York: Greenwillow.

Hoban, T. (1974). *Circles, triangles, and squares.* New York: Macmillan Publishing Co.

Hoban, T. (1983). *Round & round & round.* New York: Greenwillow.

Hoban, T. (1986). *Shapes, shapes, shapes.* New York: Greenwillow.

Huck, C., Hepler, S., & Hickman, J. (1993). *Children's literature.* Orlando: Harcourt Brace Jovanovich.

Hutchins, P. (1990). *What game shall we play?* New York: Greenwillow.

Illinois State Department of Education (1985). *State goals for learning and sample learning objectives: Language arts.*

International Relations Committee (May 1988). The U.S.A. through children's books. *Booklist,* 1532–1534.

Ivimey, J. (1987). *The complete story of three blind mice.* New York: Clarion.

Johnson, D., & Pearson, P.D. (1984). *Teaching reading vocabulary.* New York: Holt, Rinehart & Winston.

Kennemer, P.K. (1984). Reviews of fiction books: How they differ. *Top of the News, 40,* 419–421.

Kimmell, M., & Segel, E. (1983). *For reading out loud.* New York: Dell.

Kingsbury, M. (1984). Perspectives on criticism. *The Horn Book, 60,* 17–32.

Jacques, B. (1986). *Redwall.* New York: Philomel.

Lamme, L. (1976). Reading aloud to young children. *Language Arts, 53,* 886–888.

Lawson, R. (1944). *Rabbit hill.* New York: Viking Press.

Lobel, A. (1984). *A rose in my garden.* New York: Greenwillow.

Longfellow, H.W. (1893). *Hiawatha.* New York: E. P. Dutton.

Mathis, S. D. (1975). *The hundred penny box.* New York: Viking Press.

Matthews, D. (1988). *High interest, easy reading.* Urbana, IL: National Council of Teachers of English.

May, J. P. (1987). Creating a schoolwide literature program: A case study. *Children's Literature Association Quarterly, 12,* 135–137.

McCloskey, R. (1941). *Make way for ducklings.* New York: Viking Press.

McCracken, R., & McCracken, M. (1986). *Stories, songs, and poetry to teach reading and writing: Literacy through language.* Chicago: American Library Association.

McCully, E. A. (1987). *School.* New York: Harper & Row.

Meeks, M. (1983). *Achieving literacy: Longitudinal case studies of adolescents learning to read.* London: Routledge and Kegal Paul.

Milne, A. A. (1926). *Winnie-the-pooh.* New York: E. P. Dutton.

National Council of Teachers of English (1983). Forum: Essentials of English. *Language Arts, 60,* 244–248.

Noll, S. (1990). *Watch where you go.* New York: Greenwillow.

Norton, D. E. (1991). *Through the eyes of a child: An introduction to children's literature* (3rd ed.). New York: Merrill/Macmillan Publishing Co.

Norton, D. E. (1993). *The effective teaching of language arts* (4th ed.). New York: Merrill/Macmillan Publishing Co.

Norton, D. E. (1992). *The impact of literature-based reading.* New York: Merrill/Macmillan Publishing Co.

Norton, D. E., & McNamara, J. (1987). *An evaluation of the BISD/TAMU multiethnic reading program.* College Station, TX: Texas A&M University, research report.

Paulsen, G. (1987). *Hatchet.* New York: Bradbury.

Phelan, C. (1988). Poetry for young children. *Booklist, 84,* 790–792.

Potter, B. (1902). *A tale of Peter Rabbit.* New York: Warne.

Roehler, L., & Duffy, G. (1984). Direct explanation of the comprehension process. In G. Durry, L. Roehler, & J. Mason, *Comprehension instruction.* New York: Longman.

Rockwell, A. (1975). *The three bears and 15 other stories.* New York: Crowell.

Rockwell, A. (1985). *First comes spring.* New York: Crowell.

Ruddell, R. (1992). A whole language and literature perspective: Creating a meaning-making instructional environment. *Language Arts, 69,* 612–620.

Rudman, M. (1984). *Children's literature: An issues approach.* New York: Longman.

Rudman, M., & Pearce, A. (1988). *For the love of reading: A parent's guide to encouraging young readers from infancy through age 5.* Mount Vernon, NY: Consumers Union.

Rylant, C. (1991). *Appalachia: The voices of sleeping birds.* Illustrated by B. Moser. Orlando: Harcourt Brace Jovanovich.

Sawyer, W. (1987). Literature and literacy: A review of research. *Language Arts, 64,* 33–39.

Sperry, A. (1940). *Call it courage.* New York: Macmillan Publishing Co.

Strachan, I. (1990). *The flawed glass.* Boston: Little, Brown.

Sutherland, Z., & Arbuthnot, M. H. (1991). *Children and books.* New York: Harper Collins.

Taxel, J. (1988). Notes from the editor. *The New Advocate, 1,* 73–74.

Tompkins, G., & Weber, M. (1983). What will happen next? Using predictable books with young children. *The Reading Teacher, 36,* 498–502.

Toms-Bronowski, S. (1983). An investigation of the effectiveness of selected vocabulary teaching strategies with intermediate grade level students. *Dissertation Abstracts International.*

Trelease, J. (1985). *The read-aloud handbook.* New York: Penguin.

Van Allsburg, C. (1984). *The mysteries of Harris Burdick.* Boston: Houghton Mifflin Co.

Van Allsburg, C. (1987). *The z was zapped.* Boston: Houghton Mifflin Co.

Voigt, C. (1982). *Dicey's song.* New York: Atheneum Pubs.

Vos, I. (1991). *Hide and seek.* Boston: Houghton Mifflin.

White, E. B. (1952). *Charlotte's web.* New York: Harper & Row.

Wilder, L. I. (1932). *The little house in the big woods.* New York: Harper & Row.

Williams, M. (1958). *The velveteen rabbit.* Garden City, NJ: Doubleday & Co.

Wilms, D. (1985). *Science books for children.* Chicago: American Library Association.

10

Content-Area Reading

For the Reader

You might logically assume that concentration on providing excellent instruction in the various word identification and comprehension skills and strategies will automatically produce mature, flexible readers. Such is not the case. Early in the reading program, children are expected to read content material successfully and to locate and synthesize information. Although you could make a case for more than one neglected area in a school's curriculum, the area of reading in content subjects is

probably the most important. Think of your own background for a moment and answer the following questions:

- Were you directly taught how to understand text written in an expository style?

- Were you directly taught how to study in your content subjects (such as math, science, and social studies)?

- Were you directly taught how to locate and synthesize information from an almanac, an encyclopedia, and an atlas?

Were you directly taught how to interpret various maps, graphs, charts, and diagrams?

Notice the key word *directly* in the preceding statements. Many content-reading strategies receive only passing mention in our schools. However, everyone needs direct/explicit planned instruction and practice to meet the challenge of content material and to read in order to learn throughout life.

In each For the Reader section, we ask you to preview the chapter before plunging into reading. We are attempting to change your reading habits by ensuring that you take advantage of the organization of most textbooks. By now, you have probably realized the importance of previewing what you are about to read. This is but one aspect of content reading that we recommend you directly teach in your classes. This chapter presents content-area strategies along with recommended teaching procedures.

Key Ideas

- The ability to read well in a basal reader does not ensure the ability to read well in a subject area.

- Students must apply specific strategies and skills to comprehend expository text.

- How successfully a student reads content material depends on the text, the student, and the teacher.

- The major components of content reading include vocabulary development, studying strategies, reading and study skills, locational skills, and critical reading skills.

- Teachers should strive to tailor their instruction in the content areas to the needs of their pupils.

Key Terms

content reading ability   the degree to which a student can adequately comprehend and retain content or expository information.

expository text   the text structure found in content books, including (1) description, (2) collection, (3) causation, (4) problem/solution, and (5) comparison.

readability   the approximate difficulty level of written material.

graphic organizers   visual diagrams (such as flow charts, outlines, and time lines) depicting key concepts or ideas in a lesson.

metacomprehension   awareness and control of one's cognitive functioning while reading.

directed reading-thinking activity (dr-ta)   an instructional procedure for teaching a reading selection, including readiness and prediction, active silent reading, and reaction to and review of text ideas.

SQ3R   a systematized study procedure for reading content chapters. The letters SQ3R stand for survey, question, read, recite, and review.

MAJOR GOAL AND TRENDS IN CONTENT READING

The major goal of content-area reading instruction is to teach students the attitudes, skills, and strategies that will enable them to become independent learners. Effective readers not only interact with content material on a basic or literal level but seek out information in a variety of ways, depending on their goal. With the new emphases on constructing meaning in text and integrating reading instruction with the other language arts across all curricular areas, the following are growing trends in the content-reading area: content-oriented literature, integrating writing in the content areas, integrating comprehension strategies, and primary-grade emphasis.

Content-Oriented Literature

The world of literature serves many purposes, including that of a rich source of information on content-oriented themes. Students should be exposed not only to narrative literature but also expository literature (Armbruster, 1991). Whether the topic is history, different cultures, animals, science, environmental concerns, or mathematics, quality literature will not only help students understand con-

Opening up students to the world through good literature should be a goal of content reading instruction at every grade level.

tent, but will stimulate their interest and active engagement, promote reading as a lifelong activity, aid in developing reading fluency, and promote application of reading-comprehension strategies. Incorporating good expository literature into the content areas is an excellent means for reinforcing all of the language processes—reading, writing, listening, and speaking—across the curriculum. Choosing a number of expository books at various difficulty levels dealing with a particular topic is also another way of meeting the varied needs of students in any classroom.

Integrating Writing in the Content Areas

As stressed throughout the text, reading comprehension improves when the writing and reading processes are combined. Reading and writing simultaneously interact to make content learning more enjoyable and understandable. French, Danielson, Conn, Gale, Lueck, and Manley (1989) state "Reading and writing in the content areas relates prior knowledge, classroom interaction, cooperative learning, vocabulary instruction, and questioning techniques" (p. 266). Both basal and literature-based programs are beginning to capitalize on this supportive relationship.

Typically, content material is more difficult for students to comprehend, primarily because of its presentation of difficult concepts, the technical vocabulary, and the different text structures of expository writing. Combining various writing assignments—whether before, during, or after content reading instruction— can help improve students' basic understanding of ideas, inferences to be drawn from the text, and creative reactions to topics under study. This trend also must be viewed and implemented from a developmental perspective which occurs in content instruction throughout all grades.

Integrating Comprehension Strategies

With the explosion of knowledge on how readers actively and strategically interact with text, content-reading instruction now emphasizes the learning and application of this new knowledge. Intricately related to the last two trends, content reading is viewed more as a prime area for students to learn and apply various comprehension and studying strategies and reading-study skills. They need those same skills to become successful readers of expository text. In many cases, literature and writing assignments can be the vehicles to accomplish these worthwhile goals.

The regular reading program can teach many skills and strategies, but students must apply them to content subjects to comprehend content material. Reading comprehension and studying strategies and specific reading-study skills also must be taught directly during the content instructional period. Most importantly, students need ample teacher assistance in terms of initial instruction, explanation, clarification, guidance, and ongoing instruction in content-area activities to become strategic, independent learners. Students need to see content reading-study skills and strategies applied to everyday materials they encounter in their own lives (Richardson & Morgan, 1993).

Primary-Grade Emphasis

Traditionally, formal content area reading instruction was limited mainly to the intermediate, middle and high school levels. This was true despite the age-old adage that every teacher should be a reading teacher and despite the descriptions of a complete reading program as including broad areas of the instructional curriculum, an independent or recreational program, and skill and strategy development in the content areas at all grade levels. A much-needed emphasis is now occurring at the primary level. Olson and Gee (1991) reported on content instruction in the primary grades and the problems that students at this level experience with expository text. The authors surveyed primary-grade teachers regarding recommended content reading practices and strategies. They reported that "70% of the teachers found content texts more difficult than stories" (p. 300). The six highest rated practices of the teachers were "previewing concepts and vocabulary, using concrete manipulatives to develop concepts, requiring retellings, developing summaries, visualizing information, and brainstorming" (p. 300). Based on these results and recent research, Olson and Gee recommended that primary teachers use the following instructional strategies in teaching content reading:

- semantic mapping
- K-W-L: What I know, What I want to learn, What I learned
- concrete manipulative and experiences
- expository paragraph frames
- group summarizing
- visual imagery

This primary-grade emphasis on content reading instruction again reflects the developmental nature of learning to read as discussed in Chapter 1 along with Chall's Stages of Reading Development.

EXPOSITORY TEXT

Content reading ability is the degree to which a student can adequately comprehend and retain content or expository text. An adequate instructional and independent reading program does not ensure successful readers in content material. Students frequently struggle with content materials. A lack of knowledge about **expository text** is a chief reason for this difficulty (Anderson, 1984). More specific reasons include a lack of direct instruction in studying strategies and research skills, the difficulty of many content materials in terms of vocabulary and concepts, and inadequate transfer of skills from the basic reading program to content areas. In essence, students' general reading ability often does not predict how

Success in the regular literacy program does not automatically spell success in reading for content. Success in understanding any new content requires teachers to teach students needed strategies and skills.

well they will do in various content areas. Evidence of this is not new, although its ramifications for instruction are still under investigation (Readence, Beans, & Baldwin, 1981; Shores, 1943).

Organizational Structures

Students are generally more familiar with narrative writing, since most basal reader stories follow this organizational structure. Yet, students increasingly are expected to read and understand material presented in content textbooks. Most content texts are written in an expository style. While narrative materials follow a traditional story structure (such as setting, theme, plot, resolution), expository writing is organized differently. This structure is more compact, detailed, and explanatory in nature.

Meyer and Freedle (1984) identify five common expository text structures: (1) description, (2) collection, (3) causation, (4) problem/solution, and (5) comparison. McGee and Richgels (1985) discuss the importance of understanding text structure by preparing a graphic organizer for a specific passage and writing with students a passage to mirror the graphic organizer. Figure 10.1 describes each type of structure identified by Meyer and Freedle, giving a sample passage and clue words.

As a teacher of reading, you must realize that your students will not be familiar with these expository text structures. As a result, they probably will have trouble learning material presented in content subjects. Recent research supports a long-held belief that how well a text is written and how successfully readers

Structure	Description*	Sample passage	Clue words
Description	Specifies something about a topic or presents an attribute or setting for a topic.	The Summer Olympic Games are the biggest entertainment spectacles of modern times. Every four years they offer two weeks of non-stop pageantry and competition.	
Collection	A number of descriptions (specifics, attributes, or settings) presented together.	The Summer Olympics have so many different things to offer. First, there are many kinds of events: big shows like the opening and closing ceremonies, pure competitions like the races and games, and events that are partly artistic and partly competitive like the subjectively scored diving and gymnastics contests. There are old things and new things, like the classic track and field events staged in 1984 in the same stadium where they were held in 1932, and the almost bizarre sport of synchronized swimming first presented in 1984.	First, second, third, next, finally
Causation	Elements grouped in time sequence (before and after) with a causative relationship (the earlier causes the later) specified.	There are several reasons why so many people attend the Olympic Games or watch them on television. The first Olympics were held in Greece more than 2,000 years ago. As a result of hearing the name "Olympics," seeing the torch and flame, and being reminded in other ways of the ancient games, people feel that they are escaping the ordinariness of daily life. People like to identify with someone else's individual sacrifice and accomplishment, and thus an athlete's or even a team's hard-earned, well-deserved victory becomes a nation's victory. There are national medal counts and people watch so that they can see how their country is doing. Since the Olympics are staged only every four years and maybe only in a particular country once in a lifetime, people flock to even obscure events in order to be able to say "I was there."	so that, thus, because of, as a result of, since, and so, in order to

FIGURE 10.1

Expository text structures with sample passages and clue words
(From L. M. McGee and D. J. Richgels, "Teaching Expository Text Structure to Elementary Students," *The Reading Teacher, 38* [April 1985], pp. 741–742. Reprinted with permission of Lea M. McGee and the International Reading Association.)

FIGURE 10.1

Continued

Structure	Description*	Sample passage	Clue words
Problem/ solution	Includes a causative relation (between a problem and its causes) and a solution set, one element of which can break the link between the problem and its antecedent cause.	One problem with the modern Olympics is that they have gotten so big and so expensive to operate. A city or country often loses a lot of money by staging the games. A stadium, pools, and playing fields are built for the many events and housing is built for the athletes, but it is all used for only two weeks. In 1984, Los Angeles solved these problems by charging companies for permission to be official sponsors and by using many buildings that were already there. Companies like McDonald's paid a lot of money to be part of the Olympics. The Coliseum, where the 1932 Games were held, was used again and many colleges and universities in the area become playing and living sites.	*a problem is, a solution is, have solved this problem by*
Comparison	Contains no element of time sequence or causality; organizes elements on the basis of their similarities and differences.	The modern Summer Olympics are really very unlike the ancient Olympic Games. Individual events are different. For example, there were no swimming races in the ancient Games, but there were chariot races. There were no women contestants and everyone competed in the nude. Of course the ancient and modern Olympics are also alike in many ways. Some events are the same, like the javelin and discus throws. Some people say that cheating, professionalism, and nationalism in the modern Games are a disgrace to the ancient Olympic tradition. But according to ancient Greek writers, there were many cases of cheating, nationalism, and professionalism in their Olympics too.	*different from, same as, alike, similar to, resemble*

*Descriptions adapted from Meyer and Freedle, 1984, pp. 121–24.

recognize writing patterns affect student understanding (McGee & Richgels, 1985).

Readability

A possible explanation for problems in content subjects is the increased difficulty of the materials to be read. **Readability** is the approximate difficulty level of written material. The concept of readability is important for all teachers. Teachers should strive to match a book's readability with the student's instructional level. Students tend to learn the most from material that is neither too easy nor too difficult. Readability depends on factors inherent in the text (sentence structure, organizational pattern, physical presentation of the material, and vocabulary), the reader (knowledge of text structures, interest in the subject, and prior knowledge of a topic), and the teacher (the presentation). To provide effective instruction, teachers must judge the readability level of material.

Many readability formulas are available to judge difficulty of traditional text factors. Fry's readability formula (see Figure 10.2) is based on word and sentence length and is quick to use. Remember, however, that any readability formula will yield only an approximate, not an exact, level of difficulty. Indeed, using different readability formulas on the same material can yield different results. Remember, too, that readability varies within a given text.

Teachers should use a combination of a formula, personal knowledge of their students, and an informal appraisal of text characteristics to assess the suitability of a particular text. Irwin and Davis (1980) recommend an informal method for estimating the appropriateness of a textbook. Their readability checklist rates understandability, learnability, reinforcement, and motivation. Zakaluk and Samuels (1988) recommend a broader method of predicting text difficulty, by collecting and assessing information about outside-the-head and inside-the-head factors. Outside-the-head factors include the traditional text factors of word difficulty, sentence length, and adjunct aids (such as study questions). Inside-the-head factors include facility in word recognition and knowledge of the topic.

In contrast to providing a designation of grade level for readability, the cloze procedure for content material may indicate students' abilities to read a particular text. The cloze procedure yields information indicating if the material matches a student's instructional, independent, or frustration reading level. (See Chapter 11 for a description of the cloze procedure.) This procedure can be used with a large group and can quickly indicate class and individual capabilities for reading a particular content text.

COMPONENTS OF CONTENT READING

Formal education has many goals, one of which is to help students become increasingly independent within the framework of the school setting. To achieve such independence, learners must master a number of related language skills. One important cluster of skills determines success in content reading. In schools

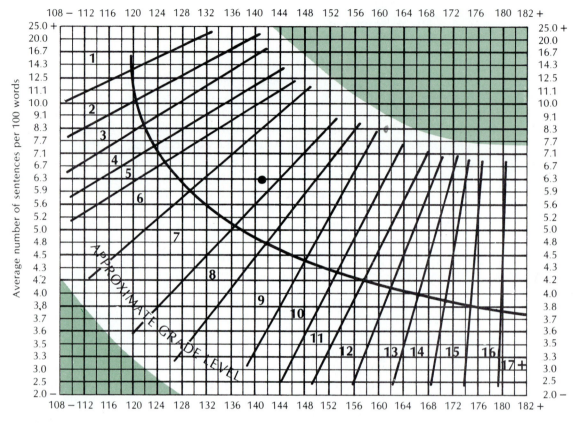

Average number of syllables per 100 words

FIGURE 10.2

Graph for estimating readability—extended (Note: This "extended graph" does not outmode or render the earlier (1968) version inoperative or inaccurate; it is an extension.)

Source: By Edward Fry. Reprinted from *The Journal of Reading,* December 1977. Reproduction permitted. No copyright.)

dominated by basic skills, instruction often gives content skills mere lip service. Although current educational trends emphasize teaching basic skills and administering tests to show that a student is literate, teachers also need to emphasize skills that enable learners to acquire information on their own.

The major functions of teaching content reading fall into three interrelated categories: (1) specific skills and strategies needed to read a chapter in a content subject; (2) specific study skills instruction; and (3) skills and strategies required for collecting, organizing, and criticizing data. Within these categories, the following five major components of content reading interact: (1) vocabulary development, (2) studying strategies, (3) reading and study skills, (4) locational skills and (5) critical reading skills.

Expanded Directions for Working Readability Graph

1. Randomly select three (3) sample passages and count out exactly 100 words each, beginning with the beginning of a sentence. Do count proper nouns, initializations, and numerals.

2. Count the number of sentences in the hundred words, estimating length of the fraction of the last sentence to the nearest one-tenth.

3. Count the total number of syllables in the 100-word passage. If you don't have a hand counter available, an easy way is to simply put a mark above every syllable over one in each word, then when you get to the end of the passage, count the number of marks and add 100. Small calculators can also be used as counters by pushing numeral 1, then push the + sign for each word or syllable when counting.

4. Enter graph with *average* sentence length and *average* number of syllables; plot dot where the two lines intersect. Area where dot is plotted will give you the approximate grade level.

5. If a great deal of variability is found in syllable count or sentence count, putting more samples into the average is desirable.

6. A word is defined as a group of symbols with a space on either side, thus, *Joe, IRA, 1945,* and & are each one word.

7. A syllable is defined as a phonetic syllable. Generally, there are as many syllables as vowel sounds. For example, *stopped* is one syllable and *wanted* is two syllables. When counting syllables for numerals and initializations, count one syllable for each symbol. For example, *1945* is four syllables, *IRA* is three syllables, and & is one syllable.

FIGURE 10.2
Continued

Vocabulary Development

Curriculum materials in content subjects confront readers with an ever-increasing number of unknown and relatively difficult words and concepts. Students must know many new, more difficult connotations for familiar words and must understand a large number of idiomatic and figurative expressions. The amount of required reading suddenly increases, and pupils must read and comprehend at a faster rate. They must also develop the flexibility to adjust their rate to both the difficulty level and the purpose.

Because of the rigid control of vocabulary in beginning reading materials, teachers frequently fail to arouse and maintain students' interest in content ma-

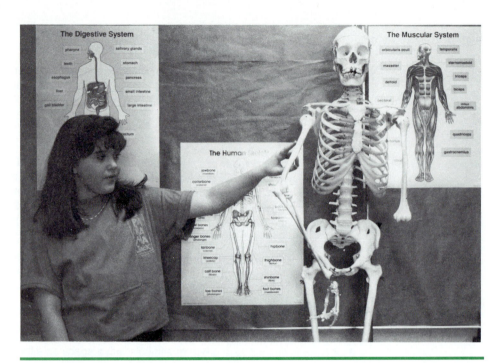

Vocabulary development in the content areas needs to include interesting and varied practice.

terials. Content textbooks introduce so many difficult words and concepts that many pupils are frustrated and lost. In addition, content vocabulary differs from vocabulary in regular reading lessons in important ways. Armbruster and Nagy (1992) report that unlike vocabulary in regular reading lessons, content vocabulary is absolutely crucial for comprehension, usually represents unfamiliar concepts, and is usually related to other content vocabulary in the same chapter.

Understanding the meaning of specialized content words and concepts requires planned, systematic instruction. Nagy (1988), summarizing recent research on vocabulary development, concludes that effective vocabulary instruction to improve comprehension includes three properties: (1) integration (relating new words with known concepts and experiences), (2) repetition (sufficient practice to know words quickly while reading), and (3) meaningful use (interesting practice that results in the ability to use new words properly).

For integrating new words with known concepts and experiences in content reading, various **graphic organizers** (visual diagrams, e.g., flow charts, outlines, and time lines) are particularly useful. Semantic mapping (Johnson & Pearson, 1984) is a popular visual technique for showing how words relate to one another. To design a semantic map, lead a brainstorming session around a particular word or topic. After listing all the words that come to mind relating to the key word or topic on the board, group the words into meaningful categories. Finally, draw a semantic map and use it as a vehicle for discussion both before and after reading a portion of text. Figure 10.3 is a semantic map completed by

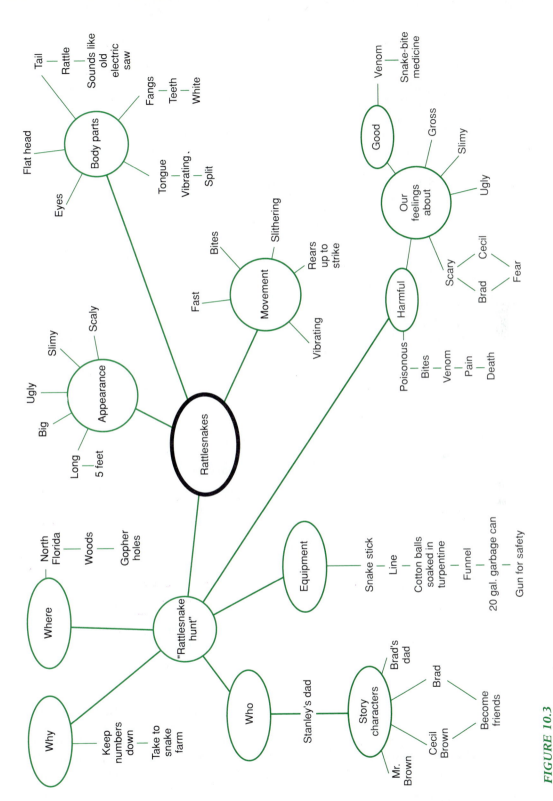

FIGURE 10.3

Group map for rattlesnakes

(From J. E. Heimlich and S. D. Pittleman, *Semantic Mapping: Classroom Applications* [Neward, DE: International Reading Association, 1986], p.28. Reprinted with permission of Joan E. Heimlich and the International Reading Association.)

sixth graders before reading a story about rattlesnakes (Heimlich & Pittleman, 1986).

Meaningful content-area reading requires students to understand new concepts continually, because this type of reading presents more difficulties per reading unit than does primary reading. One of the major problems in reading is the gap between students' store of meanings and the demands of the content reading matter. In addition, content reading contains many idiomatic expressions, abstract and figurative terms, and new connotations for familiar words. In the primary grades, even though they occur less frequently, the teacher's editions accompanying basal reader series point out these expressions. Workbooks provide instruction supplementing the reader series.

The shift to separate textbooks in the content areas reduces the emphasis on helping students with meaning difficulties—just when they need the most help. Teachers find that many students do not understand concepts even after the material has been assigned and covered in class. The following are examples of difficult concepts from fourth and fifth grade geography, science, and mathematics books:

- The native city is backward and ugly.
- Now, as in ancient time, the Mediterranean is a great connecting highway.
- The people who lived in fixed settlements made far greater progress than the nomads.
- Gradually the continent was opened. Another "jewel" had been added to the British crown.
- Business and industry were paralyzed.
- A belt of irrigated land stretches almost all the way along the coast.
- The shrinking world and new inventions have made this possible.
- Almost every farmer grows some cash crops besides food for his family.
- Ornithologists have examined the crops of many birds to find out what kind of food they eat.
- We can use a ruler to subtract fractions.

Studying Strategies

Understanding expository text depends largely upon knowledge and application of comprehension strategies to fulfill one's purpose in reading. Good readers, who are aware of what they are doing during their reading, can apply specific strategies and can monitor their progress.

Metacognition. The ability to be aware of one's cognitive functioning and apply specific strategies to fulfill one's purpose is metacognition (Babbs & Moe, 1983; Flavell, 1976). Applied specifically to reading, the term ***metacomprehension*** is the ability to be aware of and control one's reading behavior. In this sense, good readers generate and monitor purposeful reading of text. In fulfillment of this purposeful reading, metacomprehension involves not only appropriate reading strategies but also awareness and control of these strategies while reading. In understanding metacognition, it is helpful to understand the basic elements of metacognition. Following is a summary of the elements by Jones (1986):

> Metacognition in reading to learn centers around the learner's knowledge about the strategic coordination of the four variables of text, task, strategies, and learner characteristics. Text knowledge has to do with the learner's understanding of the features that aid comprehension and retention of what is read such as text difficulty, familiarity with language and content, interest in content, and structure of the text. Task knowledge deals with the learner's awareness of purposes for reading and the requirements of the assignment. The learning activities that are used to deal with the task demands, and to store and retrieve information from the text are considered strategy knowledge. The self-knowledge a learner has about himself or herself regarding ability, motivation, interest, and many personal attributes and states is considered learner characteristics. (p. 2)

Obviously, helping students engage in metacognition requires teacher intervention. Effective studying strategies in expository texts can be applied before, during, and after reading. Following are recommended studying strategies and instructional techniques.

Before reading, include the following strategies:

- Reviewing prior knowledge on the topic.
- Relating the new chapter to previous chapters.
- Relating the new material to personal experiences.
- Discussing key vocabulary and concepts.
- Reading the introduction to create a proper mind-set.
- Predicting what will be included in the text.
- Establishing an overall purpose for reading the text.
- Reviewing the pattern of the text to be read.

Teachers can accomplish the preceding strategies in various ways, including:

- *Direct/explicit instruction and thinking aloud.* Walk the students through an appropriate strategy by explaining it point by point or by modeling it. Following the direct explanation or modeling, afford sufficient practice in the strategy.
- *The directed reading activity (DRA).* Apply this teaching strategy to all content reading, not just basal materials. The elements of the readiness step (motivation, vocabulary, background, and purpose setting) help students read and learn specific content.
- *The advanced organizer.* Provide students with a short written summary and highlight new vocabulary and concepts, background information, and main ideas. Advanced organizers help students establish a correct mind-set before reading and aid them in establishing purposes for reading.
- *The structured overview.* This is similar to the advanced organizer. Present a structured overview containing the key ideas of the chapter and their relationships in a visual format (usually a flow chart, hierarchy, spoke, or pie). Discuss the key vocabulary words in the chapter before students read silently.

The importance of study skills and being able to read content text with a specific purpose were important in the early 1800s. The partial page below is from Daniel Adams, *Geography of the World*, 1830. Pupils reading the text were directed to questions the teacher would ask by the use of a superior *q*. Students were directed to ask themselves questions for each of the *q* symbols and come up with the appropriate answer.

GEOGRAPHY.

☞ The "Interrogative system" of teaching, has now become very general in almost every branch of school education. The introduction may be traced to the Scholar's Arithmetic, in 1801, many years before the appearance of Goldsmith and of Guy in our country. A further improvement in this system is here attempted, and instead of printing the question at length, which necessarily swells the book, a character (ᵠ) is introduced, intimating both to the Instructer, and the pupil, that a question is required, and this character is invariably placed BE-FORE the word or words intended to ask the question, and to which the answer, FOUND BY READING THE SENTENCE, is to be a direct reply. For example, take the first sentence; the character is placed before the words "certain knowledge;" the question then is, Had the ancients any certain knowledge of the figure of the earth? The answer, from reading the sentence, is evident, No; or, They had not.
—here the construction of the sentence suggests no particular form
put the quest'   What is said of

THE WORLD.

THE ancients had no ᵠcertain knowledge of the figure of the earth. But later discoveries, both by astronomy and navigation, demonstrate the world we inhabit to be a large opaque globe or ball, nearly eight thousand ᵠmiles in diameter. In proof of this it is only necessary to notice, that various navigators have actually sailed around it. Of these, the ᵠfirst was Sir Francis Drake, who in 1580 completed the circumnavigation of the globe, after an absence of two years, ten months, and twenty days, from England, his native land.

UPDATE

The superior *q* was in vogue more than 260 years ago and today this whole area of promoting a self-questioning, self-monitoring attitude while one reads is once again in style. Today, the new cognitive view of reading stresses interactive reading through the development of strategies students use themselves to understand, reason, and reflect on ideas in the text. As students make sense of the text, one strategy emphasized today is student-generated questions. Teachers of reading need to teach students specific ways to generate their own questions before, during, and after reading. Examples of questioning strategies recommended today include QAR, K-W-L, and Reciprocal Teaching.

- *The directed reading-thinking activity (DR-TA).* Similar in purpose to the directed reading activity, the **directed reading-thinking activity** (DR-TA) directs students' thinking about the text to be read (Haggard, 1988; Stauffer, 1975). In the first step of a DR-TA, introduce students to the material to be read and help them set their own purposes for reading by predicting what they think will be covered.

- *Semantic mapping.* This is a visual way to expand vocabulary knowledge and to show relationships among ideas (Heimlich & Pittleman, 1986). Used before reading, semantic mapping teaches new words and introduces relationships developed in the content chapter.

- *The K-W-L teaching model* (Ogle, 1986). This dialogue between the teacher and students uses prior knowledge for comprehension. K-W-L stands for (1) assessing what I *know,* (2) determining what I *want* to learn, and (3) recalling what I *learned.* Following a discussion of each of the three steps and using a portion of text, have the students write their personal responses on a worksheet that highlights the three steps.

During reading, include the following strategies:

- Turning bold-print headings into questions to guide reading.
- Answering bold-print questions before moving on to the next section.
- Rereading parts of the text that cannot be remembered (by not being able to answer bold-print questions).
- Finding the author's pattern.

Teachers can accomplish the preceding reading strategies in various ways. They include:

- *Study guides.* Study guides provide students with chapter questions to answer while reading and purposes for reading. The questions asked should balance literal, interpretive, and critical comprehension.

- *Direct/explicit instruction and thinking aloud.* Show students how to turn bold-print heads into questions using reporters questions (who, what, where, when, why and how). If students cannot recall an answer after reading a section, explain to them that they should reread the section to answer their purpose-setting questions.

- *The directed reading-thinking activity (DR-TA).* After students make predictions, ask them to read silently to prove or disprove their predictions.

After reading, include the following strategies:

- Checking comprehension by answering the end-of-chapter questions.
- Assessing the information conveyed and predicting what will happen next.
- Summarizing key points.
- Looking back or rereading parts of the text to understand particular points.

Teachers can accomplish the preceding postreading strategies in various ways. They include:

- *Study guides.* Lead a discussion of questions in the study guide.

- *The directed reading activity (DRA).* Following silent reading, ask students to answer their purpose-setting questions. Ask a variety of comprehension questions on different levels of thinking. Directly teach a reading skill or study skill related to the chapter. Then, provide independent practice activities for the skill. Check students' comprehension of the ideas in the text.

- *The directed reading-thinking activity (DR-TA).* Following silent reading, ask students questions to check the accuracy of their predictions.

- *Semantic mapping.* Rework the map that you and the students devised before they read the chapter.

- *Reciprocal teaching.* Reciprocal teaching is a dialogue between the teacher and students concerning a portion of the text (Palincsar & Brown, 1986). In this dialogue, the teaching function gradually shifts to the students. Following silent reading, model four strategies: (1) summarizing key point, (2) asking questions requiring different levels of thinking, (3) clarifying answers to questions, and (4) predicting what will be discussed in the next section of the text. Gradually let students take over one or more of the strategies, continually facilitating the process by providing timely feedback.

- *The K-W-L teaching model.* Complete the last step of this model by asking students to write down what they learned and what they still need to know.

- *Cooperative grouping.* Design discussion or assignment groups, grouping students of different ability levels. Have each group complete the end-of-chapter activity together.

Writing to Learn. Reading and writing are interdependent. As emphasized, reading is best learned through integration with the other language arts. Just as reading and writing are complementary and effective in the regular reading program, the combination yields impressive results in the content areas (Myers, 1984; Tadlock, 1978). In the content areas, writing to learn should be an integral part of the instructional program. Combining reading and writing makes students more aware of text structure and helps them understand ideas better (Holbrook, 1987). Anderson (1984) states: "Writing . . . is a way to improve students' schemata, or structured knowledge of subjects encountered in the content areas . . . fundamental to comprehending, learning, and remembering concepts in stories and texts" (p. 243).

Writing should be an integral part of content reading instruction beginning in kindergarten. Using shared experiences, student-dictated language-experience charts can be springboards for content learning and writing development. For example, students can summarize their understanding of content through writing (even invented spelling), illustrate their writing, and make an individual or class book. Kinney (1985) recommends using the language-experience approach to teach first graders about text structure. The teacher leads the discussion on a topic and a particular type of organization—for example, comparing and contrasting pairs of objects like a football and baseball—and the students dictate stories to make them aware of the text structure. The results of Kinney's study lend support to use of the language-experience approach in the content areas.

Teachers can integrate writing into content instruction in a number of ways. It is probably best to think of creative ways to incorporate writing during the prereading or postreading phases of a lesson. During the prereading portion, instruct students to write about a particular topic after reviewing their prior knowledge or brainstorming about their past experiences. Following guided silent reading, have students write to fulfill a number of purposes—to summarize main ideas, to classify information, to compare and contrast, or to predict future consequences.

Holbrook (1987) reviewed and summarized a number of specific ways to integrate writing into the content areas, including those of Smith and Bean (1980) and of Myers (1984). Smith and Bean advocate the two-step method. After discussing a topic in the prereading step, have students write two paragraphs using information from the previous discussion. Following silent reading of the text, have the students revise their first draft and discuss their revisions. Myers recommends a variety of creative writing assignments for social studies, including writing letters to the editor, assuming the role of a historical person, and interviewing and transcribing oral histories.

Different Approaches for Different Abilities. Invariably, classrooms use one content textbook for each subject and grade. This practice presents problems in accommodating differing student abilities. Because many students cannot read successfully in a particular text, teachers should understand the concept of readability and know how to measure a text's difficulty level. Teachers should teach and model reading and study skills to help students understand expository text. Finally, teachers should know various ways to tailor instruction to students who are unable to read a required text. Alternative instruction approaches that move away from reliance on a single text include providing different assignments, using multilevel content materials, providing meaningful oral reading, using educational media resources, conducting small-group instruction, assigning library books of various difficulty levels for a particular topic, and incorporating the arts in instruction.

SQ3R. In addition to individual studying strategies, many students profit from learning a specific approach to reading content chapters. Reading a content chapter resembles following a road map: Students must learn how to get from point A to point B in the shortest, most meaningful way. The best known systematized procedure for reading content chapters is ***SQ3R.***

This procedure applies many skills and strategies. In fact, many of the previously discussed studying strategies are part of SQ3R. Developed by Robinson (1961), SQ3R stands for survey, question, read, recite, and review. Students need direct instruction and a great deal of practice on each step of the procedure.

Survey encourages students to get an overall picture of the chapter before reading it by looking at the title, introduction, main headings, illustrations, and end-of-chapter questions. *Questions* helps students read with a purpose by turning each bold heading into questions. *Read* asks students to read each chapter section and to answer each purpose-setting question, keeping in mind the chapter organization and visual aids. *Recite* involves stopping periodically to answer the purpose-setting questions in one's own words. Students are encouraged to take notes during silent reading. *Review* instructs students to check their memory by reviewing their notes and reciting major points under each heading.

The steps we have asked you to follow so far in the text are a modification of this procedure. We recommend teaching the following method and practicing it with students.

1. Read the introduction.
2. Survey all visual aids in the chapter and read each bold heading.
3. Read the summary.
4. Study the questions at the end of the chapter.
5. Return to the beginning of the chapter and read.

Tadlock (1978) concurs that when teaching a study method such as SQ3R, teaches must also explain why and how the method will aid their retention of content material. She states that each step in SQ3R "is designed to facilitate the processing of incoming information (print) so the reader can deal with more of it and deal with it more effectively" (p. 111).

Reading and Study Skills

Every instructional level presents its own challenges to teachers. The emphasis on separate textbooks in the various subject areas is a chief source of instructional problems. These books call for a high level of independent reading ability and special facility in a number of reading and study skills. Following is a listing of some of the major reading and study skills needed for comprehension in the various content subjects. Students need the ability to:

1. Follow ideas and events in sequence.
2. Classify details and main ideas.
3. Identify and use the author's organizational pattern.
4. Summarize key ideas.
5. Organize and synthesize information on various topics.

Teachers and other educators constantly stress teaching various facets of reading concurrently with subject matter. Even in departmentalized schools, with one teacher responsible for social studies, another for science, another for mathematics, and so forth, the importance of integrating reading and the content subjects emerges in the slogan "Every teacher is a teacher of reading."

New teaching materials are helping both teacher and students meet the demands of content reading. For example, new basal programs integrate content knowledge, strategies, and skills into their total program. New basal teacher manuals include lesson suggestions for teachers as well as practice materials in a variety of forms including both narrative and expository literature.

The nature of reading materials and the great difference in students' instructional needs make it logical and perhaps even essential to relate some reading instruction to the social studies, science, literature, mathematics, and other subject areas. This very point was emphasized in *Becoming a Nation of Readers* (Anderson, Hiebert, Scott, & Wilkinson, 1985). The authors state: "The most logical place for instruction in most reading and thinking strategies is in social studies and science rather than in separate lessons about reading. The reason is that the strategies are useful mainly when the student is grappling with important but unfamiliar content" (p. 73).

In Figure 10.4, Pescosolido, Schell, and Laurent (1967) demonstrate how a study skill assignment requires application of several reading skills. This ex-

Task	General Skill	Specific Skill
Selecting appropriate texts	Locational Skill	use of title
Locate specific information	Locational Skill	use of table of contents
Locate page for specific information	Locational Skill	use of index
Obtaining general information in text	Comprehension Skill	determining author's pattern by reading center heads and paragraph heads
Reading for information	Comprehension Skill	finding main idea
Reading for information	Comprehension Skill	reading for detail
Reading for information	Comprehension Skill	differentiating important from unimportant
Reading for information	Organizing Skill	outlining
Reading for information	Organizing Skill	summarizing

FIGURE 10.4
Illustration of the application of reading skills in a study skills task
(From John R. Pescosolido, Leo M. Schell, and Marie-Jeanne Laurent, *Reading Approaches and Rituals* [Dubuque, IA: Kendall/Hunt Publishing Co., 1967], p. 22. Reprinted by permission of the publisher and authors.)

ample involves locating specific information about an explorer in a social studies text.

Each reading skill applied in a content area should be taught in a systematic, direct fashion. Teachers must not assume that students already know and can apply various reading skills in content areas.

The inability to apply reading skills in any subject area handicaps the reader (Forgan, & Mangrum, 1989). For example, reading science material requires classification skills, but so does reading social studies and mathematics. Ability to cope with precise, compact writing may be associated with mathematics, but it cannot be disassociated from history or literature. Poetry, Lincoln's second inaugural address, or William Faulkner's speech when he accepted the Nobel prize for literature all illustrate this idea.

Students need to draw inferences in more than one area of the curriculum. In the course of a day, a student may need to draw inferences about what happens when a decimal point is inserted between digits, how mountains located between the sea and the plains affect rainfall on the plains, and what happens to the circumference of an inflated balloon placed in a freezer.

Instruction and Practice. A major problem undermining mastery of reading and study skills is insufficient attention to these skills in both teaching and practice (see Appendix). To properly emphasize teaching of reading and study skills, teachers should use the direct/explicit instruction model and practice these skills primarily in the content areas. Instruction in connection with content subjects has many advantages, including a text organization, a functional setting, and motivation. Figure 10.5 presents a lesson on a study skill using direct/explicit instruction.

Transfer. Student difficulty in content materials may be due to the absence of interesting, varied practice. Furthermore, students do not automatically transfer skills to content materials. For example, students taught how to interpret a diagram in science require additional practice in a variety of situations before they can transfer this skill to their reading of mathematics or social studies materials. Following are examples of ways to encourage transferring the skill of interpreting a diagram:

■ Bring in supplemental materials containing diagrams of topics already studied. Ask students appropriate questions about each diagram, or allow individuals to assume the role of the teacher and explain the diagram to the rest of the class.

■ Have students make their own diagram on a topic of their choice. Make certain each diagram is labeled properly. Ask students to construct a series of questions concerning their diagrams.

Teachers can use numerous kinds of meaningful practice to promote transfer of a particular skill. Teachers must be aware of this need and provide the necessary time and opportunity to ensure the transfer.

■ **Area of Needed Reading Instruction**

Introduction to the library card catalog and its use.

■ **Intended Learning Outcome**

Students will be able to interpret information on a library index card (title, subject, author) and use the library card catalog.

■ **Past Learning**

Students have a basic understanding of alphabetical order and the Dewey Decimal System for library purposes.

Students are aware that using the card catalog is the most effective method for retrieving a book.

■ **Building Background**

Remind students that locating a book from the card catalog calls for the use of alphabetical-order skills and the Dewey Decimal System. To ensure understanding of these skills, list titles on the chalkboard and ask students to match the titles with the appropriate alphabetical section from the subject index.

Subject	Subject Index
Cats	A–Cu
Dogs	Cy–Du
	Dw–Ea

Assist the class in matching the appropriate alphabetical section written on the chalkboard with the correct subject. Use other examples for both title and author index information following the same procedure. For example:

Title	Author
Cat in the Hat	Frost, Robert
Charlotte's Web	Blume, Judy

Remind students to be sure to use the correct subject, title, or author index when they are using the card catalog.

Discuss how some index drawers are marked with two beginning alphabetical letters, such as:

A–Cu
Cy–Du
Dw–Ea

FIGURE 10.5

Direct/explicit instruction lesson

(Reprinted with the permission of Macmillan Publishing Company from *Teaching Reading: Diagnosis, Direct Instruction, and Practice,* Second Edition by William H. Rupley and Timothy R. Blair. Copyright © 1988 by Macmillan Publishing Company.)

FIGURE 10.5
Continued

Call on individuals and ask such questions as: Would the title card for *Charlotte's Web* be listed in the A–Cu, Cy–Du, or Dw–Ea drawer? Explain your answer.

Review the Dewey Decimal System for library use by providing students with a map of the library sections. Mark Dewey Decimal System labels on each appropriate section. Have students find out where various numbers, such as 100.46, 700.98, and so forth would be located. Ask students where in the room or building these books could be found. Call out other Dewey Decimal System numbers and instruct students to check the library map to find the location to ensure that they are able to use the Dewey Decimal System effectively in that particular library.

- **Teacher-Directed Instruction**

Illustrate a library index card on the overhead projector for students. Point out that the index card has various points that are important for locating a book in the library. Describe and explain each part of the index card: card number, author, title, synopsis of the book, and so forth. Stress that each part of the index card is placed in a specified section of the card. For example, the number is located in the upper right-hand corner.

Provide students with a handout that explains the purpose of the card catalog and lists and describes the function of the index card. Label and explain briefly the meaning of each part of the index card on the handout so that students will have a reference if they have trouble using the card catalog.

On the overhead projector, show a second example of an author, title, or subject card from the card catalog. Point out the various parts of their meanings to the students. Ask students the various parts and purposes of the particular card.

- **Independent Student Practice**

Take students to the library so that they can use the card catalog under the supervision of the librarian or yourself. Provide each student with a specific task, such as locating all the books by a particular author; locating a certain book when provided with only the title; and/or listing sources of information on a particular subject matter, such as rattlesnakes or boa constrictors.

- **Ongoing Diagnosis**

Observe students to evaluate their capabilities in independently using the card catalog.

- **Modifying Instruction**

Have students work in pairs to gain proficiency in using the card catalog. In addition, ask students to create a classroom library card catalog for the books in your classroom.

Locational Skills

To find answers in varied reading materials, students must understand and use all available aids. In other words, knowing how to use a book is a prerequisite for intelligent use of supplementary reading materials in the subject areas or in any unit of work. In the intermediate grades, study skills grow more important, reflecting the nature and variety of the materials used and the fact that supervision is not always readily available. Although development of study skills requires reading ability, this ability in itself does not ensure that students have mastered the study skills.

During the past few years, the availability of books, professional journals, and other printed matter has expanded tremendously. The past three decades, even when compared with the previous centuries, have seen such a dramatic advance in knowledge that the period has been labeled the knowledge explosion. Competency in any given field has taken on new meaning, and educational methods, of necessity, have changed radically to adapt to this new challenge.

No single textbook or even series of texts can completely cover a subject. The time lag between research, publication, and the adoption of textbooks causes inadequacies in even the most recent texts. To address this situation, good teachers have always provided supplementary reading materials. Today, however, providing a wide array of supplementary materials is not only desirable, but necessary. Thus, learners need study skills more now than ever, but the school's respect for these skills and its ability to teach them effectively have declined. The following discussion deals with instruction regarding locating information.

Using Books.   In teaching any study skill, the teacher at each grade level must build on what students already know. To do this, first the teacher must determine each student's ability level. A good place to begin is with the textbook adopted for a given course. Teachers can assess their students' ability to understand the text and their knowledge of specific study skills and their application.

Exercises that foster such growth are easy to devise. The major concern is how to use exercise materials in relation to the goals to be achieved. Some important learnings deal with the mechanics of learning—*how* to use a card catalog, *where* to look in an encyclopedia, *when* an appendix or glossary might be useful, and *what* is likely to be found in an appendix or glossary.

Written exercises are often used to help students understand the function of an index, table of contents, or appendix. It is common to find students who can work out correct solutions to workbook problems consisting of sample lines from an index but who still do not know how to get help from a real index. One of the best ways to teach children how to use a book effectively is to design a learning situation around a textbook they will be using throughout the year. A social studies, health, or other text can provide ample opportunities for teaching the functions of the table of contents, charts, indexes, and appendixes. The text the student is using will give him or her something concrete to return to when in doubt. Skills learned in using one text should transfer more readily to books in other areas, provided there is teacher direction and guidance.

Teachers frequently fail to detect student deficiencies in using a table of contents, index, glossary, and appendix, so they do not teach these skills. Too often, they assume that these basic skills have been taught or are being taught elsewhere. For example, as an outcome of an inservice program, one group of teachers agreed to build a one-page testing and teaching exercise consisting of 15 to 20 questions to measure students' skills in using the parts of a book. The exercise was to be specifically applicable to the textbook the students were using in one of their courses. Although students had used the books for nearly 3 months, few were able to complete the exercise perfectly. The teachers discovered glaring deficiencies and individual differences in students' ability to use these reader aids. In one class, students took from 6 to 22 minutes to do the "book-mining" exercise, with some students unable to complete the task.

Exercises such as that presented in Figure 10.6 may be used initially with an entire class and can serve as diagnostic instruments. Observant teachers will note which students have difficulty and what their problems are. Those findings should help them teach small groups and individual students the skills they need along with general concepts. This exercise was constructed for use with a sixth grade social studies text.

The exercise teaches a number of facts about the book. Question 1 takes the readers to the table of contents and requires them to associate their home state with part of a larger geographical region of the United States. Question 2 calls attention to a 16-page atlas; the next question focuses on a second, highly specialized table of contents dealing exclusively with maps.

Questions 4 through 8 deal with areas where the index may be helpful. The reader must locate pictures using key words and must be prepared to look under different headings. Topics may be listed as subheads under a more general heading. Questions 9 to 11 deal with information about pronunciation and meanings of more difficult words and emphasize that these aids are divided between the index and glossary.

Students sometimes fail to realize that most reference books and textbooks include a number of reader aids. Lack of familiarity with or inclination to use these aids inhibits students from optimizing their use of books. Although students need these skills, they do not always recognize their value.

One purpose may require students to skim the table of contents, while another demands that they read it critically. Comparing different books discloses that a table of contents may consist exclusively of chapter titles, similar to an outline composed of nothing but major topics. In some books, chapter titles precede a number of topics in their discussion order. Students may note that this is essentially a modified index containing only major headings in chronological order. In contrast, the index is in alphabetical order, dealing with narrower topics and cutting across chapters.

Every student should learn that (1) parts of the book are deliberately designed as aids, (2) these are valuable and are used profitably by efficient readers, and (3) the different parts of a book have definite purposes. Efficient readers decide instantly where to go for specific types of help. To do so, they must know what type of information each section contains, where the various aids are, and how to use each effectively. Once learned, this knowledge can be transferred and ap-

How to Use a Book

1. The region in which we live is discussed under the heading

   _____

2. The last sixteen pages in the book are called an *atlas.* Looking at these pages can you define "atlas"? _____

   _____

   _____

3. On what page can you find a listing of all maps, graphs, and diagrams found in the book? _____

4. Does the book contain a picture of Wonder Lake? _____
   How did you go about answering this question? _____

5. Is there a picture of the Grand Coulee Dam in the text?

   _____

6. Under what heading must you look to find it? _____

   _____

7. In the index there is a main heading *Exploration*. What six subheadings are found under it? _____

   _____

   _____

8. The book contains a double page map called Main Air Routes in the U.S. There is no heading "Main Air Routes" in the index. How can you find this map?

   _____

   _____

   _____

9. There are two sections of the book which provide the pronunciation of difficult words, these are _____
   and _____ .

10. The pronunciation of the following words is provided in the _____ . In the blank spaces show the pronunciation and page number where found:
    SHOSHONE _____Page _____
    COMANCHE _____Page _____
    FORT DUQUESNE _____Page _____

11. A particular page contains the *definition* of difficult words used throughout the book. That page is called the _____
    _____ and is page number ___ .

FIGURE 10.6
A study skill assignment and diagnostic test

plied to any book. Figure 10.7 is an abbreviated treatment of what a reader might expect to gain from the aids found in most books.

Using the Library. Effective use of library resources may well be one of the most underrated and undertaught skills in the entire school program. The library is where students read and receive guidance in both the use of books and research techniques. Students at all grade levels need the experience of frequent contact with a good school library.

Some teachers use the library effectively themselves but do not assume responsibility for teaching students to do so. On the other hand, a number of teachers make little personal use of library facilities.

At one school, the librarian and principal believed that a substantial portion of the teaching staff seldom used the library for personal reasons. They also found that students seemed less inclined to turn to the library for these teachers' classes.

The school incorporated a 1-hour library unit into its total in-service program. Teachers were each relieved of their regularly scheduled duties to spend an hour in conference with the librarian. The librarian discussed and pointed out

Aid	Information
Title page	The main title and possibly a subtitle. (The latter may set forth the limitations and narrow the topic.) The name of the author and where published.
Table of contents	Chapter titles possibly followed by the major topics discussed in each chapter. Is the book divided into major parts (I, II, III)? What are these? The length of the chapters gives a hint to thoroughness of the treatment.
Preface	To whom does the author address the book? What is the author's stated purpose? What new features does the author stress? What unique features does the author believe are found in the book?
Illustrations	The title, item, and page where found.
Index	The major topics in alphabetical order; minor topics under each heading; key phrases, cross-references, photographs, drawings, charts, and tables.
Glossary	Difficult or specialized terms are presented in alphabetical order with a definition.
Appendix	An organized body of facts related to the subject under consideration. For example, in a geography book the appendix may give the areas of states or nations, populations, state and national capitals, the extent of manufacturing, exports, imports, and mineral deposits.

FIGURE 10.7
Typical book aids for the reader

resources directly related to the teachers' various subjects, locating pamphlets, bound volumes, pertinent books, government documents, current magazines, and the like. The librarian also suggested ways to help the faculty member and students. The attitudes of a number of the teachers changed markedly after this experience. Some teachers visited the library more frequently, spent more time there, and checked out more materials. In addition, students in these teachers' courses began to use the library much more effectively.

It is generally conceded that teaching library usage is difficult in a classroom setting removed from the library materials themselves. However, students can learn important points about the library prior to a library visit. Several teachers in one school built a model card catalog drawer using a box for 3-by-5-inch index cards and compiled approximately 100 author cards ranging from A through Z. The teachers used this model in various classrooms, particularly in working with individual students who were not yet competent in using the card catalog. Another useful teaching device was a library checklist that teachers and the librarian devised. The list consisted of 8 or 10 specific tasks for the students to perform with teacher direction. Examples included:

1. Find the book *King of the Wind* by Marguerite Henry.

2. a. Who is the author of the book *A Child's History of Art?* _____

  _____

  b. What is the call number of this book? _____

  c. Fill out a library card for this book. _____

3. Where are the bound volumes of *My Weekly Reader* located? _____

  _____

These items provided guided practice in using title and author cards, locating books and journals on the shelves, and filling out library request cards properly. Other tasks covered specific information about the library.

To use this checklist technique effectively, small groups or individual students go to the library at specific times. The librarian briefly demonstrates and explains how to use certain facilities in the library. Each student then receives a checklist of tasks, which the librarian reviews briefly to ensure that students understand them. Such tasks should vary according to grade level and individual student needs.

Using Reference Materials. Using reference materials is an important study skill that generally is not thoroughly taught in our schools. Many students reach high school or even college with only a hazy idea of how to systematically search available materials. Although many students in the upper primary grades are ready for limited use of reference materials, teachers have a major responsibility to teach these skills in the intermediate grades.

The Encyclopedia. The use of encyclopedias and other reference books should be deliberately and systematically taught. If such materials are in the classroom, different groups of students can learn their use at various times. Instruction should parallel points already covered; for example, topics are arranged in alphabetical order, books are numbered in a series, the alphabetical range covered is indicated on the cover, and cross listings and key words must be used.

Any given unit in any content area can provide the framework for teaching efficient use of the encyclopedia. Assume a health class is considering the topic "The Adventure of Medicine." The teacher asks students to list all of the possible headings under which they might find information relating to the topic. The responses might range from one suggestion, "look under medicine," to a half page of suggestions, including medicine, surgery, disease, medical research, drugs, germ theory, space medicine, and public health. Other headings might include particular diseases, such as cancer, tuberculosis, yellow fever, diabetes, or poliomyelitis, or the names of individuals who made significant medical discoveries, such as Walter Reed, Jonas Salk, and Louis Pasteur.

An encyclopedia is a book or series of books that contains a little information about a great number of topics. A user must know what heading, or topic, to look under for particular information. Usually, an encyclopedia contains hundreds of headings that tell the reader "see _____," which is another heading under which the topic is discussed. For instance:

baking soda; *see* soda
Old Faithful; *see* Wyoming, Yellowstone National Park
Lennon, John; *see* Beatles
knee jerk; *see* reflex action
toadstool; *see* mushroom

INSTRUCTIONAL ACTIVITY

■ *Using the Encyclopedia.* Using the following drawing, have students write the number of the volumes that will likely contain the information called for in the following questions.

Vol. 1 A	Vol. 2 B	Vol. 3 C	Vol. 4 D-E	Vol. 5 F	Vol. 6 G	Vol. 7 H	Vol. 8 I-J	Vol. 9 K-L	Vol. 10 M	Vol. 11 N	Vol. 12 O-P	Vol. 13 Q-R	Vol. 14 S	Vol. 15 T-U	Vol. 16 V-Z

_____ 1. Is more money spent on newspaper advertising or television advertising?

_____ 2. Where would you find hitches, knots, and splices?

_____ 3. Where would you find timber wolves?

_____ 4. Is there a bird called a kite?

_____ 5. What is a spelling demon?

_____ 6. Where would you find data on animals that sleep through the winter?

_____ 7. What are the previous names of the city of Leningrad?

_____ 8. What is the habitat of the Eastern gray squirrel?

Maps. The ability to read maps is important in our highly mobile society. Students should have opportunities to develop this skill in various content areas. Formats for teaching map reading can involve the entire class as well as individual students, pairs, or teams of pupils pursuing given learning tasks.

INSTRUCTIONAL ACTIVITIES

■ ***Using Maps.*** Use a series of letters to represent the location of the major cities. Have students identify those cities. Draw a line connecting two cities (e.g., San Francisco and St. Louis). Have students estimate the number of miles or kilometers between them. Using numbers to represent various states, have students identify the selected states. Have them identify lakes, rivers, mountain ranges, national parks, time zones, and so on. Have students color or crosshatch a state or region that is a major producer of oil, wheat, coal, iron ore, or other materials.

Assign students the following exercises based on the simple outline map of the continental United States shown next.

Can you locate the various states and major cities on a map of the U.S?

1. The state of Missouri is represented by an X. Starting at the north and moving clockwise, name the states that border on Missouri.

2. The number 2 indicates a state formed at the outbreak of the Civil War; it is

_____ .

3. The inland state marked 3 has more water boundary than land boundary. It is

   _____.

4. The number 4 is found in the state of _____.

5. The state directly west of the state marked 4 is _____

6. Does Idaho border on Canada? (Answer yes or no.)

7. Write the name for city A. It is a state capital and the burial place of Abraham Lincoln.

8. The letter B locates a city identified with the "Birth of the Blues" and is the home of Dixieland jazz.

9. Two cities in California are marked C and D. C represents _____;
   D represents _____.

10. Write the name of the southwestern state marked with an E.

   Use the same type of activity in map study of foreign countries and regions, such as Central and South America, Europe, Africa, and Asia.

■ **Map Reading.**   Through the use of actual road maps, develop a number of map-reading activities. For one activity, plan a trip from Lisbon, Portugal, to Paris, France. Select the fastest route. Select the most scenic route. List, in order, the highways on which you will travel. Estimate the approximate distance to be traveled on each route. Plan side trips to historical sites or parks.

   Maps often contain guides for finding places or cities (Heilman & Holmes, 1978). Example A tells us how to locate Detroit. Example B locates Austin, Texas.

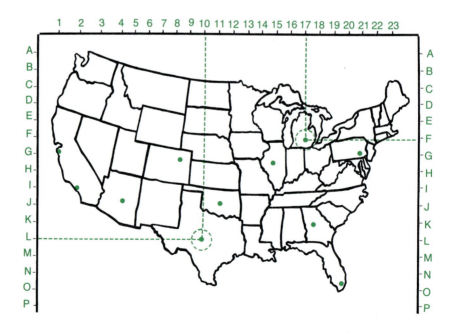

- Example A: Detroit, Michigan, is found by drawing a line down from 17 and a line over from F. The place where the two lines meet is the location of Detroit.

- Example B: Lines drawn down from 10 and over from L locate the capital city of Texas, which is Austin.

INSTRUCTIONAL ACTIVITIES

- *Find the City.* The problems that follow provide clues that will guide you to certain cities. You are to name these cities. Complete all the problems you can without using a map. Then use a map of the United States if needed. You need not draw lines on the map; use imaginary ones.

_____	H–15	The capital city of a midwestern state; Lincoln is buried there.
_____	I–1	Not a state capital, but the largest city in Southern California.
_____	J–11	A capital of a southwestern state (Will Rogers country).
_____	D–23	The capital of a state located in the northeast corner of the United States.
_____	K–17	The capital and largest industrial city of this southeastern state.
_____	C–7	Straight lines drawn from these points intersect in this state.
_____	G–21	A large city in eastern Pennsylvania (not the capital).
_____	J–4	The capital of a southwestern state.
_____	O–20	An Atlantic coastal city.
_____	G–8	The "mile-high city" and a state capital.

Critical Reading Skills

Locating information is an important part of the learning process, but it is only a small step toward the goal of assimilating material. The ability to locate information has little impact on personal or academic growth if one is unable to read critically the material located.

Teaching students how to read critically is undoubtedly the most difficult task attempted in our schools. A literate person not only possesses facts, but also can analyze information and think divergently. Analyzing and evaluating information presented in text are synonymous with critical reading. Critical reading abilities involved in content reading include:

- Knowing what the author has said.

- Grasping the validity of statements and knowing when and how to verify them with other sources.

- Differentiating between facts and opinions.

- Noting when inferences are being drawn and drawing them when they are not stated.

- Detecting author bias as well as inaccuracies that might not be traceable to bias.

- Understanding your own biases as these relate to what is being read.

- Taking into consideration an author's use of allusions, satire, humor, irony, and the like.

- Developing some criteria for judging an author's competency in the area in which he or she writes.

Undoubtedly this list could be extended. The abilities are developmental in nature, so they should be taught at all grade levels. These critical reading abilities are not important by themselves but are a means to an end. Students need considerable meaningful practice to see how these skills apply to materials they encounter in their own lives. As in all content reading instruction, teachers need to review and reinforce reading abilities continually to ensure that students become independent learners. Students will face increasingly difficult reading tasks in the content areas, and their competency will need to grow if they are to learn. This need continues through high school and beyond. How many adults are immune to propaganda, know both sides of controversial issues, and do not let their emotions color their interpretations while reading?

Inability to discern what an author is saying may well be evidence of inability to read material critically, but paraphrasing, by itself, is not evidence of critical reading, either. Restating the gist of a passage but failing to detect author bias results in a transfer of author bias to the reader. Knowing what the author is saying without realizing that some statements contradict facts is not critical reading, nor is reciting strongly expressed opinions as if these were statements of fact. Interpreting and evaluating require applying various mechanical reading skills and higher level abilities. Students need both teacher-directed instruction and systematic practice to develop effective work habits and study techniques (Stotsky, 1983).

Knowledge of Propaganda. Resisting propaganda depends to a large degree on the reader's background or knowledge of the techniques people use to manipulate the facts. Critical readers assume responsibility for questions. Although they respect language, they know that some people use it to control others' behavior. The purpose here is not to explain all of various propaganda techniques used to obscure meaning or take the reader on a detour, but to provide examples to help students detect these devices.

INSTRUCTIONAL ACTIVITIES

- ***Identifying Propaganda Techniques.*** To introduce the concept of propaganda, list a number of popular propaganda techniques. Provide illustrations and discuss them with the class. Then guide students in writing examples. Discuss these examples and elaborate upon them in relation to the earlier discussion. Following are some propaganda techniques:

- Begging the issue or throwing up a smoke screen. Here one does not discuss the real issue, but switches the discussion to other topics. For example, candidate *A* has charged that *B* has violated the law by not filing a statement of his campaign expenses. *B* replies, "A has accused me of not filing a statement of expenses. Why should he care? Is he a police officer? Have I ever lied to the voters? Who voted against raising taxes last year? I'll tell you who did—I did! And I'll tell you something else—*A* voted for the tax bill. I support every worthwhile charity in this community; I was born here; I went to school here! Can *A* make this statement?"
- Generalizing from too few cases.
- Ignoring the idea and attacking the person suggesting it.
- Using a false analogy.
- Appealing to authority.
- Relying on guilt by association.
- Using a faulty cause-and-effect relationship.
- Misusing figures or statistics.

- *Thinking Critically.* Prepare a number of propositions that might be an issue in any community. Follow each proposition with an imaginary statement that someone included in a letter to the editor. Have the students analyze and point out what the writer was up to. Following are several examples:

- Proposition: The city council should pass an ordinance requiring fluoridation of the city water supply in an effort to decrease tooth decay among children of the community. Letter to the Editor: "Of course some people favor fluoridation; they spend so much time in the Roaring Twenties Bar that they probably don't drink enough water to care how it tastes."
  Letter No. 2: "The real issue is that fluoride is a poison. We shouldn't poison our fine water supply." Beware of jumping to a conclusion: Fluoride is a poison. What is the missing detail?

- Proposition: The voters should approve a proposed school bond issue.
  Letter to the Editor: "As Lincoln said, 'You can fool all of the people some of the time,' and this is one of those times! Our schools are as good as any in the country. The people pushing this school bond proposal want to raise your taxes. I say vote this bond issue down."

- Proposition: We should adopt a city ordinance, proposed as a safety measure, that would prohibit the sale of fireworks.
  Letter to the Editor: "The Fourth of July is one of our great holidays. This proposal is unpatriotic. It is a direct slap at free enterprise. A lot of American firms make fireworks. The next thing you know somebody will try to outlaw automobiles because people get hurt in accidents."

- Proposition: The city should construct a swimming pool in the city park.
  Letter to the Editor: "The people in this town do not want a municipal pool. It is

obvious that if the people favored this harebrained idea, we would have had a pool by now!"

- Proposition: We should extend the runways at our municipal airport so that jet planes can land here. Letter to the Editor: "When we built the airport, the planners said the present layout would be adequate for at least 20 years. That was just 10 years ago. These people are experts, and we should listen to them."

Clues to Reading the News.   Teachers use newspapers and other mass media for teaching both critical analysis and the mechanical skills related to such analysis. The potential values of using such materials are numerous. There are also barriers to significant learning, including inadequate planning and the tendency to avoid discussion of controversial issues. Teachers should permit and encourage students to interpret and analyze advertisements, political cartoons, editorials, and syndicated columns. Develop clues to the news by direct instruction, focusing on discussing editorials, political cartoons, propaganda techniques, and current issues.

INSTRUCTIONAL ACTIVITIES

- *Analyzing Editorials.*   In four or five metropolitan newspapers, compare editorials that deal with a particular current issue. Assuming that there are differences of opinion, what might account for these differences? What is the political orientation of the editor or publisher? Does a particular newspaper have a standing policy on certain issues (e.g., labor and management or foreign aid)?

- *Analyzing Political Cartoons.*   Gather political cartoons that deal with the same topic from different papers and drawn by different artists. Direct students to analyze and verbalize what the cartoon is attempting to say. Student interpretation of any given stimulus will vary considerably. This will facilitate discussion and help students to see the importance of the reader's background, which includes bias, emotional attachments, and the like. Such factors always influence interpretation of a cartoon, editorial, feature article, or news story.

- *Analyzing Propaganda Techniques.*   Prepare and duplicate an editorial that contains biased statements, factual errors, and various propaganda techniques. Give each student a copy of the material and direct edits or rewrites of the editorial. Next, have the class discuss the original materials and the substitutions, deletions, and corrections that they made. In many cases, students' reactions will be markedly different, particularly if the topic is chosen wisely. In the discussion, students will be exposed to a variety of viewpoints different from their own.

- *Studying Current Issues.*   To study a current issue longitudinally:

1. Compare different newspaper and news magazine treatments of the problem.
2. Attempt to account for differences in the editorial points of view.
3. Study the interpretations of several columnists or news analysts.
4. Analyze the day-to-day statements of the decision makers or spokespersons attempting to mold public opinion. Based on the issue being studied, these might be

legislative leaders, state department officials, labor leaders, candidates for high office, the President, or White House staff.

Distinguishing Between Fact and Opinion. In content-area reading materials, students frequently must decide whether a statement is fact or opinion. Inexperienced readers develop habits that are not always helpful in this type of problem solving. One such habit is a tendency to accept what is written as factual. In addition, when a reader strongly agrees with a statement, he or she frequently accepts it as a fact. Finally, young readers may accept as fact a position that is developed logically or is repeated often enough. Thus, the statement "finding a four-leaf clover *always* brings good luck" may be doubted, but the statement "finding a four-leaf clover *can* bring good luck," may seem a bit more logical.

Probably the best way to help students learn how to differentiate fact from opinion is planned discussion of statements they encounter in textual material. This is difficult to do, however, when a teacher is limited to a particular textbook or certain materials. Another possibility is collecting statements of fact and opinion from various sources and discussing these. Obviously, all items may pertain to one subject area such as social studies, health, geography, or literature. On the other hand, exercises may deal with general statements or cut across various content areas.

INSTRUCTIONAL ACTIVITY

■ ***Fact Versus Opinion.*** Have students read each statement carefully. If the sentence states a fact, write *F* on the line in front of the sentence. If the sentence states an opinion, write *O*.

_____ Democracy is the best form of government.

_____ Wild animals will not attack if you do not run.

_____ Pollution is the most serious problem in the world today.

_____ Rich people do not pay a fair share of taxes.

_____ Football is the roughest of all sports.

_____ Different brands of aspirin are essentially the same.

_____ Compact cars are not as safe as larger cars.

_____ The United States spends too much money on arms and weapons during peacetime.

_____ People will never be able to settle on the moon.

_____ In the United States, women live longer than men.

SUMMARY /

Content reading presents many challenges to both students and teachers. To be successful in reading content materials, readers must know the characteristics and demands of expository text. To maximize student understanding, teachers must understand the concept of readability and factors that determine the difficulty of content material. To facilitate successful reading of expository text, teachers should actively teach and guide student involvement in (1) content reading vocabulary; (2) studying strategies to employ before, during, and after reading; (3) reading and study skills; (4) locational skills; and (5) critical reading skills. Skills in these five areas should be taught in a direct fashion integrated into the curriculum. Following instruction, an abundance of varied and interesting practice will help ensure that students transfer these skills automatically to expository text.

YOUR POINT OF VIEW /

Discussion Questions

1. Why is it possible that certain students may be proficient readers in science and also be incompetent readers in social studies?
2. The statement "Every teacher should be a teacher of reading" was first made more than 50 years ago. Why do you think it has not become a reality?
3. With regard to the studying strategies discussed in the chapter, how do teacher and student behaviors change before, during, and after reading strategies?

Take a Stand For or Against

1. Reading skills pertinent to specific content areas should be exclusively taught by content teachers.
2. The organizational structure of classrooms prohibits individualized instruction in the content areas.

BIBLIOGRAPHY /

Anderson, R. C. (1984). Role of the reader's schema in comprehension, learning, and memory. In R. C. Anderson, J. Osborn, & R. J. Tierney (Eds.), *Learning to read in American schools: Basal readers and content texts*. Hillsdale, NJ: Lawrence Erlbaum Associates, 243–257.

Anderson, R. C., Hiebert, E. H., Scott, J. A., & Wilkinson, I. (1985). *Becoming a nation of readers: The report of the commission on reading* (contract No. 400-83-0057). Washington, DC: National Institute of Education.

Armbruster, B. B. (1991). Using literature in the content areas. *The Reading Teacher, 45*, 324–325.

Armbruster, B. B., & Nagy, W. E. (1992). Vocabulary in content area lessons. *The Reading Teacher, 45*, 550–551.

Babbs, P. J., & Moe, A. J. (1983). Metacognition: A key for independent learning from text. *The Reading Teacher, 36*, 422–426.

Flavell, J. H. (1976). Metacognitive aspects of problem solving. In L. B. Resnick (Ed.), *The nature of intelligence*. Hillsdale, NJ: Lawrence Erlbaum Associates.

Forgan, H. W., & Mangrum, C. T. (1989). *Teaching content area reading skills: A modular program for preservice and inservie teachers* (4th ed.). New York: Merrill/Macmillan Publishing Co.

French, M. P., Danielson, K. E., Conn, M., Gale, W., Lueck, C., & Manley, M. (1989). In the classroom: Reading and writing in the content areas. *The Reading Teacher, 43*, 266-271.

Haggard, M. R. (1988). Developing critical thinking with the directed reading-thinking activity. *The Reading Teacher, 41,* 526–535.

Heilman, A. W., & Holmes, E. A. (1978). *Smuggling language into the teaching of reading* (2nd ed.). Columbus, OH: Merrill Publishing Co.

Heimlich, J. E., & Pittleman, S. D. (1986). *Semantic mapping: Classroom applications.* Newark, DE: International Reading Association.

Holbrook, H. T. (1987). Writing to learn in the social studies ERIC/RCS. *The Reading Teacher, 41,* 216–219.

Irwin, J. W., & Davis, C. A. (1980). Assessing readability: The checklist approach. *Journal of Reading, 24,* 129–130.

Johnson, D. D., & Pearson, P. D. (1984). *Teaching reading vocabulary* (2nd ed.). New York: Holt, Rinehart & Winston.

Jones, M. P. (1986). *Effects of the reciprocal teaching method on third graders' decoding and comprehension abilities.* Doctoral dissertation, Texas A&M University, College Station.

Kinney, M. A. (1985). A language experience approach to teaching expository text structure. *The Reading Teacher, 38,* 854–856.

McGee, L. M., & Richgels, D. J. (1985). Teaching expository text structure to elementary students. *The Reading Teacher, 38,* 739–749.

Meyer, B. J. F., & Freedle, R. O. (1984). Effects of discourse type of recall. *American Educational Research Journal, 21,* 121–143.

Myers, J. W. (1984). *Writing to learn across the curriculum.* Bloomington, IN: Phi Delta Kappa.

Nagy, W. E. (1988). *Teaching vocabulary to improve reading comprehension.* Urbana, IL: ERIC Clearinghouse on Reading and Communication Skills and Newark, DE: International Reading Association.

Ogle, D. M. (1986). K-W-L: A teaching model that develops active reading of expository text. *The Reading Teacher, 39,* 564–570.

Olson, M. W., and Gee, T. C. (1991). Content reading instruction in the primary grades: Perceptions and strategies. *The Reading Teacher, 45,* 298–307.

Palincsar, A. S., & Brown, A. L. (1986). Interactive teaching to promote independent learning from text. *The Reading Teacher, 39,* 771–777.

Pescosolido, J. R., Schell, L. M., & Laurent, M. J. (1967). *Reading approaches and rituals.* Dubuque, IA: Kendall/Hunt Publishing Co.

Readence, J. E., Bean, T. W., & Baldwin, R. S. (1981). *Content area reading: An integrated approach.* New York: Harper & Row.

Richardson, J. S., & Morgan, R. F. (1993). *Reading to learn in the content areas* (2nd ed.). Belmont, CA: Wadworth Publishing Co.

Robinson, F. P. (1961). *Effective study* (rev. ed.). New York: Harper & Row.

Shores, J. (1943). Skills related to the ability to read history and science. *Journal of Educational Research, 36,* 584–594.

Smith, C. C., & Bean, T. W. (1980). The guided writing procedure: Integrating content reading and writing improvement. *Reading World, 19,* 724–738.

Stauffer, R. (1975). *Directing the reading-thinking process.* New York: Harper & Row.

Stotsky, S. (1983). Research on reading/writing relationships: A synthesis and suggested directions. *Language Arts, 60,* 627–642.

Tadlock, D. F. (1978). SQ3R—Why it works, based on an information processing theory of learning. *The Journal of Reading, 22,* 110–116.

Zakaluk, B. L., & Samuels, S. J. (1988). Toward a new approach to predicting text comprehensibility. In B. L. Zakaluk & S. J. Samuels (Eds.), *Readability: Its past, present, and future.* Newark, DE: International Reading Association.

IV

Implementing a Reading Program

OVERVIEW

If all literacy instruction could be the same for all students in each grade, teaching would be easy. The complexity of teaching reading becomes obvious to teachers when they try to differentiate their instruction according to student needs. This part focuses on essential topics necessary for successful elementary school literacy programs. The three chapters will discuss assessment of students' literacy abilities, classroom management and organization, and the provision of appropriate education for culturally and language-diverse, gifted, and special-needs students. Our growing understanding of literacy development and of effective teaching have increased our appreciation of the subtleties and complexities in the learning process. This part will provide important information to help you provide effective reading instruction.

INTEGRATING PRINCIPLES OF TEACHING READING

The following principles, presented in Chapter 1, will be reinforced in this part:

- Reading and writing are interrelated and interactive processes, and literacy instruction should capitalize on this relationship.

- The use of quality literature should be an integral part of literacy instruction throughout the entire school curriculum.

- Proper literacy instruction depends on the ongoing assessment of each student's reading strengths and weaknesses.

- Teachers must provide for the needs of exceptional children in regular classroom literacy instruction.

- Teachers must be able to create, manage, and maintain an environment conducive to learning.

- Teachers of literacy must forge partnerships with the home and community to promote reading growth.

- Motivation contributes to the development of literacy.

11

Literacy Assessment

For the Reader

Do you remember the achievement tests you took when you were in elementary school? Each student had a test booklet and spent parts of several days taking the tests. Such tests are still widely used today, and many new tests are appearing every year.

The only justifiable purpose for the use of literacy tests is to obtain information about students' reading and writing abilities in order to design and improve the quality of literacy programs for them. In practice, however, some schools and teachers believe that testing programs per se have educational value. Sometimes testing becomes an end in itself rather than a basis for instruction. In some communities, a metal filing cabinet with a folder for each student represents evidence of good teaching practices. This phenomenon suggests that some teachers have forgotten that assessment alone has no beneficial effect on students. As you read this chapter, focus on how to assess students' reading and writing and how to use this information in planning and evaluating your instruction.

Key Ideas

- Ongoing assessment of students' literacy development and teachers' instruction forms the foundation for planning literacy instruction and determining its effectiveness.

- Students' reading and writing abilities can be assessed through the use of (1) norm-referenced tests, (2) criterion-referenced tests, (3) placement tests, (4) informal reading inventories (IRIs), and (5) teacher-developed procedures.

- Standardized reading tests only sample students' reading (and sometimes writing) behaviors and provide only a small piece of a much larger picture.

- Informal and teacher-developed procedures are more valuable because they use assessment strategies that are more in line with the current thinking about literacy learning.

- An effective reading teacher interacts with students as they engage in reading and writing to assess the processes the students employ.

Key Terms

norm-referenced tests standardized tests designed to compare the performance of an individual or individuals with the performance of a norming group.

criterion-referenced tests (CRTs) tests designed to measure specific behaviors performed by an individual in relation to mastery of a specific skill.

validity the degree to which test results serve the uses for which they are intended.

reliability the degree to which the results of a measurement instrument are consistent.

informal reading inventory (IRI) a series of grade-level word lists, passages, and comprehension questions ranging from preprimer through grade 8 or higher that are used to identify a student's independent, instructional, and frustration reading levels.

cloze procedure an informal diagnostic procedure that omits words from freestanding passages to identify reading levels and provide information about a reader's ability to deal with content and structure.

anecdotal records written records that describe an event or product and relate the anecdote to information known about an individual.

response journals written responses—between the student and teacher or between two students—to a learning experience and responses of others that are read.

portfolios folders that hold samples of students' work selected by the student and teacher. Can include observational notes, students' self-evaluations, writing examples, lists of books read, progress notes, interviews, and inventories.

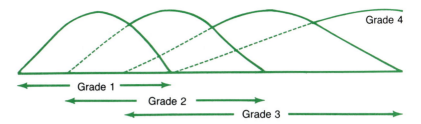

FIGURE 11.1
Graphic representation of reading abilities in the primary grades. Note that the range of abilities increases at each succeeding grade level.

MEETING INDIVIDUAL NEEDS

Ongoing assessment of students' reading and writing development forms the foundation for planning both reading and writing instruction and determining its effectiveness. Information about students' literacy strengths and weaknesses allows teachers to select instructional strategies and materials in relation to students' needs. The key here is not simply gathering information about students' reading and writing, but determining how to use the information to optimize growth for each student.

Students at any given grade level show great differences in their literacy skills and abilities. Some of them read and write at a level considerably below their grade level placement, while others have advanced literacy capabilities. Figure 11.1 illustrates the overlap between grades and the range of abilities found at the primary level.

These facts, which apply to practically every classroom, emphasize the need for differentiated instruction. One criterion that distinguishes excellent literacy programs from others is the degree to which they accommodate individual needs. Teachers must be alert to differences among students in order to follow sound teaching principles. Only various means of assessment can help teachers determine needs and plan instruction for students whose needs vary considerably. Assessment should be ongoing, since students change rapidly. An assessment conducted in September may be followed by a student having a breakthrough in some vital skill or by a failure to understand some new step in reading and writing. In either case, the earlier assessment is obsolete.

Assessment of literacy strengths and weaknesses can take a variety of forms, including standardized tests, informal tests, observation, portfolios, and interaction with learning tasks and activities. Although tests are designed for use at every grade level, no purpose would be served by a separate discussion of tests for each instructional level. The following discussion of assessment applies to the various levels of the elementary school.

STANDARDIZED TESTS

Standardized tests sample students' reading in a controlled, systematic fashion. Procedures for administering, scoring, and interpreting each test are determined under controlled experimental conditions. These procedures are usually explained in a manual accompanying the test.

Essentially, schools use two types of commercially published standardized reading tests: (1) *norm-referenced* and (2) *criterion-referenced.* Both may feature similar types of test items, but each serves a different purpose and has a different interpretation. Norm-referenced tests are used to compare a student's performance with that of a representative sample (the norming group) of students. Criterion-referenced tests compare students' performance with criteria that have been identified as skill areas or abilities that students are to master.

Commercially printed standardized tests fall into two classes: (1) those designed for group administration and (2) those designed to be administered individually. Both give credit for acceptable responses and determine the student's score by correct responses, lack of errors, and rate of reading.

Typical Features

Commercially published standardized tests usually provide a manual of directions for administering, scoring, and interpreting them. Information contained in the manual generally includes (1) an overview; (2) directions for administering; (3) directions for scoring; (4) a description of the types of scores; (5) procedures for using the results; and (6) information on development, national norms, reliability, validity, and other technical aspects.

Read the administrator's manual carefully to ensure that you understand fully each important aspect of administering, scoring, and interpreting the test. Failure to administer the test according to the manual can seriously jeopardize the *validity* of the test results. A valid test is one that measures what it purports to measure. In addition to studying the manual carefully, it is a good idea to take the test yourself. This allows you to become familiar with what the students must do when taking the test. Furthermore, by giving close attention to individual test items, you can determine how well the test fits the class based on past reading instruction. If the items do not accurately reflect past reading instruction, then the test lacks content validity and the results have little value in decisions about students' reading and writing.

Most standardized tests have a template or scoring key to facilitate rapid, accurate hand scoring of answer sheets. A large number of norm-referenced test publishers also provide computer scoring service for their test users.

Although computer scoring frees the teacher from spending time scoring each student's test, the teacher often must wait for the results. The teacher thus cannot immediately use the test results to plan and implement reading instruction.

Reliability. The consistency with which a test measures reading skills is referred to as its *reliability.* A reliable test provides a stable sample of students' reading performance. For example, if test X was administered to a student in September, you would expect that administering the test 2 or 3 weeks later would result in a similar score. If the student's score was 80 on the first administration and 15 on the second administration, however, then it is impossible to decide which score accurately reflects the student's reading ability. Such a test would be highly unreliable because it does not consistently sample students' reading skills.

Test reliability is generally reported in the administrator's manual and is expressed as a coefficient of reliability. Tests with reliability coefficients of .80 or above are considered highly reliable. Test X presented in the earlier example would have a low coefficient of reliability. Reliability is one important feature to consider when selecting or interpreting students' reading performance on standardized tests. High reliability does not ensure, however, that a test is also valid.

Validity.   As noted earlier, a valid test measures what it purports to measure. As with reliability, the administrator's manual also discusses the validity of a standardized test. Several different types of validity are important to consider in relation to the intended use of the test results, including content validity and criterion-related validity.

Content validity means that the test items are an accurate sampling of reading instruction content and the behavioral changes under consideration. A test may be called a reading test, and the test items may be easily identified as measuring reading skills, but the test still may not have content validity. Content validity means that the test measured the same aspects of reading that students had an opportunity to learn in the instructional program.

If the results from a test are used to predict future reading performance or estimate current performance in a reading task (i.e., mastery or lack of mastery in reading skill areas), then criterion-related validity is extremely important. Criterion-related validity is especially crucial in reading readiness tests, which are used to predict the likelihood of success in beginning reading tasks. The administrator's manual for readiness tests specifies criterion-related validity as a coefficient of correlation between performance on the readiness test and other standardized tests measuring beginning reading ability. The higher the validity coefficient, the more accurately the readiness test predicts later reading performance.

Norm-Referenced Tests

Norm-referenced tests compare the performance of an individual or individuals with the performance of a norming group. The norming group generally consists of a large sample of students who are representative of the national school population. These students take the test, and their performance determines the test's national norms. Following this, each student's raw score (total number of correct responses) on the test is compared to the norming data.

Several types of norms compare an individual's relative standing to a defined variable. Norming information found in the administrator's manual is based on the test's national norms. Similar norms, however, can be developed locally for a school district, school, or individual classroom. Most standardized norm-referenced tests provide for the conversion of a student's raw score to a percentile rank, stanine, and grade-level equivalent.

Percentile Ranks. Percentile ranks range from 1 to 99 and indicate the percentage of students in the norming group that scored at or below a given score. For example, if a raw score of 62 is equal to a percentile rank of 80, this means that the student did as well as or better than 80 percent of the individuals in the norming group. A percentile rank of 50 represents the median, or middle score, and indicates average performance.

Ongoing assessment of students' reading and writing development form the foundation for effective instruction.

Stanines. Stanines also indicate a student's relative standing in comparison to other students in the norming group. As the term implies, stanines range from a low of 1 to a high of 9. Stanines 1 through 3 usually indicate below-average performance, 4 through 6 average performance, and 7 through 9 above-average performance. Stanines represent a range of scores rather than a specific score. For example, a raw score of 28 at the 77th percentile and a raw score of 31 at the 88th percentile could be equivalent to stanine 7. Stanines represent units that are approximately equal; a difference between stanines 5 and 7 is about the same as the difference represented by stanines 3 and 5. Because of this, stanines can help in comparing a student's performance across various sections of a test.

Grade-Level Equivalents. Grade-level equivalents of raw scores on a norm-referenced test indicate a student's performance in relation to the average score for the grade level of the norming group. Grade-level scores are reported by school grade and tenths of the school year. A grade-level equivalent of 4.0 indicates that a student's raw score equals the score of the average fourth grader in the norming population.

A grade-level equivalent is not necessarily the same as the level at which a student should be reading. A fourth grader who scored a grade-level equivalent of 6.5 on a recently administered standardized test should not be given sixth grade work. Likewise, a fourth grader who received a grade equivalent of 2.5 probably should not be instructed at the second-grade level. In the former example, the grade equivalent suggests that this student is above average. In the latter example, the grade equivalent indicates that this student may be a low achiever for his or her grade.

Criterion-Referenced Tests

Criterion-referenced tests (CRTs) are designed to measure students' mastery of specific reading skills. Rather than comparing a student's performance to that of the norming group, CRTs view performance in relation to mastery level of one or more skills. These skills are usually stated as performance, or behavioral, objectives; for example, "Student will identify correctly the order of events found in short reading passages."

CRTs include several items for each reading objective. A student's response to these items is evaluated in terms of the number of correct items for each objective. Evaluation typically compares the student's performance to established criteria. For example, if 20 items test an objective, a student who scores 16 or more correct may have mastered the skill, 15 to 12 correct answers might indicate that review is needed, and fewer than 12 correct items could indicate a need for reteaching the skill. Some criterion-referenced tests use only one criterion of performance to indicate mastery or lack of mastery: 15 out of 20 similar items correct may mean mastery, but fewer than 15 correct is lack of mastery.

Diagnostic Tests

In addition to standardized achievement tests that contain reading subtests, standardized diagnostic reading tests are available for classroom use. These tests help teachers pinpoint specific reading strengths and weaknesses in a variety of areas. Diagnostic tests have more subtests than achievement tests. They also test items related to specific reading behaviors. The number of subtests included on diagnostic reading tests varies; however, most of them have from 5 to 10.

Many standardized tests can provide information about students' reading. All norm-referenced achievement batteries designed to test elementary students contain reading subtests. These tests usually provide a vocabulary score, a comprehension score, and a total reading score (the average of vocabulary and comprehension). Many criterion-referenced reading tests include subtests that focus on specific aspects of word identification and comprehension. With so many different reading tests, it is no surprise that many measure virtually the same aspects of reading. Nevertheless, tests vary significantly in what they measure, their intended level of difficulty, the care that went into their construction, and their ease of administration. Each of these factors influences two important attributes of reading tests: (1) how consistently they measure reading skills and (2) how well they actually measure the skills that they supposedly measure.

Cautions About Standardized Tests

Standardized tests have been criticized because they do not reflect all of the skills and capabilities associated with literacy, are often assumed to accurately measure students' learning, and provide little information on students' problem solving capabilities and learning processes (Winograd, Paris, & Bridge, 1991). Students bring much more to a reading task than a standardized test can sample. Nonetheless, many school districts and states still require the administration of standardized tests for reading and writing. Some states, such as Kentucky, have recently argued for authentic assessment, sampling both students' performance in important learning tasks (discussing books read) and students' products (writing samples).

Standardized tests only sample students' literacy in relation to the tasks (identifying words in context, selecting word definitions) and do not provide a broad view of how well an individual reads. Teachers should view results from standardized tests as only one part of a much larger picture of a student's literacy. Also, test results provide little meaningful information that teachers can use to improve the quality of their literacy instruction and better address needs of individual students. The shortcomings of standardized tests were recently noted by Early (1992/1993): "The need to know how children are doing persists—with teachers, with parents, with the children themselves—but recently gained knowledge of the reading process convinces us that standardized tests fail to measure those processes accurately, wholly, or diagnostically" (p. 306).

Informal assessment is much more valuable in helping teachers determine students' literacy development and adjust literacy instruction accordingly.

INFORMAL ASSESSMENT

Conventional literacy tests examine the products of a student's performance (such as instructional level; specific skill strengths and weaknesses; and national, state, or local ranking), not the processes a reader and writer employs. Yet, certain strategic processes characterize effective reading and writing.

The discrepancy between our knowledge of effective reading and writing and the prevailing assessment procedures has prompted many experts to recommend changes in how we assess literacy. Valencia and Pearson (1987) synthesize this position and report on the process of dynamic assessment identified by Campione and Brown (1985), stating:

Given such a view, the best possible assessment of reading would seem to occur when teachers observe and interact with students as they read authentic texts for genuine purposes. As teachers interact with students, they evaluate the way[s] in which the students construct meaning, intervening to provide support or suggestions when the students appear to have difficulty. (p. 728)

While our knowledge of various reading strategies has dramatically improved in the last 20 years, effective teachers have always known the value of simultaneous assessment and instruction. In interacting with students, effective teachers assess each student's reading strategies. In doing so, they look at the student's use of prior knowledge, story structure, headings, self-questioning, and purpose setting. They also look at how the student understands main ideas, summarizes key points, infers relationships, and rereads parts for clarification. This is called process-oriented assessment.

The most powerful assessment tool is keen teacher observation. Knowing what to look and listen for and then translating this information into instructional decisions to improve students' ability to understand text are hallmarks of an effective reading teacher.

Walker (1992) addresses this quality of assessment during instruction to emphasize the reflective and self-monitoring attitude of effective teachers:

As the diagnostic teacher assesses while she instructs, she evaluates children's present use of strategies in a specific context. Then she investigates their understanding of the reading process (i.e., how active they are). Do they use both text-based processing and reader-based processing when they are reading? If not, what can she do to help them understand the active nature of reading? When she has modified the task, do they gain more understanding and control of their reading processes? With this line of questioning, the diagnostic teacher thinks about what students already know that she can use to guide them to more integrated understanding of the reading process. (p. 44)

Classroom reading teachers can modify existing informal tests to accentuate the processes of reading rather than the products. They can add expository passages to the traditional narrative or expand the passage length to more realistically assess a student's reading skills and abilities. Before reading, they can informally assess prior knowledge by asking questions and initiating discussions with the student. After reading, they can ask questions, encourage retellings, and promote discussion to assess summarizing or inferencing abilities. Additionally, teachers can assess metacognition by asking students how they make sense of what they read.

Teale, Hiebert, and Chittendon (1987) argue that teachers need to pay particular attention to assessment and its relation to instruction during early literacy development. Encouraging teachers to work informally with children to assess emergent literacy, the authors list the following principles to ensure that assessment facilitates the curriculum goals:

1. Assessment is a part of instruction.

2. Assessment methods and instruments are varied.

3. Assessment focuses on a broad range of skills and knowledge reflecting the various dimensions of literacy.

4. Assessment occurs continuously.

5. Literacy is assessed in a variety of contexts.

6. Measures are appropriate for children's development[al] levels and cultural background[s]. (pp. 773–774)

The most powerful assessment tool is keen teacher observation.

The purpose of assessment is to pinpoint students' literacy strengths and weaknesses to aid in planning an appropriate program. Standardized tests are limited in helping the teacher identify students' literacy strengths and weaknesses. Furthermore, standardized tests alone cannot accurately assess students' literacy and the effectiveness of literacy instruction. Effective teachers use ongoing assessment in their literacy instruction. Furthermore, effective teachers employ a variety of informal assessment procedures. Informal assessment of students' literacy can include placement tests, informal reading inventories, portfolios, observation, interviews, and interaction with students.

Placement Tests

A large number of published reading materials contain student placement tests. The main purposes of these tests are to (1) facilitate assignment at the appropriate level of difficulty in the materials, (2) determine if students have progressed in their reading development, and (3) identify some reading strengths and weaknesses. In comparison with norm-referenced standardized tests, placement tests do not compare students' performance with that of students at a grade level in a wide geographic area.

Many placement tests provide criterion, or critical, scores to assist the teacher in identifying whether students have mastered various aspects of reading. Unlike standardized criterion-referenced tests, criterion scores are presented only to assist the teacher in evaluating students' performances. Furthermore, most placement tests are not diagnostic tests. Thus, they do not identify specific strengths and weaknesses.

Placement tests can help you to make decisions about students' placement in a particular level of a literature series, but they also can help you evaluate students' progress in the materials. Placement tests are content specific; that is, they test students' progress in terms of the reading materials for which the tests were developed. You should, however, evaluate and review them carefully to ensure that they closely match what is taught. Also, pay careful attention to the number of items for each skill to ensure that they adequately sample the area of reading identified. Some placement tests for literature-based reading series are attempting to incorporate more of the features of reading reflecting current thinking. Figure 11.2 is an example of recent changes in placement tests accompanying literature-based reading series.

Informal Reading Inventories

One of the more helpful tools one can use in the classroom to assess students' reading strengths and weaknesses is the *informal reading inventory (IRI)*. Essentially, IRIs take three forms: (1) commercially published, (2) accompanying reading series, and (3) teacher prepared. Regardless of the type of inventory you choose, its major purposes are to establish students' reading levels and to identify their reading strengths and weaknesses.

The typical IRI consists of graded word lists, graded reading passages, and comprehension questions.

Graded word lists consist of 10 to 20 words for each grade level represented in the IRI. Most commercially published and reading series IRIs have graded word lists for preprimer through sixth grade. A student's performance on the graded word list provides you with information for placement in the graded passages, sight vocabulary strengths and weaknesses, and strategies used to identify words presented in isolation.

Graded reading passages are series of passages, usually ranging in reading difficulty from preprimer or primer through eighth or ninth grade. Performance on the passages indicates a reader's strategies in using context, attention to

Understanding What I Read

Directions. Read the following questions about the selection you have just read. Select the answer or answers that are correct. There may be one, two, or three correct answers for each question. You may look back at the story to answer the questions.

THEME

1. What is this story mostly about?
   a. Texas cowhands name a horse Widow-Maker.
   b. Pecos Bill can do many things that other men cannot do.
   c. The wildest horse in the West is captured and tamed.
   d. There are many different tasks to do on a ranch.
   e. Cowhands are known to be jealous of each other.

1. _____

VOCABULARY

2. Why did the cowhands rename the horse Widow-Maker?
   a. The horse is wild enouth to kill a man.
   b. Men would rather die than ride the horse.
   c. The horse is the color of a black widow spider.
   d. The horse can buck very hard.
   e. Pecos Bill's wife could not ride the horse.

2. _____

PROBLEM

3. What problems does Pecos Bill face in the beginning of the story?
   a. He must find a way to capture a wild horse.
   b. He must keep other cowhands off his horse.
   c. He must tame the horse but not break its spirit.
   d. He must find the right bit for the horse's mouth.
   e. He must stay on the horse until it tires.

3. _____

CHARACTER

4. How do we know that Pecos Bill was a kind person?
   a. He does not leave Old Satan on Pike's Peak.
   b. He wants to let Old Satan ride the horse.
   c. He does not want to break the spirit of the horse.
   d. He gives his friends a prize for renaming the horse.
   e. He pats the horse gently and talks to him.

4. _____

SETTING

5. In what location is this story set?
   a. the North
   b. the East
   c. the West
   d. Mexico
   e. Texas

5. _____

SUPPORTING IDEA

6. Which of the following is NOT supported by information in the story?
   a. Pecos Bill talks to the horse.
   b. The horse is easy to capture and tame.
   c. Pecos Bill sells the horse to his good friend.
   d. The horse agrees to let Pecos Bill ride him.
   e. The horse does not mind who rides him.

6. _____

FIGURE 11.2

Example of assessment materials accompanying a literature-based reading series
(From William H. Rupley and John W. Logan, *Vistas in Reading Literature,* Silver Level [Evanston, IL: McDougall, Littell & Co., 1990], p. 31.

7. Which of the following are typical of folk tales?   7. _____
   a. The characters can be animals.
   b. The story is set in a distant time and place.
   c. The main character is a person who is alive today.
   d. The story teaches a lesson about life.
   e. The story takes place in outer space.

TEXT STRUCTURE

8. What information is given in the first paragraph?   8. _____
   a. The reason the writer wrote the story is given.
   b. The problem Pecos Bill will face is identified.
   c. The problem Pecos Bill faces is solved.
   d. The main characters are introduced.
   e. The reason for renaming a horse is told.

TEXT/LITERARY
DEVICE

9. What does the writer say to make the horse seem human?   9. _____
   a. The horse wears fine, expensive clothing.
   b. The horse begs Pecos Bill to be his master.
   c. The horse asks the cowhands to give him a new name.
   d. The horse is honored to be Pecos Bill's horse.
   e. The horse refuses to eat his oats.

10. What do the words *horse, cowhands, lasso, Texas,* and *can-*   10. _____
    yons tell you about the story?
    a. The story takes place on a ranch.
    b. The story is about life in New England.
    c. The story is about cowboys.
    d. The story could never have really happened.
    e. The story takes place in a large city.

11. Which of the following experiences would help you under-   11. _____
    stand the story?
    a. Raising horses.
    b. Climbing a mountain.
    c. Reading stories about the old West.
    d. Reading other stories about Pecos Bill.
    e. Making promises to friends.

12. Which *one* of these strategies would best help you find out   12. _____
    how Pecos Bill feels when Old Satan rides his horse?
    a. Guess from what you remember reading.
    b. Reread the story, starting at the beginning.
    c. Reread the beginning and end.
    d. Search quickly for that information.
    e. Reread every other sentence.

13. In retelling this story, which of these facts would be MOST   13. _____
    important to include?
    a. Pecos Bill is a folk tale hero who is very brave.
    b. The horse's color is white.
    c. Only Pecos Bill can ride the wild horse.
    d. The horse is very difficult to capture and tame.
    e. Widow-Maker is the son of the White Mustang.

FIGURE 11.2
Continued

meaning, identification of unknown words, and different levels of reading competence.

Comprehension questions consist of 5 to 10 questions for each graded reading passage. The questions typically cover vocabulary, main idea, inference, literal meaning, cause and effect, and sequence. The questions are intended to identify students' reading comprehension competence.

Most commercial IRIs have at least two equivalent forms. Either form may be administered orally or silently. Students' performances on the oral administration of the IRI can identify their independent, instructional, frustration, and listening capacity reading competence levels. At the independent level, the student can read materials without any assistance. The instructional level is the teaching level at which students can read materials successfully with teacher guidance. At the frustration level, materials become too difficult and, as a result, frustrating for the students. The listening capacity level indicates what students can understand when material is read aloud to them. It is identified by evaluating responses to the comprehension questions for grade-level passages that are read aloud to a student.

Reading the passages aloud and responding to comprehension questions orally allows identification of instructional, independent, and frustration levels for both word recognition and comprehension. Silent reading of the passages identifies the same reading competence levels, but only for comprehension.

Administration. Administering an informal reading inventory is easy. You should follow some basic guidelines, however, to ensure that the oral reading sample accurately represents a student's reading capabilities. The following outlines the procedures to follow when administering an IRI:

1. Prior to administering the IRI, become thoroughly familiar with the coding system used to record students' deviations from the text as they read passages orally. Figure 11.3 presents a coding system that you can use to note such deviations. It is strongly recommended that you practice using the coding system and also tape record students' oral reading to ensure accurate coding of miscues.

2. To administer the IRI, select an area that is free of distractions. Establish a relaxed atmosphere to minimize student anxiety. Tell the student that the IRI is not a test and that he or she is going to read aloud some words and stories and answer some questions about each story. Also, it is extremely to explain that you will be doing some writing as the student reads the story, because many students become highly anxious when the teacher begins to write.
   Introduce the student to the tape recorder and let the student record his or her name, the date, and something about himself or herself. Play back what is recorded to check for proper settings. This procedure usually eliminates the novelty of the tape recorder and prevents it from becoming a distraction.

3. Select the graded word list that is two levels below the student's current grade level (word lists for the students should be typed on separate note cards) and ask the student to read the list of words aloud. Encourage the student to read each word. Even if a student is not sure of a word's pronunciation, he or she

Type of Miscue	How to Mark	Example
Omission: Word, several words, parts of words or punctuation are omitted.	Circle (⬭) the word(s), part of word, or punctuation omitted.	The large ⟨black⟩ dog jumped ⟨high⟩ into the air and gra⟨bbed⟩ the ball.
Substitution: Real word is substituted for text word.	Draw a line through the word substituted and write the substituted word above the text word.	huge leaped The ~~large~~ black dog ~~jumped~~ high into the bait air and grabbed the ~~ball~~.
Insertion: Word is inserted in the passage text.	Use a caret (∧) to indicate where word was inserted and write	The large black dog jumped high into the big air and grabbed the ∧ ball.
Unknown or Aided Words: Word or words are pronounced for the reader.	Place a letter "P" over the word pronounced for the reader.	P The large black dog jumped high into the air and grabbed the ball.
Transposition: Order of words in the text is transposed.	Use a curved mark (∿) over and under the words transposed.	The large black dog jumped high into the air and grabbed the ball.
Repetition: Phrase or several words are repeated. Count as one miscue.	Place an "R" with lines extending in both directions over the words repeated.	The large black dog jumped high into the ——R—— air and grabbed the ball.
Mispronunciation: Word is pronounced incorrectly.	Write the phonetic spelling above the word or use diacritical markings to indicate the pronunciation.	largé jumpted The large black dog jumped high into the air and grabbed the ball.
Self-correction: Miscue is self-corrected by the reader. Important to note, but do not count as a miscue.	Place a check mark (✓) above the miscue.	✓ jumpted ✓ The large black dog jumped high into the air and grabbed the ball.

FIGURE 11.3
Marking system for recording oral reading miscues

should try to pronounce it. This provides some indication of the student's word identification strategies.

If the student makes a miscue on this first word list, drop to an easier list until there are no miscues. Continue administering more difficult word lists and noting student's miscues by using the coding system. Stop administering the word lists when the student's miscues reach the maximum number suggested in the teacher's manual. If you use teacher-prepared graded word lists, stop administering the lists when the student's miscues reach 30 percent or greater.

4. The highest graded word list on which the student made no miscues is the entry level for the oral reading passages. For example, if a student read from graded word lists 1 through 6 and made no miscues on list 4, then the teacher should begin administering the oral reading passage at level 4. Remind the student that he or she is going to be reading a story aloud and that after reading the story you will ask some questions about it. Some published IRIs have motivation or overview statements for each passage that you are to read to the student just before beginning oral reading of the passage. As the student reads, record the miscues on the teacher's corresponding passage.

Once the student has read the passage, remove it and ask the comprehension questions. If necessary, you may restate the questions. If the student responds to questions correctly, indicate this with a check beside the question. If the student responds incorrectly or only partially, write the response beneath the appropriate question. The student need not respond to each question on the question sheet, but he or she should answer correctly to get credit. An alternative procedure is to have the student retell the story; the teacher then judges the student's comprehension based on the retelling.

5. Continue having the student read subsequent passages and answer comprehension questions until you identify a frustration level for either word recognition or comprehension or both (see Figure 11.4).

6. To identify the student's capacity or potential reading level, have him or her begin reading at the level above the passage that produced frustration. Again, set purposes by telling the student to listen carefully as you read the story aloud and that he or she will answer some questions after hearing the story. Stop administering passages when the student answers less than 75% of the comprehension questions correctly. The highest level at which the student answered 75 percent of the questions correctly is the capacity level.

Interpretation. Use both quantitative and qualitative analysis to interpret students' performance on an IRI. Counting the number of scorable miscues in each passage and the number of incorrect comprehension questions for each passage and determining reading competence levels are the bases of a quantitative analysis.

Figure 11.4 presents two sets of criteria for determining reading competence levels. Betts' (1946) criteria for independent, instructional, and frustration levels apply to all passages, regardless of difficulty. Powell's (1976) criteria take into account passage level difficulty and permit more miscues below the sixth-grade level.

Reading Competency Level	Betts' Criteria		Powell's Differentiated Criteria					
	Word Recognition	Comprehension	Word Recognition in terms of grade-level difficulty of passage being read:			Comprehension in terms of grade-level difficulty of passage being read:		
			PP–2	3–5	6+	PP–2	3–5	6+
Independent	one miscue per 100 words (99% accuracy)	90% or greater accuracy	94% + accuracy	96% + accuracy	97% + accuracy	81% + accuracy	86% + accuracy	91% + accuracy
Instructional	five miscues per 100 words (95% accuracy)	75%–89% accuracy	87–93% accuracy	92–95% accuracy	94–96% accuracy	55–80% accuracy	60–85% accuracy	65–90% accuracy
Frustration	10 + miscues per 100 words (less than 90% accuracy)	less than 50% accuracy	86% or less accuracy	91% or less accuracy	93% or less accuracy	54% or less accuracy	59% or less accuracy	64% or less accuracy
Capacity or Potential	at least 75% accuracy		at least 75% accuracy for all levels					

FIGURE 11.4
Criteria for determining reading competence levels from student performance on an IRI

SAMPLE STUDENT RECORD SUMMARY
SHEETS AND DESCRIPTIVE ANALYSIS

STUDENT RECORD SUMMARY SHEET

Student *John Stone*   Grade *4*   Sex *M*   Age *9 – 10*
                                                    yrs. mos.

School *Merrill Elementary*   Administered by *M L Woods*   Date *1/18/88*

Grade	Word Lists	Graded Passages			Estimated Levels			
	% of words correct	WR Form *C*	Comp. Form *C*	Listen. Form *B*	**Narrative**			
Primer	100%						Grade	
1	100%	*-1 Ind.*	*-0 Ind.*		Independent		*1-2*	
2	100%	*-3 Inst.*	*-2 Inst.*		Instructional		*2-3*	
3	95%	*-7 Inst.*	*-3 Inst.*	*Inst.*	Frustration		*4*	
4	60%	*-11 Inst.*	*-5 Frust.*	*Inst.*	Listening		*5*	
5		*-18 Frust.*	*-6 Frust.*	*Inst.*	**Expository**			
6				*Frust.*	**Grade Level**			
7					Science		Social Studies	
8					WR *-1* Frust.	Comp. *-4* Frust.	WR *-11* Frust.	Comp. *-4* Frust.
9								

Check consistent oral reading difficulties:

___ word-by-word reading
___ omissions
___ substitutions ← *(makes numerous word guesses)*
___ corrections
___ repetitions
___ reversals
___ inattention to punctuation
___ word inserts
___ requests word help

Check consistent word recognition difficulties:

___ single consonants
___ consonant clusters
✓ long vowels ⎱ *medial*
✓ short vowels ⎰
___ vowel digraphs
___ diphthongs
___ syllabication
✓ use of context *(must strengthen)*
___ basic sight
✓ grade level sight

Check consistent comprehension difficulties:

___ main idea
___ factual
✓ terminology
✓ cause and effect
✓ inferential
✓ drawing conclusions
✓ retelling

30

FIGURE 11.5

An informal reading inventory student record summary sheet

(Reprinted with permission from Mary Lynn Woods and Alden J. Moe, *Analytical Reading Inventory,* 4th ed. [New York: Merrill/Macmillan Publishing Co., 1989], pp. 30, 33–35.)

DESCRIPTION OF READING BEHAVIORS—NARRATIVE AND EXPOSITORY
Narrative Reading Levels 2 and 3

Word Recognition. As John read Levels 2 and 3, I could tell that he expected to gain meaning from his reading. For example, he self-corrected many of the miscues demonstrating that he was using context clues to get meaning from the text as well as recognize words. At Level 3 he made some word substitutions that were appropriate for the meaning of the text (*banging* for *pounding, said* for *declared*), which showed that he was reading for meaning. At Level 3 he pronounced a previously miscued word correctly when it appeared later in the text, thus verifying that he was continuously searching for meaning (*become* for *belong,* but later corrected). John's most productive word pronunciation strategy was the use of initial consonants and some blends. Throughout both levels he had difficulty coping with the medial and final portions of the words. Although not an overriding problem at Level 3, uncorrected miscues did affect the meaning of the text (*read* for *read, Sunday* for *suddenly*). I am concerned that as the material becomes more complicated, the meaningful substitution strategy may not prove effective.

Comprehension. The retellings at Levels 2 and 3 contained adequate information about the passages. Both retellings showed that John thoroughly understood the sequence of events. Despite the fact that the number of miscues increased at Level 3, John's effort to read for meaning coupled with his background vocabulary demonstrated that he effectively coped at this level. After the retelling, I chose to ask all the comprehension questions to see if he had understood specific information. He responded appropriately in all instances.

Attitude. John appeared to be an intelligent, competent reader at Levels 2 and 3. Throughout the reading of both passages I could see that he was attempting to make meaning of the text. He appeared confident and self-assured as he read aloud, often subvocalizing the meaning as if he were constructing the parts of a puzzle. In summary, he coped adequately with the comprehension, and used effective word recognition strategies, causing Level 3 to be instructional.

Narrative Reading Level 4

Word Recognition. The number of miscues substantially increased at Level 4. The strategy of using the initial consonants and blends continued to be the more reliant cueing system. Difficulties persisted in the medial and final portions of the words. I could tell that his confidence was threatened because he often either waited for me to aid the word (*Gabilan*) or made a nonmeaningful whole-word substitution (*alone* for *alarm*) with no attempt to self-correct. He often glided by punctuation marks indicating that he was not grouping the author's ideas effectively. These behaviors indicate less effective coping strategies with this level of material.

Comprehension. John's retelling at Level 4 was scanty. It was randomly organized, never revealing the logic of the passage. Although John did concisely retell the main idea, when answering comprehension questions he not only had difficulty recalling some of the factual information, but also consistently missed questions requiring him to correlate portions of the text (ce) or to draw inferences from the text (inf/con). His description of many of the vocabulary words revealed their meanings, yet during the oral reading he had miscued some of them. His ability to use context clues at this level was not as effective as it had appeared at the previous level. A silent reading of Level 4, Form B rendered the same comprehension weaknesses.

Attitude. John did not look like or sound like the confident strategist he was at Level 3. He showed physical signs of stress, appearing less confident and more confused. He was reluctant to take as many risks as he had in Level 3, indicating that the coping strategies he had been using were not working as effectively.

FIGURE 11.5
Continued

continues

FIGURE 11.5
Continued

Narrative Reading Level 5

Word Recognition/Comprehension/Attitude.   John's coping strategies seemed to fall apart at this level. He made so many oral miscues that he was unable to understand most of the text. He showed obvious signs of frustration and defeat.

Listening Level (Narrative)

When I read Level 4 from Form A, John's retelling was well organized and thorough. Level 5 showed some of the same qualities, but was not as thorough as Level 4. Answering the comprehension questions I used to further probe his understanding, he again demonstrated that he clearly understood the text. In both instances, his background knowledge of vocabulary strengthened his ability to understand. The quantity of information and vocabulary at Level 6 caused John to demonstrate frustration similar to his frustration in the oral Level 4 sample. This information confirms the fact that John can comprehend slightly more challenging material when he does not have to struggle with the recognition of the words. This information should prove useful in the selection of material that is read in class, and in determining expectations for his participation.

Recommendations for Instruction (Narrative).   John should start the year at a level where he appears to be the most intelligent strategist, confident and relaxed. I recommend that he be placed in the third grade, second semester basal (3/2). Many additional independent reading experiences using trade books as well as the basal should be provided. Instructional strategies designed to help him learn more effective coping strategies in word recognition, vocabulary development, and comprehension should be provided. John should soon be challenged with grade level material. (See Instructional Recommendations, page 36.)

Science Level 4

Word Recognition.   In expository text, the same miscue patterns occurred as in narrative text. The medial and final portions of words were most often missed. Very little self-correcting took place, which indicated that John was struggling so hard with the recognition of words and the organization of the text that he was unable to monitor the meaning successfully as he had done in narrative Levels 2 and 3.

Comprehension.   Even though he had some background knowledge about comets, he still had difficulty understanding the text. The effort he had to expend to recognize the words and process the text seemed to overpower his ability to get the meaning.

Attitude.   John was obviously frustrated. Even though this was the first reading on the second day of evaluation, he yawned, wiggled around in his seat, and often glanced up to see the clock.

Social Studies Level 4

Word Recognition.   The miscues followed the same pattern as found in the science and narrative Level 4 passages.

Comprehension.   Much energy was spent on word recognition and processing the text at the cost of meaning.

Attitude.   Even though John was trying very hard, he really had difficulty sticking to the task. He told me that it was hard to remember things that happened a long time ago and that maybe his grandmother would know more about it. He was truly frustrated.

Recommendations for Instruction (Expository).   Dealing with content area text is very challenging for John. Since over half of the class experienced similar difficulties, a plan for effective instruction will include:

FIGURE 11.5
Continued

1. Providing reading experiences in alternate texts and other reading materials on each topic covered in both the science and social studies books. Films, filmstrips, and other visuals will be included. Materials should be at various levels of comprehension.
2. An instructional format that offers time for small group reading and discussion in the regular and alternate texts as well as whole group reading experiences.
3. Pairing students as reading and discussion partners when the content area text is used.
4. Instructional strategies that involve the student in predicting and analyzing possibilities of both concepts and vocabulary in the content area and alternate texts.
5. Advance organizers, both teacher- and student-made, which provide information about each reading assignment; thus, as units or chapters are introduced, students gain background experience with the content.
6. Weekly free reading time in which the teacher reads text to the students about the topics covered in the science and social studies texts, or students read and discuss the text and/or alternate texts.

Sample Student Record Summary Sheets and Descriptive Analysis   35

When both criteria are applied to a student's performance in word recognition and comprehension, Betts' criteria usually place the student at a lower competency level. Remember that reading tasks should be at a level of difficulty that maximizes students' chance of success yet should not be so easy that students lose interest. Therefore, teachers could apply both sets of criteria to students' performance. If they yield a noticeable difference in competency levels, it might be best to assign students reading materials with a difficulty between the two competency levels rather than at either extreme. This increases the likelihood that the reading task is at an appropriate difficulty level. If a student's actual reading performance suggests that the task is either too easy or too difficult, however, then move the student up or down to the appropriate level.

Most published IRIs have a form for summarizing students' performance. (See Figure 11.5 for an example.) A summary sheet enables you to identify reading levels and tally both oral reading miscues and comprehension difficulties. Also, such sheets generally provide space for briefly noting reading strengths and weaknesses. Based on the information presented in the summary sheet example, this student should be able to read library materials at the first grade level. It appears that placement in instructional materials at the third grade level would be appropriate for teacher-guided instruction. In addition, John appears to have some difficulty with substitutions, long and short medial vowels, and use of context. Comprehension problems include terminology, cause and effect, inference, drawing conclusions, and retelling. This quantitative information does not, however, provide any insights about whether these difficulties negatively affected comprehension or what word identification strategies John employed.

Qualitative analysis of students' miscues involves not only the number of miscues but also the type. Not all miscues are equally destructive to comprehension. You should note the impact of each miscue on a student's reading for meaning. Qualitative analysis enables you to determine whether a miscue interferes with meaning and to understand better the reading strategies that students use. Figure 11.6 illustrates an excerpt of level 4 from *Analytical Reading Inventory* (Woods & Moe, 1989).

Figure 11.7 illustrates a procedure for qualitatively analyzing a student's miscues. To categorize them, transfer the miscues for all passages read from the IRI to the qualitative analysis sheet and identify them by level. Write the text words and student's miscues in the appropriate columns. Compare each miscue with the text to determine if it was similar in meaning, resulted in a loss of meaning, or made sense yet resulted in a different meaning; was similar in its graphic representation and sound for beginning, middle, and ending; and was syntactically acceptable or unacceptable.

Following the categorization of miscues, analyze patterns of reading behavior, using the following questions as guidelines (Goodman, 1976):

1. Check for omissions, substitutions, insertions, and transpositions. Ask:

■ Was meaning lost or changed as a result of these miscues?

■ Was there a pattern for each type of miscue? For example, were proper nouns or inflected verbs omitted? Were adjectives inserted? Were nonsense words substituted?

Level 4 (144 words 13 sent.)

Examiner's Introduction
(Student Booklet page 49):

If you like excitement then you will enjoy reading the *Incredible Journey* by Sheila Burnford. This story is about three pets, a cat and two dogs, whose owners leave the animals when they move to another country. The animals decide to try to find their owners but face many hardships. Please read a retelling of one of the incidents from this exciting story.

The three were ~~growing~~ *getting* tired from ~~their~~ *the* long journey, and now

they had to cross a river. It was (wide and deep,) so they would have

to swim across. *it*

The ~~younger~~ *yellow* dog plunged into the icy water, barking for the

others to follow him. The older dog jumped into the water. He was ———— *R*

weak and suffering from pain, *P* but somehow he managed to ~~struggle~~ *swim*

op/posite
to the opposite bank.

The poor cat was left (all) alone. He was (so) afraid (that he) ran up *P* *and*

and down the bank wailing with fear. The ~~younger~~ *yellow* dog swam back

crying
and forth ~~trying~~ to help. Finally, the cat jumped and began

swimming near his friend.

mom/ent
At that moment something bad happened. An old beaver dam

from upstream broke. The water came rushing downstream ———— *R* ———— ~~hurling~~ *hurting*

a large log toward the animals. It struck the cat and swept him

(helplessly away.)

Comprehension Questions
and Possible Answers

(mi) ✓1. In this passage what was the difficult thing the animals had to do?
(cross a river) *swim across a river*

(f) ✓2. How would the animals get across the river?
(They would have to swim.) *swim*

(t) 3. What is the meaning of *plunged*?
(to jump in quickly) *to unclog like plunge a sink*

(ce) 4. Why did the younger dog bark at the other animals?
✓(to try to get them to follow him)

(f) 5. What is meant by the phrase "wailing with fear"?
——(to be so scared that one cries out) *Don't know*

(f) 6. After the cat jumped in, what bad thing happened?
✓(An old beaver dam broke.) *dam broke*

(ce) 7. Why did the log come hurling downstream?
——·(The rushing water brought it.) *because it floated*

(con) 8. What makes you think the animals were run down and in poor health?
✓(Stated: They were tired; the old dog was suffering from pain.) *old dog in pain*

Miscue Count:

0 _4_ i / s _9_ a _2_ REP _2_ REV _/_

Scoring Guide	
Word Rec.	Comp.
IND 1–2	IND 0–1
INST 7–8	INST 2
FRUST 15+	FRUST 4+

19 *3*

FIGURE 11.6
A marked copy of a student's performance on an informal reading inventory
(Adapted with permission from Mary Lynn Woods and Alden J. Moe, *Analytical Reading Inventory,* 4th ed. [New York: Merrill/Macmillan Publishing Co., 1989], p. 50.)

Text	Pupil	Meaning			Graphic/Sound Similarities			Syntax	
		Similar	Meaning Loss	Different	Beginning	Middle	Ending	Acceptable	Unacceptable
For Level 4									
growing	getting	X			X		X	X	
their	the	X			X			X	
wide and deep	deep and wide	X						X	
——	it	X							
younger	yellow	X		X	X			X	
suffering	P								
struggle	swim	X			X			X	
opposite	ŏp/pŏ/sitĕ		X		X				
all	——	X							
so	——	X							
that he	——	X							
and	——	X						X	
wailing	P								
younger	yellow			X	X			X	
moment	mŏm/ĕnt		X		X		X		
hurling	hurling		X		X		X	X	
helplessly	——	X							

FIGURE 11.7
Qualitative analysis of student's IRI miscue performance

- Did these miscues cause incorrect responses to comprehension questions?

- Did these miscues make sense in context when earlier or later miscues are taken into account? For example, in the text sentence, "He was so afraid that he ran up and down the bank wailing with fear," the student omitted *so,* inserted *and* between *afraid* and *that,* and omitted *that he* to say, "He was afraid and ran up and down the bank wailing with fear." It appears that the insertion of *and* may have resulted in the omission of *that he* as the student attempted to make sense of the sentence.

- Were these miscues correct syntactically? This indicates that the reader is aware of word order and sentence stucture.

2. Check for mispronunciations. Ask:

- Did the reader attempt to use a word identification skill?

- Did the reader rely too heavily on one word identification technique? That is, did the reader try to sound out every word or look at only the initial letter and guess?

- Was there a pattern to mispronunciations, such as irregular words, inflected words, proper nouns, or adjectives?

- Were mispronunciations the result of dialect differences? Dialect differences should not be scored as miscues, but they should be analyzed to determine if they possibly interfered with comprehension.

Analysis of the miscues, such as that presented in Figure 11.7, can provide important information not available from a quantitative analysis. Following are some examples of information about specific reading strengths and weaknesses available from this qualitative analysis. Based on an analysis of how John's miscues affected meaning, it appears that 11 of the 19 miscues used to identify a reading competency level did not change the meaning of the text. This indicates that while John did not read the passage verbatim, he comprehended much of its meaning. In other words, it seems as if only eight of his miscues interfered with comprehension. This difference may indicate that the passage is at his instructional level rather than his frustration level.

Furthermore, John seems to have an understanding that one must make sense from what one reads. His mispronunciations of *opposite* and *moment* suggest an attempt to use phonics to identify these words. He did not, however, ask himself if these words made sense in context. It is possible that neither of these words is part of his listening vocabulary the way they appeared in the story.

An important feature of qualitative analysis is that it considers the types of oral reading responses a student makes. Using only the initial letter cues to recognize words, a student could pronounce every word beginning with *m* as *mom.* If a student frequently substitutes words, qualitative analysis could identify (1) graphic/sound similarities (i.e., did the substituted word have similar graphic and pronunciation features as the text word?), (2) meaning features (i.e., did the substituted word have a similar or identical meaning to the text word; e.g., car for automobile?), and (3) syntactic features (i.e., was the substituted word the same part of speech as the text word?)

Qualitative analysis of miscues provides insights into the reading strategies that students use in their reading. Specific reading strengths and weaknesses become more evident as miscues are qualitatively analyzed for several orally read passages. Students' IRI performance can be qualitatively analyzed with all three types of informal reading inventories.

Cloze Procedure

The *cloze procedure* is an informal diagnostic procedure that helps identify reading levels and provides information about a reader's ability to deal with the content and structure of the information presented—syntax, word meanings, and story grammar. A cloze test is typically constructed by selecting a freestanding written passage approximately 250 to 300 words long and deleting every fifth word. The first sentence is left intact and the first deletion is the fifth word in the second sentence. Every fifth word after this is deleted throughout the passage. Each deleted word is replaced with a line of uniform length, as illustrated in the following example:

Jake saw the two horses just south of the timber ridge over by Clear Lake. He and Rusty had _____ _____ hunting these Mustangs for _____ last two days. Yesterday _____ horse ran away and _____ gone for several hours. _____ time that Jake lost _____ searching for the runaway _____ had made him think _____ they would not _____ the wild horses.
(The deleted words are *been, the, Rusty's, was, The, while, horse, seriously,* and *catch*.)

The words deleted from a passage may be any part of speech. The basic rule is to delete the fifth word regardless of its function in the sentence.

Administering and scoring a cloze test for determining reading levels are simple, straightforward procedures. Instruct students to read the passage and write in the blank the word that was deleted. Then score each of the responses as either correct or incorrect. Only the exact word is considered a correct response. Determine the percentage of correct responses by dividing the total correct replacements by the number of deleted words (e.g., 30 words correctly replaced divided by 50 words deleted would be a 60% correct replacement). Compare the percentage of correct word placement with this scale: 61% or more correct replacements for the independent reading level, 41% to 60% correct for the instructional level, and less than 40% for the frustration level (Rankin & Culhane, 1969).

Determining reading levels using the criterion of exact word replacement is intended to help you decide if students can handle the content and language structure of various reading materials, such as science, social studies, and math texts. You can better understand a reader's use of syntax, semantics, and reasoning by looking at incorrect word choices. If incorrect choices are syntactically correct (the same part of speech), the student may be analyzing words preceding and following the deletion in an attempt to supply a meaningful response. Se-

FLASHBACK

Teachers of literacy have long realized the value of gathering informal assessment information on individual students. Such information is needed to adequately plan an instructional program that meets each student's needs.

UPDATE

In addition to the teacher gathering informal assessment information on individual students for planning instruction, students are also becoming active participants in the assessment process. Portfolios are expandable folders for each student that can include a variety of literacy learning indicators. For example, students often select their "best works" to include in their portfolios. Actively involving students in the assessment process makes them more aware of their own learning.

mantically correct word choices may indicate that the reader understood the meaning but chose a different word than the author. If the words are both syntactically and semantically correct, then the reader is revealing meaning and applying a knowledge of language.

Cloze testing is an informal assessment strategy that is neither time-consuming nor difficult. Interpreting the responses may prove more valuable in securing information about a student's reading level than simply identifying the level. A fifth-word deletion may be too difficult for some students, so you may wish to delete every eighth or tenth word.

A modification of the cloze procedure is the maze procedure. Rather than supplying the deleted word, the student selects a word from a vertical array. The cloze procedure is essentially a recall task, whereas the maze procedure is a recognition task. Selective identification of words allows you to determine a student's attention to context and understanding of language. Obviously, in using this or any idea incorporated into informal testing, you must fit the levels of the pupils involved. Following is an example of the maze procedure.

<blockquote>
paddled
The boy swam his boat across the large lake,
leaned

swimming
searching for a good fishing spot. He saw a small
moved

water.
cove with tree limbs hanging over the ice.
case.
</blockquote>

Observation

Observing, interacting, and interviewing are assessment procedures that provide information beyond basic skills development. They enable the teacher to gather information specific to instruction and to students' progress while engaged in meaningful reading and writing tasks.

One of the simplest procedures might consist of having a student read aloud a short selection from a book to determine whether he or she can identify the words and construct meaning for that particular book. Such an informal assessment procedure can yield important information about students' word recognition strategies and comprehension. In addition, such interaction focuses on real literature that engages the student over longer passages of sustained reading than standardized tests generally contain.

You can use an observation form to record reading and writing behaviors. Such a form can be used to keep a record of students' literacy growth and illustrate their progress and development in specific areas of literacy. The checklist presented in Figure 11.8, for example, can be used selectively by a teacher at any grade level, can be expanded to include reading of informational text, and can be used in both literature-based or skills-focused classrooms.

Name _____ Age _____ Grade _____ Date _____

School _____ Teacher _____

Examiner _____

I. *Word Analysis*
   A. Knows names of letters
      Needs work with: _____   Yes No
   B. Attacks initial sound of words
      Deficiencies noted: _____   Yes No
   C. Can substitute initial letter sounds
      Further drill needed: _____   Yes No
   D. Can sound out initial blends and digraphs
      Deficiencies noted: _____   Yes No
   E. If root word is known, can solve words
      formed by adding prefixes and suffixes_____   Yes No

II. *Sight Words* (check if applicable)
   _____ Knows a word one time, misses it later
   _____ Guesses at unknown words
        _____ Errors frequently do not change intended meaning
        _____ Errors indicate not reading for meaning
   _____ Frequently adds words
        _____ Errors frequently do not change intended meaning
        _____ Errors indicate not reading for meaning
   _____ Omits words
        _____ Errors frequently do not change intended meaning
        _____ Errors indicate not reading for meaning

III. *Reading Habits Noted*
   _____ Reads word by word   _____ Loses place frequently
   _____ Phrasing inadequate   _____ Does not utilize punctuation
   _____ Poor intonation   _____ Lacks persistence
   Explain: _____

IV. *Sustained Reading* (basal, textbook, trade book)
   (Do quantitative and qualitative analysis using techniques presented earlier.)

	Grade Level	*Approx. Number of* Running Words	*Number of* Errors
1.			
2.			

Errors noted (example): Said *lied* for *lying; banged* for *bumped; stuck* for *start* (corrected)

Needed help with: *clown, stomach, curious, squeal*

Read with some hesitation, not smoothly, etc.

FIGURE 11.8
Reading observation checklist

continues

FIGURE 11.8
Continued

	Excellent	Average	Below Average
V. *Comprehension*			
Recall of facts	_____	_____	_____
Recognizes main ideas	_____	_____	_____
Draws inferences	_____	_____	_____
Maintains sequence of events	_____	_____	_____
Understands humor	_____	_____	_____
Interprets figurative expressions	_____	_____	_____
VI. *Oral Reading Skills*			
Relates with audience	_____	_____	_____
Enunciation	_____	_____	_____
Adequate volume	_____	_____	_____
Reads with intonation	_____	_____	_____
Phrases for meaning	_____	_____	_____
VII. *Behaviors Related to Reading*			
Attitude toward reading	_____	_____	_____
Self-confidence	_____	_____	_____
Background knowledge	_____	_____	_____
Language facility	_____	_____	_____
Originality of expression	_____	_____	_____
Range of vocabulary	_____	_____	_____
Stock of concepts	_____	_____	_____
Variety of sentence patterns	_____	_____	_____

VIII. *Other Comments* _____

_____

_____

_____

_____

_____

_____

_____

_____

_____

_____

_____

Interviews

Interviewing students about their reading and writing can provide teachers with valuable insights and help students become more aware of their own literacy interests, reading and writing strategies, and progress (McKenna & Kear, 1990). Examples of questions that teachers can use when interviewing students include:

1. What do you think makes a good reader? What do you think makes a good writer? (Indicate how student conceptualizes reading and writing.)

2. If you were to read a story about (any chosen topic), what kinds of information do you think you would find in the story?

3. When you come to a word you don't know, how do you figure it out? Show me in a story how you would figure out a word you did not know.

4. Let's look at the list of books that you have read. Which ones were your favorites? Which books did you find hard to read? Which book(s) would you like to read again and again? Why?

5. What do you enjoy most about writing? What do you not enjoy about writing? What makes writing fun or easy for you?

6. What makes understanding some stories easy for you?

7. If you have to read a science book to discuss in class, what do you think this means? Tell me how you would read a science book so we can later talk about it.

8. What do you like to write about the most? Why?

9. What does the title of a story or book tell you?

10. If we had a new student entering our class who did not know what it meant to read, how would you describe reading to him or her?

Such questions are examples of those that teachers can ask when interviewing students. Insights for both the teacher and students can be gained from such interviews about perceptions of reading and writing, strategies used for both reading and writing, and growth and development in literacy.

Besides interviewing your students orally, an interest inventory or a reading experiences inventory can provide additional information. Figure 11.9 is an example of a reading experiences inventory that a teacher can give students. Students' responses to the questions provide information about their interests, attitudes, reading habits, and perceptions.

In addition, the reading comprehension interview presented in Figure 11.10 (Wixson, Bosky, Yochum, & Alvermann, 1984) can provide information about students' perceptions of classroom reading tasks. The interview takes approximately 30 minutes to administer. You should tell students that there are not right or wrong answers and that you are just trying to find out what they think. During the interview, use probing questions to encourage the student to respond or to clarify responses. As with other informal strategies, you should look for patterns and attempt to gain insights into the student's thinking. To interpret a student's response, look at such factors as purpose for reading, concept of print, and strategies for understanding written language.

Reading Experiences Inventory

Beginning of the School Year

Read each question or statement below. Circle the letter of each item that best describes you as a reader. You may circle more than one letter. You may write your own response where a line is provided.

1. Which sentence below explains how you feel about reading?
   a. I like to read at home and at school.
   b. I like to read at home, but I do not like to read at school.
   c. I do not like to read and would rather do other things for fun.
   d. I would like reading more if I could become a better reader.

2. I like to read when . . .
   a. I am alone in a quiet place.
   b. I can talk with the other students about what I read.
   c. I know my teacher will help me with my reading.
   d. I can talk with my teacher about what I read.
   e. _____

3. It helps me with my reading when . . .
   a. I read with an older student who is a better reader.
   b. I read aloud with another student or in a reading group.
   c. I work with students who are in different reading groups.
   d. I work alone and think about what I read
   e. _____

4. It helps me with my reading when . . .
   a. my teacher gives me questions before I read to think about as I read.
   b. my teacher helps me understand the directions for my work.
   c. my teacher lets me work alone and think about what I read.
   d. my teacher directs discussion about what I have read.
   e. _____

5. How often do you read at home for enjoyment?
   a. never
   b. up to 30 minutes a week
   c. 30 to 60 minutes a week
   d. more than an hour a week

FIGURE 11.9

Example of a reading experiences inventory

(Reprinted with permission from William H. Rupley and John W. Logan, *Vistas in Reading Literature* [Evanston, IL: McDougall, Littell & Co., 1990], pp. 1–2.)

6. Which sentence below *best describes* what you do at home?
   a. I spend more time reading than I do watching television.
   b. I spend more time watching television than I do reading.
   c. I spend about the same amount of time watching television and reading.
   d. _____

7. Below are listed several types of literature. Circle the letters of ones you most like to read or have read to you.
   a. stories about animals.
   b. science fiction
   c. mysteries
   d. sports stories
   e. stories about faraway places
   f. plays
   g. poems
   h. stories about boys and girls my own age
   i. folk tales and fairy tales
   j. stories about real events in the past
   k. biographies
   l. fables
   m. myths and legends
   n. humorous stories
   o. adventure stories
   p. science and nature articles
   q. books of facts and records

8. On another piece of paper, complete the sentences below.
   a. If I read the newspaper, the sections I usually read are . . .
   b. My favorite book is . . .
   c. The best books I have read in the past year include . . .
   d. Topics I like to read about include . . .
   e. The number of books I read outside of school each month is about . . .
   f. Some magazines I like to read are . . .
   g. A reading goal I would like to set for myself this year is . . .

FIGURE 11.9
Continued

Name: _____ Date: _____

Classroom teacher: _____ Reading level: _____

Grade: _____

Directions: Introduce the procedure by explaining that you are interested in finding out what children think about various reading activities. Tell the student that he or she will be asked questions about his/her reading, that there are no right or wrong answers, and that you are only interested in knowing what s/he thinks. Tell the student that if s/he does not know how to answer a question s/he should say so and you will go on to the next one.

General probes such as "Can you tell me more about that?" or "Anything else?" may be used. Keep in mind that the interview is an informal diagnostic measure and you should feel free to probe to elicit useful information.

1. What hobbies or interests do you have that you like to read about?
2. a. How often do you read in school?
   b. How often do you read at home?
3. What school subjects do you like to read about?

Introduce reading and social studies books.

Directions: For this section use the child's classroom basal reader and a content area textbook (social studies, science, etc.). Place these texts in front of the student. Ask each question twice, once with reference to the basal reader and once with reference to the content area textbook. Randomly vary the order of presentation (basal, content). As each question is asked, open the appropriate text in front of the student to help provide a point of reference for the question.

4. What is the most important reason for reading this kind of material? Why does your teacher want you to read this book?
5. a. Who's the best reader you know in _____?
   b. What does he/she do that makes him/her such a good reader?

FIGURE 11.10
Reading comprehension interview
(From Karen K. Wixson et al., "An Interview for Assessing Students' Perceptions of Classroom Reading Tasks," *The Reading Teacher* [January 1984], p. 348. Reprinted with permission of Karen Wixson and the International Reading Association.)

Anecdotal Records

Observation checklists (see Figure 11.8) can be helpful when teachers are focusing on features of reading and writing for a number of students. *Anecdotal records*, however, provide more detail, allow for variations among students, and recognize the range in literacy capabilities within a classroom. As noted by Rhodes and Nathenson-Mejia (1992), "what is focused on and recorded depends upon the teacher, the student, and the context, not on predetermined items on a checklist" (pp. 502–503).

Guidelines (Rhodes & Nathenson-Mejia, 1992) for writing anecdotal records include the following steps: (1) describe the event or product rather than just

6. a. How good are you at reading this kind of material?
   b. How do you know?
7. What do you have to do to get a good grade in in your class _____?
8. a. If the teacher told you to remember the information in this story/chapter, what would be the best way to do this?
   b. Have you ever tried _____?
9. a. If your teacher told you to find the answers to the questions in this book what would be the best way to do this? Why?
   b. Have you ever tried _____?
10. a. What is the hardest part about answering questions like the ones in this book?
    b. Does that make you do anything differently?

Introduce at least two comprehension worksheets.

Directions: Present the worksheets to the child and ask questions 11 and 12. Ask the child to complete portions of each worksheet. Then ask questions 13 and 14. Next, show the child a worksheet designed to simulate the work of another child. Then ask question 15.

11. Why would your teacher want you to do worksheets like these (for what purpose)?
12. What would your teacher say you must do to get a good mark on worksheets like these? (What does your teacher look for?)

Ask the child to complete portions of at least two worksheets.

13. Did you do this one differently from the way you did that one? How or in what way?
14. Did you have to work harder on one of these worksheets than the other? (Does one make you think more?)

Present the simulated worksheet.

15. a. Look over this worksheet. If you were the teacher, what kind of mark would you give the worksheet? Why?
    b. If you were the teacher, what would you ask this person to do differently next time?

FIGURE 11.10
Continued

recording the general impression, (2) focus on rich descriptions rather than evaluations, and (3) relate the anecdote to information known about the child. The following example illustrates these features:

> Showed Mary how to skip a word that she didn't know in her reading as a way to figure out its meaning. She was reading a book about experiments for children and didn't know the meaning of *absorbed*. She grasped the idea quickly and read two sentences beyond the word and noted excitedly that the word must mean the liquid went from the glass up to the petals of the flower. Encouraged her to do this with other words that she might not know the meaning for.

Anecdotal records can be used effectively with individual students as well as small groups. Teachers can identify students for whom anecdotal information would be beneficial. For example, anecdotal records might help in trying to determine what is contributing to a student's disruptive behavior at the writing center, or why Jason is unwilling to edit his writing, or how well Mary is using context to figure out the meaning of unknown words.

Analysis of anecdotal records often reveals patterns of both difficulty and success for students. Teachers using anecdotal records for assessment have noted why certain organizational schemes (e.g., paired reading, interest groups, peer editing) were successful or unsuccessful, how students used or failed to use strategies for reading informational text, how certain instructional features (e.g., time allotted for an activity, modeling, scaffolding, feedback) enhanced and facilitated students' learning, and how much growth students have experienced over a period of time. One of the most important features of anecdotal records is that their use makes teachers more aware of their interaction with their students and the effects of their instruction on students' learning.

Response Journals

Although all forms of students' writing can be used in assessment, **response journals** are of important value because they integrate reading and writing. Response journals (discussed in Chapter 3) are written responses between the student and teacher or between students to a learning experience and the responses of others that are read. Response journals encourage students to think about how and what they read, and how their reading develops through writing. As students write about their reading, it becomes more personal. Through reading the teacher's responses, students become more conscious of their reading strategies and development.

Students' responses can disclose what they are understanding about what they read, their attitudes and motivation toward what they read, and the strategies they use when reading. Response journals will help teachers better understand four areas of students' reading: comprehension, reading processes, knowledge of literature, and engagement in reading.

Wollman-Bonilla (1991) summarized the assessment information teachers obtain in these four areas:

- *Comprehension:* Students' responses can reveal their understanding of characters, setting, story events, and resolutions (see the Story Grammar section in Chapter 6). Wollman-Bonilla says, "responses can illuminate the reason for comprehension problems and the types of instructional guidance [that is needed]" (p. 57).

- *Reading processes:* Information about linguistic cues (graphophonic, syntactic, and semantic) students use can be their responses. *"I didn't know what repetition meant. But after I read that Mark said, 'I'm going to do it again, and again, and again, until I can do it,' I figured out what it meant." Other responses—such as "I like the way she (author) told what kind of day it was (bright, cheery, and everything seemed*

All forms of students' writing can be used in assessment.

to sparkle). It me made think that everything was going to turn out okay for Sara"—indicate that students are forming hypotheses as they read.

■ *Knowledge of literature:* Students' knowledge of literature (language, foreshadowing, irony, etc.) helps them to predict what the text will be about. For example, Billy wrote in his journal—*"I knew Jake was going to get lost when just before the big snow storm he lost his compass."*

■ *Engagement in reading:* Indicators of engagement are questioning, relating the text to their own lives, sharing opinions, and demonstrating feeling and emotions. Examples of engagement are *"I began to cry when . . ."* *"I know how Cassie feels because . . ."* and *"I didn't like the part where . . ."*

Teachers' responses to students' journals can reinforce the use of strategies; motivate continued reading; model grammar, spelling, and punctuation; and communicate the value of reading and writing. In addition, students can be active participants in their own assessments (Wollman-Bonilla, 1991). They can use self-evaluation forms to focus on areas related to their reading. The questions used for interviews (see Interviews section) can form the core for such self-evaluations for older students (e.g., When I come to a word I don't know I figure it out by _____). Younger students can respond to questions similar to those on the reading experiences inventory (Figure 11.9) by circling *Yes* or *No* or by circling a *happy* or *sad* face. Anecdotal records can summarize students' response journals over time. Teachers can share this information with the students, their parents, and administrators to illustrate students' reading and writing development.

Portfolios

Teachers have long recognized the value of keeping samples of students' work in reading and writing as a means of assessment. However, these samples were often based solely on skill activities and, occasionally, creative writing. Literacy ***portfolios*** are a type of performance-based assessment—they represent students' engagement with real literacy tasks (e.g., reading books, writing letters, creative writing, response journals, diaries, etc.). A portfolio also can contain many of the assessment features presented earlier, such as anecdotal records, experience inventories, observation records, and conference notes (Tierney, Carter, & Desai, 1991). Flood, Lapp, and Monken (1992) looked at the features of portfolio assessment in a large suburban school district and developed a set of issues and principles for portfolio assessment (see Figure 11.11). These issues and principles provide a comprehensive overview of the concepts and basic features of portfolio assessment.

Portfolios are expandable file folders for each student that include a variety of indicators of learning to help students, teachers, administrators, and parents understand literacy growth and development. Portfolios should be kept in an easily accessible place for students and teachers; both students and teachers should contribute to them regularly and use the contents for planning subsequent learning (Valencia, 1990).

Several types of portfolios can be used for different kinds of assessment and purposes. The *best-pieces* portfolio contains samples of the students' work. Students choose which examples of their work to add to the portfolio. Often, the teacher may wish to help students select the examples by discussing with the child the features of the selection and reasons for including it in the portfolio. The major advantage of having students select their own examples for the best-pieces portfolio is that it actively involves them in the process and makes them more aware of their own learning. The teacher can use students' portfolios to engage them in discussions about why they included a particular sample, how they have grown in their learning, what they liked and disliked in books read, the quality of their writing, and their use of reading and writing strategies.

Two other types are *process portfolios* and *descriptive portfolios*. Process portfolios include students' writing—samples of finished pieces, future plans and topics, writing in progress, self-evaluation reports, and reactions to instructional features (peer editing, group process writing, etc.). Teachers use descriptive portfolios to assess students' growth as well as the effectiveness of instruction. Included in descriptive portfolios would be items such as observations, interviews, anecdotal records, response journal entries, activity work, writing and reading samples, list of books read, responses to questions and discussion activities, and other information that the teacher deems important.

Portfolios can be extremely useful in instructional decisions because they provide a broad sampling of students' literacy development over extended periods, in a variety of tasks, and in different contexts. These features are important for several reasons. First, multiple samples of students' reading and writing help better explain individual students' learning of these complex processes. Second, by collecting curent information about their students, teachers can better understand how their students regularly perform classroom tasks (Winograd & Jones, 1992).

---

1. **Definition**
   Portoflio assessment is a form of process evaluation that consists of a multidimensional profile of student progress. It is designed and collected by students, teachers and parents to gather information about students' efforts toward self-monitoring as well as students' growth and achievement in literacy endeavors. It should be fluid, continuous and authentic, to be used by teachers and students as an instructional tool for improving literacy.

2. **Purpose**
   Portfolio assessment informs teachers, students and parents about:
   the capacity and depth of each student's overall performance
   the breadth of each student's performance
   the development/growth of each student
   the willingness/attitude of each student
   the collaborative stance of each student (social aspects of literacy)
   the knowledge of literacy process and evaluative process that each student possesses (declarative [what]; procedural [how]; and conditional [why])
   the ownership for learning of each student
   the multidimensionality of the whole child

3. **Audience**
   Portfolio assessment can inform several audiences:
   students
   current teachers
   future teachers
   parents
   site administrators
   district administrators
   legislators

---

continues

FIGURE 11.11
Issues and principles for portfolio assessment
(From J. Flood, D. Lapp, & S. Monken, "Portfolio Assessment: Teachers' Beliefs and Practices," *Literacy research, theory, and practice: Views from many perspectives,* C. Kinzer & D. Leu [Eds.] [p. 121]. Chicago: National Reading Conference, 1992. Reprinted by permission.

FIGURE 11.11
Continued

4. **Structure**
   Portfolios should be designed to deal with issues of:
      individual preferences (aesthetic, functional)
      space constraints
      budget constraints
      multiple copies for various audiences
      flexibility (on-going change, choice, cleaning-out)

5. **Contents**
   Portfolios can contain a variety of information that is selected by students, teachers and parents. The contents of the portfolio will change regularly depending upon the specific focus of the assessment. Portfolios can contain:
      Writing Samples (at various stages of development)
      Projects
      Independent Reading Responses
      Classroom Textual Materials
      Response Logs
      Journals
      Self-Evaluations
      Literature Charts

Some of the basic assessment purposes of portfolios have been discussed by Defina (1992). Teachers need to determine which of the basic purposes are appropriate for their students and their instructional goals.

■ *Monitoring students' growth over time.* Contents of students' portfolios will provide information about how much they have learned in specific areas, such as descriptive writing, use of reading strategies, and so forth.

■ *Examining students' understandings about process.* Students going back to learning activities and products will help provide the teacher with insights into their understanding that a completed product (a piece of writing) requires careful deliberation, revision, and rethinking.

■ *Creating opportunities for students' self-evaluation.* Portfolio contents readily identify students' literacy strengths and weaknesses, which helps teachers address individual student needs.

■ *Observing growth of culturally and linguistically diverse students.* Diverse students' performance on standardized tests typically does not accurately reflect their literacy capabilities. Portfolios do, however, allow teachers to determine better students' growth and development in relation to literacy tasks occuring in the classroom.

■ *Observing students' language development.* Because portfolios contain samples that represent students' actual language use, they can help teachers evaluate students' language comprehension and development.

- *Evaluating and developing literacy curriculum.* Teachers can revise the curriculum based on students' learning in relation to what they know, what they have learned, and what they need to know.
- *Determining the effectiveness of literacy instruction.* The teacher can analyze items in portfolios to determine what is effective with individual students, groups of students, and the class.

Although portfolio assessment can be extremely beneficial for both teachers and students, some obstacles hinder its successful use in an elementary school. Portfolios will work successfully only if they have: (1) school-wide support, particularly from the principal, (2) no competition from other forms of assessment, such as skills tests, which can result in teachers becoming frustrated, (3) self-reliance on the part of the teacher, and (4) valid teacher judgments (Dewitz, Carr, Palm, & Spencer, 1992).

SUMMARY //////////////////////////////////////

Students' literacy ability, interests, and development in any given classroom reflect a wide range. Assessment is necessary to differentiate instruction, which, in turn, is essential for a sound literacy program. In effective literacy instruction, ongoing assessment provides the blueprint for instruction.

Formal assessment generally involves the use of standardized tests. Unfortunately, many of the standardized tests do not accurately reflect all of our knowledge about the reading and writing processes. Assessment of students' learning should include a combination of procedures that reflect what we know about literacy and use of literacy skills in meaningful reading and writing situations.

Meaningful assessment is ongoing and includes a variety of informal procedures, such as anecdotal records, informal reading inventories, portfolios, and teacher observation. Anytime students engage in a literacy activity or event—reading, writing, editing, to name a few—they provide the teacher with clues about their instructional needs and literacy growth.

YOUR POINT OF VIEW //////////////////////////////////

Discussion Questions

1. During the first week of school, you suspect that Dee cannot read the social studies text that has been adopted for class use. You wish to verify or refute this hypothesis. What assessment procedures would you use? How would you interpret the assessment information?
2. Assume that the use of standardized reading tests in the elementary grades is prohibited for the next 5 years. Suggest alternatives procedures for assessment that will help parents, children, and administrators understand students' literacy growth.
3. A new student has enrolled in your classroom and you want to plan her reading instruction. What assessment procedures would you use if no information is available from her former school?

Take a Stand For or Against

1. Critical reading is supplying "correct" responses.
2. In many schools, the potential values that might be achieved from the use of standardized tests are lost because the school is more concerned with the ritual of administering the tests than with mining the test data.
3. Informal assessment proceduress can yield as much information about an individual student's reading as can standardized tests.

BIBLIOGRAPHY /

Betts, E. A. (1946). *Foundations of reading instruction.* New York: American Book Co.

Campione, J. C., & Brown, A. L. (1985). *Dynamic assessment: One approach and some initial data.* Urbana, IL: Center for the Study of Reading, Technical report no. 361.

Defina, A. A. (1992). *Portfolio assessment.* New York: Scholastic Professional Books.

Dewitz, P., Carr, E. M., Palm, K. N., & Spencer, M. (1992). The validity and utility of portfolio assessment. In C. Kinzer & D. Leu (Eds.), *Literacy research, theory, and practice: Views from many perspectives* (pp. 153–159). Chicago: National Reading Conference.

Early, M. (1992/93). What ever happened to . . .? *The Reading Teacher, 46,* 302–309.

Flood, J., Lapp, D., & Monken, S. (1992). Portfolio assessment: Teachers' beliefs and practices. In C. Kinzer & D. Leu (Eds.), *Literacy research, theory, and practice: Views from many perspectives* (pp. 119–127). Chicago: National Reading Conference.

Goodman, K. S. (1976). Strategies for comprehension. In P. Allen & D. Watson (Eds.), *Findings of research in miscue analysis: Classroom implication,* (pp. 94–102). Urbana, IL: The National Council of Teachers of English.

McKenna, M., & Kear, D. (1990). Measuring attitude toward reading: A new tool for teachers. *The Reading Teacher, 43,* 626–639.

Powell, W. R. (1976). *Informal reading inventories: Points of view.* Speech presented at the annual meeting of the College Reading Association, Miami.

Rankin, E., & Culhane, J. (1969). Comparable cloze and multiple choice comprehension test scores. *Journal of Reading, 13,* 193–198.

Rhodes, L. K., & Nathenson-Mejia, S. (1992). Anecdotal records: A powerful tool for ongoing literacy assessment. *The Reading Teacher, 45,* 502–511.

Teale, W. H., Hiebert, E. F., & Chittendon, E. A. (1987). Assessing young children's literacy development. *The Reading Teacher, 40,* 772–777.

Tierney, R., Carter, M., & Desai, L. (1991). *Portfolio assessment in reading-writing classrooms.* Norwood, MA: Christopher-Gordon.

Valencia, S. (1990). A portfolio approach to classroom reading assessment: The whys, whats, and hows. *The Reading Teacher, 43,* 338–341.

Valencia, S., & Pearson, P. D. (1987). Reading assessment: Time for a change. *The Reading Teacher, 40,* 726–732.

Walker, B. J. (1992). *Diagnostic teaching of reading: Techniques for instruction and assessment* (2nd ed.). New York: Merrill/Macmillan Publishing Co.

Winograd, P., Paris, S., & Bridge, C. (1991). Improving the assessment of literacy. *The Reading Teacher, 45,* 108–117.

Winograd, P., & Jones, D. L. (1992) The use of portfolios in performance assessment. In J. Craig (Ed.), *New directions for education reform: Performance assessment* (pp. 37–50). Western Kentucky University.

Wixson, K. K., Bosky, A. B., Yochum, M. N., & Alvermann, D. E. (1984). An interview for assessing students' perceptions of classroom reading tasks. *The Reading Teacher, 37,* 346–352.

Wollman-Bonilla, J. (1991). *Response journals.* New York: Scholastic Professional Books.

Woods, M. L., & Moe, A. J. (1989). *Analytical reading inventory* (4th ed.). New York: Merrill/Macmillan Publishing Co.

12

Classroom Management and Organization

THE IMPORTANCE OF CLASSROOM MANAGEMENT

PREVENTATIVE CLASSROOM MANAGEMENT

GROUPING FOR INSTRUCTION
Large Groups / Skill Groups / Interest Groups / Research Groups / Cooperative Learning Groups / Ability Groups

THE PSYCHOLOGICAL IMPACT OF GROUPING

ORGANIZING A CLASS FOR INSTRUCTION

ALTERNATIVE MANAGEMENT APPROACHES
The Ungraded School / The Unit Approach

INDIVIDUALIZED READING
Background / Practices / Problems / Applications

For the Reader

Do you recall your first experience with a large group of students in a classroom? If you have not yet started to teach, do you worry about how you will handle a large group of children? In either case, you can contemplate some of the demands and constraints of a classroom. Your perceived notions of assessment teaching—pretesting, setting objectives, teaching, allowing for student practice, using a variety of materials, reinforcing abilities in a variety of situations, and posttesting—must operate in the context of a class of 20 to 35 children.

As you know, students within any group differ in a variety of ways. Within the context of the classroom, you must strive to accommodate these individual differences. Effective reading teachers understand the organizational conditions found in their teaching situations and use various grouping procedures to maximize student learning.

This chapter discusses the various options

teachers have in teaching a large group of children. Current research suggests a strong relationship between classroom management and student achievement; therefore, meeting the demands of the classroom setting will provide rewards for both you and your students.

Key Ideas

- Effective classroom management and organization correlate with increased student achievement.

- Teachers of reading must be adept at planning and organizing their classrooms.

- Effective teachers are successful managers; they are aware of the total classroom environment and practice preventative measures to maintain a good learning environment.

- Cooperative grouping promotes peer tutoring, encouragement, and achievement.

- An individualized reading approach uses the principles of seeking, self-selection, and self-pacing.

- Implementing effective reading instruction in a class requires careful planning of materials, instruction, and time to meet the needs of individual students.

Key Terms

preventative classroom management a set of practices a teacher performs to promote a classroom environment conducive to learning and to prevent inappropriate student behavior.

cooperative grouping grouping where students of different ability levels work together.

individualized reading an approach to reading that includes student selection of materials, student pacing, individual student conferences with the teacher, and record keeping by both the student and the teacher.

THE IMPORTANCE OF CLASSROOM MANAGEMENT

A history of U.S. education dealing primarily with classroom practices would be, in essence, a history of the attempts to deal with student differences. All of the principles, techniques, approaches, materials, and assessment tools of effective teachers contribute to instruction. The plural *students* is key in the previous sentence; effective teaching of reading includes organizing and maintaining a classroom environment for 20 to 35 students that maximizes their learning. Effective classroom management and organization correlate with increased student achievement. In reviewing the data from California's *Beginning Teacher Evaluation Study* in the late 1970s, Guthrie (1980) stated:

> Classroom teachers contribute to reading achievement by optimizing the scheduled time for reading and related activities, selecting materials that insure learning, minimizing the interruption of student attention, and assessing the amount of learning as a guide to assigning new materials. When these conditions are met, time in school has a handsome payoff. (p. 502)

The preceding quote underscores the interdependence of instructional and managerial concerns. A teacher can employ the best reading techniques and materials but be unsuccessful due to poor classroom management. The reverse can also happen; a teacher may implement management techniques for conditions conducive to learning but not provide differentiated instruction. Often, new teachers are judged by their ability to manage a classroom effectively. In addition, studies of new and experienced teachers indicate that classroom management is one of the most difficult and stressful elements in teaching (Lasley, 1987).

PREVENTATIVE CLASSROOM MANAGEMENT

The literature on teacher effectiveness indicates that effective classrooms are well managed and feature large amounts of quality time; that is, periods when students are actively engaged with the teacher or materials (Blair, 1988). Poor management of students, reading groups, and activities usually translates into little quality engaged time. Effective classroom managers devote considerable time to **preventative classroom management.** As Good and Brophy (1987) succinctly state: "The key to success lies in the things the teacher does ahead of time to create a good learning environment and a low potential for trouble" (p. 177).

Effective classroom managers (1) prepare and plan, (2) manage group instruction, and (3) monitor student progress. At the beginning of the school year, successful teachers devote the time and energy necessary for getting to know their students, setting instructional goals, and making sure that the students know what is expected of them. Successful teachers also plan their lessons in advance, break their lessons down into small, concise parts for presentation, and plan a variety of activities to keep students engaged in learning. Effective teachers invest time and energy into planning. As a result, they have fewer disruptions and are more productive during the reading class.

Grouping students by itself does not automatically boost student achievement. The quality of the student and teacher interaction during grouping is the

Preventative classroom management includes having all plans and materials ready to use well in advance of the actual lesson.

key. The successful teacher manages group instruction by maintaining quality learning time.

Kounin (1970) identified group management techniques of effective teachers. His findings relate to both planning the groups of students and actually conducting group discussion. Blair (1988) reported on the six qualities of successful managers that Kounin identified:

1. With-it-ness is a teacher's ability to be continuously aware of what's going on in the classroom and to communicate this awareness to students.

2. Overlapping is a teacher's ability to do more than one thing at a time in the classroom without getting frustrated.

3. Smoothness of transition is the ability to go from one activity to another or one part of a lesson to another without wasted time and or undue delay.

4. Momentum is the teacher's ability to pace lessons.

5. Group alerting is the teacher's ability to keep students' attention during lessons.

6. Accountability is the teacher's ability to know how well students are learning. (pp. 35–36)

Monitoring students during group work entails (1) interacting directly with students or checking on student progress during seatwork and (2) using physical proximity or task-related comments to ensure that the students are working productively. Monitoring students helps you realize how well your students are understanding the activity; it also serves to maintain student engagement. Monitoring can help prevent, or at least minimize, potential management problems.

Following are practical suggestions by Blair (1988) to implement the preventative classroom management areas. Consider the following suggestions in your preparation before the school year begins:

- Collect as much assessment data on students as possible.
- Decide on classroom behavior rules and procedures that are not negotiable with students. These rules may concern tardiness, dismissal, hall passes, makeup work, homework, and so forth.
- Decide how you will explain classroom behavior standards, your expectations concerning assignments, and classroom procedures.
- Organize and arrange instructional materials for easy access or distribution.
- Plan the seating arrangement to ensure a smooth transition of movement from one activity to another. When teaching, you should be able to see the whole class.
- List your rules and procedures on the chalkboard or on a bulletin board. Communicate to students the consequences of improper behavior. (p. 34)

Consider the following suggestions in your preparation to teach a lesson:

- Have all materials ready to use well in advance of the actual lesson.
- Decide on how and when you and the students will use the materials.
- Know when you will distribute materials.
- Highlight times when students will be moving around the room, planning ahead for smooth transitions.
- Plan how you will handle seatwork assignments—including giving directions, collecting finished products, and providing activities for students who finish early—and how you will monitor the students' attention to assignments. (p. 35)

Consider the following suggestions while teaching a lesson:

- Be sensitive to the timing of your explanation. Notice cues from students that indicate interest or lack of interest.
- Do not dwell too long on a topic or a response, but do not leave a question hanging.
- Anticipate problems and handle any misbehavior as quickly and positively as possible.
- Move around the room. (p. 36)

Consider the following suggestions in monitoring student progress:

- Have students show their work to you.
- Have students demonstrate any particular skill or knowledge.
- Ask students directly how they are proceeding.
- Provide meaningful praise.
- Monitor seatwork by walking around the room and stopping to work with individuals.
- Give explicit direction for seatwork assignments. Go over the first two or three examples of any assignment to be certain that students understand the task.
- Be sensitive to signs of confusion, such as unnecessary movement or talking, puzzlement, or an incorrect response to an easy question. (p. 37)

GROUPING FOR INSTRUCTION

Grouping students to achieve instructional goals facilitates literacy learning. Grouping for instruction was formerly done more for administrative convenience than anything else. Research supports the use of grouping to increase direct instruction and the amount of engaged time in the classroom, however. Yet, grouping per se is ineffective if it fails to account for individual needs. The key is how well various grouping procedures permit the teacher to teach what students need to know.

Teachers must plan and organize their classrooms according to the particular learning goals they have established for their students. Teachers can choose from three basic grouping procedures: (1) whole groups, (2) small groups, and (3) individual learning. At various times, every classroom should incorporate all types of groups.

Large Groups

Large-group or whole-class instruction is appropriate at times in any classroom. When all children need to learn certain skills, large-group instruction is a more efficient use of both teacher and student time. This grouping is appropriate for storytelling, working on art activities related to a story, and teaching various study skills (such as SQ3R; skimming; scanning; reading maps, graphs, diagrams, and charts; using reference books; and using the library effectively).

Skill Groups

This type of grouping should depend on assessment of students' specific strengths and weaknesses. Such grouping brings together a small number of students for a specific purpose. Once the skill is mastered, the group is disbanded. Skill groups formed on the basis of students' needs include those for specific word skill instruction (e.g., sounds represented by consonants) and those for specific comprehension instruction (e.g., as inferring character traits).

In interest groups, students may read a book or books on a particular subject and give a group report.

Interest Groups

Groups may be formed based on a common interest. If group members are on different instructional reading levels, cooperation among members can increase motivation and self-satisfaction. Many activities lend themselves to interest grouping. Students who read books by the same author can research that author's life or style of writing, compare stories, or complete artwork related to their books. Students who are interested in a particular subject can come together and read various books on their instructional level and prepare a group report. Others can listen to a recorded story or watch a filmstrip about a particular topic together.

Research Groups

Grouping students together to research a particular topic is similar to interest grouping. With research grouping, students collect, organize, and synthesize information from a variety of sources and produce a final product (oral report, written report, art activity, or a play). Topics may include life in our community 50 years ago, how electric lights work, exploration and settlement of the West, the growth and change of the South, John F. Kennedy, the Supreme Court, Albert Einstein, hurricanes and tornadoes, how our circulatory system works, or the United Nations.

Cooperative Learning Groups

Placing students into small, heterogeneous groups to foster cooperative learning has generated considerable interest. With the great range of differences found in today's classrooms, *cooperative grouping* can effectively increase students' engaged time. The major requirement of cooperative groups is that individual members succeed only if all members of the group do. With this arrangement, all students have a vested interest in ensuring that other group members learn. Skill, interest, and research groups can be arranged to promote cooperative learning.

Johnson and Johnson (1978) have done considerable research on the use of cooperative groups and their implications in the mainstreaming movement. The Johnsons believe all students benefit from cooperation, and this type of grouping is the only one consistent with the purpose of mainstreaming. Their extensive research comparing competitive, individualistic, and cooperative grouping structures in the regular classroom revealed the following:

- Cooperative learning experiences promote more social acceptance, liking, and friendships between handicapped and nonhandicapped students than do competitive or individualistic ones.

- Cooperative learning experiences promote higher self-esteem of all students and more basic acceptance of oneself than do competitive or individualistic learning experiences.

- Cooperative learning experiences promote higher achievement of all students than do competitive and individualistic ones. (pp. 7, 8)

Although no one set of guidelines ensures successful implementation of cooperative grouping, the following steps can help teachers initiate cooperative groups:

1. Specify the instructional objectives.
2. Select the group size most appropriate for the lesson.
3. Assign students to heterogeneous groups.
4. Arrange the classroom so that group members are close together and the groups are as far apart as possible.
5. Provide appropriate materials.
6. Explain the task and the cooperative goal structure.
7. Observe student-student interaction.
8. Intervene as a consultant to help the group solve its problems in working together effectively, learn the interpersonal and group skills necessary for cooperating, or check that all members are learning the material.
9. Evaluate the group products, using a criterion-referenced evaluation system.

An interesting spin-off involving literature-based reading, interest groups, and co-operative learning groups is the use of literature study groups (Keegan and Shrake, 1991). Heterogeneous groups meet three times during the week to discuss a particular novel that each group selected to read. Students interact with each other on various levels and complete different tasks, including writing their reactions to the novel in literature logs. The group's discussion is taped and the teacher critiques it and provides valuable feedback. Citing the students' enthusiasm and excitement for reading, the authors state: "We are convinced that literature study groups offer a framework for allowing children opportunities to discover what they know, to extend their thinking, and to develop strategies that will make them lifelong readers." (p. 547)

Ability Groups

Grouping students on the basis of previous learning in order to satisfy instructional needs is a long-standing practice in our schools. Ability grouping is an accurate description when it refers to present rather than potential achievement. It was (and still is) sometimes used to imply intellectual capacity, however. When this occurs, the grouping suggests a final judgment rather than an initial step in ongoing diagnosis.

Certain other widespread but indefensible practices have resulted in criticism of ability grouping. Once groups are established, often their composition changes very little. Also student mobility among groups does not follow any performance criteria. Often, the high, medium, and low groups all inexplicably follow the same procedures—all read, or attempt to read, the same book(s) and attempt to cover the same amount of material. Without differentiation of instruction, the grouping is assumed to be a ritual unrelated to instructional strategy.

It is realistic to assume that grouping is neither inherently good nor bad. Practices within any type of grouping may either enhance student growth or become meaningless and even harmful educational rituals. Grouping students on the basis of instructional needs can, however, provide the framework for an alert teacher to develop meaningful, differentiated instruction. Grouping can narrow the range of differences and reading problems that face a teacher during a given instructional period. As a result, teachers can focus on particular short-term goals for specific students.

Practical considerations should always influence group management. Attempting to work with five or six groups, for example, may result in instructional time blocks that are too small to be effective. Two groups may produce too heterogeneous a collection of pupils in both groups. Such problems emphasize that grouping practices should be flexible.

In *Becoming a Nation of Readers* (1985), Anderson, Hiebert, Scott, and Wilkinson concluded that "grouping by ability may slow the progress of low-ability students" (p. 92). To improve the instruction provided to low-ability groups, the authors suggest "switching group assignments periodically, using criteria other than ability for group assignment, and maybe, increasing the time devoted to whole classroom" (p. 92).

Research by Allington (1983) also indicated that students in the low-ability group often receive less beneficial instruction than students in other groups.

THE PSYCHOLOGICAL IMPACT OF GROUPING

Students sometimes consider grouping a threat. Educators have adopted various philosophies about how to group students within a classroom to avoid comparisons among children. Suggestions include calling the groups 1, 2, 3; giving the groups irrelevant titles such as bluebirds, redbirds, and robins; and referring to groups by the names of children in them. The last suggestion has the merit of being straightforward. No one is humiliated on the basis of reading ability, and it does not appear that the teacher thinks every student should have a certain ability to read. Psychologically, however, it is inadvisable for a teacher to attempt to hide differences among beginning readers. It is impossible to fool students about their reading abilities, and when the poorer readers see that the bluebirds are better readers than the blackbirds, they too start attaching a stigma to poor reading ability.

Wise teachers have different groups of students doing different things so that neither the teacher nor the students attach significance to the grouping. A first grade teacher, for example, probably did not start all children reading at level 1 on the same day. This teacher observed the students closely and identified those who were ready to begin reading. When the teacher started this group in a book, other groups also worked on reading: some on a readiness workbook, some on teacher-prepared readiness materials, and some on an experience chart. In a natural way, the teacher developed the idea that groups of students would be reading from different books and working on different workbook pages. Teachers who can do this help students in many ways:

- They help students build a foundation for independent work habits.
- They reduce competition and feelings of failure, since students are not compared with each other on the same reading tasks.
- They reduce tension and bad attitudes toward reading.
- They permit students to progress at their own rate and minimize intergroup rivalry.
- They avoid using, consciously or unconsciously, a grouping system that is too rigid.
- They break the class into groups in which some students work independently while the teacher works intensively with others.

ORGANIZING A CLASS FOR INSTRUCTION

Implementing reading instruction in a class requires careful orchestration of time, materials, and instruction to satisfy the needs of individual children. Based on assessment data, teachers must make several decisions regarding student instructional levels, their specific skill development needs, materials to use, and types of grouping to improve learning. A visitor to a typical classroom will readily see that a reading class can be organized many ways. No one way is the only correct one. The guiding principle in deciding how to organize reading instruction should be how best to accommodate students' needs in reading.

Effective teachers use different types of groups at different times to achieve desired results. Flexibility in using groups is a key, because students are different and their needs continually change. They need a careful blend of teacher-directed and independent activities for their reading ability to improve. Figures 12.1 and 12.2 suggest possible ways to organize a class for reading instruction using a basal reader approach and two or three reading groups. Although many other combinations are possible, these figures should help you visualize the decisions a teacher must make when organizing instruction. Each day's reading lesson includes both teacher-directed and independent activities. The schedules offer one possible way to distribute components of the directed reading activity (DRA) throughout a week. The organization gives students a balance of instructional and independent activities.

Regardless of group membership, differences among students always exist. Therefore, teachers need to plan time for special needs grouping. Teachers can use this time to provide instruction to students lacking in particular skills

Effective classroom managers utilize a variety of grouping plans to keep students actively engaged in instructional activities.

	Monday	Tuesday	Wednesday	Thursday	Friday
Group 1	**Teacher Directed** DRA: Readiness; Silent Reading	**Teacher Directed** DRA: Comprehension Check Meaningful Oral Rereading Specific Skill Lesson	**Student Independent Work** Supplemental Activities Activity: Kit and/or Worksheets	**Student Independent Work** Free Reading	**Teacher Directed** Special Needs Group and **Student Independent Work** Supplemental Activities
Group 2	**Student Independent Work** Supplemental Activities	**Student Independent Work** Free Reading	**Teacher Directed** DRA: Readiness; Silent Reading	**Teacher Directed** DRA: Comprehension Check Meaningful Oral Rereading Specific Skill Lesson	

FIGURE 12.1
Suggested schedule for two reading groups

	Monday	Tuesday	Wednesday	Thursday	Friday
Group 1	**Teacher Directed** DRA: Readiness; Silent Reading	**Teacher Directed** DRA: Comprehension Check Meaningful Oral Rereading Specific Skill Lesson **Student Independent Work** Workbook Activity	**Student Independent Work** Supplemental Activities	**Student Independent Work** Supplemental Activities Free Reading	**Teacher Directed** Special Needs Group
Group 2	**Student Independent Work** Supplemental Activities **Teacher Directed** DRA: Readiness; Silent Reading	**Student Independent Work** Free Reading **Teacher Directed** DRA: Comprehension Check	**Student Independent Work** Workbook Activities **Teacher Directed** Meaningful Oral Rereading Specific Skill Lesson	**Student Independent Work** Workbook Activities	and
Group 3	**Student Independent Work** Supplemental Activities	**Student Independent Work** Supplemental Activities	**Teacher Directed** DRA: Readiness; Silent Reading	**Teacher Directed** DRA: Comprehension Check Meaningful Oral Rereading Specific Skill Lesson	**Student Independent Work** Supplemental Activities

FIGURE 12.2
Suggested schedule for three reading groups

(e.g., dictionary skills, study skills, and skills with vowel sounds). Once students in a special needs group learn the targeted skill or skills, the group is disbanded.

In looking at the suggested time schedules, it is important to remember that various reading activities (both teacher-directed and student independent work) are simultaneous. What the suggested schedules do not show are the preplanning efforts to ensure (1) the success of the teacher-directed and student independent activities and (2) the smooth transition from one activity to another to avoid wasting instructional time. These efforts depend on several considerations:

1. Grouping of any type should consider the students' needs.
2. Groups should be flexible—different types should be used for different purposes, permitting students to move to other groups if they progress.
3. Groups should be task-oriented.
4. Groups should permit students to work with the teacher as much as possible.
5. Groups should be structured to keep each group working productively, even while completing activities on their own.

The last consideration is critical. Although maintaining a high level of academic engaged time with students may be easier in a teacher-directed activity, guaranteeing that students will complete activities on their own is another matter. Success in this area requires explaining clearly what students are to do and how to do it before moving to another group, circulating around the room at times to monitor seatwork and to give feedback to students in different groups, explaining in advance what students are to do if they finish an assignment early, and preparing all materials ahead of time to ensure a smooth, systematic transition when moving from one group to another (Evertson, Emmers, Clements, Sandford, & Worsham, 1984).

ALTERNATIVE MANAGEMENT APPROACHES

Part of organizing the classroom for instruction is providing for individual differences among learners. As noted, finding ways to differentiate instruction is a top priority in education. This is a justifiable preoccupation, since success in this endeavor is the key to effective school programs.

The Ungraded School

The term *ungraded* signifies an administrative-instructional organization that de-emphasizes or suspends grade-level structure and emphasizes continuous student progress. It is one approach for dealing with student differences. Attempts at ungrading have been most successful at the beginning instructional levels. Thus, much of the literature focuses on the ungraded primary school, embracing the first 3 years of formal schooling.

The ungraded primary has a highly structured curriculum that accommodates a wide range of student achievement. All tasks are placed within a series of levels arranged in ascending order of difficulty. Students move through the sequence at their own pace. As they master one level, they move on to the next, thus making continuous progress. At the end of a year's instruction, each student is located somewhere on an identified skills continuum. The next year's instruction begins at this point.

Although instruction in the conventional grade-level system is geared to the average, experience tells us that students do not cluster closely around an achievement mean. Differences in achievement are marked, and they increase with instruction. The ungraded primary starts from the premise that each student should progress at his or her own rate, and the instructional program centers on each student's need at the moment. This is accomplished by breaking the primary years into a number of units of accomplishment, or levels of competency. As students achieve competency at one level, they start working at the next level. Teachers in the program determine the number of levels and the skills for students to master at each level.

Some of the educational advantages believed to be inherent in the ungraded primary plan include the following:

- It is easier to accommodate students' reading growth if you do not consider grade-level norms the first year.
- Failure and frustration in reading are less likely if comparison and promotion are deemphasized.
- Teachers often stay with the same group of students 2 years or longer. This gives them an opportunity to know their students better. They are less likely to push students beyond their ability during the first year, since they expect to work with them the next year.
- Students always work at the level on which they need instruction; consequently, they are not likely to miss some facet of instruction because they were absent several days.
- The slower learner does not repeat the first or second grade but may take 4 years to move up from the primary level.
- The ungraded plan is flexible, allowing students to cover learning phases rapidly when they are capable of doing so and giving them more time when they need it.
- Bright students do not skip a grade; they simply go through the entire primary curriculum at a faster rate.

No grouping method automatically solves all instructional problems. If a school shifts to the ungraded plan without understanding the goals to be achieved, any potential benefits are not likely to be realized. If teachers or parents continue to think in terms of a grade-level system, the plan is doomed from the start. On the other hand, if they consider the plan's philosophy sound and believe the chief reason for adopting it is to foster growth in students' reading abilities, any problems that do arise will be surmountable.

The Unit Approach

The unit approach has a long history of successful classroom use. Although it can be considered a method of instruction, this chapter discusses it because of its classroom management aspects. Units provide many ways for coping with individual differences, differentiating instruction, and grouping pupils for specific short- and long-term activities.

This approach provides teachers with so many options that it has a wide array of titles, including resource units, teaching units, activity-centered instruction, core approach, and survey units. Teachers can integrate reading instruction and related language skills in numerous learning activities, all focusing on a specific curricular theme.

In developing a unit, teachers may discover that the first important task is finding materials at various levels. The references available vary from school to school. Basal readers at all levels can serve for such a unit, as can subject-matter texts. *My Weekly Reader* files can provide materials on many topics, and the school library and public library can be sources of books on special topics.

The teacher can devise a unit for any subject area. It can span a few days, during which students attempt to find the answer to a particular question, or it may extend over several weeks and end in some class project. The product might be a play, a school program, or a science fair with many individual and committee projects. Although the unit approach is not new, it is consistent with the aims of modern curriculum planning. Unit study can help avoid the tendency toward fragmentation of the curriculum into isolated, seemingly unrelated parts.

Units lend themselves to two types of major emphasis. The first builds students' experiences around a specific topic, such as how we get our food. Experiences might include visits to various types of farms, a cannery, a cold storage plant, a meat packing plant, a dairy, and a bakery. Students may plant and care for a garden or window box. The second major emphasis is broad reading. The early elementary grades will probably emphasize the experience approach, while the intermediate grades will shift to reading. These two methods are extremely compatible; when combined properly, they undoubtedly make for a better total learning situation.

Advantages. The potential advantages of the unit approach are numerous. Actual benefits of its use vary according to such factors as the teacher's skill, the students' reading ability and work habits, and the amount of supplementary reading material available. Following are some of the more frequently mentioned advantages of the unit approach:

- The unit serves as the framework for shaping learning experiences into larger, more meaningful wholes. The unit permits more than the superficial study of a topic and encourages application of skills in broadly varied reading.
- Units can be used in any curricular area.
- Students learn that reading is the key to learning about all subjects and not just an operation performed in the basal reader and accompanying workbooks.

- The unit approach can and should include a great variety of experiences related to reading, such as excursions, field trips, and small-group participation, in working on various facets of the problem.
- Units structure the learning situation to make reading more varied, more meaningful, and more interesting.
- Units permit readers of widely different abilities to work on different facets of the same project. Reading materials at many levels of difficulty can be used, and students need not be directly compared as readers.
- The unit approach gives teachers flexibility and freedom to work with an individual or group engaged in some reading activity at their own level. The reader with problems and the accelerated reader can work independently and successfully on something that is challenging.
- Units aid independent reading and help foster independence in research reading.

The unit approach can and should include many hands-on experiences.

A unit on weather for a fifth grade class may be used as an illustration. The teacher arouses the interest of the class through an assignment to watch weather reports on television, to find interesting pictures of weather stations, and to discuss in class stories dealing with weather. Out of this grows the decision to have a study unit on weather. Under the teacher's direction, students work cooperatively in identifying objectives, finding questions to be answered, and working on individual projects within the unit's limits.

Objectives of the unit on weather include:

- To learn ways in which weather helps or harms people.
- To learn what causes various types of weather and changes of seasons.
- To learn the causes and effects of rainfall, temperature, and fog.
- To become familiar with the instruments used in measuring or predicting weather changes.

Questions to be answered include:

- How is a thermometer constructed and how does it work?
- What is fog?
- What causes hail?
- What is lightning? Why is it followed by thunder?
- Why do we have seasons such as winter and summer?
- Why are some parts of the earth always hot and others always cold?
- Why is there very little rainfall in one part of a country and a great deal in another part?
- Why is it important for people to be able to predict the weather?
- What is a barometer? How does it work?
- What is humidity?

Activities or projects, both individual and group, include:

- Keeping a daily record of temperature. Securing temperatures registered in cities in different parts of the country.
- Preparing charts and graphs illustrating some aspect of weather, including average rainfall for different states and countries, the relationship between rainfall and the type of crops raised in a particular area, and the effect of rainfall on population density.
- Preparing maps showing occurrences of tornadoes, hurricanes, and floods during the past decade.
- Explaining and demonstrating a thermometer and barometer.
- Researching the work of the U.S. Weather Bureau in predicting weather.
- Studying the effects of weather on human dress, shelter, and diet.
- Measuring rainfall during a rain.
- Securing pictures illustrating any facet or effect of weather, such as floods, erosion, storms on land and sea, barren deserts, and permanent snow.

For the culminating activity, the class decides to have a weather fair. They display all individual and group projects, including posters, graphs, charts, picture series, student-made instruments for measuring weather, and written projects. Parents are invited to visit the class on a particular afternoon, and other classes in the school see the displays at certain times that day. Students explain their projects and derive a great deal of satisfaction from this culminating activity.

This well-planned unit provides a variety of purposeful learning experiences. The teacher structures activities so that all facets of the curriculum receive attention.

Mathematics.   In the intermdiate grades, a lack of understanding of the problems to be solved is more of a stumbling block in mathematics than is a lack of computational skills. Failure to read problems critically results in hazy understanding. In unit work, math problems emerge from the learner's immediate experiences. Problems such as finding the average rainfall, average temperature, or total foodstuffs raised are related to larger goals and become meaningful. The need for accurate measurement becomes apparent in building a barometer or measuring rainfall.

Health.   One particular topic, how weather affects our health, almost becomes a unit within a unit. The entire class participates, with students writing a brief account of anything they find in their reading that pertains to the topic. The teacher has a few references for students who need help in finding material. The health lesson also becomes a lesson in communication skills as students work on their written assignments. Students also practice their oral language skills as they report their findings to the class.

Social studies.   The discussion on health leads into social studies topics. A discussion of diet in relation to health leads to questions and discussion of how weather affects diet or production of foodstuffs. A discussion of the economic value of climate logically follows. The class discusses climate's relationship to certain natural resources, such as forestry, deposits of coal, and petroleum. The relationships among rainfall, temperature, winds, forests, and the types of crops are discussed. Methods of cultivation and crop rotation are studied in relation to land erosion.

Science.   This unit essentially is a science unit. It emphasizes how scientists predict and track the weather and the scientific instruments they use in the process. Studying the thermometer and barometer raises many scientific principles and questions, such as the principles of expansion, gravity, and pressure, and the questions of whether mercury is a metal, why it is used in the instruments, and how heat causes a thermometer to work.

Spelling.   Students learn many words incidentally as they print them on their posters or charts. The teacher assigns new words as part of the unit (such as weather, thermometer, mercury, rainfall, temperature, erosion, and bureau).

Reading.   Reading provides the vehicle for all of the other curricular activities. The unit stresses that students are getting information for health, geography, and science. The reading is purposeful. Neither the reading nor the teaching of it is the compulsive let's-get-this-workbook-page-finished approach. The teacher keeps in mind the principles of teaching reading, being particularly careful to provide a variety of supplementary materials at many grade levels.

Using the unit method in no way restricts the teacher in developing students' reading skills. In fact, once the teacher has completed preliminary planning, he or she has as much time and opportunity to help individual students or small groups as with conventional lessons.

Most unit work introduces a heavy vocabulary load, so the class must spend time on vocabulary development. As different students read and ask for help with unknown words, the teacher can prepare several lists of new words to be studied during the course of the unit. One such list might be taken from the more difficult sources and used exclusively with the advanced reading group. Vocabulary exercises for average readers and those experiencing problems can use easier words. Many new and unknown words can help in teaching phonic analysis and stressing the importance of contextual clues in solving meaning difficulties.

INDIVIDUALIZED READING

A movement? A method? A classroom organization? A philosophy of instruction? The term *individualized reading* has different meanings for different users, but it has enjoyed wide acceptance and use in our schools for many years. Paradoxically, its greatest potential strengths and weaknesses stem from the same factors. It has no concise definition, and no blueprint exists for making it work. Its success depends upon creative responses. However, its drawback is its inability to prevent teachers from developing nonproductive rituals.

Background

During the 1950s, frustration with the status quo in reading instruction reached a new high, and the climate for change seemed particularly good. The new emphasis on gearing reading instruction to individual students' needs and interests came to be known as individualized reading. Proponents of this reform movement had great enthusiasm, which was essential for change. They attacked two educational practices in particular, the use of basal readers and ability grouping.

Critics found certain indefensible practices in the use of basals and groupings. Some teachers relied on basal texts to the exclusion of other materials. When this occurred, reading and learning to read were easily reduced to deadly routines. Some students who had the ability to move through basals fairly rapidly were kept with the group, severely limiting their advancement. These students were asked to complete tasks such as workbook exercises, which added nothing to their growth in reading. Students at the other end of the achievement continuum were kept reading the same primer and first grade basals for 2 or more years even though they did not make any progress.

The other area of concern, the practice of dividing a class into three groups, was made to look like a ritual that ignored individual differences and needs. Some teachers had students read round robin, embarrassing poorer readers and providing unacceptable models of oral reading for the remainder of the group. Classes probably never enjoyed stories read under such adverse conditions. These prac-

FLASHBACK

Individualized reading is an approach based on the concepts of seeking, self-selection, and self-pacing. Willard C. Olson, who proposed these concepts in the early 1950s, believed youngsters, moving at their own pace, grow best when surrounded by a large selection of books from which to choose. This approach stresses that each child differs with respect to learning style, learning rate, and interests.

UPDATE

With a greater emphasis on literature in modern reading programs, Olson's original views on individualization are at the heart of everyday reading in today's American classrooms. Literature-driven programs have resulted in more instructional time being allocated to a variety of authentic reading situations. Realizing that comprehension is best fostered within the context of literature, that students will be achieving at different levels of ability, and that students in our classrooms are increasingly diverse, teachers are creating more situations involving literature in classrooms. Hand-in-hand with this literature emphasis goes the importance of effective classroom management techniques. With greater time being devoted to a variety of authentic reading situations, teachers of reading need to be able to create, manage, and maintain an environment conducive to learning.

tices were not inherent in the use of basals or grouping. Rather, they developed as a result of teachers and school systems.

Practices

Individualized reading rejects the lockstep instruction that tends to become standardized within the framework of the graded system and traditional graded materials. The success or failure of an individualized program rests almost exclusively with the teacher, which is one of the reasons why individualized reading is so difficult to define.

Over the years, a number of practices have become associated with individualized reading. These include students' self-selection of materials, self-pacing in reading, individual student conferences with the teacher, and emphasis on record keeping by the teacher, student, or both. One other notable characteristic is the need for a wide variety of reading material in each classroom. This becomes mandatory if students are to select books that they are interested in and can read.

Seeking, Self-Selection and Self-Pacing. Willard C. Olson's writing (1949, 1959) is frequently cited as the basis for the emphasis on seeking, self-selection, and self-pacing. Although these concepts are not new to education, the individualized reading movement has given them a new emphasis in reading instruction. The principle underlying the advocacy of self-selection is psychologically sound. Since individual differences among students in a given classroom are tremendous, the teacher cannot assume that one basal series or a single text will address all their needs.

The success of self-selection depends on several factors. First, students must have some interests they wish to explore further. This helps motivate them in the reading situation. Second, the available materials must fit their interests and ability to read independently. When these conditions are met, students should seek out the materials fitting their needs, interests, and reading levels. If they select wisely, their reading ability should grow.

Carried to extremes, this idea of individualized reading minimizes the teacher's role in guiding students to materials so that self-selection almost becomes a fetish. Teachers should not assume that students, when permitted to do so, will select materials they can read. While that may be true in a number of cases, it is not an inevitable law of child behavior.

Students' self-selection is often limited by the fact that teachers have previously chosen the 100 or 200 books found in the classroom from among thousands available. Individualized reading and self-selection do not preclude teachers from recommending books or guiding students toward certain materials, but this type of guidance does call for a high level of teacher competency. The teacher must know students' interests, their reading abilities, and the difficulty level of materials if their suggestions are to help them grow.

Economy in the teacher-learning situation must also be considered. If, after a period of seeking, students have not made a selection and settled down to reading, they may not yet be ready for self-selection. Thus, with many students, self-selection can safely be tempered with guidance.

Teacher-Student Conferences. The teacher-student conference is one of the major features of individualized reading. It is also potentially one of its great strengths. The conference is a brief session in which teachers give their undivided attention to one student. The primary goal of the conference is to ensure children that they have an appreciative audience.

The chief value of the conference is that it involves students in the reading process. For the conference be most effective, however, teachers must be more than listeners. In addition to being appreciative audiences, teachers must assume some responsibility for helping students develop values and self-understanding, goals often best achieved through judicious questioning. The conference provides a means by which teachers can learn important facts about students' psychological needs and how they fulfill these needs. Discussing reading with a respectful adult helps give students insights into their own problems and discover how others have handled such difficulties.

The conference serves as a catalyst for teacher-student rapport. For some students, the teacher's positive response to their reading is a stronger motivation than the act of reading itself. A skillful, sympathetic teacher can provide this extrinsic reward while slowly moving the student toward accepting reading as its own reward.

Preparing for the conference is essential, but one should avoid a standardized format. Veatch (1963) has listed factors that teachers should consider in setting up conferences:

- As a general rule, students should inform the teacher when they feel ready to participate in the conference.
- The teacher should be familiar with the book or story that a student plans to discuss.
- The teacher should inform students when or in what order they will be scheduled for the conference.
- All other students in the class should be engaged in some other meaningful activity. One suggestion is to have them selecting and reading books independently.
- The teacher must be prepared to ask questions that stimulate thought instead of asking only for factual information.
- The class and teacher should work out some system for students to receive help pronouncing unknown words during their independent reading.

Frequency, length, and format of conferences were the basis for many questions from teachers in the early days of the individualized reading movement. Today, we understand that practices in these areas must vary from classroom to classroom. No single proposal regarding format, frequency, or length of conferences is the best for all situations. A logical schedule for a classroom of 24 pupils may be unworkable with a class of 35. Furthermore, the length and frequency of the conference should vary with different grade levels and different ability levels within a grade. The student who has read a story consisting of only several hundred words will probably not take as much time with the teacher as the one who read *Charlotte's Web.* All conferences therefore need not use the same procedures nor last the same amount of time.

In the case of a reader who needs little encouragement to read, a brief exchange between the teacher and student may suffice on some occasions. A word of praise, a question about whether there are still a number of books in the classroom that the student wishes to read, and an offer of help when needed may be adequate. Since the sharing conference is primarily a confidence-building experience, some students obviously will need more attention than others. Some continually avoid a conference because they consider reading a threat rather than a pleasure. These students need constant encouragement and praise for their accomplishments.

Record Keeping. Record keeping received considerable attention in the early descriptions of individualized reading. This activity generally had little or nothing to do with actual diagnosis of reading needs. Rather records seemed to emphasize the number of books read and to offer proof that the system was working. In some cases, this feature became dominant, with students reading primarily to add titles to their lists. Also, it tended to invite comparisons of achievement, the opposite intention of individualized reading. Over the years, attention to this activity has diminished.

Problems

Students reading independently, selecting what they wish to read, and reading at their own pace strike some critics as quite idealistic. To keep this philosophy from becoming unrealistic, teachers must expend a great deal of effort in classroom management. Over the years, teachers have voiced a number of concerns, including:

- What types of materials are needed?
- How does one initiate an individualized program?
- When and how is ongoing diagnosis achieved?
- How is provision made for teaching the necessary reading skills?
- When the teacher is involved in teacher-student conferences, what are the other students doing? How do these students get "instant help" for their reading problems?

How the teacher handles these and other issues determines the success or failure of an individualized program.

Materials. A reading program embracing self-selection and self-pacing and tailored to individual students' interests cannot function in a learning environment that does not include a wide selection of reading materials. This is not a special problem limited to individualized reading. Any classroom or school should meet this requirement, regardless of the methodological approach or program.

Although it is difficult to say how many books are adequate, a minimum figure frequently mentioned is approximately 100 different trade book titles per classroom. These 100 books also should be changed throughout the year. Factors to consider include grade level; students' interests and abilities; class size; whether books can be rotated with other classrooms; whether the school supports a central library; and whether the same materials are used extensively in other subject areas, such as social studies and science, in preparing units.

Trade books are not the only source of materials, although they are likely to be the major source. Classrooms should contain magazines, newspapers, various reading kits, *My Weekly Reader, Reader's Digest* (skill-builder materials), and other reading materials students might choose. Reading materials should cover many areas, such as biography, science, sports, exploration, hobbies, fairy tales, medicine, space, poetry, humor, adventure, myth, and travel.

Starting a Program.   All elementary teachers are likely to be doing some things that fit logically under the heading of individualization. Any of the formal aspects of individualized reading, such as self-selection or individual conferences, can be used with one student, a small group, or an entire class. Obviously, the latter approach presents the most problems; therefore, perhaps you should start with one of the alternatives.

Prior to any conference, assemble a number of books on a reading table. Include a number of new books and books that you think will appeal to the student or students involved. Begin by calling together five or six students. Explain that they will be selecting their own books to read at their desks during the reading period. At the end of the group conference, tell the group members that after selecting the books they wish to read, they are to go to their desks and read their selections silently. Also tell students that they may keep the books at their desks until they are finished.

Within a day or two, have students meet again in the individualized group. Explain that each student is to schedule a conference with you to tell something about the book and to read a part of the book that was particularly interesting. Individuals are to tell you when they are ready for a conference.

Providing for Assessment.   Individualized reading is an approach that by its very nature calls for considerable assessment if students are to progress smoothly in reading. Some may not be able to achieve in an individualized setting without ongoing assessment.

No assessment techniques are associated exclusively with individualized reading. The individual teacher-student conference may be the major source of assessment information. Lipton and Kaplan (1978) provided the following list as a framework for diagnosing a student's oral reading patterns and strategies during a conference:

1. Has a cheerful/fearful approach to books.
2. Reads word-by-word.
3. Hesitates, then asks for help.
4. Sits passively when confronted by unknown words.
5. Uses graphic or configurational cues.

6. Uses phonemic cues.

7. Omits, inserts, or substitutes certain words, but does not alter the grammatical structure.

8. Omits, inserts, or substitutes certain words and alters the grammatical structure.

9. Omits, inserts, or substitutes certain words, but does not alter the meaning.

10. Omits, inserts, or substitutes certain words and alters the meaning.

11. Uses context cues to decode difficult words.

12. Uses regression to seek meaning.

13. Uses punctuation as an aid to meaning.

14. Demonstrates skills: a) main ideas, b) recall of details, c) making inferences, d) drawing conclusions, e) understanding vocabulary. (p. 377)

Teaching Reading Skills. The early individualized movement was in part a reaction against reading instruction that stressed skills at the expense of the total reading process. In some classrooms, all students received the same instruction, worked on the same skill-building exercises, and read the same materials. When these practices were prevalent, one could argue that instruction was predetermined rather than based on students' needs and abilities. Such uniform practices inevitably caused some students to become bored with reading instruction.

Unfortunately, the attack on uniform skills instruction for all spread to the teaching of skills themselves. Actually, skills teaching was not explicitly rejected, but this facet of individualized reading instruction was neglected. In recent years, most proponents of individualized reading have accepted the importance of skills teaching. How and when the program incorporates skills teaching remain open to question, however. Two common responses are to (1) teach some skills in the teacher-student conference, and (2) teach other skills as students need them.

The first answer represents an inefficient procedure, unless the student participating in the conference is the only one in the class who can profit from the instruction. Any reading skill that can justifiably be taught to the entire class should be taught to everyone. Students who learned with the first presentation should be doing something else when the teacher makes subsequent presentations to students who did not learn.

The basic validity of the second response (teach skills when they are needed) cannot be faulted, but it can be both vague and difficult to implement when each student in the class is reading a different book. Differentiating skills instruction need not assume that no two students or groups can profit from the same instruction. This extreme position is simply the opposite of the idea that all students in a class can profit from the same amount of time spent with the same book. Diagnosis is the best way to identify what is appropriate instruction.

Basic skills can include dozens of abilities. The major concerns for the elementary teacher include word identification, knowledge of word meanings, and application of reading skills in meaningful context.

Meaningful Class Activities. Individualized reading calls for a high degree of planning and subtle directing. The following brief listing of activities is only illustrative. The tasks are not identified by grade level, since many may be adapted to various levels. The listing includes class, group, and individual activities covering skill development, recreational reading, reading in curricular areas, and creative activities.

1. Self-selection of books or other reading materials. This may include browsing and sampling. Selection is followed by independent reading of materials.

2. Conducting library research for an individual or group report. Such an activity may relate to a unit in some other subject.

3. Planning creative writing experiences to include original stories, poems, letters to a classmate in the hospital or one who has moved away, invitations to parents to visit school, or a riddle composition to be read to the class during a period set aside for such activities.

4. Preparing artwork such as:

    a. Drawing or pasting pictures in a picture dictionary.

    b. Drawing a picture to accompany a student-dictated, teacher-written story.

The use of research groups in individualized reading programs is an excellent means to integrate literacy skills and strategies in the content areas.

    c. Preparing posters or book covers to illustrate the key point in a book or story the student has read.

5. Using workbook pages or teacher-prepared seatwork guides to develop particular skills such as:

    a. A dictionary exercise that follows an introduction of a skill, such as alphabetizing by initial letter or by two or more letters, use of guide words, pronunciation guides, or syllabication.

    b. Word analysis skills such as associating sounds with graphic symbols, noting compound words, abbreviations, and the like.

    c. Study skills involving effective use of parts of a book, such as the index, table of contents, glossary, or appendix.

    d. Study skills involving effective use of the library card catalog or reference materials.

6. Using an appropriate filmstrip with the entire class, a smaller group, or two pupils.

7. Teaching and testing word meanings.

    a. Workbook pages or teacher-prepared seatwork.

    b. Vocabulary building cards or notebooks in which students write one or more common meanings for new or unknown words they run across in their reading.

    c. Activities in which students write as many sentences as possible, using a different connotation for words listed by the teacher. For example: *light*— light in weight, light in color, light the fire, light on his feet, her eyes lit up, and lighthearted.

8. Making a tape recording of a story. A group of four to six students may each read the part of one character. Students may do practice reading and actual recording in the rear of the classroom or in any available space in the building.

9. Testing or assessment activities. The entire class or any size group may take a standardized test (or reading subtest); tests that accompany basal series; *My Weekly Reader* tests; or informal, teacher-made tests. These should be scored and studied for assessment information.

Applications

It is important to remember that the basal reading approach, not individualized reading, is the most prevalent method of instruction in our schools. However, the basic tenets of individualized reading—seeking, self-selection and self-pacing-—form a basis for any successful reading program. Every reading program should be individualized in the sense that they address students' individual needs.

    Grouping students to achieve instructional goals is part of individualizing instruction. As discussed, grouping students for particular purposes can result in improved achievement scores. This is the essence of individualized instruction. It is particularly satisfying to note that instruction can be individualized in many ways, depending on the teacher, the program, and the students.

Effective teachers use assessment procedures and teacher-student conferences. Using individual teacher-student conferences in every reading program is perhaps the greatest contribution of individualized reading. With conferences, teachers can personalize their teaching, diagnose student strengths and weaknesses, teach necessary skills, and prescribe individual assignments.

Teachers at every grade level in all reading programs should promote independent reading habits. Student self-selection and self-pacing can be integrated with the basal reading program, giving teachers and students some measure of flexibility but still retaining the structure inherent in the basal system. Students can have some freedom in choosing particular stories, and the teacher can assign workbook and reinforcement activities to fit individual needs.

Moreover, the essential elements of individualized reading closely resemble the literature-based reading program (see Chapter 9). This literary approach uses various types of literature to teach reading skills and stimulate reading as a leisure-time activity. An experimental study by Eldredge and Butterfield (1986) supported the effectiveness of a literature program incorporating many of the qualities of individualized reading. The authors concluded that a literature program is a viable alternative to traditional reading instruction. Indeed, all teachers should embody the basic tenets of individualized reading in their own teaching, regardless of grade level or reading approach.

SUMMARY /

Effective reading teachers are proficient in providing and maintaining conditions conducive to learning. These teachers practice preventative managerial strategies to reduce the likelihood of trouble and to maintain student engagement in reading activities.

Key elements of classroom management include planning reading activities, managing group instruction, and monitoring student progress. Students can be grouped several ways. Options for maximizing student involvement include flexible use of the whole group, small groups, and individual learning. Small groups can be arranged according to ability, skill, need, interest, or a research topic.

Cooperative learning groups benefit all students and are particularly relevant to successful mainstreaming. Alternative approaches to classroom management include the ungraded school, unit teaching, and individualized reading. Grouping itself is not the most important factor in learning, however. The real concerns are accommodating individual differences and increasing the degree of students' time engaged in selected tasks.

YOUR POINT OF VIEW /

Discussion Questions

1. Is it possible to overemphasize a concern for classroom management?
2. What are the disadvantages of cooperative grouping?
3. What are the major advantages and disadvantages of the unit approach? The ungraded school? Individualized reading?

4. A major feature of individualized reading is the student-teacher conference. What are some important features to consider before, during, and after such a conference?

Take a Stand For or Against

1. Being proficient in classroom management is not as important in kindergarten and grade 1 as it is in grade 6.
2. Teachers tend to view their students in terms of their placement level.
3. Ability grouping reduces the opportunities for students to learn from one another.
4. The present structure of the classroom environment prohibits cooperative learning groups.

BIBLIOGRAPHY /

Allington, R. L. (1983). The reading instruction provided readers of differing reading abilities. *Elementary School Journal, 82,* 548–559.

Anderson, R. C., Hiebert, E. H., Scott, J. A., & Wilkinson, I. A. G. (1985). *Becoming a nation of readers: The report of the commission on reading.* Washington, DC: The National Institute of Education.

Blair, T. R. (1988). *Emerging patterns of teaching: From methods to field experiences.* New York: Merrill/Macmillan Publishing Co.

Eldredge, J. L., & Butterfield, D. (1986). Alternatives to traditional reading instruction. *The Reading Teacher, 40,* 32–37.

Evertson, C. M., Emmer, E. T., Clements, B. S., Sandford, J. P., & Worsham, M. E. (1984). *Classroom management for elementary teachers.* Englewood Cliffs, NJ: Prentice-Hall.

Good, T. L., & Brophy, J. E. (1987). *Looking in classrooms (4th ed.)* New York: Harper & Row.

Guthrie, J. T. (1980). Time in reading programs. *The Reading Teacher, 33,* 500–502.

Johnson, D. W., & Johnson, R. T. (1978b). *Social interdependence and mainstreaming: A teaching module. Learning Together and Alone.* Bloomington: University of Minnesota.

Keegan, S., & Shrake, K. (1991). Literature study groups: An alternative to ability grouping. *The Reading Teacher, 44,* 542–547.

Kounin, J. S. (1970). *Discipline and group management in classrooms.* New York: Holt, Rinehart, & Winston.

Lasley, T. J. (1987). Classroom Management. *The Educational Forum, 51,* 285–298.

Lipton, A., & Kaplan, E. (1978). The pupil-teacher reading conference. *The Reading Teacher, 31,* 376–377.

Olson, W. (1949). *Child development.* Boston: D.C. Heath Co.

Olson, W. (1959). Seeking, self-selection and pacing in the use of books by children. In J. Veatch (Ed.), *Individualizing your reading program.* New York: G. P. Putnam's Sons.

Veatch, J. (1963). *Self-selection and the individual conference in reading instruction.* In *Improving reading instruction.* Joint proceedings of reading conference and summer workshop (Vol. 1). State College, PA: Pennsylvania State University, 19–29.

13

Focus on All Learners

Viola E. Florez

For the Reader

Every classroom is composed of individuals of varying intellectual ability, social or cultural background, language ability, and physical attributes. All teachers should be prepared to deal effectively with diversity. This chapter focuses attention on culturally and linguistically diverse and special students. Although such students are certainly receiving considerable attention in professional journals, newspapers, magazines, and school programs, it is important to remember that all children have specific needs and that literacy instruction should consider these needs. This separate chapter on the topic highlights this important aspect of teaching reading in today's schools.

Key Ideas

- Student differences must be a primary consideration in effective literacy instruction.

- Culturally and linguistically diverse and special students require education based on their educational needs rather than on clinical or diagnostic labels.

- Teachers must be knowledgeable of and sensitive to the dialects and languages of the students they instruct.

- P.L. 94-142, the Individuals with Disabilities Education Act, mandates a free and appropriate education for all special needs children.

- An Individualized Education Plan (IEP) must be developed and maintained for all students with learning disabilities.

Key Terms

culturally and linguistically diverse students whose culture and language or dialect are different from the primary culture or language found in the public schools.

dialect approach teaching reading using materials written in the language of the dialect-speaking students.

dual language reading approach a reading approach that provides reading instruction in the primary language of the students as well as in standard English.

mainstreaming the least restrictive school environment, which has been interpreted to mean the regular classroom.

individualized education plan (IEP) a plan of education, written for each student who has a learning disability, that details the educational program for the student. The school, student, and parents jointly develop an IEP.

gifted students students identified to have high-performance abilities and capabilities.

ACCEPTING DIFFERENCES

Proper acknowledgment of students' differences requires the teacher to adjust each student's educational program appropriately. All teachers encounter students who are different intellectually, psychologically, culturally, or physically. Knowledge of each student's background and learner characteristics is necessary for effective instruction. Teachers must remember that all students are individuals who require educational modifications based on their needs. The diagnostic teaching procedures recommended in Chapter 11 for regular classroom instruction also apply to culturally and linguistically diverse, disabled, and gifted students. Teachers must understand cultural diversity, however, to diagnose accurately a student's strengths and weaknesses.

CULTURAL AND LINGUISTIC DIVERSITY

In Chapter 3 we discussed the term *culturally and linguistically diverse*, which refers to students whose culture and language or dialect differ from that of the school. The term refers to individuals from diverse ethnic and racial backgrounds, including Native American, Mexican American, Puerto Rican, Asian, and African American. Difficulty in learning to read and write has been a major educational problem for some students from these groups.

Chapter 3 included instructional recommendations and guidelines for working with culturally and linguistically diverse students. These guidelines and recommendations can apply to all students, but they are crucial when teaching linguistically and culturally diverse students. Knowledge and application of these guidelines within the instructional approaches and strategies presented in this chapter can better serve the literacy needs of culturally and linguistically diverse students. An important instructional feature is the interrelatedness of the language arts (speaking, listening, reading, and writing) coupled with children's literature. Literature provides students with additional vocabulary and ideas to enhance their knowledge base of English (Morrow, 1992).

EARLY READING APPROACHES FOR CULTURALLY AND LINGUISTICALLY DIVERSE STUDENTS

When culturally and linguistically diverse children enter school, a major problem is likely to be a lack of school-related experiences. The school is structured to provide learning experiences that may be largely foreign to some of these children. Two potential solutions are obvious: (1) providing experiences the children need to cope with the tasks that they face in school and (2) altering the curriculum to accommodate their needs.

Although culturally and linguistically diverse students are on the same continuum as other children, they often have experiences that are different from the mainstream. For example, insufficient emergent literacy experiences and exposure to literature from their own culture or from traditional American literature may inhibit their early success in early literacy instruction. Culturally and linguistically diverse students may have such diverse emergent literacy experiences (see Chapters 1 and 4) that traditional early literacy programs do not adequately prepare them for beginning reading instruction. Sometimes even well-structured early reading activities fail with these students because they need additional or different activities. These students demand a rethinking of early reading activities to use their strengths and concentrate on eliminating their weaknesses.

The early reading and writing approaches discussed in this section attempt to redefine early literacy activities in terms of the needs of culturally and linguistically diverse learners. Their philosophy and techniques differ, but all share the goal of maximizing the probability of success in reading and writing development.

Academic Early Reading Intervention

Perhaps the most radical procedures for helping culturally and linguistically diverse students begin a successful start in literacy instruction are found in academic early reading programs. Some of these programs concentrate on the direct/explicit teaching of specific language and reading skills. This is a teaching strategy in which the teacher presents stimuli designed to elicit specific language responses. Integrating specific language activities that encourage student involvement is critical for early intervention of language development, especially for students who have limited opportunities to experience literacy outside of the classroom. A wide range of literature-based activities (see the *Basal Reader* and *Literature-Based Instruction* sections in this chapter) combined with such a program can enrich students' early reading experiences. Figure 13.1 illustrates some of the goals and direct/explicit instruction techniques for teaching specific language skills. These skill activities should not be considered the sole focus of this program. Skills can be taught throughout the school day by engaging students in meaningful language that focuses on acquisition of each goal. For example, if the teacher asks, "Where are the scissors?" students should be encouraged to respond in a manner that describes where the scissors are ("The scissors are on the big table").

The Beginning Reading Program

A beginning reading program can serve as an extension of the language development program. It can be designed to help students become familiar with letter names, associate pictures visually with their naming words, recognize and produce rhyming words, and learn and use a limited number of sight words. Cognitive embedded tasks can help relate these activities to real-life experiences.

In the alphabet learning phase of the program, children familiarize themselves with the letter names of the alphabet through identity and position statements. The child is taught first to spell words by letter sounds (kuh-ah-tuh) and is then presented clusters of words that follow the same spelling pattern (such as *cat, fat, hat,* and *bat*). Word meanings are reinforced by yes-no questions of lexical terms.

Word recognition begins with the production of isolated words in the clarification of meaning as related to the learner. A word is printed on the chalk-

GOAL 1: To move from one-word responses to complete affirmative and negative statements in reply to questions.

Teacher		Pupil
"What is this?"		"Dog."
"Say it all."		"This is a dog."
"Is this a dog?"		"Yes."
"Say it all."		"Yes, this is a dog."
"Is this a dog?"		"No."
"Say it all."		"No, this is not a dog."

GOAL 2: To respond with both affirmative and negative statements when told to "tell about something."

Teacher	Pupil
"Tell me about this ball."	"It is round."
	"It is black."
	"It is not big."
	"It is not square."

GOAL 3: To develop the ability to handle polar opposites for at least four concept pairs.

Teacher	Pupil
"If this is not up, what is it?"	"Down."
"Say it all."	"It is down."
"If this is not big, what is it?"	"It is little."

GOAL 4: To use the prepositions *on, in, under, over,* and *between* in statements describing arrangements.

Teacher	Pupil
"Where is the turkey?"	"The turkey is *on* the table."

FIGURE 13.1
A procedure for teaching specific language skills

continues

FIGURE 13.1
Continued

"Where is the long line?"　　　　"The long line is over the short line."

"Where is the number 2?"　　　　"The number 2 is *between* the numbers 1 and 3."

1 2 3

GOAL 5: To name positives and negatives for at least four classes.

Teacher	*Pupil*
"Tell me something that is clothing."	"A hat is clothing." "A chair is not clothing."
"Tell me something that is food."	"An apple is food." "A pencil is not food."

GOAL 6: To perform simple "if-then" deductions.

Teacher	*Pupil*
"If the circle is big, what else do you know about it?"	"It is white."

"If the circle is little, what else do you know about it?"	"It is black."

GOAL 7: To use *not* in deductions.

Teacher	*Pupil*
"If the circle is white, what else do you know about it?"	"It is not little."
"If the circle is black, what else do you know about it?"	"It is not big."

board and the rule "This is a word" is taught and followed by the identity statement, "This is the word *man*." Students are then encouraged to respond with complete identity statements in answering questions such as, "Is this the word *dog?*" "No, that is not the word *dog*. That is the word *man*." Gestures illustrate action words. Students are invited to suggest other words they wish to learn. If no one volunteers, the teacher supplies another word.

Word placement exercises teach visual discrimination of word forms and word meanings. The teacher labels objects with five-by-eight-inch cards and identifies them: "This card has a word on it. This is the word *toy*." Five or more words are identified in this way, and the teacher places one word card on the proper object. Students are asked, "This is the word what?" *(desk)* "So where does it belong?" *(On the desk)*. Each child has a turn at naming and placing a word. The class then identified these words on the chalkboard. The rule "If all the letters are the same, the words are the same" is taught.

Word identification exercises help students develop a small sight vocabulary useful for developing simple sentences. Students learn to recognize their own names, then they receive instruction on recognizing other children's names. They also learn names of body parts this way. New sets of words (such as *is not* and *big*) are added to construct sentences: "Joe is not big." Meaning is stressed in sentence reading by having students answer questions about their reading. "Is Joe big?" "No, Joe is not big." "Is Joe little?" "Yes, Joe is little." After students master the basic tasks, they learn to read from teacher-prepared booklets.

APPROACHES TO TEACHING READING AND WRITING TO CULTURALLY AND LINGUISTICALLY DIVERSE STUDENTS

Several approaches can provide reading instruction to students who speak a nonstandard dialect or a primary language other than English. Teachers must have an awareness of the students' cultural background and the linguistic features of their language.

The Language-Experience Approach

A frequently used approach for introducing and teaching literacy to linguistically diverse students is the language-experience approach (LEA). The language-experience approach has several advantages (Freeman, 1988). First, by using the student's oral language, the reading material reflects the student's syntax and sentence structures, eliminating much of the comprehension difficulty caused by using other beginning reading materials. Another advantage is vocabulary usage. Words used in constructing the reading materials come from the student's language and experiential backgrounds. These words reflect meaningful content for the student, facilitating the student's construction of meaning. An additional advantage is the incorporation of writing in the creating of individual- and group-experience stories.

The advantages of the language-experience approach multiply when an individual story is dictated. However, when a group story is dictated, the vocabulary and syntax both may exceed an individual student's abilities. Teachers therefore, should encourage group discussion to help linguistically diverse students construct meaning for group-dictated stories.

Teachers may wish either to incorporate the language-experience approach into their reading programs or to use it as the primary instructional program. Because of the flexibility of LEAs, they can easily be combined with other approaches. Another possibility is to begin reading instruction with the language experience approach and then gradually introduce a literature-based approach.

An instructional aide can facilitate implementation of the LEA. An aide can record and copy stories, make word cards and follow-up practice materials, read and reread stories with students, and follow up with practice activities for students who otherwise might not succeed in reading.

An Integrated Language Approach Based on Whole-Language Philosophy

Many schools are adopting an integrated language approach that uses the whole-language philosophy to teach reading and language development to culturally diverse students. The major features of this approach reflect important theories stressing natural acquisition of second languages and building on each student's linguistic strengths. Integrated language instruction incorporates literature to develop and enhance students' knowledge base. The approach also integrates language with all other aspects of language teaching, such as content-area instruction in science or social studies.

In a whole-language based classroom, students engage in reading for enjoyment and to gather information. Teachers are available to give them the help needed at a particular time, but the guidance the teacher provides enables the student to become a problem solver and to seek other resources to help solve problems. This is an important goal of the whole-language reading experience. In addition, the mentoring of students to read and locate information and how to use the information they obtain is an important feature of this approach. Students sharing their work with others and communicating their accomplishments orally or in written form are major goals of a whole-language based classroom. Workbooks and graded readers are not often used in the whole-language classroom, since the idea is that students learn from relevant, meaningful instructional materials. Students have the opportunity to learn all of the necessary reading skills, but the reading materials are student-centered and the teacher functions as the facilitator of learning.

Literature-based instruction (see Chapter 9) for culturally and linguistically diverse students can feature stories from various cultures and languages displayed around the classroom; writings of students covering the walls like ribboned wallpaper; portfolios showing drafts of creative writing pieces, such as journals of all kinds, letters, and poetry; and field notes of student activities. Integrated language instruction values all languages and students become literate in their own language and ultimately in English. Students accomplish this using real books in real writing and learning situations (Ada, 1988; Flores, Cousin, & Diaz, 1991).

Because children develop language naturally, teachers must create classrooms where students can interact with others and experiment with language. Similarly, second language learners need to construct their own meanings rather than memorize text or reiterate others' thoughts. Bilingual and English language programs should use a wide variety of instructional activities designed to encourage student interaction. These can be literature based activities that focus on developing various language and literacy skills: reading, writing, listening, and speaking. Using thematic units to teach language is an excellent way to introduce meaning that interconnects with students' lives. These units may incorporate stories that include everyday language events. Developing language through stories in the primary language and in the students' second language is important to cognitive development. Using literature to help students become literate and educated in their own language while adding another language builds students' self-concept and encourages a positive attitude toward learning. An acceptance of the student's culture and language is a major principle of second language teaching. The whole-language approach fosters this idea by promoting real, meaningful language instruction.

Teaching language to bilingual and second language learners suggests that students naturally construct new meanings from whole to part of the whole. The parts—for example, the specific skills of reading and writing—must be broken down by the learner, not the teacher, and learned as needed within the context of real books and stories and writing activities (Poplin, 1992). The whole-language orientation in a bilingual classroom should emphasize early literacy teaching of skills as a whole and within context, such as literature stories to promote meaningful literacy. Emphasizing teaching language with meaning will prevent instruction in isolated skills. Skill instruction separate from the primary literacy activities can be irrelevant and not make any sense to the student. Teachers must integrate language with real situations to stimulate a positive language learning attitude.

Stressing meaning within context and students' experiences facilitates reading comprehension. The process of learning to read involves a whole approach to literacy, which stresses the reciprocal, interactive aspects of the four language arts: reading, writing, listening, and speaking (Williams & Snipper, 1991). Engaging all of the modes of language as they interact in learning settings helps students acquire language skills. Teachers must understand all of the factors that influence students' work in teaching reading and writing to second language learners. The match between what is being taught and what is being comprehended is especially critical for the second language learner. When students are working in their primary language, a mismatch is unlikely to occur, but occasionally it does. When that happens, the student will attempt to understand meaning in various ways. Since the mental mismatch often reflects a student's cultural or linguistic background, integrating literature to supplement instruction is often recommended. The reader must make a connection between what he or she knows and what is being read or heard to comprehend it.

Predictable reading materials offer another way to develop bilingual language literacy skills. Patterned books have stories with predictable features such as rhyming and repeated phrases or refrains that promote language development (Heald-Taylor, 1987). Patterned books frequently contain pictures that may facilitate story comprehension. The predictable patterns immediately involve be-

Stressing meaning within context and students' experiences enhances their comprehension.

ginning second language readers in a literacy event in their first or second language. Books with patterned structure can provide modeling as a reading strategy, challenge students' current level of linguistic competence, and provide assistance in comprehending difficult concepts. Comprehension through the repetition of a simple sentence pattern can motivate second language learners to continue trying to learn to read. The process is important for developmental purposes. A popular patterned book is Bill Martin's *Brown Bear, Brown Bear, What Do You See?* (Martin, 1970). The fully illustrated story repeats simple patterns that second language learners can use to begin the reading process. Students become familiar with the story and language patterns and soon begin to create their own text with their own illustrations. In the early stages of second language acquisition, the use of the first and second language is critical for conceptual development. Later, as the second language proficiency develops, the student will focus on learning English. Patterned books' most important function is to offer immediate access to meaningful, enjoyable literacy experiences.

The language-experience approach should be a major component of an integrated language approach for teaching reading and writing to linguistically diverse students. In addition to the LEA, teachers should use materials from a variety of sources. Freeman (1988) recommends using the following materials for whole-language focused programs in Spanish language classrooms: (1) poetry and stories from Spanish language basal readers; (2) Spanish language trade books;

(3) Spanish language resource books; (4) Spanish language newspapers, newsletters, comics, and magazines; (5) Spanish language publications from government and health agencies; (6) telephone books, cookbooks, and television guides in Spanish; (7) books and stories written in Spanish by members of the Hispanic community; and (8) stories written by the students themselves. In addition to these sources, Freeman has compiled a list of sources for alternatives to Spanish language basals. This list is presented in Figure 13.2.

Whole-language-based teaching encourages production of student generated stories (Edelsky, 1986). The stories help develop students' self-concept simply by the creation of their own works. The language-experience approach offers students an excellent way of developing skills that integrate cooperation-fostering story writing and peer interaction strategies for language and content learning (Dixon & Nessel, 1983). Promoting story writing by second language learners will create a literate classroom with students enthusiastic about reading and writing. Allowing students to read and write everyday about their own experiences enhances literacy skills and the desire to learn. Positive literacy experiences involving reading promotes students who learn to enjoy reading and begin to seek out more information to accomplish classroom tasks in the early grades.

The Literature-Based Reading Approach—Integrating Multiethnic Literature

An important aspect of a literature-based reading program is the use of multiethnic literature to enhance reading. Multiethnic literature helps students discover the intricacies of a language, as well as the people's history and culture (Hadaway & Florez, 1987). In addition, when students read literature they encounter a multitude of characters who are both similar to and different from themselves (Norton, 1991). Each character of a story is driven by certain emotions and must deal with the problems and joys of life in various ways. How the heroes and heroines react and cope provides students with insights and information well beyond their own personal experiences.

Integrating multiethnic literature into a school curriculum for second language learners helps students realize that all ethnic groups have roots in the past and a strong heritage that is a part of their culture. Knowing about others from a similar culture encourages with a sense of pride that builds a positive self-concept for students. They may discover by reading that others from their own culture made significant contributions to society. Students encountering multiethnic literature as a part of their reading curriculum benefit academically and learn the social values and behaviors of people in society (Hadaway & Florez, 1987).

Existing reading programs can easily integrate multiethnic literature for explicit reading instruction. Teachers can share stories both orally and in written form, and instruction can coordinate language arts exercises such as vocabulary, comprehension, writing, and language development in both the first and second languages. Using literature such as the story "Bums in the Attic" from *The House on Mango Street* by Sandra Cisneros is an excellent way of increasing cultural awareness, building vocabulary and language, developing comprehension skills, and providing writing opportunities. The language used in the story provides the

Bibliographies

Dale, Doris Cruger, *Bilingual Books in Spanish and English for Children.* Littleton, CO: Libraries Unlimited, 1985. 163 pp. ISBN 0-87287-477-X.

Schon, Isabel, *A Hispanic Heritage: A Guide to Juvenile Books about Hispanic People and Cultures.* Metuchen, NJ: Scarecrow Press, 1980. 178 pp. ISBN 0-8108-1290-8.

Schon, Isabel. *Books in Spanish for Children and Young Adults: An Annotated Guide, Series II.* Metuchen, NJ: Scarecrow Press, 1983. 174 pp. ISBN 0-8108-1620-2.

Schon, Isabel, *Books in Spanish for Children and Young Adults: An Annotated Guide, Series III.* Metuchen, NJ: Scarecrow Press, 1985, 208 pp. ISBN 0-8108-1807-8.

Schon, Isabel. *Books in Spanish for Children and Young Adults: An Annotated Guide, Series IV.* Metuchen, NJ: Scarecrow Press, 1987. 301 pp. ISBN 0-8108-2004-8.

Schon, Isabel, *A Hispanic Heritage, Series II: A Guide to Juvenile Books about Hispanic People and Cultures.* Metuchen, NJ: Scarecrow Press, 1985. 164 pp. ISBN 0-8108-1727-6.

Schon, Isabel. *Basic Collection of Children's Books in Spanish.* Metuchen, NJ: Scarecrow Press, 1986. 240 pp. ISBN 0-8108-1904-X.

Catalogues

Children's Press
Libros en español para niños
1224 West Van Buren Street
Chicago, IL 60607
1-800-621-1115

Hispanic Books Distributors, Inc.
1665 W. Grant Rd.
Tucson, AZ 85745
602-882-9484

DLM Teaching Resources
55 W. 13th Street
New York, NY 10011
212-627-0099

Gessler Publishing Co.
900 Broadway
New York, NY 10003
212-673-3113

Scholastic
Spanish Big Books, Book Collections,
    Wordless Big Books
PO Box 7520
Jefferson City, MO 65102
1-800-325-6149

Lectorum Publications, Inc.
137 West 14th Street
New York, NY 10011
212-929-3833

Claudia's Caravan
Multicultural Multilingual Materials
PO Box 1582
Alameda, CA 94501
510-521-7871

Newsletters

Scholastic Language Newsletters
¿Qué Tal?; El Sol; Hoy Dia
Scholastic Inc.
PO Box 644
Lyndhurst, NJ 07071-9985

El Informador
Fiesta Publishing Co.
PO Box 9609
San Diego, CA 92019

La Luz
Alan Company
230 South Bemiston
Clayton, MI 63105

FIGURE 13.2

Sources for culturally and linguistically based reading materials

(From "Do Spanish methods and materials reflect current understanding of the reading process?" Yvonne S. Freeman, *The Reading Teacher,* March 1988, p. 660. Reprinted with permission of Yvonne S. Freeman and the International Reading Association.)

opportunity for creating a lesson on figurative language, such as similes and idioms. Also, the story's symbolism uses concrete or familiar objects and images to represent abstract and unfamiliar ideas, such as "people who live on hills sleep so close to the stars they forget those of us who live too much on earth." Idioms such as "stuck up" are often difficult for second language learners to learn and understand. Stories that integrate context with idiomatic expressions help students understand meaning. The story just described has many aspects of language teaching that would enhance the development of language and stimulate interest in reading.

The introduction of activities to expand vocabulary and conceptual knowledge can be supplemented by using literature as a means of bridging reading and language development for second language learners (Freeman & Freeman, 1993). Class discussions, role play, and brainstorming are all activities in which students can participate, increase their background knowledge, and enrich their reading abilities. Vocabulary webs provide another rich source of language development. A literature web provides students with a way of organizing their thoughts and generating new ideas and vocabulary as related to the story. Numerous activities expose students to the different linguistic and cultural components of various stories. Teachers and students can build a classroom library of literature resources to teach reading while increasing students' level of cultural awareness and expanding their social and emotional awareness by exposure to new and different styles of living and thinking.

The Oral Reading Approach

Elley (1981) describes a reading approach for linguistically diverse students that is popular in New Zealand and the South Pacific. This approach stresses high interest in reading through the use of short stories with natural language and some vocabulary control for repetition. The teacher reads the story to the group, then the teacher and students reread the story in unison. They discuss the story and read it once again. In this approach, the teacher selects individual words and phrases and emphasizes choral reading (all or several students reading in unison). Research has noted significant results for comprehension and word recognition for the students whose English proficiency is limited using this method.

Choral reading has also been used successfully in promoting language learning for linguistically diverse students. The benefits of using choral reading to enhance children's acquisition of a second language are that it: (1) creates a low-anxiety environment, (2) provides repeated practice, (3) is based on comprehensible input, and (4) incorporates drama (McCauley & McCauley, 1992).

Implementing choral reading for second language learners begins with identifying poems and adapting them for students. Poems should cover familiar topics that students can relate to. For second language learners, the poems should contain a lot of action and allow lines to be added to help clarify vocabulary and emphasize meaning.

Integrating multiethnic literature into a school curriculum helps students realize that all ethnic groups have roots in the past and a strong heritage that is part of their culture.

After the poem has been selected and adapted, McCauley and McCauley (1992) suggest the following general procedure:

- Give a quick, interesting introduction. Focus on getting students involved in talking about the poem.
- Read the poem aloud to students. Use expression, sound effects, and movements that the poem could represent.
- Make copies of the poem available to the students.
- Read the poem again to the students as they follow along.
- Read the poem with the students slowly at first, and gradually increase the speed of reading. Appropriate movements and sound effects also should be included.
- Give lines to the students when they feel comfortable with the words and movements. Students who want solo lines may be given them.
- Practice reading the poem with assigned parts.
- Recognize a job well done with applause, verbal praise, or both.

An example (McCauley & McCauley, 1992) of how movement and drama are added to "Jack and Jill" is presented next. This acting-out part of choral reading is very important for second language learners, because it aids in construction of meaning and helps text become more meaningful for them.

(Boys as they stand)	Jack
(Girls as they stand)	and Jill
(All walking)	went up the hill To fetch a pail of water
(Boys)	Jack fell down and broke his crown. Ouch! (Hold head)
(Girls)	And Jill came tumbling after. (Lean toward boys, hand gesture—i.e., hand on side of cheek—as if worried about Jack's fate, and say) Are you all right, Jack?
(Boys)	(While rubbing head) Yeah.
(Girls)	(While wiping forehead in relief) Whew!

Choral reading can be done with the whole class and ensures success for linguistically diverse students. It promotes positive attitudes toward both second language acquisition and reading.

The Basal Reader Approach

Basal reading programs are still used throughout the United States, and teachers of linguistically diverse students often choose to use them to teach reading. However, teachers should be aware of special considerations when using basal readers as the main method for teaching reading, especially to linguistically diverse students. Among these considerations are (1) special attention to developing background concepts and vocabulary in depth before reading, (2) skillful questioning during silent reading to identify and clear up misunderstandings and to enhance the students' comprehension, and (3) specific emphasis on listening to the language rather than on oral reading. Linguistically diverse students often worry about having to read orally, so they may not concentrate on the language they hear, particularly in group situations. Keeping in mind the special instructional considerations, teachers may find that linguistically diverse students can progress with their classmates in a basal reading program.

An alternative to using only a basal reader program for instruction is to use basal readers and literature together in teaching literacy. Some individuals (Delpit, 1991) have indicated that culturally and linguistically diverse students may need a bridge from the basal series to a more process-focused literature-based program. Combining features of direct/explicit instruction (see Chapters 2 and 6) with literature of the home culture of students from diverse backgrounds may benefit students.

Morrow (1992) conducted research in second-grade classrooms on how an integrated basal and literature-based reading program affected the literacy achievement of culturally diverse children. The features of her integrated program included:

1. Literacy centers within each classroom (see Chapters 3 and 7) that provided students with access to a variety of books and literacy materials. Included in the centers were multiple genres of children's literature, comfortable seating, and manipulatives (felt stories, roll movies, and taped stories).

2. Teacher-guided activities that helped students understand what they could do and should do. Included in the activities were teachers' use of modeling and scaffolding (see Chapter 6), the use of the directed reading-thinking activity (DRTA, as discussed in Chapter 8), and retellings using both books and props (felt stories, puppets, and roll movies).

3. Independent reading and writing periods were used to allow students to choose between working alone or with others, and to select from a variety of activities ranging from retelling to dramatizing stories. The basal reader portion of the literacy instruction was continued with the inclusion of the literature-based reading instruction.

Morrow's study showed that students from diverse backgrounds had improved literacy achievement. Concerns about whether students from diverse backgrounds would benefit from integrating the basal reader approach with a literature-based approach were unfounded. Components of the program that might account for its success were teachers demonstrating, facilitating, and participating in literature activities with high expectations for their students. In addition, the program featured literature that reflected the various cultural backgrounds found in the classrooms.

The Dialect Approach

The *dialect approach* teaches reading using materials written in the student's dialect. Research has not supported the use of reading materials written in black dialect, however.

Reading taught using standard materials takes dialectal and cultural differences in students into account. Currently, the best approach appears to be a conventional one, with enlightened teachers who are sensitive to students' motivations, values, backgrounds, and aspirations and who have a knowledge of the features of nonstandard dialects.

The Dual Language Reading Approach

Many bilingual programs provide reading instruction in the students' primary language as well as in standard English (e.g., Spanish and English). Many of the bilingual programs in the southwestern United States teach reading with Spanish basal programs.

Research (Weber, 1991) indicates that some instructional practices in and beliefs about teaching reading may be counterproductive to reading and language development of linguistically diverse students. Many programs use only phonics to teach reading to students with limited English proficiency (as demonstrated by many Spanish basal reading programs). Teachers of linguistically diverse students often think that a phonics approach is the only way to teach reading to second language learners. One need only observe readers both inside and outside a classroom to confirm that this is not so. If children's concept knowledge in their first language is limited, this inhibits their realization that print represents meaningful language (Neuman & Koskinen, 1992). Instruction that focuses only on decoding words in English limits students' opportunities to realize that reading conveys meaning.

Second-language learners benefit from reading programs that incorporate a range of contexts, both social and functional, in which reading begins and develops. Adapting several reading approaches can help linguistically diverse students become effective, efficient users of written English.

The *dual language reading approach* makes use of native language and literacy skills to strengthen the reading process of speakers whose English is limited. Primary language reading materials, tradebooks, basal texts, and other instructional materials help strengthen bilingual reading programs. In addition, reading activities develop cognitive structures, vocabulary, comprehension strategies, and higher cognitive levels. This focus is important for a smooth transition from first language to second language reading.

EXPANDING AND DEVELOPING MEANING VOCABULARY

Linguistically diverse students need to develop a large base of immediately recognizable words for fluent reading. They come to school already knowing words related to logos, advertisements, and print in their environment. They see print everywhere—at home, on television, while shopping, and along highways, to mention a few—that can serve as a foundation for developing language-experience stories, writing stories, and learning other words.

Krashen (1989) argues that linguistically diverse students acquire vocabulary in the second language through reading, which would suggest that a literature-based approach, an integrated language approach, or features of either combined with a basal reader approach would be more successful in expanding vocabulary than would learning words in isolation.

Teachers can choose words from the students' language-experience stories, discussions of stories read, writing activities, and environmental print. Words selected for the students should be familiar ones. Choral reading, which was presented earlier, can also enhance and expand second language learners' vocabulary (Sampson, Allen, & Sampson, 1991). Students are more likely to recognize a word in print when they can recognize either how the word functions or what it represents.

SPECIAL STUDENTS

Addressing individual student needs in reading instruction has always been an enormous task. Providing appropriate instruction for individuals within a large group demands many long hours of planning and hard work by teachers. Today, teachers are adapting their classrooms to accommodate individual needs and to provide appropriate education for special students.

Special students are those who have special needs. Included among this group are physically disabled, learning disabled, and gifted. Special students may or may not have learning difficulties; however, they often require special teaching. Such teaching is intended to ensure that special students are successful learners.

Mainstreaming

The passage of P.L. 94-142 (the Individuals with Disabilities Education Act) was one of the most significant developments in U.S. education. This law requires that individualized instruction and equal education opportunity be afforded to all children. Children with disabilities must be placed in the "least restrictive environment," which is interpreted, in many cases, as the same environment as for regular students. This trend to educate children with disabilities in the closest possible proximity to the regular classroom in which the child can succeed is often

Addressing individual student needs in literacy has always been an important consideration.

referred to as *mainstreaming.* Lewis and Doorlag (1991) define mainstreaming as:

> [The] inclusion of special students in the general educational process. Students are considered mainstreamed if they spend any part of the school day with regular class peers. In a typical mainstreaming program, special students in regular classrooms participate in instructional and social activities side by side with their classmates. Often they receive additional instruction outside the regular classroom from a special educator such as a resource teacher. (pp. 3–4)

A critical concern for a classroom teacher is: Who is going to be placed in my classroom? P.L. 94-142 defines disabled students as those who are mentally retarded, hard of hearing, deaf, speech impaired, other health impaired, deaf-blind, multihandicapped, seriously emotionally disturbed, orthopedically impaired, visually impaired, or having specific learning disabilities, who because of those impairments need special education and related services (Sec. 121 a. 530-121 a. 534). Given these components, how might a mainstreamed classroom operate? Johnson (1987) provides the following description:

> Exceptional students spend most of the day in regular classrooms, leaving occasionally to go to a resource room or resource center for educational assessments, individual tutoring, or small group instruction, or to pick up and deliver assignments prepared by the resource teacher but completed in the regular classroom. The resource teacher and the regular classroom teacher, working as a team, may schedule a student to use the resource center for a few minutes or several hours, depending on the student's learning needs. The regular classroom teacher and the resource teacher share responsibility for the learning and socialization of the exceptional students, and both take an active instructional role. The exceptional students spend more than half the day in regular classes. While the regular classroom teacher is responsible for grades and report cards, she will usually consult with the resource teacher in giving exceptional students grades. (p. 425)

The success of students placed in the least restrictive environment depends upon the cooperation of teachers, administrators, specialized personnel, and parents. In essence, however, individual teachers' ability to accommodate all students in the regular classroom determines the success or failure of such efforts. Implications for reading teachers are clear—they must employ a variety of instructional and organizational techniques to suit a wide range of student abilities and encourage the constructive interaction of special students with regular students. Teachers should understand the following principles, adapted from Gearhart and Gearhart (1989), when teaching literacy to special students who exhibit learning difficulties:

1. Tasks and activities should be meaningful to the students so they are motivated to learn. Teachers can accomplish this by explaining the relevance, and letting students actively participate in establishing objectives, procedures, time to complete, and using materials for reading instruction that are based on their interests and background.
2. Formats and modes of presentation should be varied.

3. Objectives should be explained and modeled for students. Many different modeling activities may be necessary. In addition, scaffolding using cues and prompts may be needed to help students reach the desired goals.

4. Modeling should include a variety of multisensory demonstration (hearing, seeing, feeling, etc.)

5. Students should be *active learners* when participating in activities—they should understand what to do and why to do it. Practice should be frequent and brief. Scaffolding activities can be lessened as students begin to assume their own responsibility for applying their learning.

6. Conditions for learning should be pleasant, including comfortable temperature and noise level and avoidance of activities that could lead to boredom (too easy) or frustration (too difficult).

The preceding principles suggest that most children with learning difficulties are not in need of specialized techniques, but simply good instruction. Indeed, the similarities among special children and so-called normal children are greater than the differences. Labeling children (emotionally disturbed, mentally retarded, learning disabled, and so forth) tells teachers next to nothing about how to develop an appropriate instructional program. A positive aspect of P.L. 94-142 is that it shifts the focus away from use of labels (which are usually negative and counterproductive) and toward consideration of students' educational needs.

No mystique should surround teaching of special children. These students, like all students, require instruction that emphasizes present achievement level, determination of student strengths and weaknesses, and appropriate approaches and materials. Many students carrying a fancy label have been misdiagnosed and misplaced for years in school systems. Instruction should be based on student needs, not labels. Teachers can avoid the negative effects of labeling students by simply viewing these children as different. After all, nothing is more basic in teaching than learning how to deal with differences in individual students.

The Individualized Education Plan (IEP)

The vehicle for providing the most appropriate educational program for many special students is an **individualized education plan** (IEP). An IEP is a written plan for each special child, detailing his or her educational program. In accordance with P.L. 94-142, the IEP must include the following:

■ The student's present achievement level.

■ A statement of annual goals.

■ A listing of short-term instructional objectives.

■ A statement detailing specific special educational services to be provided to the student and the extent to which the student will participate in the regular classroom.

■ Identification of the person(s) (or agents) responsible for teaching each objective.

■ The materials to be used.

Special education has undergone a varied and at times rapid transformation relative to service delivery. Maria Montessori (1870-1952), a noted Italian developmentalist and physician, was perhaps the first to introduce innovative and effective instructional strategies for exceptional and disadvantaged children. Her methods and instructional philosophy clearly influenced the development of early childhood programs for exceptional children in the United States. The practices of heterogeneous grouping, experiential education, and structured learning environments support the basis of inclusive schooling for all children.

UPDATE

Inclusion, an evolutionary concept, is based upon the concept that separate is not equal and that given appropriate services, the integration of youth serves both an educational and legal mandate. Each decade since the 1950's has offered an ever-increasing normalized learning environment for children with disabilities. To identify one or two individuals who best represent inclusion would certainly be misguided. From early normalization, through deinstitutionalization, least restrictive environment, mainstreaming, and the regular education initiative, the inclusive movement is clearly a paradigm shift that is shared and nurtured by many. The 1990's will undoubtedly be noted for its emphasis on inclusive schooling and the rights of all children to be educated together. Our recollection of Montessori not only underscores the importance of her numerous contributions, but perhaps more importantly stresses the need to integrate socialization skills with the academic needs for all children.

Note: Contributed by Dr. Michael W. Churton, Professor of Special Education, University of Central Florida, Orlando, Florida.

- The evaluation procedures.
- Project data for the beginning of program services and the anticipated duration of the services.

The IEP is an educational program that the school, children, and parents develop jointly (see Figure 13.3). Since many children with disabilities spend part or most of the day in the regular classroom, the classroom teacher must be involved in developing the IEP. As shown in Figure 13.3, the basic ingredients of an IEP are not new—they are essentially those of a good teaching plan (pretest objectives, teaching to those objectives, and the posttest). It is important to avoid thinking of mainstreaming (or least restrictive environment) as separate or different from the basic principles stated in Chapter 1. Those principles include all aspects of an IEP, and thus the process of equal education for all children. Although many problems remain unsettled regarding the implementation of P.L. 94-142, cooperative interaction among teachers, students, parents, specialized personnel, and administrators in placing every individual in a setting in which he or she may succeed will yield benefits for all students.

Gifted Students

A renewed thrust in the public schools is the development of programs for *gifted students.* In 1972, U.S. Commissioner of Education Sidney Marland defined the gifted and talented as "those identified by professionally qualified persons who by virtue of outstanding abilities are capable of high performance. These are children who require differentiated educational programs and/or services beyond those normally provided by the regular school program in order to realize their contribution to self and society" (p. 16). The U.S. Office of Education identified six areas of giftedness: (1) general intellectual ability, (2) specific academic aptitude, (3) creativity, (4) leadership ability, (5) ability in the visual or performing arts, and (6) psychomotor ability. Gifted students may demonstrate capability of exceptional performance in only one or two areas.

With specific reference to reading abilities, Howell (1987) noted that gifted students' cognitive skills are advanced beyond the activities and materials normally provided for students at their age and grade level. Common reading capabilities and behaviors of gifted students include the following:

1. A rich, well-developed vocabulary and interest in words.
2. Early reading ability prior to entering school.
3. An advanced linguistic ability in sentence construction, expression of ideas, and listening vocabulary.
4. An interest in library books and reading in a variety of topic areas.
5. An early interest in learning to write and in writing creative stories.
6. Frequent use of information sources, such as the dictionary, encyclopedia, and information text, to explore ideas and areas of interest.

Individual Education Plan (IEP)

Identification Information

Name __James S.__

School __C. L. Bishop__ Grade __2nd__

Birthdate __9/2/84__

Parents' Names __H. R. and Betty S.__

Address __1029 Langley Avenue__

__Lawrence, KS 66044__

Phone: Home __841-0920__ Office __869-4098__

Continuum of Services

	Hours Per Week	Dates
Regular class	23	9/28/91 - 6/2/91
Resource teacher in regular classroom		
Resource room	5	9/29/91 - 6/2/92
Reading specialist		
Speech/language therapist		
Counselor		
Special class		
Transition class		
Others:		
Counseling	2	9/30/91 - 5/29/92

Yearly Class Schedule

Time	Subject	Teacher
9:00	Language Arts	Miller
10:45	Math	Miller
11:30	Social Studies	Miller
12:00	Lunch	
1:00	Science	Miller
2:00	Resource Reading	Houston

Testing Information

Test Name	Date Admin.	Interpretation
Stanford-Binet	9/13/88	low average range
Key Math	9/15/88	functioning on 1.8 level
Zaner-Bloser	9/22/88	scored "low for grade"
Slingerland	9/20/88	difficulty copying near & far points
Physical exam	8/15/88	mild paralysis left hand seizure prone

Disability Area __Physical Disability__

Checklist

9-2	Referral by __Mrs. Jenkins__
9-8	Parents informed of rights; permission obtained for evaluation
9-21	Evaluation compiled
9-24	Parents contacted
9-26	IEP committee meeting held
9-26	IEP completed
9-26	Parent consent notification
9-27	Placement made

Committee Members

Teacher __Lou Astley__
__Lois Seidler__

Other LEA representative __Mrs. Belay H.__

Parents

Date IEP initially approved _____

Health Information

Vision: __Normal__

Hearing: __Normal__

Physical: __Normal__

Other: __Medication-tegratol__

FIGURE 13.3

Individualized education plan

(Reprinted with the permission of Merrill, an imprint of Macmillan Publishing Company from *Developing and Implementing Individualized Education Programs*. Third Edition by Bonnie B. Strickland and Ann P. Turnbull. Copyright © 1990 by Merrill Publishing Company.)

continues

FIGURE 13.3
Continued

Individual Education Plan (IEP)

Student's Name ___James S.___

Subject Area ___Handwriting___

Teacher ___Houston/Miller___

Level of Performance ___recognizes all manuscript letters; exhibits proper sitting & writing position; can write 7-10 letters per minute; makes erasures 50%-60% of time; handwriting is often illegible___

Annual Goals ___Print legibly all letters of alphabet (upper and lower-case); write numerals 1-10 with no erasures; write 35 letters per minute with 10% or less erasures___

	February	March	April	May	June
Objectives	1. Following a model, writes the entire alphabet legibly 2. Writes legibly numerals 1-10 in math lesson with 4 or less erasures 3. Writes legibly first and last names on all class assignments 4. Writes legibly 23 letters per minute with 30% or less erasures	1. Writes legibly Aa, Cc, Dd, Ee, Gg, Oo, Bb, Pp from dictation 2. Writes legibly numerals 1-10 in math lessons with 2 or less erasures 3. Writes 28 words per minute with 20% or less erasures	1. Writes legibly Qq, Uu, Mm, Nn, Hh, Ll, Tt from dictation 2. Writes legibly numerals 1-10 in math lessons with 1 or less erasures 3. Writes 30 words per minute with 20% or less erasures	1. Writes entire alphabet from dictation 2. Writes legibly numerals 1-10 with no erasures 3. Writes 35 letters per minute with 10% or less erasures	
Special Materials	"Beginning to Learn Fine Motor Skills" by Thurstone & Lillie				
Agent	1, 4-Houston 2, 3-Miller	1, 3-Houston 2-Miller			
Evaluation	Informal assessment 80% accuracy of objectives 1-3 on 3 consecutive days	Informal assessment 80% accuracy of objectives 1-2 on 3 consecutive days			

Individual Education Plan (IEP)

Student's Name James S.

Subject Area Handwriting

Teacher Houston/Miller

Level of Performance recognizes all manuscript letters; exhibits proper

Annual Goals Print legibly all letters of alphabet (upper- and lower-

sitting & writing position; can write 7-10 letters per minute; makes

case); write numerals 1-10 with no erasures; write 35 letters per

frequent erasures; handwriting is often illegible, slow, and laborious.

minute with 4 or less erasures.

	September	October	November	December	January
Objectives	referral/evaluation, IEP development	1. Following a model, writes legibly letters: Aa, Cc, Dd, Ee, Gg, Oo 2. Following a model, writes legibly numbers 1-5 3. Following a model, writes legibly his first name 4. Writes legibly 10 letters per minute with 50% or less erasures	1. Following a model, writes legibly letters: Bb, Pp, Qq, Uu, Mm, Nn, Hh 2. Writes legibly numerals 1-5—no model 3. Writes legibly first name—no model 4. Writes legibly 13 letters per minute with 45% or less erasures	1. Following a model, writes legibly letters: Ll, Tt, Ff, Kk, Ii, Jj 2. Writes legibly numerals 6-10 with a model 3. Writes legibly last name with a model 4. Writes legibly 14 letters per minute with 40% or less erasures	1. Following a model, writes entire alphabet legibly 2. Writes legibly numerals 6-10—no model 3. Writes legibly first and last name—no model 4. Writes legibly 19 letters per minute with 35% or less erasures
Special Materials		"Beginning to Learn Fine Motor Skills" by Thurstone & Lillie			
Agent		1, 4–Houston 2, 3–Miller			
Evaluation		Informal assessment 80% accuracy of objectives 1-3 on 3 consecutive days			

481

7. Comprehension abilities at early grade levels that exceed the literal level and demonstrate an understanding of the relationship of ideas.

8. Well-developed reading skills and abilities by the end of first grade.

Identifying gifted children and designing a curriculum to accommodate their learning needs should be accomplished through a variety of formal and informal assessment procedures. Standardized achievement tests, intelligence tests, creativity measures, actual student performance in the reading program, peer nomination procedures, and parent and teacher observations are avenues to employ for this purpose. Also, giftedness is not reserved for any one group or class of children. Teachers should not be preoccupied with ethnicity or social characteristics when identifying the gifted and talented.

For too long, gifted children were expected to be silent and follow along with the regular curriculum designed for less able students. Many reading program administrators are realizing that gifted children have unique needs, as do all students, and require differentiated instructional programs. Gifted readers are not all the same; each has unique strengths and weaknesses. As such, gifted readers need the same diagnostically based instruction afforded all learners (Carr, 1984). Indeed, many gifted children are "disabled" readers when their performance is compared to their potential. Gifted children require an instructional program that reflects their needs.

Two avenues available to meet gifted readers' needs in the classroom are reading acceleration and individualized enrichment (Johnson, 1987). Reading acceleration involves placing students at their instructional level and providing a balanced program at that difficulty level (even if it is three, four, or five grade levels above grade placement). Enrichment entails providing students with activities that delve more deeply into reading materials.

Although research supports reading acceleration, many teachers do not use this approach. One underlying reason for this lack of implementation is classroom management. If each gifted child is instructed at his or her instructional level, how does the classroom teacher organize and plan for a high percentage of academically engaged time for all students? We recommend reading acceleration if at all possible (depending on size of class, range of ability, availability of teacher aides, and individual gifted reader needs). In most cases, a careful blend of reading acceleration and enrichment can ensure appropriate instruction for gifted readers.

Whereas the reading curriculum goals are the same for gifted readers as for all readers, many individuals (Lewis & Doorlag, 1991) think the reading program should be differentiated in terms of content covered, methods taught, and pacing of instruction for gifted readers. A wide variety of literature should be used to tap gifted students' abilities and interests. Howell (1987) compiled an excellent bibliography of interesting children's books to promote vocabulary learning (see Figure 13.4).

A greater emphasis on thinking and reasoning skills is recommended for teaching gifted readers. Integrating language arts with the development of critical thinking can also be accomplished by teaching writing as a thinking process (Jampole, Konopak, Readence, & Moser, 1991). Developing writing skills as a

Basil, Cynthia. *How Ships Play Cards: A Beginning Book of Homonyms.* New York, N.Y.: Morrow, 1980.

Burchfield, R.W., ed. *A Supplement to the Oxford University Dictionary.* Oxford, England: Oxford University Press, 1976.

Gwynne, Fred. *A Chocolate Moose for Dinner.* New York, N.Y.: Windmill/Dutton, 1976.

Gwynne, Fred. *The King Who Rained.* New York, N.Y.: Windmill, 1970.

Hoban, Tana. *Push-Pull Empty-Full.* New York, N.Y.: Macmillan, 1972.

Hunt, Bernice K. *The Watchamacallit Book.* New York, N.Y.: G.P. Putnam's Sons, 1976.

Lobel, Arnold. *Frog and Toad Are Friends.* New York, N.Y.: Harper and Row, 1970.

Maestro, Guilio. *What's a Frank Frank? Tasty Homograph Riddles.* New York, N.Y.: Clarion, 1984.

Merriam, Eve. *A Gaggle of Geese.* New York, N.Y.: Knopf, 1960.

Moscovitch, Rosalie. *What's In a Word? A Dictionary of Daffy Definitions.* Boston, Mass.: Houghton Mifflin, 1985.

O'Dell, Scott. *Island of the Blue Dolphins.* Boston, Mass.: Houghton Mifflin, 1960.

Oxford English Dictionary. Oxford, England: Oxford University Press, 1933.

Parish, Peggy. *Amelia Bedelia.* New York, N.Y.: Harper and Row, 1963.

Sperling, Susan K. *Murfles and Wink-A-Peeps: Funny Old Words for Kids.* New York, N.Y.: Clarkson N. Potter, 1985.

Spier, Peter. *Fast-Slow, High-Low: A Book of Opposites.* Garden City, N.Y.: Doubleday, 1972.

Steig, William. *The Amazing Bone.* New York, N.Y.: Farrar, Staus and Grioux, 1976.

Steig, William. *Sylvester and the Magic Pebble.* New York, N.Y.: Simon and Schuster, 1969.

Terban, Marvin. *Eight Ate: A Feast of Homonym Riddles.* New York, N.Y.: Clarion, 1982.

Terban, Marvin. *In A Pickle and Other Funny Idioms.* New York, N.Y.: Clarion, 1983.

Terban, Marvin. *Too Hot to Hoot: Funny Palindrome Riddles.* New York, N.Y.: Clarion, 1985.

Viorst, Judith. *Alexander and the Terrible, Horrible, No Good, Very Bad Day.* New York, N.Y.: Atheneum, 1972.

FIGURE 13.4

Children's books for delightful vocabulary study
(From Helen F. Howell, "Language, Literature, and Vocabulary Development for Gifted Students," *The Reading Teacher, 40,* p. 504.)

logical thinking process enables gifted students to refine, synthesize, and elaborate upon their understanding of a particular topic.

Gifted students learn material faster than other learners and thus require fewer drill exercises. Yet, the overriding concern for gifted readers is that they too need instruction in various reading skills (Dooley, 1993). Providing such differentiated instruction requires diagnosis of students' strengths and weaknesses. Alexander and Muia (1982) addressed this very point when they stated, "What is most essential for program developers to remember, however, is that the learner and that learner's style are central to the curriculum. Therefore, maximum effectiveness of the gifted curriculum hinges on its ability to relate to the learner's abilities, needs, and interests" (p. 4). Further information on reading programs for the gifted can be obtained by contacting the Council for Exceptional Children and the ERIC Clearinghouse on Handicapped and Gifted Children.

SUMMARY //////////////////////////////////////

The ability to deal effectively with student differences is crucial to teaching reading. Teachers must address the needs of culturally and linguistically diverse and special students in the regular classroom. The ability of teachers to handle differences effectively translates into instructional practices that provide for each student's self-respect and that lead all students to feel secure in the classroom.

Creating success opportunities for students with limited proficiency in English requires an understanding of nonstandard dialects, characteristics of foreign languages spoken by the students in the classroom, and students' cultural values. Although speaking a nonstandard dialect or a primary language other than English can present problems in learning to read, a sensitive and knowledgeable teacher minimizes this problem.

Teachers can adapt reading instruction to the needs of speakers whose English proficiency is limited. The language-experience approach, whole-language-based approach, oral reading approach, basal reader approach, dialect approach, and bilingual reading approach can be useful in addressing the needs of culturally and linguistically diverse students.

Special needs students are increasingly taught in the least restrictive environment. Mainstreaming provides the most appropriate education for each student in the least restrictive setting, considering the educational needs of students rather than their clinical labels. A key ingredient of the legislative mandate for mainstreaming is the development of an individualized education plan (IEP) for each student with disabilities. The regular classroom teacher's total involvement in the team process is the key to successful implementation of the IEP. A special student needs the same individual approach to learning that every student needs.

Gifted students also require instruction matched to their needs. In the past, gifted students were usually not identified and their instructional needs were ignored. Today's schools are recognizing their special needs, and teachers are differentiating their reading instruction to meet these needs.

Discussion Questions

1. Brainstorm: List ways teachers can help limited-English-speaking pupils feel more secure in the classroom environment.
2. Research to date has not supported the use of dialect materials (books written in black English) to teach reading. What are some possible explanations for these negative results?
3. Mainstreaming special needs children into the regular classroom should produce a better learning environment for all students. However, mainstreaming can also make matters worse instead of making them better. What are possible reasons for this occurrence?
4. Brainstorm: List various ways to accommodate gifted students' needs in the primary grades.

Take a Stand For or Against

1. Of all the factors that influence academic achievement in the school, the dialects or language behaviors of the culturally and linguistically diverse students are the most important.
2. An IEP should be required for all students.
3. Accelerating gifted students usually results in poor social adjustment.

BIBLIOGRAPHY /

Ada, A. F. (1988). The Pajaro Valley experience: Working with Spanish-speaking parents to develop children's reading and writing skills through the use of children's literature. In T. Skutnabb-Kangas, & J. Cummins, (Eds.), *Minority education: From struggle to shame* (pp. 233–36). Clevedon: Multilingual Matters.

Alexander, P. A., & Muia, J. A. (1982). *Gifted education: A comprehensive roadmap.* Rockville, MD: Aspen Systems Corp.

Carr, K. S. (1984). What gifted readers need from reading instruction. *The Reading Teacher, 38,* 144–146.

Delpit, L. D. (1991). A conversation with Lisa Delpit. *Language Arts, 68,* 541–547.

Dixon, C., & Nessel, D. (1983). *Language experience approach to reading and writing: LEA for ESL.* Hayward, CA: The Alemany Press.

Dooley, C. (1993). The challenge: Meeting the needs of gifted readers. *The Reading Teacher, 46,* 546-551.

Edelsky, C. (1986). *Habia una vez: writing in bilingual programs.* Norwood, NJ: Ablex.

Elley, W. B. (1981). The role of reading in bilingual contexts. In J. T. Guthrie (Ed.), *Comprehension and teaching: Research reviews.* Newark, DE: International Reading Association.

Flores, B., Cousin, P. T., & Diaz, E. (1991). Transforming myths about learning, language, and culture. *Language Arts, 68,* pp.369–79.

Freeman, D. E., & Freeman, A. W. (1993). Strategies for promoting the primary languages of all students. *The Reading Teacher, 46,* 552–559.

Freeman, Y. S. (1988). Do Spanish methods and materials reflect current understanding of the reading process? *The Reading Teacher, 7,* 654–663.

Gearhart, B. R., & Gearhart, C. J. (1989). *Learning disabilities: Educational strategies.* (5th ed.) New York: Merrill/Macmillan Publishing Co.

Hadaway, N., & Florez, V. (1987). Multiethnic literature: Enhancing a reading program. *New Mexico Journal of Reading, 7* (3), 13–15.

Heald-Taylor, G. (1987). Predictable literature selections and activities for language arts instruction. *The Reading Teacher, 1,* 6–12.

Howell, H. (1987). Language, literature, and vocabulary development for gifted students. *The Reading Teacher, 40,* 500–505.

Jampole, E. S., Konopak, B. C., Readence, J. E., & Moser, B. E. (1991). Using mental imagery to enhance gifted elementary students' creative writing. *Reading Psychology, 12,* 183–198.

Johnson, D. W. (1987). *Educational psychology.* Englewood Cliffs, NJ: Prentice-Hall.

Krashen, S. (1989). We acquire vocabulary and spelling by reading: Additional evidence for the input hypothesis. *The Modern Language Journal, 73,* 440–464.

Lewis, R. B., & Doorlag, D. H. (1991). *Teaching special students in the mainstream* (3rd ed.). New York: Merrill/Macmillan Publishing Co.

Marland, S. P. (1972). Our gifted and talented children: A priceless natural resource. *Intellect, 101,* pp. 16–19.

Martin, B. (1970). *Brown Bear, Brown Bear What do you see?.* New York: Holt, Rinehart and Winston, Inc.

McCauley, J. K., & McCauley, D. S. (1992). Using choral reading to promote language learning for ESL students. *The Reading Teacher, 45,* 526–535.

Morrow, L. M. (1992). The impact of a literature-based program on literacy achievement, use of literature, and attitudes of children from minority backgrounds. *Reading Research Quarterly, 27,* 250–275.

Neuman, S. B., & Koskinen, P. (1992). Captioned television as comprehensible input: Effects of incidental word learning from context for language minority students. *Reading Research Quarterly, 27,* 94–106.

Norton, D. (1991). *Through the eyes of a child: An introduction to children's literature* (3rd ed.). New York: Merrill/Macmillan Publishing Co.

Poplin, C. E. (1992). Making our whole-language bilingual classrooms also liberatory. In J. V. Tinajero, A. F. Ada(Eds.), *The power of two languages: Literacy and biliteracy for Spanish-speaking students* (pp. 58–61). New York: Macmillan/Mcgraw-Hill.

Sampson, M. R., Allen, R. V., & Sampson, M. B. (1991). *Pathways to literacy.* Chicago: Holt, Rinehart, & Winston.

Weber, R. M. (1991). Linguistic deversity and reading in American society. In R. Barr, M. L. Kamil, P. Mosenthal, & P. D. Pearson (Eds.), *Handbook of reading research* (vol. II) (pp. 97–119). New York: Longman.

Williams, J. D. & Snipper, C. G. (1991). *Literacy and Bilingualism.* White Plains, NY: Longman.

Practice Activities and Games

Used as part of the teaching-learning cycle to reinforce and extend previously taught reading skills and strategies, activities and games are essential for student mastery. Activities and games are often thought—wrongly—to meet the requirements of effective instruction. Activities and games do not teach! Any activity, whether teacher-made or commercial, only assists instruction. Activities should only be used for supervised or independent practice or for reinforcing a reading skill or strategy. Chapters 4, 5, 6, and 10 included examples of direct/explicit instruction lessons that contained activities and games. Before allowing students to use an activity or game, the teacher must thoroughly explain to students the reading skills and strategies being practiced. The effective teacher chooses reading activities and games based on students' needs and implements these activities within a framework of a complete lesson. Viewed this way, activities and games become vehicles to enhance students' learning. Also, in conjunction with any activity or game, a particular skill or strategy must then be practiced in an authentic reading situation (i.e., reading of good literature). The following ideas for practice and application are sample activities for the various reading areas. Many of the activities designed for one reading area can easily be modified for effective use in other areas. The following suggestions should be modified to match instructional goals, teaching styles, and students' unique characteristics.

WORD RECOGNITION*

Sight Words

1. *Picture-Word Cards:* Attach pictures of dogs, cats, houses, clothing, objects, and so forth to 3" × 5" cards. These pictures can be found in major department store catalogs. Print the high-frequency service words (*is, on, to, am, was, my, our,* etc.) on 3" × 5" cards as well (one word to a card). Students can use these cards in the following ways to practice learning of high-frequency service words.

   a. The following is a game for small groups (three to five students). Stack the picture cards and word cards in two separate piles in the middle of a table and turn over the first card of each stack. Place each card next to

*Reprinted with the permission of Macmillan Publishing Company from *Teaching Reading: Diagnosis, Direct Instruction, and Practice,* Second Edition by William H. Rupley and Timothy R. Blair. Copyright © 1988 by Macmillan Publishing Co.

the stack from which it was drawn. Have the first student draw a card from each stack and decide if these cards can be played on the two that are turned up. For example, a picture of a dog and the word *is* are turned up. The first student draws a boat picture card and a *the* word card. This student could play the word cards *the* and *is* on either picture by making the phrases *the boat is* and *the dog is.* If the student plays both, then he or she gets to take all four cards; if the student plays the words on only one picture, then he or she gets three cards; if the student plays only one word card on one picture card, he or she gets to keep two cards. After the first student plays, a card from each picture stack is again turned up and the next student draws a card from each stack and attempts to play these cards. If a student cannot play the cards, they are placed off to the side. A student can only keep those cards played. The game ends when the cards stacked in the middle of the table are gone. The student with the greatest number of cards wins the game.

b. A variation of the previous game is to deal each student five word cards and five picture cards. The first student places one of the word cards and one of the picture cards face up on the table so they can be played together, such as *a shirt.* The next student can play as many of his or her cards that make sense on the two that are turned up, such as the word cards *big, is on, and, the,* and as many picture cards that make sense. For example, *a big shirt is on the dog* (picture card). If a student cannot play his or her cards on those on the table, then he or she places one picture card and one word card on the table that make sense together. The game is over when a student has played all of his or her cards.

c. The word cards and picture cards can also be used to play games such as baseball, football, basketball, and so forth. The playing field can be drawn either on the chalkboard or a sheet of oaktag. Divide the students needing sight-word practice into two teams. As each student on the team has a turn, he or she is presented with a word card and a picture card. The player must pronounce the word, use it with the picture, and decide if the phrase makes sense. If the player responds correctly, he or she gets to move his team one base, five yards, or scores two points (depending on whether the game is baseball, football, or basketball).

d. Another activity using the cards can help develop students' visual memory of a word. Write a number on the back of each card; place 10 word cards and 10 picture cards in a row on the chalktray with the number facing the students. Each student is given a turn and selects a number from the word cards and a number from the picture cards. Each card is turned over and shown to the student, who must pronounce the word and name the picture. If the word card and picture card make a meaningful phrase, then the student gets to keep them; if the phrase is not meaningful then the cards are placed back on the chalkboard with the number showing. Students take turns selecting one card from each row, paying close attention to remember which cards make sense together.

e. The picture cards and word cards can also be used individually by students to construct short meaningful sentences and to compose short stories. The word cards can also be used as flash cards.

2. *Classroom Labels:* Label objects in the classroom using short phrases such as "the doors," "the wall," "a light switch," and so forth. Direct students' attention to these phrases on a regular basis. Make sure you place the labels at students' eye level.

3. *Word Banks:* Write words of interest to individual students, such as words that students use in classroom conversation. Print the words using short phrases that are meaningful to the students and that also emphasize basic sight words, such as "my new doll," "I have a dog," and so forth. These word cards can be used for reviewing sight words, constructing short stories and sentences, and introducing derived words.

4. *Flash Cards:* Flash cards can be used with students and then their progress in correctly recognizing sight words can be graphed. Help students understand how to interpret the graph, which they should keep at their seats. Flash cards can also be sent home with students to allow parents to assist them in learning sight words.

5. *Bingo:* Bingo-type games that require students to match a flashed word with the identical word on a bingo card can help students understand which features of the word are necessary to recognize it. You can also pronounce the words and have students find the appropriate words on their bingo cards.

6. *Pronoun Referents:* Provide students with short written phrases such as the following: "It began to bark." "It is very green." "He took us to the game." Ask students to select from a list of choices those words that go with each phrase; for example, "The dog began to bark." "The grass is very green." "Father took us to the game."

7. *"Felt" Words:* Make sight words out of felt material or sandpaper. Have students practice tracing the word and saying it at the same time.

8. *Cut-Up Sentences:* Design a series of sentences using previously studied sight words. Cut up the sentences into individual words and phrases. Have students, individually or in pairs, combine the parts into meaningful sentences and then read them aloud to you or another student. A variation is to design sight-word sentences and put them in a paper bag. Have a student draw a sentence from the bag. If the student can read the sentence, he or she can keep it.

9. *Climb the Ladder:* Design a ladder out of poster board that has open slots at each step. Place sight words that have been studied during the week in the slots. Students are to "climb" to the top of the ladder by pronouncing each word and using it in a sentence. This exercise may be completed individually or with a partner. A variation is to design a baseball stadium and obtain miniature players. Have the student "at bat" look at a sight-word card. If he or she knows one word on sight, the "hit" is a single; two words in a row make a "double," three a "triple," and four a "homer." Missing a word equals an "out."

10. *Picture Dictionary:* Have students compile their own dictionary of words using pictures of words studied.

11. *Hanger Words:* Have students write sight words on poster board strips and use string to hang the words on coat hangers. Hang the coat hangers from the ceiling or chalkboard. Periodically throughout the week have students pronounce the words, write the words, and use them in a sentence. A variation is to have students arrange the words in meaningful sentences and phrases.

12. *Seasonal Words:* Ask students to list words common to the particular season of the year. For example, winter words can be listed under the headings of "weather," "animals," "sports," "clothing," and "food." A variation is to have students use these words in a creative writing lesson.

Phonics

1. *Letter-Picture Cards:* Design cards using pictures depicting the phonic elements being studied. Work individually with students or pair students together. Put each picture on one side of the card and the letter(s) represented on the opposite side. Ask students to name the initial consonant sound, final sound, or vowel sound illustrated in the picture.

2. *Make-Up Sentences:* Ask students to write sentences containing at least two words with the same sound. The students can read the sentences to you or to a classmate.

3. *Story Generation:* Have students compose a story using as many words with a particular phonic element or elements as possible. Students can illustrate the story and read it aloud.

4. *Race Track:* Out of posterboard, design a race track that has evenly divided segments containing phonic elements being studied. Using miniature model cars, students can move along the track by saying the sounds or words in each segment. Students can work in pairs or small groups to complete the game. A variation is to design a ladder with open slots at each step that will hold a word card. Students start at the bottom and try to reach the top of the ladder.

5. *Fishing for Words:* Cut out small fish from posterboard and attach a paper clip to the mouth of each fish. On each fish, write a word with a phonic element that is being studied. Using a makeshift fishing pole with a magnet at the end, have students go fishing. To keep a fish, students must pronounce the word written on the fish; otherwise, they must "throw it back."

6. *Shoe Sound Box:* In a shoe box, place small objects that begin with the phonic elements being studied. Students are to pick an object out of the shoe box and identify it.

7. *Wheel of Fortune:* Make a wheel with a spinner. Divide the wheel into equal segments having a numerical value and a word with a phonic element underlined. Have students spin the wheel and then attempt to pronounce

the word that the spinner stops on and use it in a sentence. The student who accumulates the most points wins the game. Next, the student with the most points wins a chance at a bonus prize by guessing the remaining letters of a more difficult word in which a phonic element under study has been supplied. (Allow the student to name two or three letters before guessing the word for the bonus prize.) A variation is to write digraphs and blends on the spinner and have students spin the wheel and make new words.

8. *Hangman:* In a small-group setting, write nonsense words on poster strips that illustrate phonic elements being studied. Ask a student to pronounce the word. Each time a pronunciation is missed, add another section to the body of the "hangman." The student or team to first complete their "hangman" loses the game.

9. *Auditory Discrimination of Vowel Sounds:* In order to provide practice in distinguishing among vowel sounds, have students label 3" × 5" cards with long or short vowel sounds and then display them on their desks. Next, using lists of words containing a particular vowel sound, read aloud several words and ask students to point to the card on their desks corresponding to the vowel sound heard in the words. While you continue to read different lists of words containing different vowel sounds, students are to listen to the changes and indicate that they do hear each vowel sound by pointing to the correct card on their desks.

10. *Vowel Bingo:* Design bingo cards and write a vowel sound in each box (either long or short or both). Next, pronounce words containing a vowel sound. Students are to cover up the box on their bingo card for the same vowel sound in the dictated word. A variation is to design cards for initial consonants, consonant clusters, consonant digraphs, and vowel digraphs.

11. *Yes-No Cards:* Have students design their own response cards. Read words to students that begin with the same sound and others that do not begin with the same sound. Students respond with their "yes" and "no" cards. A variation is to use these cards for practicing final consonants, vowel sounds, and special consonant combinations.

12. *Word Cards:* Design poster strips with three or four words that only have a difference in the vowel sound or last letter. Have students read the words orally. Example: *hat   hag   ham*

13. *Flannel Board Activity:* Using flannel letters and a flannel board, have students practice making individual words that contain a particular phonic element. A variation is to make a game of the activity by grouping students into teams. Make a word and have a student pronounce the word.

Structural Analysis

1. *Quizzes:* After studying root words, suffixes, and prefixes, form small groups and have students make up an exercise or quiz for another group of stu-

dents. Each group may use the following design:

Ex.	Word	Prefix	Root Word	Suffix
	unplanned	un	plan	ed
	_____	_____	_____	_____
	_____	_____	_____	_____
	_____	_____	_____	_____

2. *Word Puzzle:* Put various root words, prefixes, and suffixes on strips of poster-board. Ask students to make as many words as they can from the strips.

3. *Contractions:* Write a short paragraph containing pairs of words that can be written as contractions. Ask students to write the contraction above the words that can be written as contractions.

4. *Plurals:* Design a worksheet asking students to choose the correct plural form of a word in a series of sentences.

Example: They saw many (deer, deers) on the trip.

The (oxes, oxen) crossed the road.

5. *Plural Flash Cards:* Using 3″ × 5″ cards, write the singular form of a word on one side and the plural of the word on the reverse side. Have students use the cards by themselves, writing the plural form on a separate sheet and then checking the correctness. This activity can also be completed by pairing students together or placing them in small groups.

6. *Word Wheels:* Create a word wheel in which the outer circle names root words and the inner circle contains a spinner with prefixes. Have students spin the wheel, pronounce the word, and use it in a sentence. A variation is to use suffixes.

7. *Card Game:* After covering three or four suffixes, pass out a dozen cards labeled with root words. Have a separate deck of cards containing the various suffixes studied. The student is to pick up a suffix card and try to make a word by combining it with a root word card. If this can be done, the student can continue. A variation is to use prefixes.

8. *Syllable Flash Cards:* Design 3″ × 5″ cards with a word on one side and on the reverse side the same word divided into syllables. Have students work individually or in pairs to practice dividing words into syllables. A variation is to require students to make vowels long, short, or silent, and then explain the vowel principle that applies. Another variation is to use syllable cards and play hangman.

9. *Generating Words:* Provide students with a list of root words. Ask students to write at least four words derived from each root. To show that the students understand the meanings of the words, require students to write a sentence using the affixed forms. A variation is to give students certain prefixes or suffixes, then ask students to generate as many words as they can and use them in sentences.

Context

1. *Modified "Request" Technique:* Have students read a paragraph aloud. Afterward, ask the student the meaning of key vocabulary words. Students should be encouraged to use contextual clues to figure out the meaning of each word. Read the next paragraph and then allow the student to ask you the meaning of key vocabulary words. The process of using probing or clarifying questions should be encouraged when using contextual clues to identify unknown words. (Note: This is an excellent technique for teacher and parent volunteers to use in the classroom.)

2. *Crossword Puzzle:* Design a crossword puzzle using students' vocabulary words. Each sentence in the puzzle clues should end with a blank. Students are to think of the word that makes sense and that fits into the puzzle. You may provide students with a word list to facilitate their successful completion of the exercise.

3. *Modified Cloze:* Design short paragraphs with three or four words deleted from the sentences. Above each paragraph, list two related words for each deleted word. Ask students to read the paragraphs and fill in each blank with the correct word.

   Example: knowing   astonish   illogical
               known   astonished   logic

   _____ the answer to the question, the student raised her hand. She was _____ to find out the answer was incorrect and _____.

4. *Sentence Strips:* Prepare strips of posterboard with sentences from students' reading material (basal stories or content textbooks). Underline a word in each sentence that students are to identify the meaning of using the context of the sentence. Write a synonym for the underlined word on the reverse side of the sentence strip. Students can work by themselves or with a partner to complete this exercise. A variation is to ask students to make their own context sentence strips.

5. *Sentence Completion:* Write sentences, leaving out the verb, on posterboard strips. Have different verbs on separate strips. Ask students to select a verb that completes a sentence and that makes sense. Vary this activity by deleting nouns or adjectives from sentences. Students can work individually or in pairs to complete the activity.

6. *Finding Clues:* Design a series of paragraphs with key words underlined. Ask students to draw two lines under the words that give clues to the meaning of each underlined word.

7. *Proofreading Sentences:* Design sentences with one unknown word that you have underlined and other words that give clues to the meaning of the word. Ask students to draw two lines under the part of the sentence that gives a hint to the meaning of the underlined word.

LITERAL COMPREHENSION

1. *Picture Details:* Provide students with a short story or passage appropriate to their abilities and experiential backgrounds. Represent the major story details with pictures placed on separate cards. The pictures can represent major events, characters, settings, and so forth. For example, if in the story the main characters went to a lake to go fishing, set up a tent, wore warm clothing, and cooked their food over a campfire, then each detail can be represented on separate picture cards. Provide students with the cards appropriate to their story and include some picture cards that are not appropriate to their story. Instruct them to select cards representing the details of the story they read, which are turned into you after they complete the activity. A variation is to either record stories on audiotape or use read-along stories. Have students listen to the story and then select story details from picture cards.

2. *Finish the Story:* Provide students with a short story or several connected paragraphs to read. On a separate sheet of paper, provide incomplete information about the story's content. For example:

   This story is about Joe, who wanted a (_____). Joe's mother did not agree with Joe's choice because (_____).

   Direct students to read the incomplete information first and then read the story to fill in the missing information. Make sure students understand that more than one word is required to fill in the information that is missing.

3. *You Decide:* Give students two short stories or connected paragraphs. Direct students to read the text and then decide if information listed on separate cards belongs to either reading selection, and if so, which one. Students can read an event card aloud and other students can respond about which story contained the event, character, setting, and so on. Students who respond correctly get to keep the story card.

4. *Reporter:* Write questions about *who, what, when, where,* and *why* on separate 3" × 5" cards. Assign students a story to read, directing them to read to answer the "reporter" questions. Write the literal information appropriate to the reporter questions on separate 3" × 5" cards. For example, if the story has three characters, three separate cards should be made to answer the *who* question. Number the back of each reporter card and number the back of each story card. Place the reporter cards on one side of the chalktray with the numbers facing the students and place the story cards on the other side of the chalktray with the numbers facing the students. Have students take turns selecting a number from each group, trying to match the story card with the appropriate reporter card. For example, a student selects story card 7 and it is turned over (it reads "Joe"); then the student selects reporter card 3 (it reads "where"). Since they do not match, both cards are turned back to face the board. If the story card and reporter card match, the student gets to keep the story card and the reporter card is turned back to face the board. The activity continues until all story cards are removed from the chalktray.

5. *A Thousand Words:* Provide students with a short story or several related sentences to read. Direct them to draw a picture that best represents the main idea of the story. A variation is to have them draw a series of pictures in cartoon fashion that represent literal information found in their reading.

6. *Character:* Prepare several short descriptions of different characters. Have students read the descriptions and categorize the characters in terms of their descriptions. A variation would be to give students a web format and have them fill in each part with the descriptive words.

7. *Does It Make Sense:* Cut apart stories and paste them to a piece of cardboard. Have students arrange the stories in a manner than makes sense. A variation of this is to have students arrange all but a part of the story in a manner that makes sense. Have students read each others' stories to see if they can find the part that does not make sense. A variation is to have students experiment with the stories to see if they can be combined or organized in several ways and still make sense.

INFERENTIAL COMPREHENSION

1. *Headlines:* Prepare newspaper headlines appropriate to students' reading abilities and experiential backgrounds. Provide students with a headline and direct them to compose a story appropriate to the given headline. Before writing their stories, have students write out what would be necessary to help them in composing their stories. Use reporter-type questions to assist students in planning their stories. For example, for a headline such as "12-YEAR-OLD BOY CATCHES RECORD-SIZED FISH," students could possibly list information for *who*—name for the boy, where he lives, why he likes to fish, etc; *where*—where he caught the fish; *when*—when he caught the fish and how he felt when he caught it. Once students have listed the information related to the reporter questions, have them write their stories. This activity helps students use their experiential background to construct meaning as they read and write stories.

2. *Continuations:* Prepare a series of sentences such as "Joe earned four dollars raking leaves for his mother." Prepare an equal number of sentences that are logical continuations for each of the other sentences (e.g., a logical continuation for the previous sentence could be "He spent three dollars to go to the afternoon movie"). Have students read each sentence and select a sentence that would be a logical continuation. A variation is to have students write their own sentences that would be logical continuations of given sentences.

3. *Finish the Story:* Select a connected story and delete every other sentence from it. Students can either rewrite their own sentences that make sense for the ones that were deleted or they can select from those provided by the teacher.

    Example:

    Mary was looking forward to going to the lake with her parents. _____.

Mary had spent two weeks at the same lake last summer and made several new friends. _____

_____   _____.

4. *Who Buys It:* Provides students with a department store catalog and a list of items found in the catalog. Direct students to read the description of each item and infer the type of person or the character traits of a person who might purchase such items. A similar activity can be done by using pictures of items in the catalog.

5. *What I Know:* Provide students with a brief overview of a story and pictures appropriate to the story. Before reading the story, have students list what they know about its content. Direct students to read the story to confirm or reject the information they listed.

6. *Questions to Answer:* Provide students with brief information about a story before they are to read it. Such information could focus on the plot, characters, setting, etc. Then ask students to write a list of questions they would like to have answered as a result of reading the story. Students can write their answers to their own questions after they read the story.

7. *What I Learned:* Before students read a story, have them write down what they already know, or think they know, about the story. This information can come from reading the title, reading the first and last paragraphs, looking at the pictures, and so forth. After students read the story, have them list what they learned from their reading.

8. *Road Map:* Give students a written map of a story they are to read (this map would highlight major story information). As students read, they are to predict what comes next in terms of alternate routes on the road map. Students test their predictions as they read the story and complete their map.

9. *Who Comes to the Party:* Give students short descriptions about different characters, then tell them that one of the characters is having a party and needs help in making a guest list. Direct students to help complete a guest list by selecting people to come to the party. Students should write a brief paragraph or two about why they chose the particular group of people they did.

10. *Where Are They Going:* Cut out related items from department store catalogs and distribute them to students. Have students write a short story about where a person might be going. For example, a student who gets pictures such as a tent, fishing equipment, warm clothing, and boots might conclude that the person who bought these items was going on a camping/fishing trip and base his or her story on this information. A variation is to give students a story and have them infer what a person would purchase based on the story information.

STUDY SKILLS

1. *Using the Index:* Using a social studies or science text, ask students to find and write down the page numbers for a given list of topics. A variation is to use the same exercise involving the table of contents.

2. *Map/Graph Skills:* To learn information from different types of maps, graphs, and charts, have students design a particular map (physical, political), graph (bar, line), or chart on a topic of their choice.

3. *Dictionary Skills:* To practice the use of guide words, with a stopwatch, time students as they look up words. Repeat this exercise until students can look up a word in 10 to 15 seconds.

4. *Skimming:* After teaching how to skim an article or chapter by reading the first and last sentences of each paragraph, give students several practice articles to skim. Using a stopwatch, time their efforts. Check students' comprehension of key ideas. A variation might be to have students make a graph to use in keeping track of their skimming times.

5. *Propaganda Techniques:* Bring in magazine advertisements that illustrate the different propaganda techniques. Ask students to classify the advertisements under the correct technique.

6. *Collecting and Organizing Information:* To provide students with sufficient practice in collecting and organizing information, design a series of activities requiring students to search, organize, and report various information.

   Example: How is chocolate made?

   How does a microcomputer work?

   How would you plan a trip to Africa?

7. *Structured Overviews:* Provide students with an incomplete structured overview of a content chapter. Ask students to read the chapter and complete the overview.

8. *Fact and Opinion:* Have students read editorials on the sports page and compare the opinions with the facts about a sporting event. Ask students to list the author's opinions and facts about the event. Discuss the findings with students.

9. *Use of Encyclopedias:* Using the same encyclopedia, design a series of questions helping students find specific topics and then specific information.

10. *Scanning:* Give students a specific question from their reading materials (words, numbers, dates, figures) and ask them to scan to locate the answer. Using a stopwatch give students their scanning time. Variations are to divide students into teams and have a scanning tournament, or to use telephone books to practice scanning techniques.

11. *Table of Contents:* To illustrate how helpful a table of contents is to a reader, ask students to design a table of contents highlighting the events of their summer vacation.

12. *Maps:* Have students design a map of the classroom or their neighborhood. A variation is to study a map legend and ask students questions about its use.

Glossary

academic engaged time (time on task) classroom time in which students are actually attending to the valued learning.

academic learning time (ALT) classroom time in which students are actually attending to the work at hand with a high success rate (80 percent or more).

affixes prefixes, suffixes, and inflectional endings.

analytic phonics a phonic approach using letter-sound relationships by referring to words already known to identify a new phonic element.

anecdotal records written records that describe an event or product and relate the anecdote to information known about an individual.

assessment procedures used by teachers to identify students' literacy strengths and weaknesses in planning and executing instruction to meet the students' needs.

auditory discrimination the ability to recognize the differences in speech sounds within words.

automaticity ability to decode words with minimal effort.

basal reader reading materials that are organized and sequenced readers. The instructional sequence of skills and strategies depends on the readers and the accompanying manuals and materials.

big books books with large pictures and print that children in group settings can easily see. They use much repetition of content and language.

bilingual approach a reading approach that provides reading instruction in the primary language of the students as well as in standard English.

classics extraordinary books that last beyond their authors' lives and continue to attract readers.

cloze procedure an informal diagnostic procedure that omits words from freestanding passages to identify reading levels and provide information about a reader's ability to deal with content and structure.

computer-assisted instruction (CAI) instruction that interacts with a microcomputer.

content reading ability the degree to which a student can adequately comprehend and retain content or expository information.

contextual analysis a word-identification strategy that helps students figure out the meanings of words by how they are used in the context of sentences or passages.

contextual knowledge word knowledge derived from context.

cooperative grouping grouping where students of different levels work together.

core literature books that should be taught in the classroom through close reading and intensive consideration. These books can serve as important stimuli for writing and discussion.

criterion-referenced tests (CRTs)   tests designed to measure specific behaviors performed by an individual in relation to mastery of a specific skill.

culturally and linguistically diverse learners   students whose culture and language or dialect differ from that of the school.

decoding   identifying the pronunciation and meaning of a word.

definitional knowledge   word knowledge based upon a definition from a dictionary or glossary.

dialect approach   teaching reading using materials written in the language of the dialect-speaking students.

dialects   how people speak in different parts of the country or specific cultures. The components of dialect are pronunciation, grammar, and vocabulary.

direct approach   teaching reading by using materials written in the language of the dialect-speaking students.

direct/explicit instruction   systematic teaching in which the teacher models and demonstrates learning and gradually turns the responsibility for learning over to the student. This teaching method emphasizes students' understanding the "when" and "why" of using various capabilities and strategies.

directed reading activity (DRA)   an organized, sequenced strategy for teaching a reading selection. Three overall steps include readiness and prediction, active reading, and reaction.

directed reading-thinking activity (DR-TA)   an instructional procedure for teaching a reading selection, including readiness and prediction, active silent reading, and reaction to and review of text ideas.

emergent literacy   children's reading and writing behaviors that occur before and develop into conventional literacy.

environmental print   print in the environment, such as store names, menus, and signs, that has meaning to children.

exceptional children   culturally and linguistically diverse, disabled, and gifted learners.

experiential and conceptual backgrounds   readers' experiences that are both concrete and abstract (knowledge) as well as their reasoning abilities in using this knowledge. This is also known as background knowledge.

expository text   the text structure found in content books, including (1) description, (2) collection, (3) causation, (4) problem/solution, and (5) comparison.

extended literature   works that teachers may assign to individuals or small groups as homework or supplemental classwork.

functions of written language   to inform, entertain, and direct.

gifted students   students identified to have high-performance abilities and capabilities.

grapheme-phoneme relationships   the relationships between written letters and letter combinations and the sounds they typically represent.

graphic organizers   visual diagrams (such as flow charts, outlines, and time lines) depicting key concepts or ideas in a lesson.

homonyms   words that sound alike but are spelled differently.

individualized education plan (IEP) a plan of education written for each student who has a learning disability, that details the educational program for the student. The school, student, and parents jointly develop an IEP.

individualized reading an approach to reading that includes student selection of materials, student pacing, individual student conferences with the teacher, and record keeping by both the student and the teacher.

inferential questions questions that combine background knowledge and text information to make predictions about story content.

informal reading inventory (IRI) a series of grade-level word lists, passages, and comprehension questions ranging from preprimer through grade 8 or higher that are used to identify a student's independent, instructional, and frustration reading levels.

interactive instruction imparting new information to students through meaningful teacher-student interactions and guiding student learning.

interactive view of reading theory that readers use the information from the text, their experiential and conceptual backgrounds, and the context in which reading occurs to arrive at meaning.

language-experience approach (LEA) the approach for teaching reading that is built on children's experiences. Children dictate their experiences and the teacher writes them down or the children write their own stories as the basis for instruction.

literacy ability to read and write proficiently.

literal questions questions based on information explicitly stated in text.

literature-based reading program a program that emphasizes the ability to read all types of literature with understanding, appreciation, and enjoyment.

mainstreaming the least restrictive school environment, which has been interpreted to mean the regular classroom.

meaning vocabulary words whose meanings and concepts are represented by words already understood.

mediated instruction intervention or guidance that another person (such as a peer, parent, or teacher) provides in the teaching-learning process.

metacognition a reader's awareness of how to construct meaning and adjust strategies when he or she is not comprehending something.

metacomprehension awareness and control of one's cognitive functioning while reading.

modeling demonstration of strategies and behaviors to enhance their conceptualization.

norm-referenced tests standardized tests designed to compare the performance of an individual or individuals with the performance of a norming group.

opportunity to learn allotment of time and exposure to instruction.

oral language the language abilities of listening and speaking.

paired reading one student reads aloud as another follows along in the text.

performance-based assessment representative of literacy tasks that students face in the real world.

phonemic awareness awareness of sounds in spoken words.

phonics   word-identification strategy that uses letter-sound relationships to arrive at the pronunciations of unknown words.

plot structure   the structure used to introduce characters and conflicts and to develop a story climax.

point of view   the viewpoint that authors choose when they tell a story, including the details they describe and the judgments they make.

polysemous words   words having different meanings (such as air in air ball and to air one's views).

portfolios   folders that hold samples of students' work selected by the student and teacher. Can include observational notes, students' self-evaluations, writing examples, lists of books read, progress notes, interviews, and inventories.

predictable books   books in which students can grasp easily what the author is going to say next. They use much repetition of content and language.

preventative classroom management   a set of practices a teacher performs to promote a classroom environment conductive to learning and to prevent inappropriate student behavior.

process-oriented assessment   determination of a student's reading strategies to comprehend text.

readability   the approximate difficulty level of written material.

reading   an active process of constructing meaning from written text in relation to the experiences and knowledge of the reader.

recreational reading groups   students grouped on the basis of their interests to discuss the same book, books by the same author, or books with similar characteristics.

reliability   the degree to which the results of a measurement instrument are consistent.

response journals   written letters or dialogues that students share with each other and their teacher on a regular basis.

scaffolding   teacher support that enables students to complete activities that they would have difficulty completing on their own.

scaffolds   "forms of support provided by the teacher (or another student) to help students bridge the gap between current abilities and the intended goal" (Rosenshine & Meister, 1992).

schema (plural, schemata)   the background knowledge structure for an idea, object, or word meaning.

schema theory   a theory that attempts to explain how we learn, modify, and use knowledge acquired through our experiences.

semantic clues   a contextual-analysis strategy using the meanings of known words in a sentence or passage to identify an unknown word.

semantics   the meaning features of a language.

shared reading   students see the text as it is read aloud to them—usually from big books—and are invited to read along.

sight vocabulary   words that a reader recognizes and comprehends instantly.

silent sustained reading (SSR)   a scheduled period of silent reading in the classroom. During this time, both teachers and students may read a book or any form of print without interruption.

skills   learning that is specific in nature and amenable to behavioral objectives.

slots   attributes of a schema that must be recognized for a reader to activate that schema.

SQ3R a systemized study procedure for reading content chapters. The letters SQ3R stand for survey, question, read, recite, and review.

story schema readers' mental representation of story parts and their relationships. Story schema is also referred to as story grammar and story structure.

strategy learning that is less specific and represents higher level cognitive thinking to be used in interacting with text information.

structural analysis a word-identification strategy that focuses on visual or structural patterns and meanings that change as a result of adding inflectional endings, prefixes and suffixes and combining root words.

style an author's choice and arrangement of words to create plot, characterizations, setting, and theme.

syllabication the division of a word into its basic units of pronunciation.

syntactic clues a contextual-analysis strategy using the knowledge of word order in our language to identify an unknown word.

syntax the word order or grammar of a language.

thematic units integrating content (science, math, social studies) using literacy to facilitate children's learning of important concepts and ideas.

theme the central idea that ties the plot, characterizations, and setting together in a meaningful whole.

validity the degree to which test results serve the uses for which they are intended.

visual discrimination the ability to note similarities and differences, particularly in letters and words (e.g., the difference between *b* and *g* and the difference between *bat* and *bit*).

whole language a style of reading instruction based on the idea that students learn best when literacy is naturally connected to their oral language.

whole-word approach a word-identification strategy that focuses on learning words as wholes rather than by any form of analysis.

word identification the process of arriving at the pronunciation of a word, given the printed letter representations (also known as decoding).

About the Authors

Arthur W. Heilman served as director of the University Reading Center at The Pennsylvania State University from 1962 to 1979 and is now Professor Emeritus. He received his B.A. from Carthage College and his M.A. and Ph.D. from the University of Iowa. Dr. Heilman has authored numerous books, including *Phonics in Proper Perspective,* seventh edition (1993) and *Improve Your Reading Ability,* fourth edition (1983). He is also the author of numerous articles in reading journals. He is active in various professional organizations, including the International Reading Association, the College Reading Association, and the National Conference on Research in English.

Timothy R. Blair is Professor in Reading in the College of Education at the University of Central Florida. He received his B.S. in Elementary Education and M.S. in Reading from Central Connecticut State University. His Ph.D. was awarded in Elementary Education with a major in Reading at the University of Illinois. He is a former elementary classroom teacher and reading teacher at the elementary, middle and high school levels. Dr. Blair is the author of *Emerging Patterns of Teaching: From Methods to Field Experiences* (1988) and has coauthored three college textbooks on reading methods, diagnosis, and remediation. He is also the author of numerous articles in professional journals. He is active in various professional organizations, including the College Reading Association and the International Reading Association.

William H. Rupley is Professor in Language, Literacy, and Culture in the Department of Educational Curriculum and Instruction at Texas A&M University. He has been an elementary classroom teacher, coordinator of undergraduate reading education programs, and director of the Language and Reading Laboratory at Texas A&M University. Dr. Rupley received his B.A. from Indiana University, his M.S. from St. Francis College, and his Ph.D. from the University of Illinois. He has coauthored three textbooks: *Reading Diagnosis and Remediation: Classroom and Clinic,* third edition (1989); *Teaching Reading: Diagnosis, Direct Instruction, and Practice,* second edition (1988); and *Phonic Competencies for Reading Teachers: Steps to Literacy,* third edition (1993). He is the author of articles in professional reading journals and is editor of *Reading Psychology: An International Quarterly.* He is active in several professional organizations, including the International Reading Association, National Reading Conference, and American Educational Research Association.

Index

Boldface page numbers indicate an entry defined in context. Italic page numbers indicate an illustration.

observing literacy behavior of, 236–241
parents reading to, 229
Children and Books (Sutherland & Arbuthnot), 310
Children's Literature (Huck, Hepler, & Hickman), 310
Children's Literature: An Issues Approach (Rudman), 310
Chittendon, E. A., 389
A Chocolate Moose for Dinner (Gwynne), 483
Christopher, J., 319
Churton, M. W., 477
"Cinderella," 324
Cinquains, 159–160
Circles, Triangles, and Squares (Hoban), 321
Cisneros, S., 467
Classification of terms, 94–95
Classroom, language-rich environment in, 64–75
Classroom centers, as feature of language-rich classroom environment, 68–69
Classroom management and organization, 424–453
  affecting teacher effectiveness, 43
  alternative approaches to, 438–444
  grouping for, 427–448
  importance of, 424–453
  individualized reading for, 444–453
  preventative, 427–430. *See also* Grouping
Clay, M. M., 19, 233, 260, 262
Cleary, B., 318
Clements, B. S., 438
Clements, N. E., 284
Cloze procedure
  as informal assessment tool, **406**, 408
Cocchiarella, M., 138
"The Cock and the Mouse and the Little Red Hen," 319
Cognitive reading, 9
Cohen, C. L., 327
Cohen, R. G., 38
Collection, as expository text structure, 344, *345*
Colt, J., 305
Commeyras, M., 31
Comparison, as expository text structure, 344, *346*
Competence levels in reading, criteria for determining from student performances on informal reading inventory, 396–397, 402
The Complete Story of the Three Blind Mice (Ivimey), 321
Compound words, 124–125
Comprehension, 13, 166–217

assessed from information contained in response journals, 416
conceptualizations of, 169–175
content-area reading and, 342–343
direct/explicit instruction for, 182–193, *185–186*
inferential, practice activities and games for, 495–496
instruction of, 175–177
interactive view of, 169
interviews to determine, 411
literal, practice activities and games for, 494–495
monitoring of, 177
oral language and, 205–206
questioning strategies to promote, 177–182
questions and, 209–211
readers' theater and, 206
reading and writing strategies for, 207–216
reading interview to determine, *414–415*
schema theory of, 169–174
strategies and skills, *212–215*
visual arts and, 206–207
visual displays of text for, 202–205
Computer-assisted instruction (CAI), **292**–294
  software for, 293–297
Computers
  as instructional procedure for teaching literacy, 292–297
  uses of, 292–293
Concept books, for increasing vocabulary, 321
Conceptual and experiential background. *See* Experiential and conceptual background of readers; Knowledge
Conflict
  external
    plot structure for, 327, *328*
    plot structure for *Sir Gawain and the Loathly Lady* (Hastings), 327, *328*
  person-versus-self
    plot structure for, 327, *329*
    plot structure for *On My Honor* (Bauer), 327, *330*
Conflict webbing, for selection of literature, 324, *326*
Conn, M., 342
Consonants, 104–112
  blends of, 108–111
  digraphs of, 110–112
  sounds of, 104–108
Content-area journals, 313
Content-area reading, 338–376
  components of, 347–375

Perkins, G., 315
Perrault, C., 311
Personal language, *66*
Person-versus-self conflict, plot structure for, 327, *328*
Pescosolido, J. D., 29, 31
Pescosolido, J. R., 359
Phoneme, 56
  definition of, 57
  relationship to grapheme, 56
Phonemic awareness
  and beginning reading programs, **232**–233
  in direct/explicit instruction, 253–254
Phonics, 56–57, **83**, 95–118
  analytic, **98**
  in direct/explicit instruction, 98–99, **255**–257
  practice activities and games for, 490–491
Phonology, 56–57
Phrases, 127
Picture books
  for increasing vocabulary, 321
  modeling for, 331
Picture dictionary, 90–91
Pictures, for building background knowledge, 257–259, 262
Pieronek, F. T., 276
Pinnell, G. S., 66
Pittleman, S. D., 351, 352, 355
Placement tests
  as informal assessment tool, 391
  for literature-based reading, 391, 392–393
Play, print concepts associated with, 230
Play centers, 243–244
Plot
  literary, 197
  as literary element, 313–314
  structures of
    for external conflict, *328*
    as literary elements, 327, *328*
    for person-versus-self conflict, 327, *329*
    for person-versus-self conflict for *On My Honor* (Bauer), 330
Poplin, C. E., 465
Population
  cultural diversity in student, 7
Portfolios
  assessment of, 418–421, *419–420*
  best piece, 418
  descriptive, as informal assessment tool, 418–419
  as informal assessment tool, 407, **418**–421

process, as informal assessment tool, 418
Potter, B., 315
Powell, W. R., 396
Predictable books
  for developing reading skills, 319–321
  literature and, **248**
Preface, as aid for readers, *366*
Prefixes, 122–124
Prereading
  for comprehension, 207–208
  stages of development in reading instruction for, *20*
Preventative classroom management, **427**–430. *See also* Grouping
Print
  acquiring concepts about, 228–232
  associated with art, 230
  associated with play, 230
  decontextualized use of language associated with, 230–231
  environmental, **229**–230
  meaning associated with, 231
Probable passages strategy, for comprehension, 207
Problem/solution, as expository text structure, 344, *346*
Process knowledge, product knowledge and, 64
Process portfolios, as informal assessment tool, 418
Product knowledge, process knowledge and, 64
Propaganda, 372–374
Push-Pull Empty-Full (Hoban), 483

Question-and-answer relationships (QAR), 178–181
  as questioning strategy, 354
  types of, *180*
Question cards, *210–211*
Questioning strategies, 354
Questions
  comprehension and, 209–211
  generation of, comprehension and, 176
  inferential, **177**–178
  literal, **177**
  reporter, 91–92
  strategies to promote comprehension, **177**–182
  teacher-identified, 177
  teacher responses to, 181–182

Rabbit Hill (Lawson), 318
Rand, M. K., 244